*Redemptive-Historical
Hermeneutics and Homiletics*

WEST Theological Monograph Series

Wales Evangelical School of Theology (WEST) has produced a stream of successful PhD candidates over the years, whose work has consistently challenged the boundaries of traditional understanding in both systematic and biblical theology. Now, for the first time, this series makes significant examples of this ground-breaking research accessible to a wider readership.

Redemptive-Historical Hermeneutics and Homiletics

Debates in Holland, America,
and Korea from 1930 to 2012

Yung Hoon Hyun

Foreword By
Eryl Davies

WIPF & STOCK · Eugene, Oregon

REDEMPTIVE-HISTORICAL HERMENEUTICS AND HOMILETICS
Debates in Holland, America, and Korea from 1930 to 2012

Copyright © 2015 Yung Hoon Hyun. All rights reserved. Except for brief quotations in critical publications or reviews, no part of this book may be reproduced in any manner without prior written permission from the publisher. Write: Permissions, Wipf and Stock Publishers, 199 W. 8th Ave., Suite 3, Eugene, OR 97401.

Wipf & Stock
An Imprint of Wipf and Stock Publishers
199 W. 8th Ave., Suite 3
Eugene, OR 97401

www.wipfandstock.com

ISBN 13: 978-1-62564-567-8

Manufactured in the U.S.A.

All scripture quotations, unless otherwise indicated, are taken from the Holy Bible, New International Version®, NIV®. Copyright ©1973, 1978, 1984, 2011 by Biblica, Inc.™ Used by permission of Zondervan. All rights reserved worldwide. www.zondervan.com The "NIV" and "New International Version" are trademarks registered in the United States Patent and Trademark Office by Biblica, Inc.™

Contents

Foreword by Eryl Davies | vii
Preface | xi
Acknowledgments | xiii
List of Abbreviations | xv

1. Introduction | 1
2. Redemptive History: Hermeneutical Roots | 31
3. The Dutch Debate: Homiletics and Redemptive History | 75
4. The American Debate: Homiletics and Redemptive History | 134
5. Confusion and Definitions: Homiletics and Redemptive History | 173
6. The Debate in Korea: Homiletics and Redemptive History | 216
7. Conclusion, With Samples of Korean Redemptive-Historical Preaching | 260

Bibliography | 289
Name Index | 315
Scripture Index | 321

Foreword

I COUNT IT A privilege to have been invited by the author to write this Foreword. I have known the Rev. Dr. Yung Hoon Hyun for several years and have visited him in his seminary in Korea on occasions. It has been a joy to fellowship with Dr. Hyun, especially while I functioned as his main university research supervisor in Wales during his PhD studies. It has been a joy to know him and supervise the progress and direction of his research. Dr. Hyun was an outstanding student, possessing considerable academic ability and skills. I have respected also his godliness and commitment to the Lord and His church.

Original

This book represents a major and original contribution to learning in the area of Reformed hermeneutics and homiletics. The task which Dr. Hyun set himself in his research was intellectually arduous and ambitious. His task was to reexamine and explore the background and development, as well as the influence, of redemptive-historical hermeneutics and homiletics, particularly in the twentieth-century, with special reference to Korea. No one else has covered the subject so comprehensively, competently and sympathetically as Dr. Hyun, yet without bitterness or a party spirit. His approach is non-polemical. At the same time, he has been prepared to challenge assumptions and theories, but to do so with solid arguments and compelling evidence, which now demand serious attention by preachers and scholars, especially in Korea.

Appeal

For that reason I appeal to scholars, preachers, and seminary teachers to study carefully the content of this book in order to understand the subject better, but also for the more important reason of preaching the Word of God in a way which glorifies God and nurtures the church. There is much to benefit from in reading this book.

Subject

What, then, is the subject handled in this book? Dr. Hyun is concerned over the content and quality of reformed preaching in Korean Presbyterian churches. A crisis in preaching has arisen due to various factors, including the preacher's concern for his own interests and status, dependence on Western scholars and traditions, and even also the influence of Confucian shamanism. Theological interest in homiletics, therefore, in Korea is considerable. In a masterly way the author describes and evaluates critically the various approaches to preaching within Korean Presbyterianism (chapter 6). As the majority of Korean Presbyterian theologians have been trained in the West, there is a range of different, often conflicting, approaches to homiletics. Dr. Hyun shows us in detail how Korean theologians introduced and recycled the views of Western scholars in Korea from the 1950s. In this context, he introduces and outlines the history of what he describes as "redemptive-historical hermeneutics," which he demonstrates became a crucial part of the Korean debate about the nature of preaching.

In chapter 2, Dr. Hyun identifies and explores in depth the European and American elements which contributed to redemptive-historical hermeneutics. He then proceeds, in a superb chapter (chapter 3), to describe and analyze critically the debate on the subject from the 1920s, following Abraham Kuyper's death, demonstrating the deep division between two contrasting expressions of Dutch Calvinism, namely, the "old" Calvinism and Neo-Calvinism. His contribution is original here in several respects, not least in recognizing the crucial importance of cultural issues affecting the Dutch debate. Chapter 4 examines the more recent American debate, and once again the author demonstrates that this was distinctive and not a continuation of the Dutch debate, as most scholars have imagined. I particularly enjoyed chapters 5 and 6, and to be reminded of the advance of the church in Korea in recent decades,

Korean interaction with Western theologies, and Dr. Hyun's assessment of Korean preaching. His conclusion is that most Korean theologians and preachers have "misunderstood redemptive-historical preaching." The book closes with an interesting sample of how redemptive-historical preaching can be applied culturally within Korean society; the sample majors on Won-Tae Suk.

Should you read this book? If you are a Korean preacher and theologian then the answer is a positive one. This book will help you understand, and grapple with, important issues relating to preaching and to avoid the confusion which prevails in Korean Reformed churches even today. This book should become a text-book, and studied as an essential part of ministerial training in Korea, for it will stimulate students to improve their own preaching and seek to be God-honoring in the proclamation of the Word. What about Western preachers and theologians? Well, we need to be more informed about the "crisis" in preaching in countries like Korea, while at the same time endeavoring to make our own preaching edifying and God-centered for churches in the West and elsewhere.

I commend this book as a major theological contribution to homiletics and hermeneutics for Korean Reformed churches. It is my prayer that it will have a powerful impact upon seminaries, theologians, preachers, students, and congregations to the glory of the Triune God.

Rev. Dr. D. Eryl Davies
Cardiff, Wales, May 2014
Formerly Principal of Wales Evangelical School of Theology (WEST), 1985–2006
Currently Research Supervisor, WEST / University of Wales

Preface

A MAN IS LIKE his inward thoughts (Prov 23:7). What a man thinks depends on how he views the world and other people. Our Lord describes our eye as the lamp of our body, so that if our eye is healthy our whole body will be full of light, but if our eye is unhealthy our whole being will be full of darkness (Matt 6:22; Luke 11:34). Here the "eye" means, I believe, how we view the world, that is, our worldview.

My longstanding theological queries have been concerned with why one theology differs from another although they derive from the same texts, the Scriptures, and why Reformed theology, in my view, does not produce more reformation in personal and church life. I was fortunate to encounter two good tutors who kindly guided me with Christ's loving care to find the answers for myself. One opened my eyes to the Scriptures by giving me an awareness of God's sovereignty and thought in His revelation. The other further opened my eyes so that I came to understand why theology does not work in congregations, and to know how to overcome, or reform, the seemingly invincible gap between theology and life.

This book is the first major product of my theological research after twenty years of study and struggle with those theological questions. The major theme of this book is the redemptive-historical (RH) perspective, which I believe is a suitable way to bridge the gap. Only the Scriptures can change God's people and enable them to be complete and equipped for every good work (2 Tim 3:16-17) and the RH perspective is an honest approach to properly examining those texts. This approach has also brought in some harmful by-products, like the RH homiletical debates between its advocates and opponents in Reformed groups, especially in Holland, America, and South Korea, which need to be resolved. As a student of Reformed theology, I felt an obligation to handle this matter and so I eventually undertook this project.

The first step of my theological journey comes to a close here and I must now prepare for the next stage. All I have learned from my seven-year project is that I know nothing but God's grace. By God's grace I have completed the project and I give deep thanks to Him and glorify His name.

Acknowledgments

I would like to thank Dr. Eryl Davies who, as my supervisor, guided my research with prayer and hearty care. I much enjoyed the time with him in Wales Evangelical School of Theology (WEST). I would also like to extend my gratitude to the principal of WEST, Rev. Jonathan Stephen, Dr. Tom Holland, Dr. Robert Letham, Rev. Iwan Rhys Jones, Dr. Mark Pickett, Dr. Sung-Ho Choi, Ms. Anwen Davies, Mr. and Mrs. John and Gill Lang, and Mr. Kevin Green, who have all helped me with prayer and support in various ways. I especially appreciated the Christian love and help provided by Rev. Nigel Birt. I would like to give special thanks to Ms. Linda Baynham who joyfully bore the hard work of editing the manuscript.

I have greatly appreciated the real Christian love of Pastor Dae-Keun Min and the members of Bridgend Korean Church as I have much enjoyed fellowship with them during my stay in the UK. Dr. Young-Jin Choi and his wife Eun-Hye Kim, and also Pastor Pyeong-Soo Kim and his family have supported me much and become close friends of mine in South Wales, the lonely land. I thank God for them.

I am deeply grateful to all the members of Goryo Theological Seminary (GTS), where I have served as a part time lecturer since 1998 and a full time lecturer since 2009. Above all, I give profound thanks to Rev. Dr. Won-Tae Suk, my great teacher and the former principal of GTS, who allowed me three years leave and scholarship to study for my PhD in Britain and who constantly encouraged and challenged me, with prayer, to pursue my academic journey unyieldingly. I also give my heartfelt thanks to the members of GTS, especially the president Dr. Goo-Won Kang, Professor Gil-Kon Kim, Keith-Suk, Yeon-Cheol Chung, Hyun-Sang Lee, Myung-Gil Whang, Jung-Cheol Lee, and Koo-Seok Kown who have prayed much for me and my work. The fellow workers of GTS and the classes from 2010 to 2014 merit my love and deep gratitude. I am especially grateful to Seung-Choon Chai, the exhorter, who has sincerely prayed for me and heartily served memorable meals in GTS.

Finally, I express my deepest gratitude to my loving wife, Sung-Sook Hong, and my only daughter, Ye-Rim, for their sacrifice and patience during the seven long and tough years of my study in Britain and Korea. I give my foremost thanks to my mother who prayed much for me in her lifetime and now is resting beside our Lord Jesus Christ. Soli Deo Gloria!

Abbreviations

AV	*Authorized Version*
BRPR	*Biblical Repertory and Princeton Review*
CS	*Christianity & Society*
CTJ	*Calvin Theological Journal*
CTM	*Concordia Theological Monthly*
EDT	*Evangelical Dictionary of Theology*
EvT	*Evangelische Theologie*
GKN	Gereformeerde Kerken in Nederland (Reformed Churches in the Netherlands)
GM	*Gereformeerd Mannenblad*
GPTS	Greenville Presbyterian Theological Seminary
GTJ	*Goryo Theological Journal*
GTT	*Gereformeerd Theologisch Tijdschrift*
JBL	*Journal of Biblical Literature*
JR	*Journal of Religion*
JBR	*Journal of Bible and Religion*
NDCT	*A New Dictionary of Christian Theology*
NDT	*New Dictionary of Theology*
NT	New Testament
NWTS	Northwest Theological Seminary

OPC	Orthodox Presbyterian Church
OT	Old Testament
PCK	Presbyterian Church in Korea
PCUSA	Presbyterian Church in the USA
PE	*Pro-Ecclesia*
PRTS	Puritan Reformed Theological Seminary
RH	Redemptive History / Redemptive-Historical
RHP	Redemptive Historical Preaching
RSV	*Revised Standard Version*
TBT	*The Banner of Truth*
TTR	*The Theological Review: A Theological and Homiletical Quarterly*
WCC	World Council of Churches
WTJ	*Westminster Theological Journal*
WTS	Westminster Theological Seminary

Translation of Korean Titles and Quotations

All Korean book and periodical titles and quotations are entered in English and have been translated by the author.

1

Introduction

FIRST OF ALL I describe my aims in this book, before defining key terms and then providing a brief outline of the homiletical controversy in Holland, America, and Korea concerning redemptive-historical Reformed preaching.

Aims

My first aim is to describe the background to, and development of, the debates in Reformed circles, especially in Holland, America, and Korea, concerning redemptive-historical preaching. I regard this as a necessary aim, if only for the reason that, in Korea especially, many preachers and scholars who argue over redemptive-historical preaching do not appreciate the complex history of the debate or the relationship between the Dutch and American debates. It is too often wrongly assumed in Korea, but also in the West, that the Dutch and American debates in the 1930s and 1980s respectively were similar, if not almost identical. In addition, in order to engage in detailed research concerning the relationship and differences between the Dutch, American, and Korean debates, it will be helpful to provide a clear outline of that history later in the chapter.

My second aim is to explore critically, and compare, the distinctive features of both the Dutch and American debates relating to redemptive-historical preaching. Many scholars, like Edmund P. Clowney (1961),[1]

---

1. Clowney, *Preaching and Biblical Theology*.

Sidney Greidanus (1970),[2] and Cornelis Trimp (1986),[3] critically examined the original Dutch debate, but their examinations are now dated and have crucial weaknesses in their treatment which I identify and discuss in chapters 3 and 4. A new debate relating to redemptive-historical preaching occurred in America in the late 1980s and continues until today, necessitating a reexamination of the original debate in relation to the new debate. This preliminary research is also essential for the proper examination of the redempive history debate in Korean churches, because the latest Korean debate follows a similar course to that of the previous two debates, as I intend to show.

Recent surveys of the Dutch and American debates, like those of John Carrick (2002)[4] and Stefan T. Lindblad (2005),[5] are, however, inadequate for several reasons. Firstly, a participant in the American debate, such as Carrick, is unable to be detached from his preference for one of the debating parties. Secondly, Carrick's research is inappropriate because it focuses mainly on the limited issue of his own concern, that is, the issue of the imperative mood in the biblical text. Such an approach thus fails to explore the comprehensive characteristics of both sides in the debates. Thirdly, Lindblad attempts to be more fairly objective in dealing with both debates, but he is concerned much more with the American than with the Dutch debate. Moreover, he identifies the American debate theoretically with the Dutch one, but this is misleading because each debate has its own distinctive features, with different theological roots and contexts. These factors must be respected in seeking a competent understanding of both debates, and their distinctive features must be recognized. No study has been undertaken which compares the two debates alongside an acknowledged and thorough recognition of their respective theological roots and ecclesiastical contexts. In this respect, my research is necessary and original.

My third aim is to examine the influence of the Dutch and American controversies on redemptive-historical preaching in Korean Reformed homiletics. The redemptive history debate in Korea, which occurred in the late 1990s, expressed a dependence of Korean Reformed preaching on the previous two redemptive history debates in Holland and America.

---

2. Greidanus, *Sola Scriptura*.
3. Trimp, *Preaching and the History of Salvation*.
4. Carrick, *Imperative of Preaching*.
5. Lindblad, "Redemptive History and the Preached Word."

Scholars like Sung-Jong Shin[6] and Sung-Kuh Chung[7] identified the homiletical problems in the Dutch Reformed churches in the 1930s with those in Korean pulpits today. However, this approach is misleading because the theological and cultural contexts of the Korean churches are different from those of the Dutch churches involved in the debate. Consequently, the current redemptive history debate in Korea has been somewhat confused regarding subsequent developments in the West. I deem it necessary to examine the influences of both the Dutch and American debates on Korean redemptive-historical preaching.

My final aim is to sample Korean Reformed preaching, with a view to identifying, comparing, and evaluating any distinctive features which may be found in redemptive-historical preaching in Korea. There has been a general agreement amongst participants in the Korean debate that Korean redemptive-historical preaching requires further reflection and development. I have chosen Won-Tae Suk's case as an example of redemptive-historical preaching in Korea. This will be investigated in chapter 7.

Definitions

I now turn to the definition of key terms used in this work. This exercise is essential because some of these terms are understood differently by scholars. I am eager to achieve precision in my own use of these terms in order to avoid any possible misunderstanding.

Redemptive History

This term has been given different connotations, even by those who claim to use and advocate the redemptive-historical method. A number of key works were published between 1945 and 1970 dealing extensively with this theme, including, for example, Oscar Cullmann's *Christ and Time* (1945) and *Salvation in History* (1965); Eric C. Rust's *Salvation History* (1962); and Isaac C. Rottenberg's *Redemption and Historical Reality* (1964). Although these works are now dated and restricted in their treatments of the subject, they have been influential. For example, Cullmann dealt with redemptive history only as an hermeneutical tool, while

---

6. Shin, "Problems of the Korean Pulpit," 54–55.
7. Chung, "Principles and Methods of Redemptive-Historical Preaching."

Rust and Rottenberg mainly discussed historical and biblical aspects retrospectively.

Furthermore, there have been some significant publications and debates on this subject since 1970, such as those by George Eldon Ladd, *A Theology of the New Testament* (1974); Leonhard Goppelt, *Theology of the New Testament* (1976); David L. Baker, *Two Testaments, One Bible* (1976); Gerhard Hasel, *New Testament Theology* (1978); Herman N. Ridderbos, *Redemptive History and the New Testament Scriptures* (1988); and Robert W. Yarbrough, *The Salvation Historical Fallacy?* (2004). I submit, therefore, that there is an urgent need to provide a more comprehensive analysis, as well as evaluation, of the use of the term *redemptive history* over this long period, and to explore how it has been applied. Korean scholars have also expressed different views about the origin, development, and present status of this method for about sixty years, with many theological students in Korea being confused about the subject. I am therefore eager to bring greater clarity and precision to the current debate in Korea.

The term *redemptive-historical* can be defined simply as the "history of God's redemption." Here, the word *history* is ambiguous, signifying either a chronological record of significant events, or a philosophical explanation of them. The German language usually differentiates *Historie* from *Geschichte*, with the former describing the process of outer events and the latter the inner aspect.[8] The latter term focuses on the meaning of events without questioning their historical reality. This distinction has consequently introduced crucial theological issues which will be discussed later. While the word *history* may be open to ambiguity, I understand it here as both the "process of the outer events and its constitutional account," a definition which also accords with the general Christian understanding of history, which presents both historical events and their historical interpretation, even though general historians confine it to historical facts which are scientifically verifiable.[9] The latter part, the interpretation of history, would reflect the individual's worldview or foundational philosophy. Generally speaking, the Christian worldview includes scientific, external events, and also the internal purpose and meaning of them, in the term *history*.

In this context, the term *God* is used to designate exclusively the Triune God, who is "the Object, as revealed in Scripture, of the Christian

---

8. Rust, *Towards a Theological Understanding of History*, 3–4.
9. Butterfield, *Christianity and History*, 3.

Church's confession, worship and service."[10] The other key word, *redemption*, signifies, as in biblical theology, Christ's saving of His people from their sins through giving His life as a ransom.[11] While some scholars[12] doubt whether the Graeco-Roman terminology of the word *redemption* (*lytron*) corresponds exactly to the biblical meaning, and suggest its sociological usage, as in the deliverance of slaves or the political salvation of the oppressed, nevertheless Scripture expresses the action of Christ as setting His people free from their sins through His sacrificial death, yet in terms of Old Testament (OT) teaching and events.[13] Tom Holland asserts,

> While the vocabulary of the New Testament could be found throughout the Hellenistic world, it did not have the same meaning when it was used in a religious sense within the Jewish community . . . It was Greek in its alphabet and vocabulary, but Hebrew in its mindset and essential meaning."[14]

Scripture also implicates "the fulfilment of God's purpose in all things of His created world" in the key word *redemption*.[15]

With regard to the term *redemptive-history*, I understand it provisionally as the history of the Triune God's redemption of His people and the created world through His Son Jesus Christ, which was revealed in the Scriptures and fulfilled in space and time, but is to be fully accomplished at the end time.[16] This definition complies with Gerhard Vos's understanding of redemptive history, for "it has to do with that pattern of decisive divine activity subsequent to the fall until the coming of Christ by which God is exercising his lordship over the whole of history in the interest of accomplishing his eternal purpose for the entire creation."[17]

This understanding of redemptive history is so crucial that I will discuss it in more detail in the next chapter. Certainly, the term is understood in many different ways as, for example, in the same way as the

---

10. Packer, "God," 274–277.

11. Matt 1:21, 20:28; Mark 10:45.

12. Hill, *Greek Words and Hebrew Meanings*, chapter 3; Brown, *New International Dictionary of New Testament Theology*, vol. 3, 177–223.

13. Marshall, "Redemption," 560.

14. Holland, *Contours of Pauline Theology*, 52. This dissertation follows Holland's methodology of interpreting biblical words.

15. Eph 1:7–10.

16. There are many diverse definitions of the word by different theological groups. My definition here is a tentative one according to Eph 1:7–12.

17. Gaffin, "Introduction," xxi.

term, *history of Israel's religion*.[18] However, technically and provisionally, I define the term as the history of God's redemption as biblically described. The term *redemptive history* will be used here interchangeably with the terms *salvation history* or *history of redemption* or *history of salvation*. The word *salvation* has a much broader meaning than redemption. The latter refers to the specific act of Christ in giving His life as a ransom for those under the bondage of sin and divine wrath, thus setting them free.[19] The former term represents more widely the divine provision for our human plight.[20] Nevertheless, both terms will be treated here in the same way as in the technical terms *history of salvation* and *history of redemption*.

The German term *Heilsgeschichte*, however, which used to be translated into English as *holy history* or *salvation history*,[21] should not be regarded as being identical with our term *redemptive-history* in this research, because the German term specifically denotes a metaphysical history without factuality, and so inevitably leads to unnecessary confusion. Furthermore, Rudolf Bultmann contends that by using this word Paul transformed the Greek mythological idea of cosmos into God's salvation of sinners in Scripture.[22] According to Bultmann, salvation history, that is, *Heilsgeschichte*, must be demythologized to get to the reality of God's salvation of a human being. Thus the word *Heilsgeschichte* in its use has theologically sceptical overtones. I differentiate this term from the more biblical interpretation of redemptive history.

Hermeneutics

Anthony Thiselton moves cautiously "towards a definition of hermeneutics"[23] and understands the term *biblical hermeneutics* as that

---

18. Rad, *Old Testament Theology*, vol. 2: *Theology of Israel's Prophetic Traditions*, 90–112.

19. Marshall, "Redemption," 560.

20. Marshall, "Salvation," 610–611.

21. Piper, *God in History*, xix. According to Piper, this term was designed and developed by the *Heilsgeschichtliche Schule* (the School of Holy History) in the south of Germany, which flourished for a hundred years from the middle of the eighteenth century; its principal representatives were Johann Albrecht Bengel, Johann Tobias Beck, J. Chr. K. von Hofmann, and Karl August Auberlen.

22. Bultmann, "Heilsgeschichte und Geschichte," 659–66, quoted in Bultmann, *Existence and Faith*, 264–84.

23. Thiselton, *Hermeneutics*, 1.

which "investigates more specifically how we read, understand, apply and respond to biblical texts." He notes how post Friedrich Schleiermacher (1768–1834), biblical hermeneutics raises biblical, philosophical, literary, and social questions in a "concern for the whole process as it involves author, text, and reader as an act or event of communication,"[24] thus distinguishing it from exegesis. For Thiselton, hermeneutics "explores the conditions and criteria that operate to try to ensure responsible, valid, fruitful, or appropriate interpretation." There are valuable insights here, and the discouragement of "tight, brittle, fully formed systems of thought that are closed" against revision or development.[25]

The term *hermeneutics* as used in this research refers to the principles of the interpretation of biblical texts; this is consistent with Thiselton's definition and also the general understanding of the term as "the science and art of biblical interpretation."[26] To call hermeneutics a science raises a question, as it suggests, for example, rules or principles. Thiselton reminds us that formulating rules for hermeneutics is no longer popular, although it "persists today," especially amongst conservative scholars who accept an infallible biblical canon. I acknowledge myself to be within this group, but I want, however, to underline the fact that I recognize the notion of fallible human interpretation and I am both self-critical and critical of other conservative scholars who appear reluctant to acknowledge that their fallible interpretation is in need of adjustment. In viewing hermeneutics as a science, I also understand it to be an art, so that its communication is flexible and dynamic rather than rigid or mechanical.

In the New Testament (NT) the word *hermeneuein* is used for significant terms like the "translation of words" (John 1:38, 42, 9:7; Heb 7:2), and the "interpretation of tongues" (1 Cor 12:10, 14:26–28). People in Lystra referred to Paul as *Hermes* because he was the chief speaker (Acts 14:12). Luke used the cognate word to testify of Jesus Christ, who interpreted the OT prophets to the two disciples on the Emmaus Road (Luke 24:27). From these biblical usages the word *hermeneutics* throughout church history came to mean the appropriate principles of interpreting Scripture.

The term *hermeneutics* differs from *exegesis* in that the former is the theory of biblical interpretation but the latter is the application of

---

24. Ibid., 2.
25. Ibid., 15.
26. Virkler, *Hermeneutics*, 15–16.

that theory to specific biblical texts. Hermeneutics is concerned with the critical examination of the theological and philosophical assumptions and presuppositions which influence exegetical practice, while exegesis deals with the specifics of grammar, vocabulary, syntax, and the historical context of the text.[27]

Homiletics

The technical term *homiletics* relates to the art of preaching, and is the study of the composition and delivery of a sermon that conveys God's message from Scripture to specific Christian congregations. The Greek word *homileticos*, from the stem *homilein*, means "to consort" or "hold converse with." *Homily*, its derivative word, signifies a short discourse addressed to a congregation and fundamentally related to a passage of Scripture.[28] Thus homiletics, as a study of a homily, deals essentially with Christian preaching. Traditionally, Reformed theology has defined preaching as *explicatio et applicatio verbi Dei*, that is, "the explication and the application of the Word of God."[29] It is basically composed of *kerygma* (proclamation of redemption), *marturia* (witness to redemption), *didache* (teaching about redemption), and *homilia* (application of redemption).[30] Homiletics is, therefore, very closely related to these four factors and vitally connected with hermeneutics.

In Reformed homiletics, the proper interpretation of a given scriptural text is the basis for preaching. Jesus Christ also made himself understood by means of the Jewish Scriptures, that is, the Old Testament. Peter and Paul interpreted OT texts prior to preaching Christ's crucifixion and resurrection in Acts 2. Scripture is, thus, a book of interpretation and the preaching of God's Word. In taking Scripture as a text for preaching, a preacher must first interpret it and then preach its message accordingly. Biblical hermeneutics actually controls biblical homiletics, and vice versa.[31]

---

27. Davis, *Foundations of Evangelical Theology*, 246.
28. Stacey, "Homiletics, Homily," 270.
29. Carrick, "Redemptive-Historical Preaching," 153.
30. Ridderbos, *Redemptive History and the New Testament Scriptures*, 50. The first three factors are derived from Ridderbos, to which I have added a fourth, because these four factors are broadly recognized as the essential conditions of biblical preaching.
31. Packer, "Preaching as Biblical Interpretation," 189.

The term *preaching* comes from the Latin *praedicare*, meaning to proclaim, announce, and declare. A similar word in the Greek New Testament is *euaggelizesthai*, which includes the technique of the art of preaching.[32] Here the word *preaching* implies the practical communication of truth from the biblical text about God as it affects the hearer's life.[33] I prefer to use the term *preaching* rather than *sermon*, because preaching is more dynamic, involving an encounter with God in His person, His works, and His words.[34]

Reformed

The word *Reformed* is here understood as the traditional system of theology which John Calvin (1509–1564), the Genevan Reformer, established through his writings, and which those scholars who followed him developed in church history.[35] The Reformed tradition began originally with Huldrych (or Ulrich) Zwingli (1484–1531), the first Reformer in Zurich, but afterwards the influence of Calvin was greater in the later development of its legacy. Thus the term *Reformed* is used synonymously with Calvinism, distinguishing it from the theologies of Martin Luther (1483–1546) and the Anabaptists.[36] Reformed theology ultimately focuses on the sovereignty of the Triune God and attempts to bring the whole of life under the sway of God's supremacy.[37]

Historically, the Reformed tradition finds its roots in Calvin's celebrated textbook, *The Institutes of the Christian Religion*, or church documents based on it. These documents are the early catechisms and confessions of faith of the Reformed churches in Northwest Europe, Switzerland, France, Holland, Germany, Hungary, and the British Isles.[38] They include the Heidelberg Confession (1563), the Helvetic Confessions (1536, 1566), the Belgic Confession (1561), the Gallic Confession (1559),

---

32. Shedd, *Homiletics and Pastoral Theology*, 33.

33. Packer, "Introduction: Why Preach?" 10. A similar definition is found in Stott, *Between Two Worlds*, 266, quoted in Krabbendam, "Hermeneutics and Preaching," 229.

34. Krabbendam, "Hermeneutics and Preaching," 229.

35. Reid, "Reformed Tradition," 997–99.

36. These three are the constituents of the Protestant Reformation, but only the Reformed group is of particular importance in the English-speaking world.

37. Letham, "Reformed Theology," 569–72.

38. McGrath, *Christian Theology*, 60–61.

the Scots Confession (1560), the Thirty-Nine Articles of the Church of England (1562, 1671), the Canons of the Synod of Dort (1618), the Westminster Confession of Faith and Catechism (1647), and the Formula Consensus Helveticus (1675).[39] Some of these documents, for example the Heidelberg Confession and the Westminster Confession, which are still subordinate standards of faith in most European Reformed churches, have provided the foundations for churches also in the United States, South Africa, Australia, and New Zealand. In this way the Reformed tradition has not only expanded its influence in the Western world, but also exercised its influence more powerfully on churches in newly developed countries like India and South Korea.[40] The influence of the Reformed tradition has been considerable on very diverse aspects of thought and life, such as education, politics, economics, and culture, in many countries throughout the past centuries, but much of its contribution has been gradually secularized, with the essentials of its theological legacy often diluted and even discarded.

Theologically, the features of the Reformed faith have been reexamined and reaffirmed, but also questioned and sometimes revised by some sections of the Reformed community. Following the challenge of the Dutch theologian Jacob Arminius (1560–1609) and his followers to the Reformed tradition, theologians met at the Synod of Dort in 1618 to condemn Arminianism by reasserting the five major points of the Reformed faith, which form the popular acrostic TULIP.[41] The Reformed faith is much more comprehensive than these five points and many attempts have been made to identify certain characteristics of this faith. R. C. Sproul (1939–), an American Calvinist theologian, describes "the foundations of Reformed theology" as (1) centered on God; (2) based on God's Word alone; (3) committed to faith alone; (4) devoted to the Prophet, Priest, and King, that is, Jesus Christ; (5) represented as covenant theology. To these he added the five points of TULIP.[42] John R. De Witt perceived the basic outline of Reformed theology as (1) its doctrine of Scripture; (2) the sovereignty of God; (3) the invincibility of God's grace; (4) the Christian life lived according to biblical doctrine; (5) a clear understanding of the relationship between law and gospel; (6) a positive

---

39. Letham, "Reformed Theology," 569.

40. Reid, "Reformed Tradition," 997.

41. Total depravity of man; Unconditional divine election; Limited atonement of Jesus Christ; Irresistible grace; Perseverance of the elect until the end.

42. Sproul, *Heart of Reformed Theology*, 1–13.

and affirmative view of the "cultural mandate"; (7) a distinctive emphasis on preaching.[43] In contrast to these Henry Meeter (1886-1963), author of *The Basic Ideas of Calvinism*, emphasized only one principle, which he felt governed the other elements as a unifying system—"the absolute sovereignty of God."[44]

I am aware that the term *Reformed* is used widely as well as narrowly, as in my case. David Cornick provides a competent and useful survey of the Reformed tradition and asks "who are the Reformed?"[45] He reminds us that in one sense all Protestant churches are by nature Reformed and the terms *Reformed*, *Protestant*, and *evangelical* were used almost synonymously in the sixteenth century.[46] In that sense Reformed was a kind of theological umbrella for various groups. By 1660 the Reformed community had spread extensively to countries such as France, the Netherlands, Scotland, Poland, and Hungary, with a Presbyterian polity being adopted in many areas.

There was migration of many Reformed Christians and leaders during the seventeenth century, due to persecution, but a century or so later the Enlightenment,[47] with its allegiance to human reason over revelation and tradition, and, later, the Evangelical Revival, both contributed in different ways to modifying or developing a new expression of Reformed theology, as in the case of Jonathan Edwards (1703-1758). Schleiermacher later had enormous influence in interpreting Christian dogma in terms of religious experience, and Cornick is justified in regarding him as the considerable force behind "the development of twentieth century liberal theology."[48]

The theological plurality within Reformed communities and scholarship became more apparent, and in that context the neo-orthodoxy

43. De Witt, *What is the Reformed Faith?* 3–24.

44. Meeter, *Basic Ideas of Calvinism*, 15–23.

45. Cornick, *Letting God Be God*, 22–52.

46. Ibid., 11.

47. The Enlightenment refers to the dominant intellectual tendency in Western culture in the eighteenth century. Although there are diverse expressions of the Enlightenment, it largely consisted of four principles: (1) commitment to reason as the proper tool and final authority for determining issues; (2) stress on nature and the appeal to what is "natural;" (3) widespread acceptance of an idea of progress; (4) rejection of the authority of tradition. Immanuel Kant (1724-1804) saw his days as an age in the process of enlightenment, which required human freedom to make use of reasoning without any direction from another. Cf. Pailin, "Enlightenment," 179–180.

48. Cornick, *Letting God Be God*, 49.

of Karl Barth (1886–1968) emerged following the First World War of 1914–1918. He brought in his distinctive emphasis on the otherness and majesty of the Triune God, with the Scripture "becoming" the Word of God in moments of encounter with the Word, that is, the Lord Jesus Christ. On the continent of Europe, the term *Reformed* is now often associated with Barth and his distinctive theology.

Clearly I am using the term *Reformed* more narrowly to describe Reformed Presbyterian churches in the Netherlands, America, and Korea which have adhered more strictly to Calvin's theology and owe allegiance to the Reformed confessions, including the Westminster Confession of Faith. This is the section of the Reformed community where, in the twentieth century, a controversy occurred concerning preaching and its relation to the redemptive-historical method of interpreting and preaching Scripture.

I also acknowledge that the term *Reformed* is often used interchangeably with that of *evangelical* in parts of Europe. Historically the term *evangelical* can be traced back to the Reformation era in the sixteenth century and was initially used to refer to those writers wishing to revert to more biblical beliefs and practices than those associated with the medieval church.[49] Luther made use of the term to avoid his followers being called by his name. The term has now come to be widely used to refer to a major trans-denominational movement, especially in English-language churches and their theology, which lays emphasis upon the supreme authority of Scripture in the Christian life.[50] The word *evangelical*, however, like the other two terms, also came to be adopted and applied to diverse theological traditions such as German Pietism, the British Methodist Revival, the Great Awakening in the United States, the Pentecostal Movement, and Protestant fundamentalism.

John Stott (1921–2011) has distinguished the major marks of evangelicals as being "Bible people" and "gospel people."[51] Robert Johnston, writing of American evangelicalism, explained that evangelicals are those who believe the gospel is to be experienced personally, defined biblically, and communicated passionately.[52] David Bebbington suggested four key features as common characteristics of evangelicalism: conversionism (an

---

49. McGrath, *Evangelicalism and the Future of Christianity*, 11.
50. McGrath, *Christian Theology*, 110–13.
51. Stott, *What is an Evangelical?* quoted in Tidball, *Who Are the Evangelicals?* 12.
52. Tidball, *Who Are the Evangelicals?* 15.

emphasis on the "new birth" as a life-changing religious experience); biblicism (a reliance on the Bible as ultimate religious authority); activism (a concern for sharing the faith); crucicentrism (a focus on Christ's redeeming work on the cross).[53] D. Martyn Lloyd-Jones (1899–1981), an influential leader of the British Reformed wing of evangelicals, differentiated evangelicals from others in several ways. For example, preservation of the gospel (primarily recognition of the Bible as the sole authority); learning from history (recognizing the great Reformation but not being slaves to it); maintaining negatives (not embracing the wrong things); lack of subtractions or additions (no deviation from the pure gospel) help to explain the distinctive characteristics of evangelicals.[54] According to Lloyd-Jones, the priority of the evangelical is to submit to the Bible and to emphasize spiritual rebirth, church revival, evangelism, and preaching. These distinctions are also common to Reformed theology.

Notwithstanding these theological similarities, the two terms are not identical in their usage and connotations. People who prefer the term *evangelical* often tend to dislike confessional statements as being too theologically tight or exclusive. They strive to avoid theological narrowness and heterodoxy of doctrines and beliefs in order to place more stress on the gospel, evangelism, and social activity. It is therefore helpful to distinguish the term *Reformed* from that of *evangelical*, but there is an additional reason to maintain the distinction.

This important reason is found in the context of the Korean Reformed church. Unlike in Europe or America, the two terms are distinguished and only infrequently used interchangeably in Korean churches. For Koreans, the word *evangelical* includes the various traits of historic neo-evangelicalism and its development, which appeared and developed as a movement distinct from theological fundamentalism in the United States in the 1930s.[55] Historically, those preferring the term *evangelical* have embraced diverse theologies and criticized the narrowness of the Reformed group in Korea. Those maintaining the term *Reformed* tend to be more strict in essential doctrines like the inspiration of Scripture, the virgin birth of Christ, and the penal death and physical resurrection of the Lord; they embrace the original historic faith and theological tradition of the Reformers, especially Calvin and his successors. Because these

53. Bebbington, *Evangelicalism in Modern Britain*, 13–19.
54. Lloyd-Jones, *What is an Evangelical?* 33–42.
55. Erickson, *New Evangelical Theology*, 30–37.

two terms, *evangelical* and *Reformed*, are rarely used interchangeably in Korean churches, unlike in Western churches, I must distinguish them at this point.

The term *Reformed church* relates to Protestant churches in Korea which have believed and taught as their subordinate standard the Westminster Confession of Faith and the Shorter and Larger Catechisms since their first acceptance in Korea in 1907. The Reformed churches in Korea have focused especially on God's sovereignty in creation, providence, and salvation, and on the supreme authority of the Bible in all matters of faith and practice. This Reformed theology was dominant during the explosive growth period of the Korean church for several decades in the twentieth century, and so Korean Protestant churches, especially Presbyterian churches, are likely to call themselves Reformed and strive to keep these traditional doctrines.

Presbyterian

By the term *Presbyterian*, I understand a form of regional church government by presbyters, which consists of teaching elders, generally called pastors, and ruling elders.[56] Presbyterianism seeks to restore biblical church order, acknowledging Christ as the supreme head of the church and the only mediator between God and man, who rules in His church through His Word and by His Spirit through His appointed officers, who are regarded as presbyters. Above all, the authority of God's Word is used to establish and build biblical church order. Accordingly, the office-bearers who deliver God's Word in the church should be respected and supported.

Characteristically, Presbyterianism in Korea is strongly Calvinistic, and has been so from its beginnings because most of the early missionaries were Calvinists. However, Calvinistic or Reformed theology in Korea cannot be limited to a specific denomination, being spread over several theological groupings beyond church denominations, including Baptists. There are more than one hundred denominations in Korea which organize themselves under the term *Presbyterian*, but some of these do not practice Presbyterian polity or embrace Calvinism. I use the term *Presbyterian* in this research to refer to a church group, often calling itself Presbyterian, which both faithfully teaches Presbyterian polity and embraces Calvinism.

---

56. Clowney, "Presbyterianism," 530–31.

Original Research

I suggest there are five areas of research in this book which offer an original and important contribution to learning.

Firstly, although others have surveyed and evaluated the Dutch debate they have done so from a polemical or restricted theological position. Although I embrace Reformed theology, and previously followed the redemptive-historical method, I do not owe allegiance to any one side and recognize weaknesses on both sides of the debate. For that reason I am able to be more objective and critical.

A second contribution of this research is that I identify cultural and theological factors, as expressed through Pietism and Kuyperian teaching, as being the major cause of the Dutch controversy. I submit that other scholars have failed to recognize this adequately. One example of the latter is Greidanus, who refers to the cultural and theological background without exploring it because of his preference of majoring on the debate itself. I regard that as a serious omission and one which makes it more difficult to appreciate the debate's complexity.

A third area where this research offers an original contribution is in challenging the common assumption that the Dutch debate was simply continued in, or transferred later to, America. Only in a minor way was this true, and then only through Dutch immigration to America. However, this factor did not affect the American debate directly at all. Scholars have failed to recognize the uniqueness of the American debate. For example, the American debate was governed largely by eschatology, whereas this was not true in the Netherlands where there was a greater christocentric emphasis.

A fourth and related contribution of this research is that no one else has compared the Dutch and American debates. The reason for this is because scholars have tended to bracket the two together as being part of one continuous debate. But that is not borne out by the facts, as I demonstrate, and even Greidanus discusses only the Dutch debate and was not in a position to compare both debates.

A final and major contribution to learning in this research is that no one else has studied and compared both the Dutch and American debates critically while at the same time relating them to the debate in Korean churches. The Korean debate mirrors the Dutch and American debates, but little original work has been done and usually there has only been a mere recycling of the positions taught in the Dutch and

American debates. Consequently, there is considerable confusion, as well as misunderstanding, in Korean Presbyterian churches concerning this subject. My desire is that this original research with regard to the Dutch and American debates and its application to Korea may promote more understanding of the issues involved and contribute to greater precision in theologizing, as well as more effective preaching.

Background: Redemptive History in New Testament Theology

I assume in this research that the concept of redemptive history is rooted in the Bible.[57] Paul interpreted the plan of salvation as God's "economy of salvation" in his epistles.[58] Luke, as a careful investigator of gospel history, testified how the plan of God's salvation proceeded through Christ's and the apostles' actions.[59] Gerhard von Rad (1901–1971), an OT theologian, highlights the texts of Deut 26:5–9 and Josh 24:17–18 as being the confessions of God's saving activity in history.[60] Walter C. Kaiser (1933–), a retired professor of the Old Testament, found that the rudimentary points of the OT texts, for example, Gen 3:15, 9:25–27, 12:1–3; 2 Sam 7; Jer 31, consist in the single plan of God. God's promises point, from God's single plan, to a seed, a race, and a blessing of universal proportions. The progress of revelation and history are processed in that plan.[61] Willem VanGemeren, a leading theologian of redemptive-historical hermeneutics, claims that the NT authors were excited at the new era of Christ, in which all the acts of God, all the revelation of His promises and covenants, all the progression of His kingdom, and all the benefits of salvation are present.[62] This suggests, at least, that the concept of redemptive history was originally embedded in both the Old and New Testaments.

---

57. For example, Joseph tells his brothers "God sent me ahead of you to preserve for you a remnant on earth and to save your lives by a great deliverance" (Gen 45:7), giving a hint of this concept. See also Dan 2:44–45 and Isa 43:1–21.

58. Eph 1:4–14.

59. Luke 1:1–4; cf. Flender, *St. Luke*, 90–91.

60. Rad, *Theologie des Alten Testaments*, vol. 1; cf. Rust, *Salvation History*, 15.

61. Kaiser, *Toward an Old Testament Theology*, 39.

62. VanGemeren, *Progress of Redemption*, 27.

This biblical concept of redemptive history was retained by the Apostolic Fathers. For example, Ignatius of Antioch (35–107)[63] borrowed the NT term *oikonomia* (Eph 1:10), interpreted as "God's saving plan," to speak of the divine plan which was fulfilled in Christ.[64] Irenaeus of Lyons (125–200) also used the term and highlighted the concept of redemptive history to defend early Christianity from Gnosticism.[65] Augustine of Hippo (354–430) also found the concept of redemptive history in the Bible and used it to explain that human history is the process of the struggle between two cities—the city of God's people and the city of God's enemy.[66]

Joachim of Fiore (1135–1202)[67] also acknowledged the fact of redemptive history in the Bible and emphasized the eschatological structure of world history, which was divided into three ages or "states," according to the actions of the Holy Trinity.[68] The first state was from Adam to Isaiah; the second, the period of Christ, which began from the time of Isaiah's prophecies concerning the Messiah; and the third, the period of the Spirit, which began with Benedict (ca. 480–ca. 547), the founder of the spiritual life of monasticism.[69] This division is arbitrary, with no justifiable basis, but it assumes the notion of redemptive history throughout Scripture.

The Reformers developed the redemptive history concept by recovering the doctrine of the supreme authority of the Bible over Christian thought and life, under the logo *sola scriptura*. The development of biblical redemptive history can be perceived in their emphasis on the providence of the sovereign God, with three creational realities, namely, time, history, and culture, all converging theologically in the biblical doctrine of divine providence.[70] Calvin especially spoke of it as the secret plan by which God governs not only the redemption of His people but also all the events of the world.[71]

---

63. Ignatius, also known as Theophorus, was the third Patriarch of Antioch after Peter and Evodius; cf. Eusebius, *Church History*.

64. Cullmann, *Salvation in History*, 76.

65. Trimp, *Preaching and the History of Salvation*, 29.

66. Augustine, *Basic Writings of Saint Augustine*, vol. 1, 406–7.

67. Joachim was a Cistercian abbot and a significant theorist of history in the twelfth century.

68. Voight, "Joachim of Floris." Joachim taught that there had been a reign of the Father from the creation to the birth of Christ, and a reign of the Son, which would come to an end in 1260, followed by a reign of the Holy Spirit.

69. Bebbington, *Patterns in History*, 59.

70. Spykman, *Reformational Theology*, 270.

71. Calvin, *Institutes of the Christian Religion*, 1.16.1.

In the Post-Reformation era, Johannes Coccejus (1603-1669) developed the redemptive history concept more in terms of the history of God's covenant, which was called "federal theology."[72] For him, the entire human race stands in a federal relationship with God. The first Adam was the federal head of all posterity under the covenant of works into which God entered with him, but this first Adam failed to meet the conditions. The second Adam, Jesus Christ, is the federal head of all believers under the covenant of grace into which God entered with Him, promising Him the salvation of all believers as the reward of His obedience.[73] This perspective gives adequate attention to the unifying covenant of grace, spanning the entire period of redemptive history from the fall of man to the return of Christ, and it depicts the stages of salvation through which God leads the covenant people to eternal life and glorification. All these theologians found the theological concept of redemptive history in Scripture, even if they did not actually use that term.

In the late seventeenth and eighteenth centuries biblical interpretation related to the two most significant movements, Pietism[74] and Rationalism,[75] which appeared as a reaction to the previous orthodox Scholasticism, in which the Scriptures were looked upon as being beyond history and only as proof-texts supporting church doctrines. J. A. Bengel (1687-1752),[76] a pietist theologian, in his famous *Gnomon of the New Testament* (1742), emphasized God's economy as God's eternal plan of salvation of His people. For Bengel, the concept of redemptive history is not explicitly mentioned, but is implicitly expressed in Scripture as the providence of God over the whole history of salvation.[77] Rationalism

---

72. Cf. Asselt, *Federal Theology of Johannes Coccejus*.

73. Collins, "Federal Theology," 444.

74. Pietism means here the historical movement from Southern Germany in the seventeenth and eighteenth centuries which, seeking for "heart religion," reacted against the formalism and scholasticism of post-Reformation Christian religion, especially Lutheran orthodoxy. Philipp Jakob Spener (1635-1705) is the initiator of this movement, called *Collegia Pietatis*. Cf. Noll, "Pietism," 924-26.

75. Rationalism means here the philosophical movement expressed by thinkers like Descartes, Spinoza, and Leibniz in the seventeenth and eighteenth centuries in Europe. See Habermas, "Rationalism," 985-87; McGrath, *Christian Theology*, 60-61, 78-79.

76. Chi, "Modern Theology and the Concept of Redemptive-History," 199.

77. Weborg, "Bengel, J(ohann) A(lbrecht)," 289-94. Bengel was a German Lutheran NT theologian and pastor who founded Swabian Pietism, which was a branch of the contemporary German Pietism Movement. He suggested a new perspective of

began especially with Rene Descartes (1596-1650); it assumed reason to be a higher position than revelation and was even used to determine what parts of revelation were to be accepted as true.[78] Later, rationalists like J. S. Semler (1725-1791), J. P. Gabler (1753-1826), and G. L. Bauer (1755-1806) viewed the Bible solely as a human product in the history of religion, and subsequently the situation of biblical hermeneutics became more complex than before.[79] Scripture was no longer considered as the inerrant Word of God but as a merely human historical record which must be scrutinized under human critical sciences. This historical-critical principle of interpretation led many scholars to abandon traditional beliefs. For example, G. E. Lessing (1729-1781) rejected Christianity as having, as he thought, no verifiable truth of history, but nevertheless requiring unconditional assent to historical events.[80]

The nineteenth century saw the intrusion of the philosophy of G. W. F. Hegel (1770-1831)[81] into biblical hermeneutics and the rise of a new approach to redemptive history. F. C. Baur (1792-1860) developed a dialectical theory of interpreting the history of the early church, following Hegel's philosophy of history.[82] Thus Baur tended to undermine the reliability and historicity of Scripture.[83] This understanding firmly founded the Tübingen School[84] and also influenced William Wrede (1859-1906), who launched the History of Religions School in Göttingen.[85] In reaction to this rationalistic historicism, J. C. K. von Hofmann (1810-1877), J. Beck, and K. Auberlen, of the Erlangen School, emphasized "holy

---

biblical interpretation that sees God's consistent economy of centering creation and redemption in the Scriptures, rather than seeking subjective and dogmatic messages. He asserted that there is a persistent stream, named "Heils-Geschichte," according to God's logically objective principles, and this concept later deeply affected the school of redemptive-history.

78. Virkler, *Hermeneutics*, 69.
79. Davis, *Foundations of Evangelical Theology*, 270.
80. Kent, "History," 259.
81. Hegel, one of the most influential German philosophers, claimed that history is a forum in which the contradictions of finite thought are exposed between antithetical movements, and then through divine action they are repeatedly resolved into a higher level of cultural and spiritual status of synthesis; cf. De Vries, "Hegel," 544.
82. Ladd, *Theology of the New Testament*, 15.
83. Bray, *Biblical Interpretation*, 328-29.
84. Ladd, *Theology of the New Testament*, 15.
85. Bray, *Biblical Interpretation*, 336-37.

history" (*Heilsgeschichte*) as the best method of doing theology.[86] For them, all Scripture was bound together in this holy history because every event looked backwards, but also to the present and future.[87] This was first and foremost an organic view of history which was applied systematically to the field of hermeneutics.[88] However, they advocated a compromise between the predominant historical criticism and the traditional faith of Christianity in the authority of the Bible, but at the expense of the Reformed understanding of inspiration.[89] On this account B. Childs (1923–2007)[90] suggested that the theological origins of Hofmann's method of interpretation were rooted in the extensive influence of historical criticism and Hegelian philosophy.[91] The German term *Heilsgeschichte* could not therefore be recognized as being conservative or Reformed, because of its development under the umbrella of historical-criticism.

From the early period of the twentieth century there have been new movements of biblical hermeneutics influencing scholarship.[92] Among them, the most noteworthy groups relating to redemptive history are neo-orthodoxy, the Bultmannian School, and the New Hermeneutic. Firstly, neo-orthodoxy, ushered in by Barth at the end of the First World

---

86. Harrisville, "Von Hofmann," 376–80. Cf. Rottenberg, *Redemption and Historical Reality*, 29. Hofmann suggested that redemptive history could be a unifying theme congruently lined up in the whole Scriptures and that all Christians could recover real biblical faith through it. Strictly speaking, their concept was not a biblical perspective, due to their rationalist Hegelian philosophy.

87. Ramm, *Protestant Biblical Interpretation*, 80.

88. Preus, "Preface," xii.

89. Hofmann, *Interpreting the Bible*, 15–17.

90. Childs was a professor at Yale (1966–1988) and a leading exponent of biblical theology and canonical criticism. He integrated traditional thought with critical consciousness in developing his theme.

91. Childs, *Biblical Theology of the Old and New Testaments*, 17.

92. For about a century, from the end of the nineteenth century until the 1970s, historical criticism was broadly accepted as the only scientifically respectable way to study the Bible, but after the First and Second World Wars new types of religiously committed scholarship began to grow rapidly.

INTRODUCTION

War,[93] endeavored to see beyond history into "the spirit of the Bible."[94] Thus, for Barth, the true aim of interpreting the Scriptures is to reach "the Word of God," that is, Jesus Christ, behind the text. Encountering "the Word of God" became the primary theme in Barth's magnum opus, *Church Dogmatics* (1932–1967).[95] According to Barth, man's fallible words of proclamation could become God's Word when Christ is present in the words by the power of the Holy Spirit.[96] This means that the Bible should not be directly identified with God's self-revelation, for it is only a human witness to the "event" of God's Word.[97] This is a dynamic view of revelation on which neo-orthodox hermeneutics depends. According to this system, the resurrection of Christ is a real objective event, but the objectivity lies in the real man-God relationship behind the ordinary history (*Historie*), which is the dimension of *Geschichte*. For this reason, this methodology is called a "new objectivism" by S. M. Ogden.[98] This dualistic view of history, however, cast its shadow over the contemporary hermeneutics and homiletics of redemptive history. We shall discuss this in more detail in the following chapters.

Secondly, Bultmann (1884–1976) contended in his famous essay, "New Testament and Mythology" (1941), that the interpreter must unmask the myth and recover the original existential meaning of Scripture

---

93. Bray, *Biblical Interpretation*, 337–38. Barth absorbed the advanced liberal theology of A. von Harnack (1851–1930). He became a pastor in the Swiss town of Safenwill in 1912, but soon realized that he could not preach liberal theories in the parish, and realized that his teacher supported the German war aim. This made him think that the theories he had learned were wrong. He made an intensive study of Romans during the war years and the fruit, *The Epistle to the Romans*, came out in 1919 to shock the theological world.

94. Barth, *Epistle to the Romans*, 6–7. Barth said in his book, "By genuine understanding and interpretation I mean that creative energy which Luther exercised with intuitive certainty in his exegesis; which underlies the systematic interpretation of Calvin; and which is at least attempted by such modern writers as Hofmann, J. T. Beck, Godet, and Schlatter."

95. McGrath, *Christian Theology*, 98–99. *Church Dogmatics* is probably one of the most significant theological writings of the twentieth century.

96. Cobb, *Living Options in Protestant Theology*, 174.

97. Van Til, *Christian Theology of Knowledge*, 67.

98. Ogden, *Christ without Myth*, 55, quoted in Van Til, *Christian Theology of Knowledge*, 353–55. Ogden, a critic of Bultmann, defined Bultmann's approach as "objectivism," and Van Til later added "new" to this term in *A Christian Theory of Knowledge*.

in order for it to be acceptable to the modern mind.[99] Bultmann taught that the essential matter of history is not the temporality but only the contents of Christ's *kerygma* and the believer's reaction.[100] His understanding of history and of human existence led him to incorporate into his system an interpretation, mainly based on Martin Heidegger's existential philosophy, to determine what the myth says to contemporary readers.[101] In Bultmann's existential method, redemptive history in the Scriptures cannot be objective because they are, he claimed, written for man's existential decision. Thus there can be no possibility of objective redemptive history in Bultmann's hermeneutical system, but only an existential understanding of it. We shall also discuss this in more detail in the next chapter.

Thirdly, the New Hermeneutic, another existential movement from the 1950s, represented by Heidegger (1889–1976), and by the hermeneutical trio of Gerhard Ebeling (1915–2001),[102] Ernst Fuchs (1903–1983), and Hans Georg Gadamer (1900–2002),[103] sprang partly from Bultmann's scepticism about the NT, and was developed further, but differently, by its exponents. They considered that Bultmann's concept of history was confined to nineteenth century positivism, and that the twentieth century required a new concept of history, as developed by Wilhelm Dilthey (1833–1911) and R. G. Collingwood (1889–1943), in which only man's totality, the emotions and volition as well as the mind, forms the subject-matter of history. For acquiring the new subjective significance of history, they eventually devised "a new quest for the historical Jesus," which allegedly reaches a deeper level of historical reality.[104] Thence history is

---

99. Ramm, *Protestant Biblical Interpretation*, 87–88.

100. Bultmann, *Jesus and the Word*, 11–19; cf. Cullmann, *Salvation in History*, 40–45.

101. Bray, *Biblical Interpretation*, 468. Heidegger had a great influence on Bultmann through his classic work *Being and Time* (1927), which provided a philosophical framework for current hermeneutical theories.

102. Ebeling began his theological study in Marburg, where Bultmann introduced him to the methods of historical-criticism, form critical analysis of text, and also the wide field of exegetical, church-historical, and systematic theological research. His lifelong preoccupation with Luther's hermeneutics began in Marburg and is a new, mainly critical, way of approaching Luther; cf. Betz, "Gerhard Ebeling," 347–48.

103. Gadamer's philosophical development was strongly affected by Heidegger's teaching at Marburg from 1923 to 1928. Gadamer worked as Heidegger's assistant during that period, and submitted his research dissertation, "Plato's Dialectical Ethics" in 1928, under the guidance of Heidegger. Cf. Malpas, "Hans-Georg Gadamer."

104. Robinson, *New Quest of the Historical Jesus*, 71.

no longer objective positivist historiography. This view allegedly lessens the tension between history and faith, but the relation between *Historie* and *Geschichte* came to be more delicate.[105] The task of historiography, then, is to grasp the meaning for participants, and it is related to each participant's existential language.

In the New Hermeneutic, thus, the reality of redemptive history would be found in the speeches of participants of the events.[106] Language becomes a way of interpreting their world and experiences, since the deepest essence of man consists in this linguisticality (*Sprachlichkeit*), which means person to person "participation and communication."[107] For this reason the proponents of the New Hermeneutic understand biblical hermeneutics to be an account of the way in which God's Word becomes a language event.[108] The interpreter should participate in that event and redescribe it in his own language. Heidegger claimed that language is the "house" or "custodian" of Being or God, and so the interpreter's task is to find the "place where God can come to speech for us."[109] Only as the respective horizons of the text and interpreter interact can the words of the text become a language-event in relation to authentic human existence, which is the ultimate goal of hermeneutics.[110]

The New Hermeneutic has revealed the barrenness and aridity of liberal theology and its critical, negative approach to the Bible, but is itself guilty of a subjectivism which relativizes revealed biblical truth.[111] Another weakness of this method is the application of the language-event to exclusively imperative, direct language, and the discrediting of informative and descriptive language. Criticizing this position of Fuchs, Thiselton says,

> Fuchs refuses to define the content of faith . . . He is afraid of the Word as convention or as a means of conveying

---

105. Van Til, *New Hermeneutic*, 76.

106. Ramm, *Protestant Biblical Interpretation*, 90–91. This new concept is different from the traditional one in that, historically, hermeneutics meant the various rules given for interpreting ancient documents. For instance, sacred hermeneutics listed the special rules for interpreting Scripture, but in the New Hermeneutic the rules are not as important as "the language event."

107. Van Til, *New Hermeneutic*, 74–75.

108. Davies, "New Hermeneutic," part 1, 48.

109. Heidegger, *On the Way to Language*, 85.

110. Davies, "New Hermeneutic," part 1, 54.

111. Davies, "New Hermeneutic," part 2, 30.

information . . . Fuchs carries this so far that revelation reveals nothing . . . Jesus calls, indeed, for decision . . . But surely his Words, deeds, presence, and messages rested upon dogma, eschatological and theocratic.[112]

This existential method of interpretation influenced the homiletical struggles between redemptive-historical preaching and exemplary preaching; the former mainly focuses on the description of God's redemptive acts in the given text, while the latter mostly deals with the direct existential meaning of the Word of God to all who hear it. We discuss this in more detail in chapters 3 and 4.

Outline

In the twentieth-century, the debate concerning redemptive-historical preaching first occurred in the Dutch Reformed Church in the 1930s. This period saw the rise of a new movement of Calvinistic philosophy, founded by Herman Dooyeweerd (1894–1977) and D. H. Th. Vollenhoven (1892–1978), professors at the Free Reformed University in Amsterdam.[113] Johan H. Bavinck (1895–1964), a professor of missiology at Kampen from 1939, and at Amsterdam from 1955 to 1964,[114] described this new movement as a "new direction," because it reveals various elements of earlier pietism and mystical subjectivism in Dutch church life, and rejuvenates these ecclesiastical matters in a new direction.[115]

Some of the participants in the New Direction, for example, K. Schilder, B. Holwerda, H. J. Spier, and C. Veenhof, propagated a new way of interpreting and preaching the Bible, which was claimed to be the redemptive-historical approach. This new method stimulated many Dutch preachers to depart from the usual or traditional way of preaching, which may be called "exemplary preaching." However, supporters of the exemplary method, like J. Douma, Ph. J. Huyser, K. Dijk, and Bavinck, endeavored to retain it as a legitimate way of biblical preaching. Douma,

---

112. Marshall, *New Testament Interpretation*, 326.

113. Frame and Coppes, *Amsterdam Philosophy*, i–vi. Dooyeweerd and Vollenhoven also founded the Association for Calvinistic Philosophy in 1935, which functioned as a base camp for the new movement.

114. Bavinck was a nephew of Herman Bavinck (1854–1921), Professor of Systematic Theology in Amsterdam Free University from 1902 until his death in 1921.

115. Bavinck, *De toekomst van onze kerken*, 9, quoted in Greidanus, *Sola Scriptura*, 22.

one representative of the exemplary preaching group, said "Calvin considered himself to be called by God to preach sacred history also in an exemplary manner. And not only Calvin but all Reformed preachers held that conviction."[116] Notwithstanding its solid tradition and honoured practitioners, the proponents of redemptive-historical preaching laid a scathing critique against exemplary preaching. Eventually the critique gave rise to what is in fact the homiletical controversy.

The conflict raged through the Reformed Church in Holland during the 1930s and lasted until the early 1940s. The attack by the redemptive history group on their opponents' methods was at times excessive, for instance in saying that their methods were "not a ministry of the Word of God."[117] This was based on their excessive zeal for the ground motive, *sola scriptura*, in which they were not simply accepting its formal acknowledgement but wanted it to function exclusively (*sola*) in their preferred way in the interpretation and preaching of the Reformed Church.

However, this zeal for the Word waned around 1940, due to the arrest of Schilder by the Nazi authorities in 1940, and also due to the prohibition of the publishing of *De Reformatie*, the major voice for the redemptive history approach. From then on articles from both camps failed to attract any significant reaction. Worse still, the Dutch church, to which both parties of the debate belonged, split into two denominations in 1944 because of other doctrinal issues.[118] One denomination continued as the original Reformed Church of Holland, while the other was the so called Liberated or 31 Reformed Church of Holland.[119]

---

116. Douma, "Exemplarische prediking," no. 3336, quoted in Greidanus, *Sola Scriptura*, 29.

117. Dijk, *Pro-Ecclesia* 6, 279 quoted in Greidanus, *Sola Scriptura*, 44.

118. The synod of 1936 gave six subjects to a committee to investigate for "differences of theological perspective." These were: common grace; the covenant of grace; the immortality of the soul; the pluriformity of the church; the natures of Christ; self-examination at the Lord's Supper. Cf. Greidanus, *Sola Scriptura*, 25.

119. Both churches claimed the name "Gereformeerde Kerken in Nederland," but for the sake of convenience the secessionists are known as "the Liberated." The designation "31," which stands for Article 31 of the Church Order, to which Schilder appealed to repudiate the decisions of the synod, is also attached to the secessionists, including Schilder. In contrast, the other remaining group is called a "synodocratie." This 31 Article faction closely related with Koshin Presbyterian Church and is one of the reasons the Koshin denomination emphasizes redemptive-historical preaching so much. We will discuss this matter in more detail in chapters 4 and 5.

After a long analysis of the debate in *Sola Scriptura*, Greidanus claimed there was a "failure of both sides."[120] C. Trimp, Professor Emeritus at the Theological University of the Reformed Churches in Holland (Liberated), Kampen, considers that the debate is not yet over, but has been occasionally overshadowed by differences of theological perspective which affected the church separation in 1944.[121] Other assessments, like that of W. D. Jonker, of Stellenbosch University, also point to weaknesses and limitations in the redemptive history position, but the debate is complex and difficult to understand and will be discussed in greater detail in chapter 3.

The impact of the Dutch controversy extended beyond the borders of the Netherlands, at first to the English speaking world, then to other areas like South Korea. The Dutch debate directly influenced Clowney and his book *Preaching and Biblical Theology*.[122] This book in turn influenced the pulpits of Reformed churches in North America, centering on Westminster Theological Seminary, both in Philadelphia (founded in 1929), and in California (founded in 1979), where he had served as Professor of Homiletics.

Relying on Vos's concept of biblical theology, and considering the Dutch controversy, Clowney emphasized that biblical theology must be understood as the unfolding of redemptive history, specifically the whole of God's self-disclosure in Christ. Therefore, a preacher who highlights this history is leading the hearers to Christ, but otherwise he fails to do adequate preaching and falls into ethical or anthropocentric instruction. Clowney thus contends that the Christ-centered perspective of biblical theology must be applied to interpreting the Scriptures and in exercising a preaching ministry.[123] This new model of Christ-centered redemptive-historical preaching has been introduced to a wider Reformed and evangelical audience through his other writings since 1961, when *Biblical Theology and Preaching* was published, and more notably by *The Unfolding Mystery: Discovering Christ in the Old Testament* (1988) and then *Preaching Christ in All of Scripture* (2003). Clowney expected biblical theology to play a formative role in the ministry of God's Word

---

120. Greidanus, *Sola Scriptura*, 211–12.
121. Trimp, *Preaching and the History of Salvation*, 136–38.
122. Clowney, *Preaching and Biblical Theology*, 78–86.
123. Clowney, *Preaching Christ in All of Scripture*, 33.

and his expectation was realized, but it also became the cause of a further homiletical debate, this time in North America.

Due to Vosian biblical theology and Clowney's legacy, a special emphasis on the redemptive history principle appeared in North America. James T. Dennison and his brothers Charles G. Dennison and William D. Dennison are representatives of the so called "extreme wing of the redemptive historical school."[124] James Dennison, editor of *Kerux: A Journal of Biblical-Theological Preaching*,[125] and Professor of Church History and academic dean of Northwest Theological Seminary (NWTS), Lynwood, Washington, says "Biblical-theological preaching will bring our people to the arms of Jesus . . . Preaching which does any less is bankrupt . . . anything less is the promotion of the earthly agenda of the preacher."[126] "Biblical-theological" preaching means, here, the exclusive redemptive-historical preaching. Dennison insists it is none other than God Himself who speaks to us in His Word, and who displays His own person and work in redemptive history.[127]

However, John M. Frame, a professor at Reformed Theological Seminary, Orlando, demonstrates the fallacy of this redemptive history school, saying,

> James Dennison objects to the term 'application,' because he believes it had connotations in theologies like Schleiermacher's and Bultmann's. But criticizing language on such grounds is an instance of the genetic fallacy . . . And the alternative 'living in the text' is really too vague to denote a purposeful ethical preaching thrust."[128]

John Carrick,[129] Professor of Applied and Doctrinal Theology at Greenville Presbyterian Theological Seminary, describes the failures of redemptive-historical preaching. For Carrick, it fails to note and implement in its

---

124. Carrick, *Imperative of Preaching*, 134.

125. *Kerux* was first published in 1986 by James T. Dennison, Jr. while he worked as a librarian and lecturer in Church History at Westminster Theological Seminary in California from 1980 to 2000, and is committed to the hermeneutical methodology of Geerhardus Vos, the discipline of biblical theology, and redemptive-historical preaching.

126. Dennsion, "What is Biblical Theology?" 32–41.

127. Ibid., 40.

128. Frame, "Ethics, Preaching, and Biblical Theology," 3.

129. Carrick was formerly minister of Cheltenham Evangelical Church, UK and Matthews Orthodox Presbyterian Church, North Carolina, USA.

preaching the indicative-imperative pattern or structure of the NT.[130] He explains the reasons in another book, *The Imperative of Preaching*: "The extreme wing of the redemptive-historical school demonstrates an idealization—indeed, almost an idolization—of Geerhardus Vos as a preacher which must be challenged."[131]

A theological conference was held at Greenville Theological Seminary on 12–14 March 2002, in which the two parties in the controversy had an opportunity to seek reconciliation. However, rather than achieve reconciliation, the discussion deepened their division and differences. Although influenced by the Dutch debate initially, the American debate has not developed in the same way as the Dutch debate, due to being wholly dependent on Vos's biblical theology and Clowney's legacy. It is thus more difficult to assess this debate. We will examine the criticisms of both parties more thoroughly in chapter 4.

In Korea, a corresponding homiletical debate occurred between scholars of the Reformed churches in 1998. A few critical articles about redemptive-historical preaching, in *Geu-Mal-Seum* (meaning "The Words,") ignited the controversy. Chang-Gyun Chung said,

> Scripture is the record of history of God's redemption . . . In this respect it can be said that biblical preaching should be necessarily of the redemptive-historical method and characteristically Christ-centered. Thus preachers must make efforts for redemptive-historical preaching while equipping themselves with the hermeneutical methodology of Reformed biblical theology."[132]

Jong-Kil Byun explained analytically that the methodological differences between redemptive-historical and exemplary preaching essentially lie in whether the practice of taking a human example for us today from a specific text of biblical history, like Abraham's lie (Gen 12:10–12), should be thoroughly discarded or broadly accepted. For Byun, the false opposition to correct exemplary preaching causes considerable theological confusion.[133]

These discussions, in *Geu-Mal-Seum*, stimulated more criticism of the redemptive-historical method. Jee-Chan Kim claimed that the method neglects an essential grammatical-literal analysis of the text and

---

130. Carrick, "Redemptive-Historical Preaching," 156–57.
131. Carrick, *Imperative of Preaching*, 138.
132. Chung, "Ground of Redemptive-Historical Preaching," 13.
133. Byun, "Meaning and Limit of Redemptive-Historical Preaching," 23.

goes directly into a canonical-theological interpretation.[134] For him, this swallowing up of the primary grammatical-literary interpretation is the outcome of the redemptive historical approach in Korea.[135] Shortly afterwards, Hae-Moo Yoo refuted Kim's assertion that there were defects in the Korean style of redemptive-historical preaching, maintaining that it had not yet been fully introduced to the Korean pulpit and thus required further development rather than to be discarded. Kim responded that Yoo had misconceived his view of redemptive-historical preaching, for his intention had been to criticize it constructively and build up a proper redemptive-historical preaching approach which would be through the right process, namely, the grammatical-literary approach.[136] I suggest there is confusion and misunderstanding over these respective terms and the related language used in this Korean debate.

The Korean homiletical debate arose from reading about the Dutch and American debates, with a consequent consideration of their influence on Korean churches. The essential content of the debate is similar to earlier ones. Sung-Jong Shin described it:

> The problems of the Korean pulpit that I am discussing are not my own, but, in truth, Greidanus dealt with them in his book, and I am just transposing the situation to Korea and reconsidering it . . . It would not be a small challenge to the Korean pulpit to check if our preaching is really biblical.[137]

However, the context of the Korean debate is different from that of the earlier Western debates and needs to be carefully examined, along with the historical and theological background. We will discuss this in more detail in chapters 5 and 6.

The Korean homiletical debate reveals several characteristics, while highlighting also some questions. It occurred later and has been governed by the Dutch and then American debates. Is the Korean debate dependent on these? If so, to what extent? Furthermore, there are many misunderstanding over the redemptive historical method, even though Korean participants in the debate refer to the original controversies. What are these misunderstandings? Again, while participants in the Korean debate agree in their desire to embrace and develop the

---

134. Kim, "Is it Right to Keep Redemptive-Historical Preaching in This Way?"
135. Sho, *Debate of Redemptive-Historical Preaching*, 9–15.
136. Kim, "To Answer Hae-Moo Yoo's Refutation."
137. Shin, "Problems of the Korean Pulpit," 54–55.

right method for hermeneutics and homiletics, why did their efforts in the previous debates fail or stagnate? How can we move forward in this Korean debate? These will be some of the major questions discussed here, and especially how we can contribute positively to this debate in Korea.

In this chapter I have described my aims, defined key terms, described briefly the background to, and history of, the redemptive historical method, and outlined briefly the redemptive historical homiletical debates in Holland, the United States, and Korea. As part of the background to the redemptive historical homiletical debates in the Netherlands and America, I intend in the next chapter to describe the hermeneutical roots of redemptive history.

2

Redemptive History

Hermeneutical Roots

We have now examined various understandings of the term *redemptive history* in Korean Presbyterian churches as they relate to Western theologians and their influence. I established that the understanding of redemptive history depends on one's view of Scripture. Now I want to identify the hermeneutical roots of the concept of redemptive history by tracing the way in which the history of God's redemption has been perceived in Scripture by key scholars. This is necessary in order to understand the redemptive historical concept further, and also to remove the confusion which currently exists in regard to the concept, especially in Korea.

Delimitations

Scholars have offered their own explanations concerning the relation of history and Christianity, but some of these are not immediately relevant to this research for two reasons. Firstly, the various philosophical and humanist approaches to the subject deviate from our major theme which focuses primarily on biblical hermeneutics and homiletics. On the one hand, philosophers of history normally ask if history has any meaning or goal towards which it is ultimately moving, and how changes in history take place.[1] On the other hand, other humanist scholars are interested in

---

1. Nash, *The Meaning of History*, 5–11. According to Nash, the proposed

how people think of history in a specific period, and how it differs from one culture to another. For example, Herbert Butterfield (1900–1979) depicted the relationship between Christianity and history[2] by suggesting that Christianity has distinctive religious doctrines centering in historical events like the crucifixion and the resurrection of Jesus Christ, events which provide an interpretation of the whole drama of human life and thus affect one's ability to face and understand other historical events. Butterfield presented a distinctive concept of history in his *History and Human Relations*, in which he describes history as judging human evil and distortions, like German Nazism, which is one essential characteristic of history.[3] David Bebbington also clearly articulates a Christian view of history in his *Patterns of History*, while introducing traditional ideas about the course of history. These are, according to Bebbington, the ancient notion of history as a revolving wheel; the Christian concept of history as a straight line under the control of God; the idea of progress which appeared in the period of the Enlightenment; historicism as a reaction against the Enlightenment; and Marxism as a socialist theory of history.[4] Both Butterfield and Bebbington deal with a Christian concept of history in significant and helpful ways, but they do not discuss in detail the hermeneutical aspect, that is, how we obtain that historical concept from the text of Scripture. Butterfield and Bebbington suggest a Christian understanding of history as being the most acceptable, but this research needs to proceed further to examine the theological and hermeneutical grounds of a Christian understanding of history, namely, its origin, nature, development, and application.

---

explanations about the momentum of history are Hegel's "world hero," Vico's "divine providence," Marx's "economic determinism," and Toynbee's formula of "challenge and response."

2. Butterfield, *Christianity and History*, 1–8. Butterfield abstracted the relationship between the two saying, "History must be a matter of considerable concern to Christians in so far as religion in this way represents the attempt to engage oneself with the whole problem of human destiny . . . Christianity in any of its traditional and recognisable forms has rooted its most characteristic and daring assertions in that ordinary realm of history with which the technical student is concerned."

3. Butterfield, *History and Human Relations*, 37–65. According to Butterfield, before the First World War, men even imagined that they could control the course of history and mould the shape of the future, but at the very peak of the disaster they came across the most crucial problem of all: that humans might be able to determine evil.

4. Bebbington, *Patterns in History*, 43–67. Bebbington suggests that Christian history exclusively talks of God's providence controlling human history in a straight line to the goal that God had set originally in His creation of the world.

Secondly, while a general exploration of a Christian concept of history would be helpful for comparing differing philosophies of history, it is not relevant to my study of redemptive history as an aspect of biblical hermeneutics; the latter needs to be approached theologically, not philosophically. For example, a French historian, Trygve R. Tholfsen, sketches the origins and development of a Christian understanding of history, referring to some scriptural figures like Jeremiah, Ezekiel, and Paul.[5] The objective of that delineation is, however, to trace the historical thinking of people through human history, from ancient time to the modern period. The arbitrary methodology Tholfsen employs is simplistic and makes the Christian concept of history so generalized that it may disregard the diversity and complexity of theological views about redemptive history in the Bible, with which we are concerned in this research. Some of these approaches by philosophers are thus inappropriate for this study because their scope and methodology are radically different.[6] In this chapter, I now intend to focus exclusively on the hermeneutical background to redemptive history in the discipline of biblical theology.

This research needs additional delimitation to a more specific area of biblical interpretation because the subject itself is too broad to be handled adequately here. Since Bauer first separated the discipline of biblical theology into OT and NT theology,[7] there have been considerable developments and, accordingly, increased complexity in both disciplines. Some scholars, like Vos and B. Childs, claim to deal with both testaments as a unified subject, but most scholars handle them separately and sometimes to such an extent that it seems that OT and NT theology are totally different from each other. For example, Hasel treats basic issues of NT theology separately from OT theology, even though he admits that many basic issues in the former are related to those in the latter.[8] On the other hand, Vos had begun his biblical theology with the OT but could not finish the whole scope of NT theology within his life time, while others, like D. L. Baker, deal with both testaments as a unity, but his description

---

5. Tholfsen, *Historical Thinking*, 1–17, 60–92.

6. In general, historians have sought for certain philosophies of history about how people understand history in the context of a specific culture and religion. Our sole concern in this research, however, is the history of God's redemption and how theologians perceive it in Scripture, not in human culture. Therefore, those aforementioned philosophical and historical approaches cannot be within the range of our research.

7. Childs, *Biblical Theology of the Old and New Testaments*, 5.

8. Hasel, *New Testament Theology*, 10.

of the redemptive history theme is superficial.⁹ It is therefore more appropriate for the purpose and focus of this book to limit our survey on redemptive history scholars to NT theology alone.

Historical Background: Redemptive-Historical Hermeneutics

The earliest biblical interpreters, such as the Jewish rabbis and scribes, presupposed that God is the author of Scripture and that each incidental detail in it has a secret meaning.[10] They developed several principles of the ancient Jewish exegesis, which remained at the time of Christ as well as in the apostolic and later periods. These Jewish principles are the "literal, midrashic, pesher, and allegorical."[11] Philo (20 BC–54 AD) was famous for using the allegorical tradition in Alexandria, striving to reconcile Jewish Scripture with Greek philosophy.[12] The word *allegory* means, by definition, something different from what is actually written, allowing the transpositon of morally unacceptable things in myths into the thought-forms of the contemporary culture.[13]

Christian scholars in Alexandria were influenced by this prevailing method of interpretation. Bernard Ramm (1916–1992) explains that allegorism had originally been developed by the Greeks and influenced Christians in Alexandria, where there was a considerable Jewish population at the time.[14] The exegetical school of Alexandria embraced these allegorical legacies. Clement of Alexandria (150–215) and his pupil Origen (185–254), for example, are the most prominent representative

---

9. Vos, *Biblical Theology*, 3–4; cf. Baker, *Two Testaments, One Bible*, 257–270.

10. Virkler, *Hermeneutics*, 48.

11. Longenecker, *Biblical Exegesis in the Apostolic Period*, 28–50. A literal method was considered to be foundational for any other type of interpretation. The midrashic method combined texts containing similar words and gave them an interpretive significance, while the pesher interpretation, which existed particularly among the Qumran communities, was almost identical with the midrashic but focused more on the eschatological significance. The allegorical exegesis found what it regarded as the true meaning by extended metaphor beneath the letter in Scripture.

12. Scholer, "Introduction to Philo Judaeus," xi–xviii. Scholer says that Philo is significant for understanding first century AD Hellenistic Judaism because he is the main surviving literary figure of Hellenistic Judaism of the Second Temple period of ancient Judaism.

13. Kannengiesser, "Biblical Interpretation in the Early Church," 6.

14. Ramm, *Protestant Biblical Interpretation*, 24–25.

theologians of this school.[15] This allegorism was typically a trait of the gnostic interpretation of Scripture, which Irenaeus criticized as being "inverse exemplarism,"[16] and which disregarded the historicity of events in Scripture. This allegorical tradition, however, continued in various forms in the history of hermeneutics, giving rise to exegetical problems which weaken the factuality of God's saving events in Scripture.

The school[17] of Antioch started over against that of Alexandria, avoiding both the letterism of the Jews and the allegorism of the Alexandrians.[18] Theodore of Mopsuestia (350–428) and John Chrysostom (349–407) belonged to the latter group.[19] The proponents of this school denounced allegorical exegesis as depriving Scripture of its historical character, insisting on the historical reality of the biblical revelation, and they accordingly staunchly defended the principle of the literal and historical interpretation of Scripture.[20] For them, the historical narratives of Scripture should not be confused with allegory, but be understood literally, with the possible addition of a spiritual element. This school could be said to be the first hermeneutical group in history to focus on the historical event itself as the means of exploring spiritual and theological truth.[21]

The hermeneutics of the Western church[22] were influenced by both of these schools. For example, Jerome (340–420) contributed significant-

---

15. Berkhof, *Principles of Biblical Interpretation*, 20. Clement suggested five principles of interpretation: historical, doctrinal, prophetic, philosophical, mystical. Mystical was subdivided into three: literal, moral, and allegorical or mystical. In practice, Clement mostly employed allegory, believing it was only allegory that yielded true knowledge.

16. Norris, "Irenaeus," 41. The term means that an interpreter tries to transpose human exemplars into the historical events of Scripture.

17. Here "school" means a group of exegetes and theologians who shared a common theology and exegesis.

18. Simonetti, *Biblical Interpretation in the Early Church*, 67–69. Here "letterism" or "hyper-literalism" is different from literalism. For example, when we read in Scripture "The eyes of the Lord are on the righeous" (Ps 34:15), the letterism of Alexandria would attribute an actual eye to God, while the literalism of Antioch understands it as referring to God's omniscience.

19. Kaiser and Silva, *Introduction to Biblical Hermeneutics*, 221. Even though the principal representatives of the Antioch school—Diodorus, Theodore, John Chrysostom, Theodoret—differ in some details from one another, the general tendency of their approaches to interpretation can be summed up as literalism and anti-allegorism.

20. Virkler, *Hermeneutics*, 62.

21. Kaiser and Silva, *Introduction to Biblical Hermeneutics*, 221; cf. Ramm, *Protestant Biblical Interpretation*, 49.

22. The term "Western Church" is used in contrast to "Eastern Church" after

ly to the Latin world by his translation of the Vulgate Bible, embracing Origen's allegorical methods to a large degree.[23] Augustine also had a great influence on the Western world with his allegorical tendency.[24] He articulated twelve principles of sound biblical interpretation, but in practice he tended towards excessive allegorizing.[25] For example, Augustine justified an allegorical interpretation by suggesting that 2 Cor 3:6, "for the written code kills, but the Spirit gives life" (*RSV*), unquestionably supports an allegorical interpretation as the life-giving method, while other interpretations kill spiritual life.[26] Augustine indulged himself much in allegorical interpretation and therefore influenced many in the Middle Ages.

Biblical interpretation in the medieval age continued the hermeneutical theories of the Early Fathers.[27] The emphasis on both ecclesiastical tradition and authority over biblical interpretation was strengthened and further solidified. The major figure in this era was Thomas Aquinas (1225–1274), who defended the literal sense of Scripture yet emphasized its symbolism, because the heavenly aspect was thought to be expressed

---

Christendom in the Patristic period (100–451) became geographically and linguistically divided in the Roman Empire. This division developed tension between the Christian leadership at Rome and Constantinople and resulted in the great East-West Church schism in 1054. Cf. Needham, *The Age of the Early Church Fathers*, 102–103; Sohm, *Outlines of Church History*, 59–66; McGrath, *Christian Theology*, 5–7.

23. Bray, *Biblical Interpretation*, 92. Even though Jerome claimed to reject allegorism, his writings indicate that he remained tied to this tradition.

24. Simonetti, *Biblical Interpretation in the Early Church*, 103–8. According to Simonetti, Augustine became a strong allegorist because he converted to Christianity due to hearing Ambrose's allegorical exegesis of the OT, or as a result of the Manichean controversy.

25. Berkhof, *Principles of Biblical Interpretation*, 22. Cf. Ramm, *Protestant Biblical Interpretation*, 36–37. Augustine was illuminated by the allegorical interpretation of the OT by Ambrose when he struggled with the coarse literalism of the Manicheans. Cf. Virkler, *Hermeneutics*, 61. Virkler explained this point by affirming that Augustine's forsaking of his own principle of interpretation in practice made his exegetical commentaries some of the least valuable parts of his writings.

26. Ramm, *Protestant Biblical Interpretation*, 35. According to Ramm, this is obviously a misinterpretation of the biblical statement, which implies that the gospel under the Holy Spirit gives life while the written Law of the OT kills. Ramm says "This abuse of this Scripture has continued throughout history and to this hour." He says that neo-orthodoxy uses it in declaring "Existential interpretation gives life, literal interpretation is the wooden, lifeless letter."

27. Grant, *Short History of the Interpretation of the Bible*, 119. Grant described the position of church officers at that time as institutionalized and the majority of priests ignorant of how to understand the Bible.

in earthly terms.[28] This attitude mostly relied upon the ecclesiastical tradition of the early church leaders, like Athanasius.[29]

In the Reformation period this traditional approach was gradually abandoned.[30] Reformers, such as Luther and Calvin, rejected the allegorical method of interpretation with a renewed emphasis on the sole and supreme authority of the Bible. Luther warned, "Allegory is a sort of beautiful harlot, who proves herself especially seductive to idle men."[31] Calvin also described allegory as "a contrivance of Satan," while insisting on an essential rule of Reformational hermeneutics, "Scripture interprets Scripture."[32] This Reformed rule, *sola scriptura*, afterwards became a touchstone of Protestant biblical hermeneutics. To approach the original text of Scripture, a study of its languages was required and an understanding of the historical background and context of the text were emphasized. This approach is theoretically simple but practically demanding, because considerable research and preparatory work are prerequisites for its success. Most of Scripture may become clearer under the rule of "self-interpretation," but in some parts of Scripture, such as in apocalyptic literature, the rule is more difficult to apply. Nevertheless, various understandings about the rule and its application, for example Hofmann's *Heilsgeschichte* theology and Vos's Reformed theology, have been developed by using it. Thus we need to identify and survey the hermeneutical roots of redemptive history in relation to this historical background.

Post Reformation Hermeneutics and Redemptive History

Following the Reformation, and especially after the Enlightenment, redemptive-historical hermeneutics in Protestantism developed in three main ways: in historical criticism, existentialism, and Reformed biblical

---

28. Kaiser and Silva, *Introduction to Biblical Hermeneutics*, 222.

29. Bray, *Biblical Interpretation*, 105. According to Bray, Athanasius was the first exegete who placed the church strongly in the center of Christian hermeneutics. This feature remains characteristic of the hermeneutics of both the Roman Catholic and Eastern Orthodox churches.

30. Berkhof, *Principles of Biblical Interpretation*, 65.

31. Luther, *Lectures on Genesis*, Comments on Gen 3:15–20.

32. Farrar, *History of Interpretation*, 347. Calvin also stated that "it is the first business of an interpreter to let the author say what he does say, instead of attributing to him what we think he ought to say."

theology. A similar classification can be found in Jong-Kil Byun in 1997: the existential method of Barth and Bultmann, the employment of the Erlangen School and its followers, like Cullmann, and the approach of Dutch Reformed theologians like Schilder and Holwerda.[33] Byun does not, however, elucidate the grounds for his classification, except to emphasize the difference between the approaches of the Erlangen School and the Dutch Reformed group. According to Byun, the former and the latter both emphasized the redemptive-historical approach for interpreting Scripture, but the Erlangen School was influenced by Hegel's philosophy of history while the Dutch were not. Byun's weakness is that he does not argue convincingly for these divisions in the redemptive-historical hermeneutical approach.

The post-Reformation hermeneutics of redemptive history has been developed under a discipline generally described as "biblical theology,"[34] which emphasized the role of history in viewing Scripture. Biblical theology concerns that theology which is found in the Bible in its own historical setting and thought forms, while systematic theology seeks to organize the teaching of the Bible and suggest its relevance for today.[35] Biblical theologians search for the original significance or authorial intent of the given scriptural text in its own historical context. Ladd pointed out that the Bible has the obvious intent of telling a story about God and His acts in history for man's salvation.[36] James Barr affirmed, however, that there are so many different concepts of "revelation through history" that it would be illegitimate to arbitrarily group together such diverse positions into several preset domains.[37] Ladd and Barr, therefore, differ from each other in viewing the original intent of Scripture, and the "history of God's saving acts" in Scripture may be interpreted differently by biblical

---

33. Byun, *Holy Spirit and Redemptive History*, 22. This book was originally Byun's doctoral dissertation at Kampen in 1992, titled "The Holy Spirit Was Not Yet: A Study on the Relationship between the Coming of the Holy Spirit and the Glorification of Jesus according to John 7:39."

34. Vos, *Biblical Theology*, 5–10. Vos defined biblical theology as the branch of exegetical theology which deals with the process of the self-revelation of God deposited in the Bible. Here "the process" means successive, progressive, and organic acts of God in the course of history. Thus this discipline naturally cannot but emphasize the historical aspect.

35. Piper, "Biblical Theology and Systematic Theology," quoted in Ladd, *Theology of the New Testament*, 20.

36. Ladd, *Theology of the New Testament*, 25.

37. Barr, *Old and New in Interpretation*, 65–66.

theologians. Although the idea of the redemptive-historical concept was actually rediscovered by biblical theology,[38] the understanding of it has not been identified exclusively with any single hermeneutical program in the development of biblical theology.

The term *biblical theology* initially denoted a theology contained within the Bible, or a theology which accorded with the Bible.[39] It was also used originally to refer to a collection of proof-texts supporting systematic theology. Further, it was employed by the Pietistic movement as against the more dogmatic approach to Scripture on the part of the hyper-scholasticism in the Lutheran Church in the mid-seventeenth century. The term began to embrace its modern meaning when Gabler defined it with historical character.[40] The crucial element in Gabler's definition of biblical theology was the need to search for what the biblical writers originally meant about divine matters in its own historical context.[41] Here historical-critical methodology was introduced to interpret the Bible.

Bauer expanded practically on the methodology of Gabler in his study of OT and NT biblical theology. Previously, Semler had established the key principle of historical criticism by affirming that the Word of God and Holy Scripture are not identical.[42] The sharp distinction between God's words and the human form of Scripture became a major characteristic of historical criticism. Baur developed this historical-critical methodology further by incorporating Hegel's historical philosophy into biblical theology, and then its principle was firmly formulated by E. Troeltsch in the so-called "historicism"[43] approach, of which the central idea is that all human cultures including religion are moulded by history.

---

38. The idea of redemptive history is originally embedded in Scripture, and then scholars advocating it find its concept through their study of the Bible. See chapter 1.

39. Ebeling, *Word and Faith*, 79–97.

40. Vos, *Biblical Theology*, 9.

41. Baker, "Biblical Theology," 96–99. Gabler had introduced the new discipline in his inaugural lecture at the University of Altdorf on 31 March 1787. He himself never wrote a biblical theology, but the principle set the basis for future work on the subject.

42. Kümmel, *New Testament*, 63, quoted in Hasel, *New Testament Theology*, 21.

43. Kroner, "History and Historicism," 131–34. Historicism cannot be simply defined in a sentence because it has been intricately linked with various concepts of literature, philosophy, arts, etc. However, in biblical study, historicism points to a certain overvaluation of the historical view, which stresses that the function of history is to attain objective truth from past sources.

Biblical theology, as a modern discipline, rediscovered historical aspects of the Bible by the principles of historical criticism, and also influenced readers to see the biblical text through a longitudinal perspective rather than a cross-sectional one, taking notice of the specific context of time, location, the relation with before and after. This view, however, involved renouncing the verbal inspiration and supreme authority of the Bible which was the legacy of Reformers like Luther and Calvin. The school of *Heilsgeschichte*, an allegedly conservative party, strove to defend the traditional role of the Bible and eventually designated two distinctive and remarkably compatible divisions of history, that is, *Historie*, which is verifiable through historical investigation, and *Geschichte*, which is not provable, but acceptable only through one's faith in the same way as people accepted ancient Greek myths. Since then this school has appeared successful in gaining ascendancy in the field of biblical theology; however, its residual overvaluation of history was criticized by both conservative and liberal sides as they were unable to free biblical study from the prevailing historicism in the late eighteenth and nineteenth centuries.

From the early mid-twentieth century, a revolutionary movement in biblical theology emerged, with its major concern shifting to the theological or existential meaning for individual believers rather than to historical objectivity, which had prevailed over biblical hermeneutics in the nineteenth century. This movement actually took place against the preceding historicism and facilitated the new theological tendency, Dialectic / Existential Theology.[44] The previous purely historical approach dealt only with historical aspects of the Bible, tending to ignore the theological dimension, with a significant gap emerging between its scholars and ordinary Christians who wanted practical theological messages from the Bible. Barth experienced this chasm so keenly in his own parish that he felt the need to develop a new way of interpretation in order to hold the more valid aspects of the Bible;[45] this was expressed in his *Epistle to the Romans* (1919), which launched his famous dialectical theology. The similar question of how the historical factuality of the Bible relates to personal existence troubled Bultmann, for whom historical criticism was a theological base that explicated the inner meaning of the biblical message, the *kerygma* being the authentic theological agenda. He finally

---

44. Baker, "*Biblical Theology*," 96–99.
45. Barth, *Epistle to the Romans*, v.

formulated an "existential interpretation" by means of his own method.[46] Both Barth and Bultmann succeeded in degrading the monolithic historicism of the nineteenth century, but eventually minimized the importance of the historical reality of Christianity, focusing only on the kerygmatic or existential aspects of revelation.[47] Their approaches have greatly influenced succeeding scholars in the formation of new methods like the New Hermeneutic, and the "sociological approach."

When existentialist theology appeared and began to thrive, conservative scholars also began to raise their voices against the prevailing theological liberalism. Vos, for example, responded to works like Wrede's *The Messianic Secret* in order to defend what he regarded as the Reformed faith in his early writings such as *The Teaching of Jesus Concerning the Kingdom and the Church* (1903) and *The Self-Disclosure of Jesus* (1926). F. W. Grosheide, a Dutch theologian, ardently vindicated a crucial Reformed principle in his book, *De eenheid der Nieuw-Testamentische gods-openbaring* (*The Unity of the New Testament Divine Revelation*).[48] In the late 1940s, Vos formulated a redemptive-historical approach as representing Reformed biblical theology, in his *Biblical Theology: Old and New Testaments* (1948). He firmly embraced the doctrines of the Westminster Confession of Faith at a time when the Presbyterian Church in the USA attempted to revise its creed.[49] Ladd supported Vos and the traditional biblical-historical approach as the only possible way of dealing adequately with the reality of God and His breaking into history.[50] Childs pointed out that biblical theology had reached a crisis because the biblical norms, overly combined with a liberal criticism, had resulted in dismal failure.[51] Hasel then suggested the biblical-historical standpoint as a better starting-point for biblical theology.[52] These scholars set a distinct foundation for further advanced theological reflection on the so called redemptive historical perspective, or biblical historical view, which is essentially different from both historicism and existentialism in their approach to the history of redemption.

46. Macquarrie, "Demythologizing," 150–51; cf. Bultmann, *Jesus Christ and Mythology*; Macquarrie, *Existentialist Theology*.

47. Morgan, "Bible and Christian Theology," 124–25.

48. Webster, "Geerhardus Vos," 312.

49. Dennison, "Geerhardus Vos," 83–92.

50. Ladd, "Search for Perspective," 41–43.

51. Childs, *Biblical Theology in Crisis*.

52. Hasel, *Old Testament Theology*, 85.

There have been, therefore, at least these three strands of hermeneutics within redemptive history in the history of biblical theology: historical criticism, existentialism, and Reformed biblical theology. There are three reasons in support of this classification. Firstly, historical criticism has been important within the post-Reformation strands of biblical hermeneutics; it also provides an extensive foundation for modern biblical interpretation and has a specific relation to the nineteenth century's redemptive-historical hermeneutic. Secondly, the existentialist reaction to the historical-critical approach is another important trend which must be acknowledged for it offers a new perspective for redemptive history in the Bible. This methodology is currently influential in biblical hermeneutics and raises controversial issues for Western hermeneutics, as well as for the Korean church. Thirdly, while historical criticism and existentialism have powerfully influenced the theological world, the other distinct movement has arisen and succeeded in Reformed theological circles. This latter movement is substantially different from the other two approaches of historical-criticism and existentialism in that it starts from the Reformed perspective of God and His revelation.

Even though the classification of the above three approaches relating to redemptive history is rarely found in Western literature, I suggest that it is assumed in the writings of most scholars of biblical theology. For example, Gerald Bray identified the branches of biblical interpretation in history as historical criticism and its by-products or alternatives, which include existentialism and evangelical, or conservative, responses.[53] Hasel also described the history of NT theology, taking these three categories as crucial criteria.[54] For Hasel, the major methodologies of NT theology are the thematic, existentialist, historical, and salvation history approaches. This classification implies that the second is at least distinct from the third, and the third from the fourth, suggesting that existentialism and historical criticism are different from one another in the history of biblical theology. Reformed biblical theology, then, must not be confused with the salvation historical approach, and should also be differentiated from the other two approaches.

---

53. Bray, *Biblical Interpretation*, 7–12, 480–90. Bray singled out "the conservative attack," "canonical criticism," and "the new hermeneutics" as "alternatives to historical criticism."

54. Hasel, *New Testament Theology*, 18–71.

We shall now discuss in more detail the individual roots of historical criticism, existentialism, and the Reformed biblical theology of redemptive history.

Historical Criticism

The term *historical criticism*, also referred to as the historical-critical method, expresses an hermeneutical approach to the Bible which dominated the academic field from the late-eighteenth century until recently.[55] An increasing number of scholars, however, now regard this approach as being unacceptable.[56] For example, Childs criticized the theological inadequacies of historical-critical approaches to the Bible, as they accept the widespread historicist's method to acquire the illusory historical objectivity, rejecting the Scriptures as the canonical books as received by the Christian church, and thus failing in forming a proper biblical theology.[57] George Lindbeck has also pointed out the irrelevancy of historical criticism: "It is now the scholarly rather than the hierarchical clerical elite which holds the Bible captive and makes it inaccessible to ordinary folk."[58] Walter Wink also claimed that historical criticism is bankrupt, because it has reduced the Bible to a dead letter: "Our obedience to technique has left the Bible sterile and ourselves empty ... it was based on an inadequate method, married to a false objectivism ... separated from a vital community, and has outlived its usefulness as presently practiced."[59] On the other hand, proponents of historical criticism, like James Barr and John Roberts, still want to retain the essentials of this approach as a sound tool for a reasonable interpretation of Scripture. Scholars, then, vary in their hermeneutical approaches and this illustrates how difficult it is to obtain a clear-cut, unquestionable delineation of historical criticism. I confine

---

55. Grant, *Short History of the Interpretation of the Bible*, 123.
56. Möller, "Renewing Historical-Criticism," 150–52.
57. Childs, *Biblical Theology of the Old and New Testaments*, 5–9; *Biblical Theology in Crisis*, 141–42. Childs has been a major critic of historical criticism throughout his career. J. M. Roberts considers Childs's criticism of historical criticism restrained and measured compared to the charges levelled against the method by other biblical scholars such as Walter Wink, who calls biblical criticism bankrupt in *Transformation*, 4–15, quoted in Roberts, "Historical-Critical Method," 131–32. Cf. Childs, "Interpretation in Faith," 432–49.
58. Lindbeck, "Scripture, Consensus, and Community," 16.
59. Wink, *Transformation*, 1–15.

myself here to discussing only the key points relating to the hermeneutics of the history of salvation, namely, the general understandings of historical criticism, its origin and development, its influence on biblical hermeneutics, and its relation to redemptive-historical hermeneutics.

The definition of historical criticism is almost as controversial as its desirability, but it usually assumes that a proper meaning of the biblical text must be determined only by specific historical conditions. According to Gordon Wenham,[60] the historical conditions which make an interpretation of the text genuine or valuable are acquired through three preliminary elements: the techniques of dating documents, the verification of information about past events, and the reconstruction of past events and their explanation.[61] Ramm described historical criticism as a scientific and critical inquiry regarding the authorship of the book, its date of composition, its historical circumstances, the authenticity of its contents, and its literary unity.[62]

John Barton outlined four features which are central to the historical-critical study of the Bible. These are: genetic questions, questions regarding the original meaning, historical reconstructions, and disinterested scholarship.[63]

The genetic question is a query about when, and by whom, books were written, what their intended readership was, and how they become biblical books. Ladd agrees: "To be a critic means merely to ask questions about the authorship, date, place, sources, purpose, and so on, of any ancient work."[64] The term *original meaning* refers to what the original text had meant to its first receivers, and not what it might mean to modern minds. The search for an original meaning requires the prior understanding of the historical context of the given text. For example, επισκοποις και διακονοις[65] in Phil 1:1 originally referred to quite different officials to what people might think of today; thus for the historical

---

60. Wenham was until 2005 Senior Professor of Old Testament at the University of Gloucestershire, a post he held for 10 years. He currently lectures at Trinity College, Bristol.

61. Wenham, "History and the Old Testament," 42.

62. Ramm, *Protestant Biblical Interpretation*, 9–10. Ramm says that historical criticism is a necessary biblical science if we desire a faith that is neither gullible nor obscurantistic.

63. Barton, "Historical-Critical Approaches," 9–19.

64. Ladd, *New Testament and Criticism*, 36–39.

65. Which means "to bishops and deacons" (*RSV*).

REDEMPTIVE HISTORY

context their different usages need to be understood. The term *historical reconstruction* points to collecting and analyzing the sources of scriptural texts and rewriting what is presumed to have happened in the past. So, for example, a critic could extract the alleged earliest sayings of Christ from the Synoptic Gospels, or other sources like the Pseudepigrapha, then attempt to arrange them in diachronic order to fit into the original stories about Christ. The term *disinterested scholarship* claims to be value neutral in trying to approach the text without prejudice for an historical-critical inquiry, seeking only objective facts as a non-biased observer, without any presupposition affecting the interpretation of texts.[66] Barton's delineation of the historical-critical method presents us with a reasonably objective and balanced definition, that is, disinterested scholarship seeking the original meaning of a given text by the specific processes of genetic questions and historical reconstruction of sources.

Historical criticism is technically one branch of biblical criticism; the latter has two major areas: higher and lower criticism. Lower criticism is used to refer to textual criticism, which analyzes individual copies of Scripture in order to ascertain the original texts. Higher criticism has been considered to refer to literary and historical criticism, involving a critical literary analysis of the biblical books themselves. F. F. Bruce (1910–1990) observed that textual criticism was called "lower criticism," in that it represented the lower courses in the edifice of biblical theology, while the "higher" presupposed the findings of the "lower."[67] Thus historical criticism belongs to higher criticism, which is a more radical discipline of biblical criticism. Here we need to understand the technical term *criticism*, which refers generally to the scientific investigation of literary documents in regard to such matters as origin, text, composition, and history.[68] The Greek word for criticism, *krisis*, means simply "a judgment" and appears in the work of historical criticism as intelligent judgments about the questions of historical, textual, literary, and philological authenticity in dealing with the Bible. Ladd explained helpfully that questions of criticism for the NT include, for example, the authorship of the Gospel of Matthew, its purpose, which sources the gospel used, and why it is similar to Luke and Mark.[69] For Ladd, these questions are necessary

---

66. Barton, "Historical-Critical Approaches," 11–12.
67. Bruce, "Biblical Criticism," 93.
68. Merriam-Webster, "Criticism."
69. Ladd, *New Testament and Criticism*, 37–38.

for criticism; to be non-critical means ignoring these questions. Ladd expresses the point well:

> To be non-critical means simply to ignore altogether the historical dimension of the Bible and to view it as a magical book. If the Bible has come to us through historical events, persons, and situations, criticism is necessary to understand the historical process through which the sovereign God has been pleased to accomplish both self-revelation and the salvation of men.[70]

To be critical, therefore, means being attentive to the historical dimensions of Scripture and, here, the term *historical* means something other than ecclesiastical traditions or church dogmas. The Bible, then, is an historical document and needs to be examined as such. However, in biblical studies the term *criticism*, as we have seen, came to signify approaches conflicting with traditional approaches to the Bible. Biblical criticism, therefore, sought a better understanding of the Bible as the Word of God in its historical setting, but employed a "scientific" method involving the renouncing of the inspiration and supernatural elements of the Bible. The Bible is, therefore, considered a document like any other.[71] Historical criticism embraces other branches of biblical criticism, such as textual criticism, literary criticism, source criticism, redaction criticism, and form criticism; these various kinds of criticism are subsidiary to the all-embracing discipline of historical criticism.[72] We now need to outline briefly the origin and development of historical criticism.

Origin and Development

Historical criticism finds its origin mostly in the eighteenth century Enlightenment.[73] The latter is a term generally understood as referring to

---

70. Ibid., 38.
71. Goppelt, *Theology of the New Testament*, vol. 1, 256.
72. Wenham, "History & the Old Testament," 42.
73. Bruce, "History and the New Testament," 84. Hasel in *New Testament Theology*, 28 also attributes the turning point of biblical theology into a historical science with "purely historical" or "historical-critical" approaches to the age of the Enlightenment. Goppelt in *Theology of the New Testament*, vol. 1, 256 asserts that the historical critical investigation of Scripture arose out of the awareness and reflection of historical thought, which was initially the product of the eighteenth century and the Enlightenment. Barton in "Historical-Critical Approaches," 16 asserts that it would be foolish to deny historical criticism's debt to the Enlightenment. However, he thinks there would

the specific emphasis on human reason and autonomy characteristic of Western European and North American thought during the eighteenth century. Alister McGrath adds that the term *Enlightenment* embraces a cluster of ideas and attitudes characteristic of the period 1720–1780, such as the free and constructive use of reason in an attempt to demolish the oppression of the past.[74] The terms *age of reason* or *rationalism* are, thus, often used to refer to the Enlightenment.[75] For example, Donald Guthrie (1915–1992) viewed historical criticism as originating in rationalism: "The age of reason gave rise to modern criticism, for it was then assumed that criticism was not only a legitimate but even a necessary process for subjecting the biblical text to the scrutiny of human reason."[76] This rationalism primarily regarded the natural world as a closed, mechanical system which excluded the supernatural power of God and miraculous events like Christ's resurrection, standing in antithesis to Christian supernaturalism, which accepts God's intervention in, and ruling over, the natural world and human history.[77]

Rationalist scholars like Gabler and Bauer sought religious ideas from the Bible consistent with the universal laws of reason, and were called historical-critical rationalists. They vigorously developed biblical theology as a "purely historical" discipline.[78] The second generation of scholars advocating historical criticism, such as Baur, Wilhelm De Wette (1780–1849), and D. F. Strauss (1808–1874), were influenced by the historical philosophy of Hegel and shifted their major concerns from universal truth in the Bible to the historical development of the concepts of the gospel and Christ in the early church.[79] They were usually less interested

---

be possibilities of tracing historical criticism other than to the Enlightenment, for example to the Reformation.

74. McGrath, *Christian Theology*, 87.

75. "Age of reason" could also refer to the Middle Ages and "rationalism" can refer to any tendency in which the doctrine that the external world can be known by reason alone is held as the major underlying principle.

76. Guthrie, "Historical and Literary Criticism of the New Testament," 86. According to Guthrie, rationalism set man firmly on the throne over all else, including God's revelation. Cf. Anderson, *Bible and Modern Criticism*, 22–25. Previously Anderson (1841–1908) thought higher criticism originated from scepticism rooted in rationalism.

77. Richardson, *History Sacred and Profane*, 187–90. "Supernaturalist" is the antithesis of "rationalist."

78. Hasel, *New Testament Theology*, 24–25.

79. Ladd, *Theology of the New Testament*, 15.

in the truth of Scripture than in the historical processes of Christianity. This amalgamation of purely historical criticism with an Hegelian dialectical philosophy gave rise to a new movement of scholarship, the Tübingen School, which rejected traditional orthodox Christianity and embraced mainly its ethics.[80]

This historical critical scholarship of "Gabler-Bauer-Baur" developed a more radical historical approach, referred to as the history of religions approach. Otto Pfleiderer (1839–1908), William Wrede, Wilhelm Bousset (1865–1920), Adolf von Harnack, and Herman Gunkel (1862–1931) are representative of those who investigated the religious experiences of early Christianity, paying attention to the wider religious environment like Hellenistic mysticism.[81]

This purely historical discipline of Gabler-Bauer-Baur developed into the formulation of Ernst Troeltsch (1865–1923), as historicism.[82] Troeltsch proclaimed that the historical-critical method has, as its presupposition, a whole world view, which means history has continuity itself.[83] For Troeltsch, a unique event like Christ's resurrection cannot be an integral part of the historical continuum, thus the alleged "privileged position" of Christianity is unacceptable.[84] In 1898 he proposed three principles for proper historical research. Firstly, the principle of criticism or methodological doubt: historical inquiry is not in the realm of ab-

---

80. Harris, *Tübingen School*, 262. Harris actually classifies Baur as an atheist. According to his evaluation, Baur chose wrong historical-total views and distorted the historical sources of early Christianity. For example, Baur thought that Christ's teachings were just an expression of His religious consciousness and not yet theology, and that later Paul, as a Hellenistic Christian, made them a theology (thesis) following opposition of Jewish Christians, like Peter and James; finally the harmonized Old Catholic Christianity emerged from the struggle in the second century.

81. Bray, *Biblical Interpretation*, 336–40; Hasel, *New Testament Theology*, 51. For example, H. Weinel, Wrede's pupil, in his *Biblische Theologie des Neuen Testaments*, placed the greatest emphasis on the "religion of Jesus" as an "ethical religion of redemption" in contrast to the "mythical religion of redemption," both of which united in the "religion" of earliest Christianity. Cf. Ladd, *Theology of the New Testament*, 17–19. Bousset also sharply differentiated, in his *Kyrios Christos*, the faith of primitive Christianity that held Christ to be the transcendent Son of Man of Jewish apocalyptic, from the views of Hellenistic Christianity, which held Christ to be a divinity, like the Greek cult lords.

82. Goppelt, *Theology of the New Testament*, vol. 1, 256.

83. Hasel, *New Testament Theology*, 51, quoted in Goppelt, *Theology of the New Testament*, vol. 1, 31.

84. Troeltsch, *Protestantism and Progress*, 35, quoted in Rottenberg, *Redemption and Historical Reality*, 40.

solute certainty but only has relative probability. Secondly, the principle of analogy: all past events have in nature their similar event today, and thus we can have historical knowledge. Thirdly, the principle of correlation: historical events are all interrelated to each other by the sequence of cause and effect.[85] According to Troeltsch's historicism, Christianity and its truths are considered to be no more unique and so events like the exodus should be modified in the context of history as a whole.[86] History, for historicism, sits on the throne of biblical study, instead of revelation, and relativizes all absolute truth; this is a fully developed historical-critical methodology, freed from the theological interests of orthodox Christianity.

Influence

Historical criticism has greatly affected biblical hermeneutics and Bray explains these influences on biblical scholars, claiming it became common in the English-speaking world from 1890, and that by 1945 virtually all professional biblical scholars had accepted its principles, although some still continued to draw conservative conclusions.[87] This opened a new epoch of biblical theology as historical science and its investigation provided scholars with an awareness of the origin, transmission, background, and literary forms of the texts.[88] Many biblical scholars, such as Barr and Barton, still appraise its availability and usefulness.

On the other hand, others, like Goppelt, point out the problems in applying historical criticism to biblical hermeneutics, and he identifies three main questions relating to the historical-critical investigation of Scripture which ought to receive serious attention from scholars. The first concerns the quest for the original, historical Jesus. The second is the quest for the church's primitive beginnings. The third question concerns the quest for the original historical message, namely, the essential content of the NT and of early Christianity.[89]

Answering these questions, Strauss reinterpreted the gospel records of Christ as being mythically transformed and enlarged by a Jewish

---

85. Collins, "Is a Critical Biblical Theology Possible?" 2.
86. Wells, "Historical Critical Method," 19.
87. Bray, *Biblical Interpretation*, 223.
88. Wells, "Historical Critical Method," 19.
89. Goppelt, *Theology of the New Testament*, vol. 1, 257–259.

prophet (or rabbi) and put into the faith of the early Christian community.[90] Albert Schweitzer found, in his *The Quest of the Historical Jesus* (1906), the historical Jesus as the life of an apocalyptic prophet in Jewish religion; in the end his conclusions were in contradiction to the figure of Christ in the gospels. Baur's reconstruction of early Christianity claims it underwent a struggle between Petrine Jewish Christianity and Pauline Hellenistic Christianity, reaching a peaceful harmony in second century Catholic Christianity. Albert Ritschl (1822–1899) interpreted the essence of Christianity as purely spiritual and ethical instruction, which was proclaimed by Christ's life and mission.[91] These questions are primarily sceptical about Bible texts and seek to replace them with historically more original ones assumed to be more acceptable to modern scholars.

However, the purely historical did not always involve being objective, and its critical investigations are not always acceptable to the modern Christian mind. One reason is that the sources on which historical critics depend are fragmentary and so cannot provide a completely verifiable reconstruction of the "purely historical" Jesus and Christianity. Ladd pointed out that these proponents approached the Bible with specific philosophical or theological ideas.[92] Troeltsch also admitted that "an entire world view" was operative as a rational presupposition,[93] while Hasel affirms that historical research has always been conditioned by the current philosophy of the time.[94]

The most significant influence of historical criticism on biblical hermeneutics has been the instillation of its contemporary philosophies, such as the rationalism of Descartes and Spinoza, with Kant's synthesis, followed by the dialectic philosophy of history of Hegel, into biblical hermeneutics. Historical-critical scholars, like Baur and De Wette, propagated the supremacy of human reason by using the reminiscent Latin term, *crisis*, to identify the rationalist approach to the Bible as "scientific," and by disparaging the conservative exegesis as being "uncritical" and "narrow."[95] The rationalists' closed system of world-view excludes *a priori*

---

90. Hasel, *New Testament Theology*, 31.
91. Goppelt, *Theology of the New Testament*, vol. 1, 260–261.
92. Ladd, *New Testament and Criticism*, 40.
93. Goppelt, *Theology of the New Testament*, vol. 1, 263.
94. Hasel, *New Testament Theology*, 52.
95. Harris, *Tübingen School*, viii–ix.

supernatural events in Scripture and challenges exegetes to explain them psychologically and spiritually.

Historical criticism has unquestionably undermined, or reinterpreted, the authority of the Bible, while it has developed as a distinctive discipline of biblical study through the last two centuries. Salvation history, which the Bible describes as centering in Christ, is downgraded to "prehistory" or "supra-history," like the sagas, myths, and legends of the Hellenistic world.

Heilsgeschichte Theology

The so-called "school of *Heilsgeschichte*"[96] in the nineteenth century appeared in the midst of, and as a reaction against, a flourishing historical criticism, which began in an alleged conservative circle, in Erlangen, Germany. Adherents included G. Menken (1768–1831), J. Beck (1804–1878), G. Thomasius (1802–1875), and Hofmann. The preeminent figure of this school, Hofmann,[97] who was Baur's peer, and also a theological rival,[98] wanted to keep the authority of Scripture, in which he found a linear salvation history that unfolds for the redemption of all mankind.[99]

According to Hofmann, biblical hermeneutics requires full consideration of the uniqueness of Holy Scripture as a body of literature before the application of modern techniques of scientific exegesis to the Bible.[100] For Hofmann, "a correct appreciation of Holy Scripture" recognizes first of all "its totality," namely, *Heilsgeschichte*, and emphasizes simultaneously "its intrinsic unity" that forms the object of biblical hermeneutics.[101]

Unlike scholars, like Baur and the Tübingen School scholars, who followed historical criticism and applied general principles of historical investigation indiscreetly to Scripture, Hofmann claimed to start with the

---

96. This has also been called the Erlangen School.

97. Hofmann was a confessionalist who studied first at Erlangen and then at Berlin, where he was influenced by Schleiermacher and Hegel, and most greatly by the historicism of Leopold von Ranke (1795–1886), which gave him the balance between the motives of individuals and the underlying processes of history. Due to these influences, Hofmann had a greater interest in history and literature than in philosophy throughout his career. Cf. Bray, *Biblical Interpretation*, 282–83.

98. Yarbrough, *Salvation Historical Fallacy?* 58–59.

99. Ladd, *Theology of the New Testament*, 16.

100. Hofmann, *Interpreting the Bible*, 1–4.

101. Ibid., 4–19.

consideration of the specific character of Holy Scripture, that is, "holy history," consisting in the historical fact of salvation in Christ and its biblical proclamation. Afterwards, Hofmann's endeavors to safeguard the authority of Scripture and to maintain the Reformation rule of interpretation gave birth to the new hermeneutical principle of the Erlangen School, namely, *Heilsgeschichte*.

For the Erlangen School, individual and spiritual regeneration is the precondition for all theological knowledge; the Erlangen theology primarily emphasized this immediate experience of rebirth, which practically complemented, and partly connected with, the influence of Schleiermacher.[102] For this School, the three factors of individual experience of rebirth, Scripture, and confession became the prerequisites for theology and biblical hermeneutics.

According to Hofmann, the threefold essence of Christianity, which is "in the immediate experience of the rebirth of the Christian, in the history and existence of the Church, and in Holy Scripture," constitutes the proof of theology.[103] Hofmann thought of human history as the product of God's love, which could be understood only through personal conversion to Christ, after which Scripture gave confirmation.[104] Thus, Holy Scripture was considered to witness to this history of God's love and its application.[105] The individual biblical texts can then be rightly interpreted only from this perspective of holy history (*Heilsgeschichte*). This perspective seemed to provide a bridge back to the classical Reformed position.

However, Hofmann's *Heilsgeschichte* theology turned out to be an offspring of its preceding Hegelian philosophy.[106] He synthesized the prevailing hermeneutical tool, historical criticism (thesis), with the orthodox or traditional concept of Scripture (antithesis). Hofmann considered that Scripture should be investigated by the proper methods of literary and historical criticism, but within the traditions and confessions of the church. This implies that if a scientist found the biblical accounts of creation incompatible with the conclusions of science, then the interpreter should see the story, such as Genesis chapter 1, as showing God's creation of the world in order to edify the belief of

---

102. Welch, *Protestant Thought in the Nineteenth Century*, vol. 1, 219.

103. Hofmann, *Schriftbeweis*, 1:23, quoted in Welch, *Protestant Thought in the Nineteenth Century*, vol. 1, 221.

104. Bray, *Biblical Interpretation*, 282–283.

105. Welch, *Protestant Thought in the Nineteenth Century*, vol. 1, 222.

106. Childs, *Biblical Theology of the Old and New Testaments*, 17.

the Israelites. Scripture provides the authoritative witness solely to the saving truth, not to scientific details.

For Hofmann, the descriptions in Scripture about nature, geography, and world history are not free of error, or infallible, but are significant only to the extent that they relate to *Heilsgeschichte*, because the purpose of the Bible is to witness exclusively to the process of God's salvation of sinners. Here, in the *Heilsgeschichte* theology of Hofmann, a remarkable harmony between the traditional view of the authority of the Bible and the contemporary critical method seems to have been achieved.

While striving to retain in some way the authority of the Bible, *Heilsgeschichte* theology divided the traditional concept of history into the two different parts of *Historie* and *Geschichte*. The former concerns verifiable historical facts, while the latter is able to embrace the unverifiable details only by faith. Eventually the biblical descriptions of the history of God's redemption became the dualistic composite which consists of two different historical meanings. One is historically verifiable and acceptable to modern historians, for example, the Jewish apocalyptic prophecies about the Messiah and the historical life of Christ, who was proclaimed as the Messiah, but during the period of the Roman Empire was acknowledged by the Jewish people as only a prophet or a rabbi. The other is historically unverifiable, but understood as the specific area of Christianity, the so called *Heilsgeschichte*, which only those adhering to the faith of the Christian religion accept and understand.[107] The history of God's salvation in Scripture then became the history which can be scientifically researched and verified, but also the history which cannot be attainable by positivist study but only by religious faith.

Nevertheless, there remains a hermeneutical problem in the theology of holy history. To what extent should the biblical descriptions of God's acts be understood as *Geschichte* or *Historie*? What is the criterion for differentiating one from the other? For Hofmann and the Erlangen School, the judgment depends solely on the basis of historical criticism. To apply the prevailing rationalist tools to the Bible, *Heilsgeschichte* theology had to modify seriously the Reformation rule of interpretation, that is, Scripture interprets Scripture.

Otto Piper, a follower of Hofmann, admits that the authority of the Bible does not lie in its claim to be verbally inspired, but rather in that "the Bible confronts us with facts that are more comprehensive and more

---

107. Hofmann, *Interpreting the Bible*, 64–65.

important than anything else we know."[108] Therefore, *Heilsgeschichte* theology cannot be said to be a genuine successor of the Reformed tradition of interpretation, but rather a revision of it by adopting rationalist historical criticism. In the next section, we discuss another important development, that of existentialism, as we continue to examine NT hermeneutics relating to redemptive history.

Existentialism

Hermeneutical existentialism started in the early twentieth century as a reaction to rationalist historical criticism. Alvin Plantinga suggests that historical criticism turned out to be a failure in such a way that traditional Christians feel no need to modify their beliefs in the light of its alleged results of investigation.[109] David Steinmetz also argues that the historical-critical method, as practiced for the last two hundred years, has failed to win over the Christian community and many of the Reformed faith, not because of their ignorance or conservatism, but because of its own inadequacy to deal with the nature of biblical texts.[110] The conflict between faith and reason continued in biblical hermeneutics throughout the twentieth century and the existentialist approach emerged from this conflict.[111]

The two theological movements seeking to resolve the conflict between the dogmatic rationalism, which was dominant over the last two centuries, and the traditional faith of Protestantism, were the aforementioned *Heilsgeschichte* theology and the existential approach. Scholars, like Hofmann and Bultmann, were forced to select either the critical-historical or the religious-psychological stances to Scripture.[112] The *Heilsgeschichte* theologians brilliantly combined the two poles of the conflict between historical reason and traditional faith, while emphasizing more the historical perspective in approaching biblical revelation. Consequently, revelatory history results in a dualistic form with regard to the scientifically verifiable *Historie* and the unverifiable *Geschichte*. The

---

108. Ramm, *Protestant Biblical Interpretation*, 79–83.

109. Plantinga, "Two (or More) Kinds of Scripture Scholarship," 55.

110. Steinmetz, "Superiority of Pre-Critical Exegesis," 38; quoted in Clark, *Recovering the Reformed Confession*, 13.

111. Plantinga, "When Faith and Reason Clash," 9–15; also quoted in Plantinga, "Two (or More) Kinds of Scripture Scholarship," 56–57; Helm, *Faith and Understanding*, 3–8. Cf. Swinburne, *Faith and Reason*, 198–201.

112. Braaten, *History and Hermeneutics*, 23.

existential approach, however, focused on the psychological change of an individual encountering God. The new conflict between the *Heilsgeschichte* and existentialist schools of thought arose from the differences in approach toward biblical redemptive history.[113] Existentialism places the primacy of biblical interpretation on seeking for one's own being in one's relation to God through the text, not on God's saving acts in His relation to man in history. In order to reach the existential meaning of each individual being, theologians of this persuasion distinctively deal with biblical texts and redemptive history in the Bible. We now need to examine the definition and characteristics of existentialism in order to identify its influence on biblical hermeneutics and its relation to the redemptive historical approach.

Meanings and Definitions

Existentialism is a term which found its first usage in Jean-Paul Sartre's explicit expression of it as "self-description."[114] Philosophers labelled with this term are preeminently Karl Jaspers (1883–1969), Martin Heidegger (1889–1976), Martin Buber (1878–1965), and Nicholas Berdyaev (1874–1948), while Søren Kierkegaard (1813–55) and Friedrich Nietzsche (1844–1900) can be recognized as precursors of this movement. According to Mary Warnock, this term is conventionally used to cover a kind of philosophical activity which flourished on the European continent, especially in the 1940s and 1950s.[115]

However, the term *existentialism* does not construct a particular system of philosophy.[116] McGrath observes that it refers primarily to a way of philosophical thinking, emphasizing the real-life experience of individuals.[117] This way of thinking can appear in such wide areas as in the atheism of Sartre, the catholicism of Gabriel Marcel (1889–1973), who converted to the Roman Catholic Church, and the orthodoxy of Berdyaev. Emmanuel Mounier traces a family tree of existentialism and

---

113. Rottenberg, *Redemption and Historical Reality*, 30. Cf. Braaten, *New Directions in Theology Today*, vol. 2, 18.

114. Crowell, "Existentialism."

115. Warnock, *Existentialism*, 1–5.

116. Copleston, *Contemporary Philosophy*, 125.

117. McGrath, *Christian Theology*, 146–47.

shows well its very extensive kinship with roots stretching back to the pre-Christian era.[118]

The philosophy of existentialism tends to emphasize one's own subjective awareness and decision rather than objective opinions or a community's traditional view.[119] Warnock claims she found the true voice of existentialism in Heidegger,[120] for whom one's true existence depends on one's own recognition and decision of what he or she chooses to act. Heidegger extensively discussed, in his *Being and Time* (1927), an inquiry into "true existence" (German: *Dasein*), rejecting science as an inadequate approach to human existence.[121]

While the term *existentialism* cannot be defined precisely, one working definition is:

> Without denying the validity of scientific categories (governed by the norm of truth) or moral categories (governed by norms of the good and the right), "existentialism" may be defined as the philosophical theory which holds that a further set of categories, governed by the norm of *authenticity*, is necessary to grasp human existence."[122]

This definition is helpful in general, but we need to discuss it more specifically with regard to existentialist theology.

Existentialist Theology: Origin and Characteristics

The early twentieth century saw the rise of a new theological movement which was driven by a group of theologians like Barth, Bultmann, Reinhold Niebuhr, and Paul Tillich, who were influenced by existentialist philosophy.[123] Barth, in his early period when writing *The Epistle to the Romans*, was influenced by Kierkegaard's existentialism and accepted its essential concept of "the wholly otherness" of God.[124] Bultmann's theology

---

118. Mounier, *Existentialist Philosophies*, 3.

119. Allen, *Existentialism from Within*, quoted in Copleston, *Contemporary Philosophy*, 127.

120. Warnock, *Existentialism*, 54–55.

121. Heidegger, *Being and Time*, 21–35.

122. Crowell, "Existentialism."

123. Not all these theologians like being called an "existential theologian," especially Barth. Cf. Cook, "Existentialism," 244.

124. Cobb, *Living Options in Protestant Theology*, 201–2. Barth's theology

was influenced by the more developed existentialism of Heidegger, rather than that of Kierkegaard.[125] Tillich depends to a small degree on both Kierkegaard and Heidegger, but draws heavily from the existential movement in the wider sense.[126] Niebuhr is independent from them, but his affirmations equally deserve the label "existentialist."

Philosophical existentialism poses the fundamental questions of human existence: what is the meaning and the cause of human existence? Existentialist theologians apply these questions in turn to their theology. The origin of existentialist theology is naturally found in existentialist philosophers like Kierkegaard and Heidegger. What are then the special characteristics of this theological movement? The essential features of existentialist theology are rooted in philosophical existentialism and the thought trends of the late nineteenth and early twentieth centuries. As we have seen, rationalist objectivism and historicism prevailed in the nineteenth century and the illusion that true and objective knowledge of almost anything can be achieved through scientific investigation dominated people's thinking. However, Kierkegaard had a strong hostility against this assumption, for he believed human ethics and science are enslaved and had thus lost their spontaneity and the true life of inwardness.[127] He declared that subjectivity is the real domain of true human existence: "It is with subjectivity that Christianity is concerned, and it is only in subjectivity that its truth exists, if it exists at all."[128] After experiencing two world wars and subsequent disillusionment and despair, the modern existentialist sought to reject the possibility of objectivity and concentrated on the more subjective meaning of human existence. Heidegger began to urge Christian theology to change its ground motif from the external to the internal, that is, existential:

---

underwent so many significant changes that one should be careful to examine his theological tendency in a specific period. From the 2nd edition of *The Epistle to the Romans*, the whole tone of Barth's theology was set against his previous position. However, the earlier influence of Kierkegaard cannot be denied at any period of his life.

125. McGrath, *Christian Theology*, 146–47. McGrath points out that the origins of existentialism primarily lie in the writings of Kierkegaard, but Heidegger contributed the most important part in the development of existentialism in terms of theology, providing Bultmann with the basic idea for developing a Christian existentialist account of human existence.

126. Tillich, *Theology of Culture*, 76–111.

127. Warnock, *Existentialism*, 8–9.

128. Kierkegaard, *Kierkegaard's Concluding Unscientific Postscript*, 116, quoted in Warnock, Existentialism, 9.

> Theology is seeking a more primordial interpretation of man's Being towards God, prescribed by the meaning of faith itself and remaining within it. It is slowly beginning to understand once more Luther's insight that the "foundation" on which its system of dogma rests has not arisen from the inquiry in which faith is primary, and that conceptually this "foundation" not only is inadequate for the problematic of theology, but conceals and distorts it.[129]

For Heidegger, contemporary Christian theology was building its dogmatic system on wrong foundations, that is, objective historical proof, and thus it needed to reorient the Christian faith to Luther's perspective which is concerned with individual subjective faith rather than with objective matters. Bultmann accepted this challenge and established existential presuppositions to reinterpret the Christian faith,[130] so that Christian theology was understood as the clarification of the content of faith, representing it as conscious knowledge.[131] Theology then becomes the study of the existential meaning of human faith and constructs subjective knowledge from it. The most important agenda of Bultmann's theology, therefore, becomes the question of whether the Christian faith today is best articulated from an anthropological perspective or not.[132] Bultmann admits that his basic question on approaching the Bible is to seek for the answer to questions about human existence. Although existentialist theology is surely asking about God, it does so in so far as God is only significant to man as existing.[133] Afterwards the individual human being, not God Himself, is the central thrust of existentialist theology in its essence.

In existentialist theology, what a man believes is not as important as how he believes it. As long as he has a self-consciousness of his own existence and realizes a truth for himself, whether the truth is objective or not does not matter. In the next section we discuss in more detail the influences of existentialist theology on biblical interpretation, especially on redemptive history.

---

129. Heidegger, *Being and Time*, 30.
130. Macquarrie, *Existentialist Theology*, 8.
131. Bultmann, *Theology of the New Testament*, 190.
132. Morgan, "Introduction," xiv.
133. Macquarrie, *Existentialist Theology*, 11.

Influences on Biblical Hermeneutics

Barth was influenced by the existentialism of Kierkegaard when he rewrote *The Epistle to the Romans*, and this influence appears in his preface. He confessed that if he had a system it would be Kierkegaard's "infinite qualitative distinction" between time and eternity, and thence the relation between such a man and such a God became Barth's major theme of the Bible and the essence of his philosophy.[134] Barth named this God-man encounter "the Crisis of human perception" and sought to locate this in the figure of Christ. Barth's theology of "crisis" expressed an objection against the objectivism of the historical method in the nineteenth century,[135] in which God and human were confused and God's revelation and human words were mingled.[136] Barth emphasized God's distinctiveness from man, as God the "Wholly Other," or the "Hidden One," who is revealed in the Bible. This emphasis on the distinctiveness of God was focused in Barth's interpretation in time for the second edition of his book, which was published in 1922.

In Barth's theology of crisis, God's encounter with humans in Jesus Christ was highlighted as well as God's "otherness." God had revealed himself in Jesus Christ as the reconciler, and at the point of the revelation of God heaven and earth meet: "In this name (Jesus Christ) two worlds meet and go apart, two planes intersect, the one known and the other unknown."[137] The Bible proclaims this crisis of intersection between God and man in Jesus Christ and all individuals will stand under this encounter in Christ for God's judgment or reconciliation. This is the real "crisis" of man, which can be a turning point for sinners from danger to God's grace, and reconciliation with Him. Barth says that this crisis of God's judgment in Christ is "both negation and affirmation, both death and life."[138] At the point of the Christ event, man is forced to respond to God's challenging Word, that is, the revelation of God Himself, and therefore for Barth all theology was a dialogue between God and mankind.[139] Barth's theology has thus been called a dialectical theology. However, this

---

134. Barth, "Preface to the Second Edition," 10. See also Cochrane, *Existentialists and God*, 31.

135. Parker, *Karl Barth*, 42.

136. Rogers and McKim, *Authority and Interpretation of the Bible*, 410–11.

137. Barth, *Epistle to the Romans*, 29; cf. Parker, *Karl Barth*, 44.

138. Barth, *Epistle to the Romans*, 69.

139. Rogers and McKim, *Authority and Interpretation of the Bible*, 411.

approach was in essence different from Hegel's dialectical philosophy of historical evolution because Barth majored on the existential encounter between God, as the "Wholly Other," and the individual human.

Bultmann's hermeneutical approach to the NT was fundamentally influenced by Heidegger's existentialist presuppositions. The two preliminary concepts of Heidegger's existential system, *Fragestellung* and *Begrifflichkeit*, are of considerable importance for examining Bultmann's hermeneutical presuppositions. Bultmann claims that his own existential approach to the Bible follows the writers of the NT, such as Paul. According to Bultmann, Paul begins the Epistle to the Romans by describing the desperate situation of human existence, and then focuses his teaching on man in relation to God.[140] For Bultmann, Pauline theology deals with God as a God who is significant for man and man's salvation; Paul's theology thus becomes anthropology.[141] This claim of Bultmann's was admittedly based on Heidegger's basic presuppositions, the so-called *Fragestellung* (the manner of putting the question) and *Begrifflichkeit* (a category of ground concepts under which we understand what confronts us in experience).[142] For Heidegger, every inquiry of human existence (*Fragestellung*) must be dealt with in a category of existential concepts (*Begrifflichkeit*), not in a category of science.[143] Thus if one lacks an appropriate existential concept beforehand, then one's interpretation of the being of man in the Bible will be distorted. Bultmann, therefore, initially embraces these existential presuppositions of Heidegger for the right interpretation of the being of man in the Bible, and affirms that the approaches of biblical writers are identical with his own.

Bultmann has also adopted the distinction of Heidegger between "inauthentic" and "authentic" existence as a basic principle for interpreting human existence in the NT.[144] An inauthentic existence means a man is merged in the external world and thus loses himself, while an authentic

---

140. Bultmann, *Theology of the New Testament*, 296; cf. Macquarrie, *Existentialist Theology*, 12.

141. Ibid., 191.

142. Macquarrie, *Existentialist Theology*, 14.

143. This presupposition is directly related to the definition of existentialism described in the previous section. Heidegger seeks, by this assumption, to show that the structure of the being of man differs from the being of objects in nature, and must be differently understood and described. Cf. Macquarrie, *Existentialist Theology*, 14.

144. Heidegger, *Being and Time*, 76.

existence means a man is free for his world and thus gains himself.[145] Bultmann also applies these two kinds of human existence to the NT: unredeemed existence or redeemed existence.[146] Those possessing the former lose their true being through the external things of the world, like material prosperity or moral actions, while those possessing the latter gain their true being through trusting in God. This distinction concerning human existence then becomes a motif for Bultmann's interpretation of the NT, so that this existentialist approach highlights the authentic life of humankind and calls for the readers or hearers to be existentially confronted with God for attaining their true being. The "demythologization" becomes a necessary method in interpreting redemptive events in Scripture for the modern man in the existentialist hermeneutical program of Bultmann and his followers, especially in the New Hermeneutic.[147]

By this existentialist approach, traditional faith seems to be preserved from rationalist attack on the authority of the Bible, and consequently on beliefs in biblical history. Bultmann proclaims that he stands on the same ground as Luther in his hermeneutical approach. However, this existential faith depends on man's self-consciousness in relation to God and his own decision, while traditional Christian faith depends on God's self-revelation and on God's sovereign endowing of illumination on believers.

However, I do acknowledge that the tension between faith and reason, and also between theology and history, which undergirded theological study from the eighteenth century, is offered a solution in this existential approach. Scholars like Macquarrie appraise that this existential synthesis of theology with history, especially in Bultmann's demythologizing program, makes a valuable contribution to the development of NT theology.[148] Barton concurs that Bultmann's achievement in combining the most rigorous critical scholarship with a committed theology remains the best model for biblical study.[149] This existentialist approach has, in fact, affected, and continues in, the New Hermeneutic, which we referred to in chapter 1.

---

145. Macquarrie, *Existentialist Theology*, 40.

146. McGrath, *Christian Theology*, 146–47.

147. Bultmann, *Jesus Christ and Mythology*, 45; cf. Hasel, *New Testament Theology*, 83–84.

148. Macquarrie, *Existentialist Theology*, 243.

149. Barton, *Biblical Interpretation*, 124.

Criticism of existentialist approaches mostly majors on a loss of any genuine understanding of God's revelation, due to its amalgamation with a philosophy which is at root anthropocentric and atheistic.[150] For example, Bultmann thought he had found a criterion, which is based on the existential presuppositions of Heidegger, for distinguishing the authentic *kerygma* from inauthentic ones. He argued that the resurrection described in 1 Cor 15:1–11 is not as consistent with Paul's underlying existential approach as in other writings and thus cannot be fundamental to Paul's letter. This argument is questionable and the reasoning suspect. Bray claims that Bultmann's work resulted in a complete distortion of the genuine, fundamental message of Scripture, while it strove to hold personal belief within the canon of Scripture.[151] It went so far as to deny the incarnation of Christ and thus has been criticized by scholars like Cullmann and Ridderbos as undermining, or even removing, objective biblical history. We now discuss the relationship of existentialist theology to redemptive history.

Relationship to Redemptive History

Existentialist theology primarily, then, has little to do with objective history or, more specifically, with redemptive history in the Bible. The existentialist interpretation starts with the question, "What does the Bible say about my personal existence?" because it is always seeking for the self-understanding of one's existence in the concrete moments of the "here and now."[152] However, an existentialist theologian, as a modern man, cannot but refuse the whole concept of the world of the gospel, because it is thought to be fundamentally mythological.[153] Bultmann developed his

---

150. Cook, "Existentialism," 244.

151. Bray, *Biblical Interpretation*, 429, 441. Bultmann has also been attacked for making the *kerygma* a disembodied abstraction, which in theological terms amounts to a denial of the incarnation.

152. Bultmann, *Jesus Christ and Mythology*, 56.

153. Ibid., 15. Here Bultmann calls the conception of the world of the Bible mythological, because it is a different conception of the world from that which has been formed and developed by science since its inception in ancient Greece, and which has been accepted by modern men. Bultmann's definition is arbitrary and unacceptable because the ground for the judgment, modern science, is not suitable for God's real world.

demythologizing approach as an hermeneutical method for interpreting those stories with supernatural details.[154]

In existentialist theology, history is significant only when it relates to individual existence; an existentialist faith, which makes it possible for one to gain authentic existence, depends therefore on one's direct encounter with God through the *kerygma* of Christ. The external and objective description of the history of salvation, from creation through Christ's crucifixion and resurrection to the end of the age, consequently has nothing to do with such an existential encounter. Bultmann insists that the concept of history should be based on either a modern critical understanding or on individual faith,[155] and so he and his pupils like Fuchs and Ebeling, leading proponents of the New Hermeneutic, opposed the *Heilsgeschichte* theology approach[156] which tried to recognize salvation history in the Bible.[157]

This existentialist theology, therefore, essentially renders a very different view of history in the "history of salvation" from that of *Heilsgeschichte* theology. Bultmann observes that the term *history* in the phrase the "history of salvation" is unclear and he cannot see the occurrence of salvation in that history.[158] For him, man's encounter with God cannot be found in a succession of objective events, which Cullmann described as the history of salvation. That is why Bultmann and the New Hermeneutic theologians firmly reject any possibility of adopting the view of the history of salvation.[159] Bultmann explains that the connection of history and myth in the NT was influenced by the preceding Jewish apocalypticism, which is by no means something specifically Christian.[160] History of salvation in the NT is, then, nothing other than Jewish apocalyptic speculation, which is transformed into the Christian philosophy of history by *Heilsgeschichte* theologians like Cullmann.[161] History of salvation, in this existentialist program, is transformed into a subjective history.

154. Ibid., 45.
155. Bultmann, "History of Salvation and History," 277.
156. Cullmann, *Salvation in History*, 48.
157. Welch, *Protestant Thought in the Nineteenth Century*, vol. 1, 221–22.
158. Bultmann, "History of Salvation and History," 274.
159. Yarbrough, *Salvation Historical Fallacy?* 196.
160. Bultmann, "History of Salvation and History," 279. Bultmann acknowledges here that the concept of salvation history is embedded originally in the writings of the NT, even though the NT writings were influenced previously by Jewish apocalypticism.
161. Ibid., 280.

For example, the history of Christ in the gospels should be, in Bultmann's theology, the history of subjective moments of an individual's encounter with God.[162] The history of Christ in the NT is then no more the history of the historical Christ of "there and then":

> Salvation history in Bultmann is actually totally devoted to this "here and now" of encounter; it becomes salvation-historically, that is, the encounter with God in his word which occurs continually in one's existence. God never encounters me objectively . . . therefore there can also no longer be any such thing as historical fact that would be revelation.[163]

We find here a fundamentally different concept of salvation history from the one of *Heilsgeschichte* theology; it is no more an objective, factual history, but only a clothed *kerygma*, with Jewish and Hellenistic myths. Bultmann is more candid in saying that "precisely the events and persons that constitute salvation history are, in the NT sense, not historical but mythological phenomena."[164]

This concept of the history of salvation has strengths and weaknesses. Positively, it provided a distinctive interpretation of history which addresses the conflict between history and theology, giving an answer to the "quest for the historical Jesus."[165] For example, Bultmann contends that "Jesus Christ is the eschatological event, the action of God by which God has set an end to the old world. In the preaching of the Christian church the eschatological event . . . does become present ever and again in faith."[166] Thus, a modern man is able to confront God's eschatological event in this dehistoricized preaching and to sustain his own existential faith without struggling with incredible historical events like the virgin birth and the resurrection. For these reasons, this existential approach may be evaluated as a remarkable development of biblical theology in the twentieth century.

---

162. Hughes, "Truth of Scripture," 182.

163. Flückiger, "Heilsgeschichte und Weltgeschichte," 41, quoted in Yarbrough, *Salvation Historical Fallacy?* 197.

164. Maier, *Biblical Hermeneutics*, 199.

165. Rust, *Salvation History*, 45. According to Rust, Bultmann is anxious to retain Christ as a concrete historical figure, who is also the eschatological emissary of God. Bultmann considers his agenda was accomplished through the demythologization of biblical history.

166. Bultmann, *Presence of Eternity*, 151, quoted in Rust, *Salvation History*, 46.

There are, however, decisive problems in this approach, which has been seriously criticized by many NT scholars like I. Howard Marshall and Guthrie. Marshall rightly points to the reductionism in Bultmann's treatment of gospel history, which is based on Bultmann's scepticism regarding the greater part of the record and his conviction that the history of what Christ did is irrelevant for the Christian faith.[167] Guthrie also criticized Bultmann's approach to history—his "dialogue with history,"[168]—as being entirely subjective and depriving the NT of significant events relating to the historical Christ;[169] in this approach there are no more than forty of the sayings of Christ that would be regarded as authentic.[170] According to Guthrie, Bultmann and his followers' view of the historical Christ is akin to that of Docetism, which early Gnosticism adopted,[171] and so the charge of syncretism, that is, of combining biblical history with contemporary philosophy, cannot be avoided. After changing his theological position, Barth also criticized Bultmann's approach as clamping the gospel in the vice of philosophical existentialism.

Ultimately, how to conceive the history of salvation in the NT comes down to one's presupposition. Cullmann presupposes that the Bible is the product of salvation history and thus should be recognized in its own character, the whole of salvation history.[172] Bultmann, however, primarily considers the Bible as being oriented only for human existence and thus thinks its interpretation should be done through existential presuppositions. These preconceptions are, however, admittedly preoccupied with human philosophies rather than with Scripture itself. We now turn to discuss another approach to Scripture, that of perceiving redemptive history from the perspective of Reformed biblical theology.

Reformed Biblical Theology

Reformed biblical theology, as a new expression of biblical theology, first appeared with Gerhard Vos (1862–1949) in the nineteenth century, and was firmly established within Reformed circles during the first half of

---

167. Marshall, *New Testament Theology*, 42.
168. Bultmann, *Jesus and the Word*, 3.
169. Guthrie, *New Testament Theology*, 44.
170. Cf. Bultmann, *History of the Synoptic Tradition*.
171. Guthrie, *New Testament Theology*, 47–48.
172. Welch, *Protestant Thought in the Nineteenth Century*, vol. 1, 222.

the twentieth century. When Vos gave his inaugural address at Princeton Theological Seminary in May 1894, his new biblical theology was launched. Vos provided clear definitions and a significant discussion of the new science in his inaugural speech titled "The Idea of Biblical Theology as a Science and as a Theological Discipline."[173] Vos developed it further in his *magnum opus*, *Biblical Theology: Old and New Testaments* (1948), which became extremely influential, establishing a new trend in biblical theology in Reformed circles.

Use of the conjugate term "Reformed" with "biblical theology" is debatable. Conventional biblical theology, which dominated the scholarly world for two centuries, was not influenced by Reformed theology. On the other hand, Bray claims that Vos developed a specifically evangelical version of biblical theology, using a theologically broader term than "Reformed."[174] Richard B. Gaffin names Vos as "the father of a Reformed biblical theology."[175] The term "Reformed" attached to the conventional term "biblical theology," refers to a new trend in biblical theology which was originated, and developed, by Vos's Reformed theological principles and his predecessors.

This new version emerged as a reaction against the conventional biblical theology previously described. Before this new science appeared, there had been a tension between history and theology in the approach to interpreting Scripture. *Heilsgeschichte* theology and existentialist theology occurred as scholastic solutions for moderating this tension between historical and theological aspects in the study of biblical theology. Both approaches failed because they did not recognize the inerrancy and inspiration of Scripture and thus did not appeal to Reformed minds such as that of Vos. It was in that context that Vos developed his new version of biblical theology. We now turn to discuss the distinctive features of Vos's new way of approaching biblical theology.

Origin and Development

Reformed biblical theology, by which I mean Vos's version of biblical theology, is considered as originating in the *Heilsgeschichte* theology of the nineteenth century. R. L. Webster affirms that Vos followed the

---

173. Originally published: New York: Randolph, 1894.
174. Bray, *Biblical Interpretation*, 545.
175. Gaffin, "Introduction," xiv–xv.

Heilsgeschichte method for the presentation of biblical theology, while other orthodox scholars held to a purely historical method.[176] Gaffin assumes that the period of doctoral study in Germany must have stimulated Vos's interest in biblical theology.[177] J. Dennison also designates several rationalist scholars, like A. Dillmann (1823–1894), H. J. Holtzmann (1832–1910), and T. Nöldeke (1836–1930),[178] as those who had probably influenced Vos during his study in Germany from October 1885 to April 1888.[179] Gaffin's assumption about the influence of German scholars on Vos's biblical theology seems to be fairly well supported by Dennison. However, Vos's interest in biblical theology might have been influenced by his rationalist teachers during his studies in Germany, but no direct connection can be established between Vos's approach and *Heilsgeschichte* theology or its representative theologians like A. Schlatter (1852–1938).

Vos's idea of biblical theology was hardly influenced by the dominant approach of German biblical theology, even if his postgraduate study was done in that environment, like J. Gresham Machen (1881–1937) who did postgraduate study under a leading liberal NT theologian, W. Herrmann (1846–1922),[180] but retained his confidence in the historical accuracy of the gospel narratives.[181] Here is Vos's own statement on this matter:

> The modern tendency to transform Biblical theology into an out-and-out historical science, represented by such men as Wrede, has a certain degree of justification; although . . . it proposes to make our science a purely naturalistic and secular branch of study, a mere subdivision of the history of religions.

176. Webster, "Geerhardus Vos," 304–17.

177. Vos, *Redemptive History and Biblical Interpretation*, xii.

178. Nöldeke was a professor at Strasbourg (1873–1906) and then supervised Vos's doctoral dissertation, "Die Kämpfe und Streitigkeiten zwischen den Banu ʿUmajja und den Banu Hasim" (The Fight and Quarrels among the Banu ʿUmayya and the Banu Hasim), which researched a textual collation of an Arabic manuscript. His major work *Untersuchungen zur Kritik des Alten Testaments* (1869) demonstrated the unity of the basic writing by which K. H. Graf (1815–1869) developed new ground in OT criticism, that is, redaction criticism of the Pentateuch. Cf. Bray, *Biblical Interpretation*, 278–85.

179. Dennison, "Geerhadus Vos," 82–83.

180. Johann Wilhelm Herrmann, a professor at Halle and later at Marburg, saw God as the power of goodness and Christ as an exemplary man. He produced a typical idealistic liberal theology which Karl Barth later opposed.

181. Calhoun, *Princeton Seminary*, 230. Machen said that Herrmann believed hardly anything essential to Christianity yet exuded an incredibly impressive piety. This perplexed Machen, but he would go to his room, take out the Gospel of Mark and read it from beginning to end in one sitting and his doubts would fade.

> But surely we are not reduced to the alternative of following either the old systematizing or the new evolutionary principle of treatment. From the latter we need only learn to place greater emphasis upon the historical nexus of the several types of truth deposited in the Scripture, without thereby abating in the least our conviction concerning the supernatural genesis and growth of the body to which they belong.[182]

Vos respected modern biblical theology as an historical science, but he rejected some of its principles. His biblical theology was, however, not developed in a vacuum and Gaffin claims that Vos's work in biblical theology indicates originality in wrestling with the matter of biblical interpretation in the Reformed tradition.[183] This does not mean, however, that Vos was the innovator of Reformed biblical theology. For Gaffin, the term "Reformed tradition" primarily refers to Vos's original training for the Christian ministry, first in the Theological School of the Holland Christian Reformed Church in Grand Rapids (1881–1883), then at Princeton Theological Seminary (1883–1885). At the time, Princeton Seminary had members of faculty, like B. B. Warfield, Charles Hodge, and W. H. Green, who staunchly represented the historic Calvinism of the Westminster Standards.[184] Vos held to this confessional tradition firmly, even during his studies in Germany.

Peter J. Wallace argues that the foundations of a Reformed biblical theology cannot be attributed only to Vos's own efforts.[185] He points out that before Vos's development of biblical theology there were also direct precursors of that approach in the Reformed tradition, especially in the old Princeton Seminary, such as Hodge (professor from 1822 to 1878), Joseph Addison Alexander (professor from 1834 to 1860) and William Henry Green (professor from 1851 to 1900). Hodge had also studied for two years (1823–1824) in Germany under critical biblical theologians and had introduced their ideas to Princeton Seminary, but mainly to criticize them.[186] Alexander was largely indebted to E. W. Hengstenberg

---

182. Vos, *Presbyterian and Reformed Review* 11, 702, quoted in Gaffin, "Introduction" xii.

183. Gaffin, "Introduction," xii.

184. Webster, "Geerhardus Vos," 305.

185. Wallace, "Foundations of Reformed Biblical Theology," 41–69.

186. Hodge, *Life of Charles Hodge*, 202–5. Cf. Dawns, "Liberalism." Hodge was warned by Archibald Alexander that if he lost the deep impression of divine truth and fell into scepticism he would lose more than he gained from the German professors

(1802–1869) for his approach, and contributed to the Princeton theology his understanding of biblical history as one "grand organic whole" which provides the structure of biblical revelation.[187] Green continued in Alexander's perspective and upheld the idea of a christocenric interpretation of the OT.[188] Wallace thus articulatesd the foundation and framework for OT theology at Princeton which had been laid by the 1890s by these three scholars, emphasizing the flow of the history of special revelation.[189] While acknowledging this important background, it is correct to affirm that what Vos did in his contribution was to weave their concepts of redemptive history, together with Reformed covenant theology, into a biblical theology of both testaments. Whereas his predecessors devoted themselves solely to criticizing the harmful aspects of critical biblical theology,[190] Vos, in contrast, established a positive approach with Reformed principles. Gaffin, with some justification, has called Vos the father of Reformed biblical theology, while Wallace considers Alexander deservedly "the father of Reformed OT theology."[191]

Vos's approach represented a new epoch in biblical theology and was in fact closely connected to the conflict in the Presbyterian Church in the USA (PCUSA). While Vos was teaching in the Theological School of the Dutch Reformed Church for five years (1888–1893), PCUSA was inclined to revise the Westminster Confession of Faith under the influence of critical biblical theology, with higher criticism becoming a major controversial issue in the church from 1880 to 1910.[192] For example, the famous "Briggs Affair" (1880–1893) occurred between conservatives and modernists in the church.[193] There was, therefore, a theological battle

---

and libraries. Hodge kept this warning in mind.

187. Alexander, "Plan and Purpose of the Patriarchal History," 24–39.

188. Green, "Theology of the Old Testament," 103–20. Cf. Green, "Structure of the Old Testament," 161–87.

189. Wallace, "Foundations of Reformed Biblical Theology," 44.

190. Webster, "Geerhardus Vos," 313.

191. Wallace, "Foundations of Reformed Biblical Theology," 61.

192. Dennison, "Geerhardus Vos," 83–84. Vos told Kuyper in a letter in 1890 that the revision of the Westminster Confession obviously revealed a decline of historic Calvinism in the PCUSA. At the time Vos had been teaching didactic and exegetical theology at his alma mater for five years, and then moved to the Old Princeton school to take up a new chair in Biblical Theology to fight biblical criticism.

193. Longfield, *Presbyterian Controversy*. Cf. Rian, *Presbyterian Conflict*; Loetscher, *Broadening Church*. When Charles A. Briggs (1841–1913), a major advocate of higher criticism in the church, gave the inaugural address for the first ever Professor

line formed between the two sides, and Vos was invited by the Princeton school to a major teaching position and concentrated his efforts in the area of biblical theology, partly as a tool to respond to the more critical biblical theology.[194]

Characteristics and Influence

The characteristics of Reformed biblical theology were initially described in Vos's inaugural address and his *Biblical Theology* in 1948. When Vos defined biblical theology as "the exhibition of the organic progress of supernatural revelation in its historic continuity and multiformity,"[195] it presupposed Scripture to be God's supernatural revelation, with its intrinsic organic progression in history—an approach, of course, distinct from that of critical scholars like Gabler, Wrede, and Heikki Räisänen, in that they gave history priority over theology, while Vos takes both together.[196] Vos's method is also unlike the approaches of existentialist theologians such as Barth and Bultmann, or *Heilsgeschichte* theologians like Hofmann and Piper, in that these two groups basically adopted critical methods into their respective hermeneutical systems to deal with Scripture as a product of human history, whereas Vos retained a strong Reformed perspective on Scripture and theology.

Firstly, according to Vos, the term *biblical theology* needed to be redefined. Theology is, for Vos, "the science concerning God," that should be shaped by none other than God Himself, and thus is His self-revelation, inasmuch as the things of God are known only by the Spirit of God. In other sciences, man takes the first step to subject the objective world to his reason, but in theology this relation between subject and object is reversed, because without God revealing Himself no one can acquire a proper knowledge concerning God.[197] Here there is a profound differ-

---

of Biblical Theology at Union Theological Seminary in 1891, he openly announced that critical biblical theology had now definitively proven that the Pentateuch had not been written by Moses, and that the doctrine of inerrancy of Scripture taught in the Old Princeton school was wrong, as well as the Westminster Confession. Briggs called for other proponents of higher criticism to gather together to sweep away the dead orthodoxy from the church.

194. Gaffin, "Introduction," xi.
195. Vos, "Idea of Biblical Theology," 15.
196. Thileman, *Theology of the New Testament*, 27.
197. Vos, "Idea of Biblical Theology," 4–5. In Gabler's tradition of historical

ence between Vos's concept of theology and those of critical theologians like Gabler and Bultmann.

Secondly, the word *biblical* in biblical theology has, for Vos, recovered the meaning it had before it was revised in the eighteen century. Unlike Gabler, who announced in 1787 that biblical theology should be a "historical discipline,"[198] Vos refused to eliminate the revelation-principle of the Bible.[199] The predicate *biblical* in biblical theology meant, for him, recognizing Scripture as God's reliable self-revelation.

Thirdly, Vos's approach primarily highlights redemptive history, with its organic progression, as the principle for doing biblical theology adequately. Recognizing redemptive history, with its progressive nature, was a crucial key to the interpretation of Scripture for Vos, because revelation is the product of God's objective acts of redemption in history—redemptive acts which are connected to each other as a whole, advancing from beginning to end under the one great goal of God: the fullness of His glory in the whole universe.[200] Vos described this point with four major features of revelation: "the historic progressiveness," "the actual embodiment in history," "the organic nature of the historic process observable in revelation," and "practical adaptability."[201] These four features all refer to the relation of revelation to redemptive history, and become the basic concepts of his biblical theology. Vos proposed several guiding principles for keeping biblical theology from degenerating into historical science, such as: (1) the recognition of the infallible character of revelation; (2) the objectivity of the groundwork of revelation; (3) the dependency of biblical theology on the full acceptance of "plenary inspiration."

Vos's biblical theology is, therefore, characterized by three suppositions: theology cannot but be shaped by God's self-revelation; biblical study should recognize first Scripture's own characteristics, namely, the inspiration, the supernaturalism and the infallibility of God's self-revelation; biblical theology can properly proceed on the principle of redemptive history, with its organic progression which is structured in the whole of Scripture. Here are the essential characteristics of Vosnian biblical

---

criticism, theology is about specific people's religious experience of God; in Bultmann's approach, theology exclusively deals with man's subjective understanding of God. Thus Bultmann admittedly professed that biblical theology should be purely anthropology.

198. Matera, *New Testament Theology*, xx.
199. Vos, "Idea of Biblical Theology," 15.
200. Ibid., 8.
201. Vos, *Biblical Theology*, 5–7.

theology, with its presuppositions concerning the relationship between special revelation and redemptive history. Because of these specific features, Vos wanted to call this discipline the "history of special revelation," a term which expresses more precisely what this science aimed to be.[202]

Covenant theology in the Reformed tradition also assumes an indispensable position in Vos's biblical theology, functioning as the governing hermeneutical principle in Vos's program. For Vos, covenant is the foundation of salvation and the guarantee of the historical progress of God's redemption and its resulting church. There was essentially a threefold covenant in Reformed tradition: the covenant of works, the covenant of redemption, and the covenant of grace. This covenant was established as a dominant hermeneutic principle in federal theology, which first appeared with Cocceius in the seventeenth century,[203] and was then incorporated into the historical progression of revelation, which had been a key concept in OT studies at Princeton for over fifty years before Vos.[204] In his biblical-theological study, Vos combined Cocceius's federal theology with the concept of the historical progression of revelation, which his predecessors like Alexander and Green had affirmed, and eventually brought out his distinctive perspective of redemptive history which centered on the covenant. Before Vos's program appeared, covenant theology was not seriously handled in critical biblical theology, or even in the works of Vos's Reformed predecessors, but it takes a central position in Vos's hermeneutical system, with redemptive history. By means of this new combination, Vos contributed more to the Reformed strand of biblical theology than before, strengthening the ties with the Westminster Confession.

Vos's biblical theology had a significant influence on scholars within the Reformed circle, like John Murray, Herman Ridderbos, and Willem VanGemeren. For example, VanGemeren confesses that his idea of redemptive history came from Vos's discipline. Murray, Cornelius Van Til, and Ned Stonehouse all embraced Vos's idea of biblical theology, and

202. Vos, *Biblical Theology*, 14. Vos admitted, however, that it is difficult to change a name which has the sanction of usage.

203. Bray, *Biblical Interpretation*, 186. Cocceius discovered the idea of the covenant in Scripture and developed it in terms of a succession of historical periods and events in his *Summa doctrinae de foedere et testamento Dei (The Doctrine of the Covenant and Testament of God)* in 1648, which became the standard for a later generation. Bray considers him the ancestor of both salvation history and modern millenarianism.

204. Taylor, *Old Testament in the Old Princeton School*, 262, quoted in Wallace, "Foundation of Reformed Biblical Theology," 68.

Gaffin, Ridderbos, Meredith G. Kline, and James, Charles, and William Dennison attempted a further development of Vos's original insights.²⁰⁵ Vos's approach posited a solid foundation on which later scholars could build their studies of biblical theology in the Reformed tradition and, owing to Vos's foundational work, the historical and the theological came together within the Reformed confession. This is, in my judgment, a most significant contribution of Vos's approach to biblical interpretation.

I suggest that the influence of Vos's method has been seriously underestimated, or neglected, by critical scholars. For example, Eric Rust, who wrote *Salvation History* in 1962 in America, did not refer at all to Vos or his methodology, although he dealt with the specific theme of salvation history at length and quoted extensively from Cullmann and Bultmann.²⁰⁶ Hasel also discussed the redemptive history theme significantly in his *New Testament Theology*, but Vos's concept of redemptive history was not introduced at all, except in presenting him twice in unrelated sections as an author treating both the OT and NT simultaneously.²⁰⁷ Piper, a professor at Princeton Seminary in the 1930s and 1940s, must have known of Vos, yet he ignores him and refers to *Heilsgeschichte* theologians like Hofmann and Cullmann for his idea of a redemptive history perspective. Piper claimed wrongly that the only group in Protestant theology to maintain the central significance of salvation history was the school of *Heilsgeschichte*.²⁰⁸

Nevertheless, the legacy of Vos's biblical theology has been greatly appreciated by theologians in the Reformed confession. For example, Ladd quotes often and extensively from Vos's works, as does Ridderbos.²⁰⁹ Likewise, Vos's works and numerous monographs provide a standard and dependable source of reference, especially his *Biblical Theology*, which has extensively influenced scholars and pastors in Korean Reformed churches.

---

205. Dennison, "Geerhardus Vos," 91.
206. Rust, *Salvation History*, 313–15.
207. Hasel, *New Testament Theology*, 171, 201.
208. Piper, *God in History*, xix.
209. Webster, "Geerhardus Vos," 316–17.

Conclusion

In this chapter, I have identified and discussed the hermeneutical roots of redemptive history, especially historical criticism, existentialism, and Reformed biblical theology. I explained that the method of Reformed biblical theology has influenced the Korean Reformed church in hermeneutics and homiletics. This will be the background for our understanding of the Korean homiletical debate.

In the next two chapters, we discuss the homiletical debate in Holland and America as an essential background to the Korean debate.

3

The Dutch Debate
Homiletics and Redemptive History

BEFORE WE DISCUSS THE Korean debate on redemptive history we need to explore further the nature of the related Dutch controversy and the American response because these debates converge on how to view the Bible and then apply it to preaching. As indicated in chapter 1, redemptive-historical preaching and its subsequent controversy in Korea was primarily influenced initially by the Dutch debate, but it is also closely related to the American discussion about redemptive history. By exploring the essential features of the two preceding debates we can assess the extent to which they influenced the Korean debate.

The Debate: Dutch Reformed Churches in the 1930s and 1940s

Methodologically, I intend to use Greidanus's *Sola Scriptura* (1970), Trimp's *Preaching and the History of Salvation* (1986), and William Renninger's doctoral dissertation "The New Testament Use of Old Testament Historical Narrative and the Implication for the Exemplary Interpretation of Old Testament Narrative" (2000) as major resources to survey the Dutch debate, with supporting materials such as Clowney's *Preaching and Biblical Theology* (1975) and N. H. Gootjes's "Introduction to Greidanus's *Sola Scriptura* (1989)." This investigation will also employ primary sources by the leading figures in the debates, such as Schilder, Holwerda and M. B. Van't Veer, which appeared originally in Dutch journals such as *De Heraut* and *De Reformatie*.

There are significant reasons for adopting this methodological approach. Firstly, Greidanus, Trimp, and Renninger have provided the most comprehensive and reliable information about the debate. Originally, the arguments of participants in the debate appeared extensively in various Dutch magazines and journals throughout the 1930s and 1940s. These three scholars, especially Greidanus, have arranged the scattered articles helpfully in their books, using the most useful and relevant materials on this subject. Gootjes[1] himself suggests that we should refer to the writings of Greidanus and Trimp if we wish to examine the details of the Dutch debate.[2] He introduces the former by claiming, "Greidanus collects most of the arguments of the Dutch debate and presents the whole aspect of them. This presentation becomes the most useful part of that book."[3]

Secondly, Greidanus and Trimp are both recognized as being well qualified to record and explain the details of the Dutch debate because of their background and close connection with the past controversy. Greidanus has dealt with the theme of the historical texts of the Bible, which directly relates to the debate, and Trimp had been teaching homiletics since 1970 at the Theological University of the Reformed Churches in the Netherlands (Liberated), which itself emerged from the denominational schism relating to the debate. Greidanus's original aim in writing his doctoral dissertation was to explore the past controversy concerning how to preach on historical texts in the Bible,[4] while Trimp intended in his writing to continue, or develop, the discussion in the Dutch Reformed churches today.[5] Greidanus's book was written in English, with the intention of widening the discussion internationally, whereas Trimp's book was written in Dutch in an attempt to revive the debate in the original Dutch context.[6] These two books thus complement each other well and are considered major resources for the survey of issues relating to the debate. For example, Lindblad recommends these two books as being most

---

1. Gootjes is a former Dutch Professor of Systematic Theology in Koshin University in Korea, and now a Professor of Dogmatology at the Theological College of the Canadian Reformed Churches.
2. Gootjes, "Luke 4:16," para. 16.
3. Gootjes, "Book Introduction," 13–14.
4. Greidanus, *Sola Scriptura*, 1.
5. Trimp, *Preaching and the History of Salvation*, 12.
6. Ibid., 11–12.

relevant for a more detailed survey of the Dutch debate,[7] while Hendrik Krabbendam suggests that for an excellent discussion of the debate we should refer to Greidanus's *Sola Scriptura*.[8]

Thirdly, it is extremely important to note that the Korean debate on this subject has been influenced almost entirely by Greidanus's *Sola Scriptura*. As we examined in chapter 1, Sung-Jong Shin was the first to recycle Greidanus's explanation of the Dutch debate in pointing to the problems of Korean Protestant preaching. Sung-Kuh Chung also acknowledged that the concern for redemptive history was mainly introduced to Korean Reformed churches after he himself had taught redemptive-historical preaching in the ThM program while using Greidanus's English book at Chong-Shin Theological Seminary in the 1980s.[9] The book subsequently considerably influenced the Korean homiletical debate. It is thus appropriate that *Sola Scriptura* should be taken as a major source for examining the influence of the Dutch debate on the Korean discussion about redemptive-historical preaching.

However, a survey which depends entirely on only a few sources would be subject to major criticism, possibly due to prejudice, regarding the omission of both additional major data and different evaluations. To meet such a criticism, I am using other supporting materials, as indicated above. For example, Gootjes provides his own opinion about Greidanus's methodology in approaching the debate, while criticizing serious weaknesses in translation, which we will discuss later. Clowney also offers a succinct, but different, explanation, while Renninger gives his own review of the debate and also an evaluation of the arguments of those involved in it. Others, like Cornelis Pronk[10] and Stefan Lindblad,[11] also describe the controversy from their own perspectives. In addition to these, articles by Holwerda[12] and Van't Veer[13] will significantly strengthen our exploration of the subject because they were participants in the debate. I submit that all these sources together are appropriate, necessary and comprehensive because the authors are reliable guides who worked from the various pri-

---

7. Lindblad, "Redemptive History and the Preached Word," part 1: Introduction, 16.

8. Krabbendam, "Hermeneutics and Preaching," 230.

9. Chung, *Reformed Homiletics*, 348.

10. Pronk, "Preaching in the Dutch Calvinist Tradition."

11. Lindblad, "Redemptive History and the Preached Word."

12. Holwerda, "De heilshistorie in de prediking."

13. Veer, "Christologische prediking," 117–67.

mary sources and well understood both the situation and the debate. My methodology is therefore appropriate for our purpose of examining the context and development of the Dutch controversy, and then of exploring further how, and what part of, the Western debate influenced Korean Protestant scholars.

Background

The debate over redemptive-historical preaching occurred within a most complex situation, which was interwoven with philosophy, theology, and ecclesiastical matters in the Dutch Reformed churches in the 1930s and 1940s. Sung-Kuh Chung, a leading proponent of redemptive-historical preaching in Korea, explains that Barth's existential interpretation of Scripture and consequent preaching gave rise to redemptive-historical preaching, while the Dutch pietistic expression of subjectivism and mysticism was also the background to the birth of redemptive-historical preaching in the Netherlands.[14] According to Chung, the introduction of Barth's dialectical theology provoked several different responses in the Dutch churches—one welcomed it as a reforming measure criticizing the previous Kuyperian theology, another sought for a harmonizing approach between Kuyper and Barth, while others wanted to eradicate the influence of Barthian theology from their churches. For example, Schilder came to emphasize redemptive-historical preaching as a reaction against the anti-historical tendency of Barth's dialectical theology. In addition to this, subjectivism, individualism, and mysticism, which were previously embedded in Dutch Pietism,[15] were also thought to be extinguished in the reformation movement by Schilder's reform group. Chung's analysis is, however, mostly dependent on Greidanus's explanation given in his *Sola Scriptura*.

Greidanus finds the actual reasons for the Dutch homiletical debate in a philosophical movement, referred to as the New Direction. According to Greidanus, a group of Dutch theologians, mostly belonging to the New Direction, began to criticize the traditional preaching in Dutch

---

14. Chung, "Principles and Methods of Redemptive-Historical Preaching," 20–22.

15. Dutch Pietism originated from the Dutch Second Reformation (*De Nadere Reformatie*) in the seventeenth and early eighteenth centuries, and should not be misconceived as being affected by German Pietism. We discuss this later in this chapter. Cf. Beeke, *Quest for Full Assurance*, 291–92.

Reformed churches in the early 1930s.[16] Their objections were mainly directed at the preaching methodology which dealt with biblical characters in historical texts as mere models or examples to be imitated, without an explanation of the historical context of those texts. This practice was customary on the part of preachers at that time. The New Direction charged this so-called exemplary preaching with weakening, and even disparaging, the whole nature of biblical history, that is, redemptive history, by not doing justice to biblical texts. Their scathing critique was intended to dispel what they imagined were unbiblical tendencies from church pulpits, but eventually this met with the protest of traditional preachers who argued that such factors should be retained in preaching. Afterwards, this passion for a radical change in church preaching gave rise to the Dutch homiletical debate, the so-called "exemplary versus redemptive-historical" controversy. This is Greidanus's outline for the background of the Dutch debate, but it is unclear because it does not provide a sufficient context and fails to identify the roots of that philosophical movement. We therefore need to further explore the New Direction movement, to examine its main features and its specific connection to the Dutch church situation.

The New Direction movement was led by the famous philosopher Herman Dooyeweerd and his brother-in-law D. H. Th. Vollenhoven in the early 1930s.[17] John Frame calls this movement the Amsterdam Philosophy, because it started at the Free University of Amsterdam where these two scholars had taught and from where their influence spread widely to places like North America and South Africa.[18] Dooyeweerd's trilogy *Wijsbegeerte der wetsidee* (1935–36)[19] and Vollenhoven's book *Het Calvinisme en de reformatie van de wijsbegeerte* (1933) crucially influenced the formation of the Association for Calvinistic Philosophy

---

16. Greidanus, *Sola Scriptura*, 23.

17. Ibid., 22.

18. Frame and Coppes, *Amsterdam Philosophy*. Frame says the title *Amsterdam Philosophy* is his own; the original title "The Philosophy of the Idea of Law" is cumbersome for easy reference, while "Dooyeweerdianism" is somewhat offensive, and titles like the "Reformational" or "Radical Christian Philosophy" are unsuitably honorific in the context of a theological debate. Accordingly, Frame selected the more neutral title.

19. These volumes were published between 1953 and 1958 in an English edition, translated by Freeman et al., with the title of *A New Critique of Theoretical Thought*, in Amsterdam and Philadelphia by Presbyterian and Reformed Publishing.

(1935),[20] which listed many famous scholars, like Van Til (1895–1987)[21] of Westminster Theological Seminary (WTS), Philadelphia, and H. G. Stoker[22] of the University of Potchefstroom, South Africa, and to which most proponents of redemptive-historical preaching, like Schilder, Holwerda, Spier, and Veenhof, belonged, and exposed their dislike of traditional exemplary preaching.[23] S. G. De Graaf (1889–1955), the author of *Promise and Deliverance*, was a member of that school and also expressed similar distaste for an individualistic interpretation of biblical texts and subsequent exemplary preaching.[24] That the Dooyeweerdians were commonly uncomfortable with the traditional preaching suggests that there should be a connection between this philosophical position and the idea of redemptive-historical preaching.

Dooyeweerd's philosophy is complex and detailed and it is beyond the scope of this book to undertake an extensive evaluation of it. Dooyeweerd himself assumed that many, even with philosophical training, would be deterred from studying his philosophy because of its complexity, obscurity, and new terminology.[25] All I intend to do here is to underline Dooyeweerd's emphatic and foundational claim that no human thought can be autonomous or neutral, but is always oriented towards, and committed to, certain religious systems like Buddhism or atheism, which can be understood as religions intended to negate the concept of God. There is no neutral ground. For Dooyeweerd, philosophy should provide a theoretical insight into the inter-modal coherence—a reference to the totality of all aspects of the temporal world.[26] In other words, philosophy ought to explain how to interrelate selfhood with other modal

---

20. This association later became the Association for Reformational Philosophy, which remains in the Netherlands but has achieved worldwide influence.

21. Van Til had once been an editor of the journal of the Association of Calvinistic Philosophy, *Philosophia Reformata*, and is listed as a member of the school in Dooyeweerd's book *In the Twilight of Western Thought*. However, he became increasingly critical of this philosophical movement in the later days of his life.

22. Hendrik Gerhardus Stoker (1899–1993) was born in Johannesburg and taught philosophy from 1925 to 1970 in Potchefstroom University whilst being a renowned Calvinistic philosopher.

23. See Frame and Coppes, *Amsterdam Philosophy*.

24. Graaf, *From Creation to the Conquest of Canaan*, 24.

25. Dooyeweerd, *New Critique of Theoretical Thought*, vol. 1, v–ix. Dooyeweerd acknowledged in his foreword that his philosophy is complex, but only because it breaks with traditional philosophical views (viii–ix).

26. Ibid., 4.

aspects, like the physical, the logical, the historical, the social, the economic, the aesthetic, and the moral aspects, and that of faith. Dooyeweerd claims to have discovered, in his study of philosophy, the "transcendental ground-motives" at the foundation of all philosophical thought, which brought forth the different theoretical views concerning the structure of reality, that is, "the modal aspects of human experience."[27] All theoretical thought finds its fundamental root in the thought of God and Scripture or, otherwise, in human reason. Dooyeweerd, therefore, offered a critique of humanist philosophy with its claim to self-sufficiency:

> . . . I wish to repudiate any self-satisfied scientific attitude in confronting immanence-philosophy . . . I should not judge immanence-philosophy so sharply were it not that I myself have gone through it, and have personally experienced its problems. I should not pass such a sharp judgment on the attempts at synthesis between non-Christian philosophy and the Christian truth of faith, had I not lived through the inner tension between the two and personally wrestled through the attempts at synthesis.[28]

For Dooyeweerd, there is a fundamental antithesis between the Christian ground-motive and that of non-Christians.[29] Any attempt to integrate these two contrary motives thus inevitably fails. That is why he wanted to develop an authentically Christian philosophy, based purely on "God's law," over against the synthesis of Christianity and the non-believing classical philosophy of earlier ages, as adopted by Augustine, Thomas Aquinas, Kant, and Søren Kierkegaard. Thereby, Dooyeweerd's philosophy of "cosmonomic (*wetsidee*: logis or law) idea"[30] has consistently emphasized radical separation from the influence of apostate humanistic philosophy and the full adoption of a genuine Christian ground-motive of creation, fall, and redemption.

In Dooyeweerd's cosmonomic philosophy, God created all things and beings in the cosmos and gave His law to be obeyed according to His sovereign will, with respect to the created reality. Here the law (*wetsidee*

---

27. Ibid., v–vi.
28. Ibid., viii.
29. Ibid., 86, 157.
30. Ibid., 93. From the outset of his philosophy, Dooyeweerd introduced the Dutch term *wetsidee* (idea logis or law) for the transcendental ground idea, or basic idea, of philosophy. He took "cosmonomic idea" as the best English term for it. Cf. Shepherd, "Doctrine of Scripture in the Dooyeweerdian Philosophy," 18–23.

or cosmonomic) meant the totality of God's ruling acts over all his creatures, including nature and history, as well as grace and salvation.[31] These laws distinguish one sphere from another, just as laws of nature, such as gravity, are different from the laws of grace. Thus each created sphere should be differentiated from other spheres and controlled by its own distinctive law, which God sovereignly gave to it, and to which the name "sphere sovereignty" was given. For instance, not only church and state, but also school, business, family, and other aspects are sovereign spheres and have a unique character, depending on a respectively different sovereign law, even though they probably interrelate with, or support, each other.[32] Accordingly, it is not until one grasps the ground-motive of Scripture that one understands the totality of these law-spheres, which together form the structure of the cosmos.

The ground-motive of creation, fall, and the redemption of Christ was, for Dooyeweerd, reckoned not as a petrified ecclesiastical doctrine, but as the driving force to change fundamentally the life of Christians and their worldview. He claimed that if our hearts were acquainted with this central meaning of Scripture, we would then be beyond the scientific problems of both theology and philosophy.[33] For example, one such problem was a distorted view of history, namely, historicism, with its related Western culture, illustrated in German Nazism and Italian Fascism, as described in Spengler's *The Decline of the West* (1918). In handling this, Dooyeweerd reinterpreted the history of Western civilization as three continuing periods—the ancient pagan, the medieval Christian, and the modern secular culture periods—by reflecting a crisis in the very spiritual foundation of Western culture.[34] He suggested the ultimate answer to this problem is found only in the central revelation of Scripture, that is, creation, fall, and redemption through Jesus Christ. The attempt to resolve the problems of the earlier synthesis between Christianity and humanist philosophy thus became the major agenda for reformation in this philosophy.

For Dooyeweerdians, the reformation means radically rooting out the synthetic elements embedded in the thought and life of most Christians, and fundamentally rebuilding them on the foundation of a

---

31. Johnson, *Dutch Reformed Philosophy in North America*.
32. Klapwijk, "Struggle for a Christian Philosophy."
33. Dooyeweerd, *In the Twilight of Western Thought*, 125.
34. Dooyeweerd, *New Critique*, vol. 1, 208; vol. 2, 291–93; cf. McIntire, *Legacy of Herman Dooyeweerd*, 28–29.

Christian ground-motive. However, dominant Western thought and culture had been, for Dooyeweerd, mostly based on secular philosophies like those of Plato, Aristotle, Descartes, and Kant, while even Christian thought, like that of Kierkegaard, at best accommodated itself to non-Christian systems, especially the dualism of "nature and grace" or "body and soul."[35] Dooyeweerd insisted that Scripture had not been used adequately to integrate Christian thought and life, but was used only for purposes of Pietism in developing the Christian life and experience. That is why his philosophy sought a revolutionary reformation in all spheres of human life, including the sciences, law, economics, politics, theology, and especially ecclesiastical life, through the scriptural ground-motive.[36]

Ecclesiastical renewal was primarily required to achieve Dooyeweerdian reformation, and was to proceed by centering on the religious community. The contemporary church's thought was, however, in Dooyeweerd's view, significantly mingled with a humanistic apostate motive. For example, the Greek motive of "form and matter" or "nature and grace" permeated Western thinking and also that of Christians, thus making them likely to separate the church from the world. Dooyeweerd contended that this dualistic view, traced back to Greek philosophy through medieval Roman Catholic scholasticism, affected Barthian theology and also contemporary Christians.[37] Dooyeweerdian reformation thus sought for fundamental disintegration of that synthesis of Christian motive from the Greek ground-motive. The church should not separate herself from the world and confine her congregation to the spiritual realm. The Christian ground-motive should be pervasive in the secular

---

35. Wolfe, *Key to Dooyeweerd*, vi–xiii. Wolfe tried to present the key thoughts of *A New Critique of Theoretical Thought*, Dooyeweerd's *magnum opus*, in some 2000 pages in three volumes, in a manner understandable to the average reader. According to Wolfe, Dooyeweerd's works actually undertake a Christian refocusing of the entire corpus of theoretical thought, like "time and space," "motion and energy," "the biotic," "the economic," "the aesthetic," "law," and "faith," exclusively on the divine revelation of Jesus Christ.

36. Dooyeweerd emphasized his turning point by saying, " . . . I came to understand the central significance of the 'heart,' repeatedly proclaimed by Holy Scripture to be the religious root of human existence. On the basis of this central Christian point of view I saw the need of a revolution in philosophical thought of a very radical character." (Dooyeweerd, *New Critique*, v) ; cf. Kalsbeek, *Contours of a Christian Philosophy*, 19–20.

37. Dooyeweerd, *Roots of Western Culture*, 140. Dooyeweerd described the Early Church as influenced by Greek and Near Eastern ground-motives, as in Gnosticism and Marcion.

life of Christians as well as in their church life. To achieve this reformation, the church needed to radically change in dogmatics and homiletics according to the scriptural ground-motive. There should not be any division between the secular and the sacred. This movement called for the integral unity of the Christian life in and outside the church, which is why Dooyeweerdians had a deep concern for their culture and for the externals of religion. However, its effect was to de-emphasize individual piety and subjective experiences of God. This is the philosophical background of the redemptive-historical approach, which does not tolerate more emphasis on internal experience in traditional preaching. What then is the theological background of redemptive-historical preaching?

Theologically, the New Direction movement has a close relationship to the Neo-Calvinism of Abraham Kuyper (1837–1920), who profoundly influenced the theological, educational, and political climate of the Netherlands from about 1870 to 1920.[38] Dooyeweerd's thought system was in fact the expansion of Kuyper's theological principles,[39] which are evident in Kuyper's famous Stone Lectures given at Princeton Theological Seminary in 1898.[40] Kuyper articulated the principles of his world view, which reinforced the principles of Calvin in his *Institutes of the Christian Religion*. This view is called Neo-Calvinism in many journals, such as the daily *Standaard* and the weekly *Heraut*, but Kuyper did not himself develop a systematic Christian philosophy. Dooyeweerd and his colleagues undertook that task and developed a Christian philosophy which became the New Direction movement. Kuyper's theology, therefore, can be un-

---

38. On Kuyper's seventieth birthday in 1907 it was said, "The history of the Netherlands, in Church, in State, in Society, in Press, in School, and in the Sciences of the last forty years, can not be written without the mention of his name on almost every page, for during this period the biography of Dr. Kuyper is to a considerable extent the history of The Netherlands." (De Vries, "Biographical Note," 6.)

39. Kuyper's influence on Dooyeweerd can be outlined in three points. Firstly, Dooyeweerd grew up in the home of Calvinistic parents whose thought and life were deeply affected by Kuyper. Secondly, he also studied at the law school of the Free University of Amsterdam, which Kuyper founded in 1880 in order to cultivate intellectually competent Christian leaders who would confront the dominant modernism of the nineteenth century. Thirdly, in 1922 Dooyeweerd was appointed assistant director of the Kuyper Institute in The Hague, a newly established research center of the Anti-Revolutionary Party, which Kuyper had once led for political reformation, and, later, in 1926, Dooyeweerd became Professor of Legal Philosophy at his alma mater, serving until his retirement in 1965. In view of these points, no one can deny Kuyper's influence on Dooyeweerd. Cf. Kalsbeek, *Contours of a Christian Philosophy*, 14–19.

40. McIntire, "Herman Dooyeweerd in North America," 60–61.

derstood as the significant background to redemptive-historical preaching. Cornelis Pronk, a pastor of the Free Reformed Church in North America,[41] supports this point: "The 'redemptive-historical' school of preaching . . . was, and is, espoused by men influenced by Dooyeweerd's philosophy of the Law-Idea. This philosophy in turn, has its roots in the Neo-Calvinism of Dr. A. Kuyper."[42] We now need to survey the phenomenon of Neo-Calvinism.

Neo-Calvinism

The Neo-Calvinism of Kuyper has been a contentious theological position in the Netherlands and in North America, raising critical issues like "common grace"[43] and "presumptive regeneration."[44] It is beyond the scope of this work to discuss Kuyper's theology extensively, but I want to refer to aspects which relate to redemptive-historical preaching as this will assist the exploration of our subject. Kuyper also emphasized that historic Calvinism should be applied to all spheres of the Christian life. We observe the key features of his theological thought in his *Lectures on Calvinism*, which formed the Stone Lectures. He says:

> . . . If the battle is to be fought with honour and with a hope of victory, then principle must be arrayed against principle; then it must be felt that in Modernism the vast energy of an all-embracing life-system assails us, then also it must be understood that

---

41. The Free Reformed Church in North America is the counterpart of its mother denomination the Christelijke Gereformeerde Kerken (Christian Reformed Church, different from the Christian Reformed Church in the United States).

42. Pronk, "Preaching in the Dutch Calvinist Tradition."

43. "Common grace" for Kuyper means that God blesses humanity with intellect, gifts, and a disposition for developing human culture, without differentiating believers from non-believers. Remarkable achievements of secular scholarship, science, and astonishing works of unbelieving artists or musicians have all been attained by the use of God's gifts. In view of this doctrine of common grace, a Christian should be involved actively in all spheres of human life, to promote the cultural mandate. However, critics of Kuyper, such as Pronk, argue that the doctrine of common grace emphasizes too much the cultural mandate (Gen 1:28) and eventually it de-emphasizes the evangelistic mandate of Christ (Matt 28:18–20).

44. "Presumptive regeneration" implies that the Holy Spirit's work of regenerating an elect person precedes his or her own conversion experience and thus the regeneration of covenantal children should be presumed before their baptism. Kuyper argued that baptism should be administered on the presumption that regeneration has preceded it. Cf. McGoldrick, *God's Renaissance Man*, 132–37.

> we have to take our stand in a life-system of equally comprehensive and far-reaching power . . . When thus taken, I found and confessed, and I still hold, that this manifestation of the Christian principle is given us in Calvinism. In Calvinism my heart has found rest. From Calvinism have I drawn the inspiration firmly and resolutely to take my stand in the thick of this great conflict of principles.[45]

Kuyper here expresses, rather pointedly, the motive and cause of his theological efforts as a struggle with modernism.[46] Modernism, for Kuyper, meant a comprehensive life system, which was in reality an anti-Christian movement that began with the French Revolution (1789–1799)[47] and then greatly affected Western culture, including Dutch politics and religion, by embracing rationalism and the theory of evolution as espoused by Darwin. Experiencing waves of that type of modernism in higher education at Leiden University, and becoming a modernist himself in his early days before conversion, Kuyper well knew the enemy against which he was determined to fight vigorously as a young pastor in the late 1860s.

Kuyper found in historic Calvinism the effective means of combating the dominant modernism, claiming to understand Calvinism as a powerful life-system, applying it to all areas of life for Reformed believers. He said, "We cannot be passive and silent towards those who reject God's Word and our holy faith."[48] He hoped to restore God's genuine authority and glory over the church and also over the created world. The principle of God's sovereignty in Calvinism had thus been an impetus and a key in Kuyper's theology, from which other principles, like antithesis, sphere sovereignty, common grace, and social reformation, were developed. He did not want Calvinism to be limited to an individual's faith alone, but wanted to expand and proclaim its message to the whole world and reach

---

45. Kuyper, *Lectures on Calvinism*, 11–12.

46. Kuyper spent all his life combating modernism. When he gave the Stone Lectures he confessed that he had been spending all his energy in the struggle with modernism for nearly forty years until 1898.

47. There were sacrilegious slogans used in the French Revolution such as "We no longer need a God" or "No God, no master." These slogans implied that removal of the king and all authority in religion would emancipate from all curses and give liberation to people. Kuyper thought that God employed the revolution to end the tyranny of the Bourbons, but its principle of being thoroughly anti-Christian spread like a cancer, undermining the Christian faith. Cf. Kuyper, *Lectures on Calvinism*, 10.

48. McGoldrick, *God's Renaissance Man*, 38.

out to all spheres of human life. He thus actively pursued his Calvinistic reformation through journalism, education, and political action for half a century, from 1870–1920. His reformation efforts appeared successful.

However, Kuyper viewed some Reformed believers as being reluctant to follow his principles, being prepared to confine themselves to their confessional faith. This made him more strongly urge the Reformed community to purge out the latent pietistic dualism, for example, the separation of Sunday from the workweek and the spiritual from the physical.[49] He claimed that if they were real Calvinists they could no longer dismiss spheres in the general world, like science, art, and politics, as "corrupted things."[50] Kuyper's theology came to emphasize the cultural mandate rather than personal faith, or the more objective and cosmological aspects of religion rather than subjective, individual experiences. Kuyper himself, of course, had a high view of one's experience of God, especially conversion, but his followers increasingly came to devalue individual experiences. The roots of certain traits of redemptive-historical preaching, especially the strong aversion to experiential preaching, with its pietistic emphasis on subjectivism, individualism, and spiritualism, can therefore be traced back through Dooyeweerdian philosophy to Kuyperian theology, often referred to as Neo-Calvinism.

Ecclesiastically, Neo-Calvinism and the New Direction movement have been specifically embedded in the history of secessions in the Dutch Reformed Church. A brief examination of the history of the church is now required to further our discussion. The earliest Protestantism began in the Low Countries at the time of the Spanish monarchy under Charles I (reigned 1516–1556) and Philip II (reigned 1556–1598), through the influence of Lutheranism from Germany. However, Calvinism had begun to supplant Lutheranism during the Eighty Years' War (1568–1648), by means of which Dutch noblemen sought to preserve political freedom and combat excessive taxation. Dutch Calvinists exerted significant leadership in that war, and eventually saw the birth of the Dutch Republic (1581–1795). The Dutch political and military leaders, like William of Orange (1533–1584), had appreciated the contribution of Dutch Calvinists towards achieving independence and thus willingly supported the establishment of the Calvinists' church as the official religion of the Netherlands in 1579.

---

49. Bratt, *Dutch Calvinism in Modern America*, 16.
50. Ibid.

In the meantime, in 1571, a synod of Calvinistic leaders subscribed to the *Belgic Confession of Faith* (1561) and the *Heidelberg Catechism* (1562) as their doctrinal standards. The Synod of Dort (1618–1619) produced the *Canons of Dort*, affirming strict Calvinistic orthodoxy while condemning the views of Arminius and his followers, that is, Arminianism.[51] The Dutch Reformed Church (Nederlandse Hervormde Kerk) was then firmly established on the basis of historic Calvinism, formalizing its principles under the three doctrinal statements as the Three Forms of Unity, and for a while enjoying state support.

However, as rationalism became popular in Dutch universities like Leiden and Groningen, by the late-eighteenth century the church found some of its pastors were being imbibed with theological liberalism, which rejected the supernaturalism of the Bible and taught ideas contrary to the Reformed faith. After the French Revolution of 1789, the French army, led by Napoleon, occupied the Netherlands from 1795 to 1814. The Dutch Reformed Church was deprived of its prime and beneficiary position by King Louis Bonaparte, who favored Roman Catholicism.[52] After the country regained independence in 1814 and newly established the kingdom of the Prince of Orange,[53] the church began to suffer from state control and saw the dominance of rationalists in the universities and also in the church. When the first national synod discarded the *Canons of Dort* in 1816, the national church began to deviate from historic Calvinism and opened itself to theological liberalism. There were still, however, some people, like Hendrik de Cock (1801–1842), who kept their Reformed faith as taught by the Calvinistic standards of the Three Forms of Unity. They eventually left the Nederlandse Hervormde Kerk, and united as Reformed believers in the first secession (*Afscheiding*, 1834) from the national church. These secessionists then formed a new denomination, the Christian Reformed Church (*Christelijke Gereformeerde Kerken*) in 1836, proclaiming separation from state control, and subsequently suffering severe persecution by the state until 1840.[54]

---

51. McGoldrick, *God's Renaissance Man*, 21.

52. Ibid., 23.

53. The first king of the Kingdom of the Netherlands, William I (reigned 1815–1840), promoted religious unity without regard for Reformed doctrine, and this program caused the Dutch Reformed Church to deteriorate theologically, according to Guillaume Groen van Prinsterer (1801–1876) who supported the secessionists in theory, but did not participate in action. Cf. McGoldrick, *God's Renaissance Man*, 28.

54. Free Reformed Churches of North America, "Our History," paras 1, 2. The Free

Despite experiencing the first secession, the national church continued to deteriorate spiritually. The church and the universities in which Christian leaders were educated and trained were under state control and staffed with modernist teachers and pastors.[55] When Kuyper entered the University of Leiden in 1855, the most distinguished school at that time in the Netherlands influenced him with unbelief regarding the supernatural characteristics of the Bible. After converting to the orthodox faith during his first pastorate from 1863 to 1867 in the small town of Beesd, and with the help of uneducated but godly parishioners like a woman named Pietje Baltus (1830–1914),[56] Kuyper realised that his once revered modernistic knowledge was unhelpful to the church and he consequently saw the need for a new reformation movement. By the middle of the nineteenth century, the schools, like Groningen University, which had provided pastors for the national church, had become more radical than before in denying major doctrines like the deity of Christ. They considered Christ's only mission was to lead humanity to God and thus to set Himself as an ethical model.[57]

Around the late 1860s, a group of Reformed believers within the national church rose to oppose this radical theological movement, with Abraham Kuyper as a leader of that campaign in Utrecht (1867–1870) and afterwards in Amsterdam. Thinking that the reformation would be unsuccessful without a Christian university in which the biblical worldview was foundational in building up all the related subjects of study, Kuyper founded the Free University of Amsterdam in 1880 to provide the national church with Christian leaders grounded in the Reformed faith. However, graduates of the university were refused ordination in the national church as the Dutch government demanded that they pass state examinations to approve their degrees. To make matters worse, the

---

Reformed Churches in North America is the American counterpart of the Christian Reformed Church in the Netherlands, and C. Pronk is one of its leaders in North America.

55. For this reason the first secessionists opened a theological seminary at Kampen in 1854, in order to educate their ministers in Reformed doctrines.

56. McGoldrick, *God's Renaissance Man*, 36–37. At the suggestion of Baltus, Kuyper read through Calvin's *Institutes of the Christian Religion*, by virtue of which he experienced his own conversion and found the concept of God as father and the church as mother of believers. After his conversion he said, "My life goal is now the restoration of a church that could be our mother."

57. Vanderlann, *Protestant Modernism in Holland*, 12–16, quoted in McGoldrick, *God's Renaissance Man*, 30.

national synod officially decided in 1883 that subscription to the Three Forms of Unity would no longer be required for a pastoral candidate, which meant that the church would no longer adhere to the historic Reformed doctrines. Kuyper and other orthodox believers expressed deep sorrow (*doleantie*) and appealed to the synod to reverse the decision and return to the traditional principles of Christianity. However, they faced opposition from the council, and even the dismissal of their seventy-five leaders from the national church.[58]

The foremost mark of the true church was, for Kuyper, the faithful proclamation of God's Word, "faithful" meaning complete commitment to Scripture. For him, the true church stands firmly on this foundational mark, in opposition to other religious bodies which succumb to the allure of humanist modernism, which Kuyper considered a deadly poison to the church. Kuyper declared, "The Church is a strictly spiritual monarchy, a kingdom under the absolute kingship of Christ."[59] This meant that the church should not be subservient to other authorities, like a secular state or populism, but to Christ Himself, as presented through the preached Word and the sacraments. The government of the church should adhere to this essential principle, otherwise it would not be a benefit to Christ and His kingdom. For example, if the church government tolerated false doctrines, and thus led its members to deviate from her confession of revealed truth, profaning the sacraments, and diluting the preaching of God's Word, the church would then be denying the kingship of Christ.[60] Kuyper's strong belief in the true church is the major reason for him and his followers not conforming to the government of the national church, which had rejected Reformed doctrines. Afterwards, Kuyper and his followers (the so-called Doleantie) left the national church in 1886 and formed a new denomination, the Dolerende Kerk (Sorrow Church), with about two hundred congregations nationwide,[61] even though Kuyper had never intended this schism to occur, unlike the first secessionists.[62] This was the second secession in the history of the Dutch Reformed Church.

58. McGoldrick, *God's Renaissance Man*, 94.
59. Kuyper, "Pamphlet on the Reformation of the Church."
60. McGoldrick, *God's Renaissance Man*, 127–30.
61. The national church (the Dutch Reformed Church (Nederlandse Hervormde Kerk)) consisted of about five hundred congregations at that time; about 40 percent of the total members joined the second secession under Kuyper.
62. Kuyper had criticized the first secession of 1834 as separating too hastily, without pursuing reformation long enough for restoration of the truth in the church.

The two resultant denominations, the one seceding in 1834 and the other in 1886, united under the name of the Reformed Churches in the Netherlands (Gereformeerde Kerken in Nederland (GKN))[63] in 1892, and this new denomination became the actual seat of the New Direction movement and the redemptive-historical preaching debate. Greidanus explains that the GKN, between the First and Second World Wars, gave birth to a new school of thought, that is, the New Direction.[64] Trimp pointed more specifically to the distinctive theological tendencies inherited respectively from the Afscheiding (Separation, 1834) and the Doleantie (Sorrow, 1886), which remained in the newly united church and from which the redemptive-historical preaching debate came about.[65] What were the differences? According to Pronk, even though both parties showed strong allegiance to traditional Calvinistic principles of faith, including Presbyterian polity and the Three Forms of Unity, they were distinguishable in some of their theological tendencies. For example, the Afscheiding tended to favor experimental preaching, but the Doleantie was inclined instead towards the so-called redemptive-historical preaching. Pronk says, "Broadly speaking, Dutch Calvinistic preaching may be divided into two categories."[66] The one is the old school, or traditional Calvinists, and the other the so called Neo-Calvinists. William Young confirms this fact:

> The central contrast to be drawn concerns the role of experimental religion in the Reformed Faith. The scene of the Reformed Faith in the Netherlands exhibits a remarkable phenomenon: i.e. a sharp cleavage between Calvinists emphasizing sometimes in an extreme fashion, experimental religion, even cultivating a kind of mysticism, and on the other hand, the Kuyper-Calvinists, including the followers of Schilder as well as the leaders of the Gereformeerde Kerken (Reformed Churches), who tend to exhibit a marked aversion to experimental religion and to

---

However, when he had no choice but to leave the church in 1886, he concluded that the national synod had become irrecoverably separated from biblical principles, and thus faithfulness to Christ required secession. Cf. McGoldrick, "Every Inch for Christ," 91–99, quoted in McGoldrick, *God's Renaissance Man*, 92.

63. The *Hervormde Kerk* was the national church (the Dutch Reformed Church) and the newly merged denomination employed another Dutch word "*Gereformeerde*" to preserve the meaning of the term "Reformed."

64. Greidanus, *Sola Scriptura*, 22.

65. Trimp, *Preaching and the History of Salvation*, 138–39.

66. Pronk, "Preaching in the Dutch Calvinist Tradition," vol. 53, no. 5.

> restrict their interests to the doctrinal and practical aspects of religion. The former, i.e. the Old Calvinist circles, in addition to the smaller communities named Oud-Gereformeerd (Old-Reformed), include the flourishing Gereformeerde Gemeenten (Reformed Churches), the Christelijk Gereformeerde Kerken, (Christian Reformed Churches) and a substantial orthodox element in the Hervormde Kerk (Reformed Church) . . .⁶⁷

The Dutch homiletical debate had its roots in the underlying discordance between Neo-Calvinists and the Old Calvinists, which was occasionally expressed in relation to preaching, even though they hoped to be loyal to basic Calvinistic principles. Whereas these two distinct Calvinist groups belonged to the one denomination (GKN), the latent theological differences between them were a portent for future conflict.

After Kuyper's death in 1920, the church faced spiritual decline, with church attendance falling under preaching which had little spiritual power or conviction. Despite Kuyper's reformative endeavors having significant influence on all areas of life including politics, education, and social services, they did not work effectively in the church.⁶⁸ Kuyper's followers, such as Schilder, then emerged to reform the whole of church life, especially preaching, and this movement became a central stream of the so called New Direction.

Members of the New Direction began to oppose the conventional way of preaching in which the elements of earlier Pietism and mystical subjectivism still remained. The fervent opposition of the New Direction to the exemplary preaching of the Old Calvinists cannot be clearly grasped without an understanding of this ecclesiastical background. We now proceed to an exploration of the exemplary preaching which the New Direction opposed.

Exemplary Approach

According to Greidanus, the title *exemplary preaching* was originally designated by Holwerda, a proponent of redemptive-historical preaching, who said in 1940: "This method I would call the 'exemplary' method because it dissolves biblical history into various independent histories

---

67. Young, "Historic Calvinism and Neo-Calvinism," 48.
68. De Jong, "Introduction," para. 5.

which are examples for us."⁶⁹ However, Trimp judged Holwerda's interpretation of the word *example* to be incorrect and thought the subsequent discussion could be misleading. Trimp opined that the word *example* has a wide semantic range, and thus cannot be limited to one selective meaning, as Holwerda assumed.⁷⁰ On the contrary, the diverse usage of the word *example* justifies seeing history as being exemplary. According to Trimp, the word example (*exemplum*) may refer etymologically to a characteristic example, or a single part of the whole body from which we can learn about the whole. In other words, example, in historical texts of the Bible, means a characteristic but related part of the whole history of redemption, and thus a single history cannot dissolve into many independent histories by way of examples. This is Trimp's argument against Holwerda's definition of the word *example* at the outset of his discussion on exemplary preaching.

However, the etymological approach to understanding the title *exemplary preaching* does not help us to reach the kernel of the debate concerning the exemplary versus redemptive-historical controversy. The multi-faceted accusation of Neo-Calvinists against traditional preaching cannot simply be explained in terms of linguistics. Holwerda also acknowledged later, in 1949, that it is not the terms but rather the issues which are at stake, and these should be central for discussing the Dutch homiletical debate.⁷¹ I concur with that statement. The term *example* was chosen by Holwerda for the sake of brevity in an attempt to typify the two different methods in Dutch Reformed preaching.⁷² What were, then, the distinguishing characteristics of the exemplary preaching which the New Direction opposed?

In examining the various criticisms of exemplary preaching, I submit there are two major points made. One is that it dehistoricizes biblical

---

69. *Gereformeerd Mannenblad*, vol. 18, 27, quoted in Greidanus, *Sola Scriptura*, 19. According to Holwerda, the word *exemplum* (derived from the Latin verb *eximere*) refers to "one of many similar things," and "exemplar from a collection of similar articles." However, this thought was changed later, with greater emphasis on the issue itself than on the terminology of the word *example*.

70. Trimp, *Preaching and the History of Salvation*, 96–101. Trimp explained the meaning of the word *exemplum* from the Latin verb *eximere*, as did Holwerda, but the former extracted different meanings from it: test, sample, proof, token, specimen, model, and ideal. Trimp thinks that the word *example* never has the sense of a levelling factor as Holwerda's conception of the word does.

71. Holwerda, *Historia Revelationis*, 114, quoted in Greidanus, *Sola Scriptura*, 20.

72. Holwerda, "History of Redemption," 4.

history, while the other is that it fails to do justice to the historical texts of the Bible. Both points are interrelated and can be understood as one argument—that the exemplary approach used biblical texts incorrectly in sermons. Alternatively, exemplary preaching was criticized mainly for violating biblical history with its anti-historical or ahistorical tendencies, which might be affected by other religious trends rather than by the historic Reformed tradition. The New Direction thus began intentionally to highlight the ground-motive of the sixteenth century Reformers, that is, *sola scriptura*, over those dehistoricizing tendencies and this led to an over-emphasis on redemptive history. Afterwards, this movement irritated people who wished to retain exemplary preaching. Whether or not this movement, the New Direction, was loyal to the Bible and beneficial to the churches is an important question. An examination of whether or not exemplary preaching had really weakened a true perspective of biblical history is directly related to the question of beneficial effect regarding the New Direction, no matter what the word *exemplary* meant originally or practically.

The origin of this exemplary preaching must be discussed. Greidanus suspects that it might have originated from nineteenth century theological liberalism, with its specifically subjective personification of biblical history.[73] For example, the theology of Schleiermacher[74] majored on the religious consciousness of biblical characters, often drawing out their moral or psychological experiences from the biblical texts rather than majoring on God's message in redemptive history.[75] Thus, for Greidanus, the obvious assumption is that exemplary preaching and liberal theology go hand in hand, because liberal theologians, like Schleiermacher,

---

73. Greidanus, *Sola Scriptura*, 9.

74. Friedrich Schleiermacher (1768–1834), "the father of liberal theology," grew up and was educated under the influence of German Pietism but, after graduating at Halle University, the center of German pietists, he eventually rejected conservative doctrines and developed a kind of liberal pietism which focused more on human feelings than objective history. He found a contact point for Christianity with unbelieving cultural despisers and wrote a book, *On Religion: Address in Response to Its Cultured Critics*. This book laid, in a sense, the foundation for liberal theology, asserting that the essence of religion lies not in rational proofs of the existence of God and supernaturally revealed dogmas, but in a fundamental, distinct, and integrative element of human life and culture—the feeling (*Gefühl*: inner awareness) of being utterly dependent on something infinite that manifests itself in and through finite things. Cf. Clements, *Friedrich Schleiermacher*, 7–12; Olson, *Story of Christian Theology*, 543.

75. Olson, *Story of Christian Theology*, 542–53.

Ritschl,[76] and Harnack,[77] are inclined to extract mainly ethical examples from biblical texts, rather than focus on redemptive history.[78]

However, the roots of exemplary preaching actually appeared in the Early Church Fathers, such as Clement[79] and Justin,[80] who used the OT as the book of ethical models for Christians. Bultmann called attention to the fact that the exemplary approach was already practiced in the first and second centuries.[81] As early as the end of the first century, Clement of Rome (died 99 AD) used Scripture as a source of primarily moral examples.[82] Origen, another of the Early Church Fathers, also found ethical models in Scripture.[83] According to Huyser, a proponent of the exemplary approach, Reformers like Calvin and Luther also proposed to utilize biblical history in an exemplary way.[84] This exemplary approach has a long history within groupings such as Lutherans, Calvinists, Puritans, Pietists, Methodists, and Baptists. We should therefore be careful not to condemn too hastily every method labelled with this term.

---

76. For Albert Ritschl (1822–1899), the Christian faith does not manifest anything supernatural and dogmatic in the Bible events, but experiences transformation of oneself through ethical action inspired by Christ's pattern. For Ritschl, Christian theology deals solely with human morality, not with historical facts. Cf. Mackintosh, "Introduction to Albrecht Ritschl," iv-v.

77. Adolf von Harnack (1851–1930) described the essence of Christianity in three great ideas: the kingdom of God as the rule of God in the hearts of individuals; God the Father as infinitely valuing every human soul; and, the higher righteousness as loving each other. Cf. Harnack, *What is Christianity?* 55.

78. Greidanus, *Sola Scriptura*, 9.

79. Clement of Rome, *1 Clement*, 40; 41; 58:2.

80. Justin Martyr (ca. 100–165), in his *Dialogue with Trypho the Jew*, deals with the OT Law as the eternal moral law, the prediction of Christ, and the ceremonial law, as still valid. Cf. Bultmann, *Theology of the New Testament*, vol. 1, 112–114.

81. Bultmann, *Theology of the New Testament*, vol. 2, 130.

82. Mayer, "Clement of Rome and His Use of Scripture," 537, quoted in Dockery, *Biblical Interpretation Then and Now*, 49–50. Mayer notes, "Perhaps Clement can be classified as basically a Hellenistic exegete who had been trained to study ancient documents primarily to obtain moral examples from them by separating the events from their original historical contexts and demythologizing all possible offensive connotations." Clement also held forth Christ in his writing *1 Clement* (ca. 96) as a model for piety (1:2), for humility (16:2), and for self-emptying (7:4; 12:7; 21:6; 49:6).

83. Grant, *Interpretation of the Bible*, 65.

84. Huyser, "Exemplarische prediking," 211. Huyser briefly described the history of exemplary preaching from Chrysostom to Spurgeon (205–211), quoted in Greidanus, *Sola Scriptura*, 10.

To search for the historical root of the exemplary approach is an almost impossible task, because this way of interpretation and preaching can be recognized at various times and places, in history as well as in Scripture, and was even employed on occasions by Christ and the apostle Paul. Greidanus is also sceptical about the origins of the exemplary method being found in any specific period or group, because he thinks the exemplary approach appears whenever preachers look for a relevant illustration or role model to be applied to contemporary hearers.[85]

The matter at issue in the Dutch debate is not the example itself but the way of using it to interpret historical texts of the Bible in sermons. The opponents of exemplary preaching also accepted the necessity of examples or illustrations for accommodating biblical stories to the contemporary congregation. Holwerda also used biblical examples of marriage to illustrate types of Christian marriage to engaged couples.[86] It is natural and necessary to use examples from biblical history for teaching, reproof, correcting, and training the people of God in righteousness. What were, then, the elements in the exemplary method which posed such a problem that they dehistoricized biblical history?

Trimp presupposes that two elements of biblical hermeneutics, namely, allegory and typology, need to be clarified before examining the exemplary method. According to Trimp, allegory always involves twisting historical facts into a timeless moral teaching, while typology is consistently based on taking history seriously.[87] The former sets an analogical connection between the text and reality, with symbol and human imagination thus disregarding real history. For example, John Bunyan's *Pilgrim's Progress* symbolizes a Christian's life in the world, without asking if it is real story or fact. However, typology employs evident similarities between events or persons of an earlier history and those of a later period. For example, the historic event of Moses's lifting up the serpent in the wilderness was a type, or a prefiguring, of Christ's crucifixion. This distinction is arguably available in various works and dictionaries.[88] However, these two distinct elements of allegory and typology have been embedded in the Latin word *exemplum* and both have been used

---

85. Greidanus, *Sola Scriptura*, 9.

86. Holwerda, *De betekenis van verbond en kerk voor huwelijk, gezin en jeugd*, 23–65, quoted in Greidanus, Sola Scriptura, 57.

87. Trimp, *Preaching and the History of Salvation*, 32–33, 66–67.

88. Cf. Hanson, *Allegory and Event*; Martens, "Revisiting the Allegory/Typology Distinction," 283–317; Aune, "Allegory" and "Typology."

interchangeably, and thus confusingly, with the exemplary approach. According to Hanson, there were two kinds of allegory in antiquity—Hellenistic and Palestinian; the former knows nothing of typology, whereas the latter is full of typology.[89] This Hellenistic, or Alexandrian, allegory had had harmful effects on biblical hermeneutics, as we explored in chapter 2, in the section "Historical Background: Redemptive-Historical Hermeneutics."

One probable element, in the so called exemplary method, to which the New Direction objected, was the allegory which disregarded historical facts in the Bible. Van't Veer says,

> When one reads the works and sermons of the Barthians, it seems at times as if the allegory of the first centuries and typology of the Middle Ages have been revived in a new shape. The 'literal' or 'historical' meaning of a Scripture passage is of little importance.[90]

Thus, some Neo-Calvinists opposed dialectical theology from its beginning in Holland in the 1920s. For example, Schilder saw it as an internal threat to traditional Calvinistic theology and informed young Neo-Calvinists of its danger.[91] Calvin considered redemption as the reestablishment of the original creation, but dialectical theology created a scheme which placed God and creature in conflict. In the Calvinistic philosophy of the New Direction, a philosophy driven by the underlying motive of creation, fall, and redemption, there is no place for any dualism between God's grace and nature. In dialectical theology, however, history, which is considered to belong to the realm of nature, is set against God's acts of redemption, which are the expression of God's grace.[92] There might be no

---

89. Hanson, *Allegory and Event*, 63–64: "But Alexandrian allegory has in all its forms one feature in common with Hellenistic allegory; it is unhistorical. It does not use typology. Its ultimate aim is to empty the text of any particular connection with historical events."

90. Veer, "Christological Preaching on Historical Materials of the Old Testament," 10.

91. Schilder, *Zur Begriffsgeschichte des 'Paradoxon'*, quoted in Greidanus, Sola Scriptura, 29–30.

92. Torrance, *Karl Barth*, 136–37. Barth's theology has frequently been criticized as deistic dualism because in it God as "wholly other" is set in antithetical relation to the world of nature and history. However, Torrance justifies Barth, saying " Barth was convinced that the subordination of evangelical Christianity to 'cultural Protestantism' . . . [was] due to the assimilation of God to nature and of revelation to history, and thus the reduction of theology to anthropology, that had been going on since the end

possibility of a genuine history of God's redemption in such a dialectical system.[93] The notion of *Urgeschichte* (primal history), initially designated by Søren Kierkegaard's philosophy of dialecticism, had been a significant part of the early thought of Barth,[94] and gave a special place to the contact of revelation with history, that is, of eternity with time.[95] This dualism of dialectic theology permeated the Dutch theological world, with the result that the renewed emphasis on redemptive history was an actual reaction against it. For the New Direction, redemptive-historical preaching was like an antidote against the toxic ahistorical preaching of dialectical theologians. Consequently, those who did not follow the redemptive-historical method became the object of the criticisms made by the New Direction. However, whether exemplary preaching and its proponents had been practically influenced by Barthian theology, or not, needs to be investigated later in this chapter.

The other significant foe targeted by the New Direction was that of the continuing problems which had been present for a long time within the GKN since its union in 1892. Those problems arose because of implicit theological differences in a non-homogeneous organization. According to Greidanus, there were four religious tendencies which left their mark on the Dutch Reformed church. These were Dutch Pietism,[96] which had the characteristics of subjectivism, individualism, and spiritualism;[97] an

---

of the eighteenth century. Hence he made up his mind to call a halt to it by tearing up the Protestant synthesis and creating such a *diastasis* between God and man . . . "

93. In dialectical theology, the term "redemptive history" must be a contradiction because the revelation of God's redeeming acts means the end of history. Cf. "Existentialist Theology" section in chapter 2, with special regard to Barth's theology.

94. We need to be careful in examining the theology of Barth because it underwent several periods of significant modification and change. Cf. Bowden, *Karl Barth*; Bromiley, *Introduction to the Theology of Karl Barth*; Barth, *Karl Barth (1886–1968)*; Morgan, *SPCK Introduction to Karl Barth*. As the writing of *Church Dogmatics* progressed, Barth's view of redemptive history changed from the earlier idea of *Urgeschichte* to a modified form closer to the traditional *Heilsgeschichte* theology of Hofmann, which I described in chapter 2.

95. Van Til, *New Modernism*, 10. Van Til claimed that the notion of primal history is the child of the philosophical dialecticism of Kierkegaard, which is the child of Kantian criticism.

96. Beeke, *Quest for Full Assurance*, 286–309: Here, Dutch Pietism was considered to have had unfavorable influences on its followers, but there are other opinions concerning this matter. We discuss this subject in more detail later.

97. Here "subjectivism" means accentuating the experience of the Christian; "individualism" having no eye for the significance of covenant and church; and

Anabaptist sect, with its dualism of nature and grace leading to subjectivism and spiritualism; objectivism, with its rationalist overtones; and, finally, Spinozism, which lent its support to either rationalism or mysticism.[98] There were some significant unorthodox theological elements in the GKN in the 1930s, which were rooted in the original churches prior to union. The New Direction sought to purge out those unfavorable elements from the church, judging that the exemplary method was actually embracing them.

In addition, Trimp refers to several enemies of the Reformed faith, against which Bavinck and Kuyper were anticipating the history of revelation, or biblical theology, being a useful weapon.[99] The first enemy was the denial by biblical criticism of the historicity of facts recorded in the Bible; the second was a mechanical atomistic use of isolated verses, which usually served to support traditional dogmatics; the third was a moralistic view of Scripture, in which the Bible was regarded as only a resource for religious or ethical models. The Neo-Calvinists, who followed Bavinck and Kuyper, naturally laid emphasis on the discipline of the history of revelation, that is, biblical theology, and accordingly expressed a strong aversion to its enemies. Exemplary preaching was suspected of being in affiliation with some or all of these opposing tendencies in the Dutch homiletical debate.

Exemplary preaching became the major target which New Direction members endeavored to remove from the church. There were, however, several theologians who claimed to be genuine Calvinists and who upheld the exemplary method while opposing the New Direction. The clash between the two sides developed as the exemplary versus redemptive-historical preaching controversy. We need to investigate whether either approach has a real problem, or harmful effect, and assesses whether or not the debate was controlled by factors other than the genuine Reformed motive of *sola scriptura*. We now discuss the criticism of exemplary preaching in more detail.

"spiritualism" reducing Christian living to the inner or spiritual realm. Cf. Greidanus, *Sola Scriptura*, 33.

98. Greidanus, *Sola Scriptura*, 33.

99. Trimp, *Preaching and the History of Salvation*, 63. Biblical theology appeared as a new discipline in the theological field in Holland in the late 19th century.

Criticisms of the Exemplary Approach

Criticisms of the exemplary approach were many and broad, while critics, like Schilder, Holwerda, D. Van Dijk, and Van't Veer, varied in their critical opinions. For example, Schilder, the so called father of redemptive-historical preaching,[100] introduced the breadth and complexity of biblical motifs, especially concerning redemptive history, whereas Holwerda was interested more in the exegetical analysis of those motifs.[101] Schilder developed his major concern of preaching the Christ of Scripture, while Holwerda primarily handled the hermeneutical questions of redemptive history. Van't Veer attacked specifically the subjectivism and psychology which preoccupied the sermons of his contemporaries in the 1940s but, in contrast, Holwerda emphasized the danger of objectivism, with its strongly doctrinal sermons.[102] These differences between the critics demand careful examination.

Greidanus provides extensive analysis of objections to the exemplary approach, classifying them into five categories: objections to the exemplary view of Scripture; its method of interpreting historical texts; its preaching of historical texts; exemplary-subjective preaching; using preachers in Scripture as examples.[103] In contrast, Renninger divides

---

100. Runia in his book *Het hoge woord in de lage landen*, 116, identifies Schilder as "the father of the so-called salvation-historical preaching." Schilder was not the only one to acclaim this type of preaching, for many others, such as Van Dijk, Holwerda, Van't Veer, and Veenhof, also supported him on the issue. Runia said that, nevertheless, Schilder deserves to be called "the father" because he was the first writer who publicly and systematically, especially in the weekly paper *De Reformatie*, propagated it as the only valid method of interpreting historical texts of Scripture. Cf. Renninger, "The New Testament Use of Old Testament Historical Narrative," 38.

101. Trimp, *Preaching and the History of Salvation*, 86.

102. Ibid., 90–91.

103. Greidanus, *Sola Scriptura*, 56–120. The first objection relates to viewing the primacy of Scripture as a source of illustration and recognizing individuals in the historical text as examples for contemporary believers. The second objection is to "the illustrative interpretation," "the fragmentary interpretation," and "the atomistic interpretation." The third objection to the exemplary preaching of historical texts relates to "biographical preaching," or anthropocentric preaching, and "the historical equation mark," that is, "psychologizing," "spiritualizing," "moralizing," and "typologizing." The fourth group of objections relates to exemplary-subjective preaching: "the objective-subjective combination," "the explication-application dualism," "the subjective preaching," "multiple application," and the "faculties of man." The fifth objection is to using preachers in Scripture as examples, such as the apostolic sermons in 1 Cor 10, Heb 11, and Jas 5:16–18.

them into three groups: hermeneutical/theological objections; objections to the exemplary use of OT historical material in the NT; homiletical considerations.[104] Trimp distinctively arranges the criticisms under the three individual critics: Schilder, Holwerda, and Van't Veer.[105] In my judgment, Greidanus's division provides more valuable detailed information, but it is complex because it mixes various criticisms with refutations alongside them. Trimp provides a brief but insightful analysis, yet I regard it as unacceptable due to its lack of information, while Renninger's arrangement of the resources is interesting but requires more detailed information. I prefer to arrange the criticisms into three groups, but utilizing Greidanus's headings: theological, hermeneutical, and homiletical objections.

Firstly, the theological objections to the exemplary approach relate to its view of Scripture and interpretation of biblical texts. Renninger summarizes and classifies these objections into eight themes.[106] Substantially similar criticisms can be found in the corresponding section in Greidanus's *Sola Scriptura*. According to Greidanus, both sides of the debate honored the authority of Scripture and redemptive history but had "different views of historical texts of Scripture,"[107] the essential difference between them being whether or not historical texts can be used illustratively. The exemplary side thought it possible to utilize historical texts as relevant illustrations for contemporary believers, while redemptive history advocates disagreed. For example, J. Schelhaas, a proponent of the exemplary approach, suggested that the Lord possibly had a certain history recorded in order to picture the human response to His words and deeds, rather than to illuminate His progressing revelation.[108] In contrast, Schilder claimed that the intent of the biblical historical narrative is to unfold God's progressive plan of salvation in Christ at a specific juncture

---

104. Renninger, "New Testament Use of Old Testament Historical Narrative," 25–37.

105. Trimp, *Preaching and the History of Salvation*, 75–91.

106. Renninger, "New Testament Use of Old Testament Historical Narrative," 25–32. (1) The exemplary approach does not recognize the nature and purpose of biblical historical narratives nor their ramifications for the method of scriptural interpretation. (2) It dehistoricizes historical narrative. (3) It fails to understand the relationship between historical matter and dogmatic, ethical, and other kinds of material. (4) It fragments Scripture's one history into many independent histories and thereby disregards both the unity and the progress of redemptive history. (5) It atomizes Scripture. (6) It is anthropocentric instead of christocentric. (7) It fails to see the true tie that links believers with the text. (8) It is an illegitimate method, even if it edifies.

107. Greidanus, *Sola Scriptura*, 60.

108. Schelhaas, *GTT* 42, 126, quoted in Greidanus, *Sola Scriptura*, 61.

in the whole history of redemption, and this should be respected.[109] The debate was thus actually rooted in a different homiletical use of Scripture, and specifically of historical texts.

Secondly, hermeneutical objections arose with the emphasizing of the redemptive-historical approach to historical texts over against the exemplary approach. According to Trimp, as early as the 1920s Schilder began to highlight the need for the redemptive-historical approach over against the ethical view of Scripture, and also against a psychologizing approach to biblical narratives.[110] Schilder criticized those who did not recognize the Bible's unity, in which one progressive history of God's redemption is recorded: "They break down Holy Scripture into a series of spiritual, edifying fragments. The one Word of God is shattered into many words about God, and the one work of God is dissected into many works which are related somehow to God and religion."[111] He blames the exemplary approach from the early 1930s, in his magnum opus *Christ in His Suffering*, because it failed to place biblical characters in the line of redemptive history and consequently neglected their significance in the Bible.[112] Schilder's work stimulated younger ministers like Holwerda and Van't Veer to participate in this theological debate.[113]

Holwerda argued that those interpreting historical texts in an exemplary manner need no longer be concerned about their historicity, and thus could join the opposing camp. He endeavored to show why this happened: "If a historical text serves to illustrate and depict concretely a certain 'truth,' then the factual character of such an event is not overly important since that illustration can equally well be given in a parable or allegory."[114] However, it is not necessarily true that an illustration of Christ's sacrifice for many in terms of a dying wheat seed in John 12:24 makes the factual crucifixion of Christ Himself less important. Holwerda

---

109. Schilder, "Kerkelijke leven: puten van overeenkomst (I)," 18; quoted in Renninger, "New Testament Use of the Old Testament Historical Narrative," 26.

110. Trimp, *Preaching and the History of Salvation*, 78.

111. Schilder, *Christus in zijn lijden*, vol. 1, 29; cf. English ed. *Christ in His Suffering; Christ on Trial; Christ Crucified*, vol. 1, 39.

112. Schilder, "Iets over de eenheid der heilsgeschiedenis," 36, quoted in Renninger, "New Testament Use of the Old Testament Historical Narrative," 29.

113. Trimp, *Preaching and the History of Salvation*, 85–86.

114. Holwerda, *Dictaten*, vol. 1, 21, quoted in Greidanus, *Sola Scriptura*, 61. Holwerda describes "the enemy" here as being men like S. R. Driver (1846–1914) who deduce their "moral and spiritual lessons" from the biblical narratives "whether they are strictly historical or not." Cf. Driver, *Book of Genesis*, 247.

overly criticizes his opponent here. He also attacked an atomic interpretation that lifted an atomic element like doubt or faith from a given text to apply it to people today, thus disregarding the uniqueness and the total message of the text. Holwerda explained, "One can preach the same sermon on, for example, Matthew 11:1–6 (the doubt of John the Baptist) and John 20:24–29 (the doubt of Thomas) on the similar theme of 'Jesus Delivers from Doubt,'" and "one can apply Genesis 22 (Abraham's faith tested) in the same way as Matthew 15:21ff (the Canaanite woman's faith tested)."[115] This atomistic handling, in fact, may not do justice to the uniqueness of a particular text.

Van't Veer,[116] deeply influenced by Schilder, especially blamed the exemplary approach for fragmenting the one continuous history. He viewed the struggle between the seed of the woman and the seed of the serpent (Gen 3:15) as the embryonic form of the whole gospel; redemptive history unfolded from this promise all the way to its fulfilment in Christ.[117] Van't Veer pointed out: "This exemplary method results in an artificial addition of the Christological element rather than an inference from the Christological character of the one redemptive history. It is done in the form of typology, allegory, or parallel . . . "[118] The adherents of the exemplary approach contended that redemptive history is a unified structure with Christ at its center, but this did not inhibit them from treating individuals separately in historical texts.[119] Van't Veer replied to this contention: "The knowledge that this history is a unified structure should have kept them from this (fragmental) approach."[120] In addition, Van Dijk claimed that the historical text is descriptive, but the exemplary approach treats it as prescriptive.[121] To sum up, these critics criticized the exemplary approach for not rightly recognizing the nature of historical

---

115. Holwerda, *Begonnen*, 92, quoted in Greidanus, *Sola Scriptura*, 64.

116. Van't Veer published his study on Elijah (1 Kgs 17–18) entitled *My God is Yahweh* in 1939, and set forth his hermeneutical and homiletical insights on redemptive-historical preaching in his comprehensive essay "Christological Preaching on Historical Materials in the Old Testament."

117. Renninger, "New Testament Use of Old Testament Historical Narrative," 30.

118. Veer, "Christological Preaching," 15.

119. Douma, "Calvijn over historische stoffen," no. 3292, quoted in Greidanus, *Sola Scriptura*, 63.

120. Veer, *GM* 19 (1941), 66, quoted in Greidanus, *Sola Scriptura*, 63.

121. Dijk, "Tot onze leering," 295, quoted in Renninger, "The New Testament Use of the Old Testament Historical Narrative," 27.

texts, resulting in an illustrative, fragmentary, and atomistic interpretation of them.

Thirdly, the homiletical objections relate to hermeneutical problems which the exemplary approach has in dealing with historical texts. Sermons constructed by the exemplary approach, which Holwerda criticized as being "illustrative, fragmentary, and atomistic," were described critically as being only "biographical" or as having a faulty "historical equation mark." David J. Burrell, a scholar of homiletics, appraised biographical sermons as having an inexhaustible supply of sources in Scripture.[122] However, redemptive-historical proponents objected to these biographical sermons as being in essence anthropocentric. As early as 1926, T. Hoekstra, a Dutch homiletician, criticized non-christocentric sermons as being inappropriately called "sermons."[123] The exemplary approach also aimed at preaching christocentric sermons but wanted to achieve this by focusing on man in his relation to Christ. For example, Schelhaas contended that Scripture is all about God's work in and through Christ, yet the people therein must be pictured and portrayed because the scriptural texts certainly do write about them.[124] According to Greidanus, advocates of the exemplary approach wanted a sermon which is both christological and relevant, but the relevancy was being sought not from the christological but from the empirical. The sermon then becomes more anthropocentric, so that Joseph, Moses, David, Peter, or Mary become central rather than Christ.[125] Schilder provided an alternative to this anthropocentric method in his trilogy:

> It is not . . . Mary's maternal grief but the passion of her Son, of God's Son, her Lord, which is being proclaimed to us here, which must save us. The moment we put Mary and her grief at the centre of our thinking, we have done injustice to the Son.[126]

He remarked regretfully that for both the Roman Catholic and the Protestant there has never been complete emancipation from the concrete

---

122. Burrell, *Sermon*, 95; cf. Perry, *Manual for Biblical Preaching*, 106.

123. Hoekstra, *Gereformeerde homiletiek*, 172, quoted in Greidanus, *Preaching Christ from the Old Testament*, 2. Hoekstra says, "In expositing Scripture for the congregation, the preacher . . . must show that there is a way to the centre even from the farthest point on the periphery. For a sermon without Christ is no sermon."

124. Schelhaas, "Christus en de historische stoffen in de prediking," 127ff.

125. Greidanus, *Sola Scriptura*, 67.

126. Schilder, *Christ Crucified*, 339–40.

presentation of images, rather than God's Word.[127] According to the Heidelberg Catechism (96–98), he argued, God wants His people instructed not by dumb images but by the living preaching of His Word. Schilder actually accused the exemplary approach of even being somewhat idolatrous, which is a strong and exaggerated criticism but indicates the depth of feelings the debate generated.

The "historical equation mark" in the criticisms of exemplary preaching means that a preacher refers to historical texts while disregarding the historical gap between people in the texts and people today, by means such as psychologizing, spiritualizing, and moralizing. This kind of approach is called critically the historical equation mark. Schilder warned against psychologizing as early as 1930, saying, for example, that a preacher should not describe Peter's denial of the suffering Christ psychologically, to stimulate the hearers' minds, for he is then not preaching on the suffering Messiah which the text intends to convey.[128] Holwerda added that the warning against psychologizing was in fact an objection to a method which concealed the real meaning of the given text.[129]

Spiritualizing an historical event or figure in historical texts is akin to taking the Red Sea event as the deliverance from our personal spiritual bondage, or viewing Jacob's physical struggle at Peniel as our spiritual hardship.[130] Spiritualizing had been extensively used by preachers in the medieval period and was occasionally appraised as attaining to a deeper meaning rather than a literal exegesis.[131] Van't Veer objected to this tendency by saying that the drawing of analogical lines between Abraham, Jacob, Moses, David, and other biblical characters, and people today, fails to respect the historical nature of the texts to which those biblical figures belonged, and fails to appreciate that this history reveals Christ in His coming into the world.[132] This spiritualizing method actually opens

---

127. Ibid., 37.

128. Schilder, *Christ on Trial*, 198.

129. Holwerda, "History of Redemption," 11.

130. Greidanus, *Sola Scriptura*, 77. There are many more examples of spiritualizing: the physical blindness of the two men in Matt 9 becomes our spiritual blindness; the woman's reaching to touch Christ's garment becomes our spiritual reaching to touch the spiritual Christ; the Cana wedding invitation to the earthly Christ becomes our invitation to the heavenly Christ.

131. Horton, "What Are We Looking For in the Bible?" 4–8. Horton says, "This is to return to the allegorizing method of Alexandria that had enjoyed so much success in medieval preaching and was overthrown by the Reformation."

132. Veer, "Christological Preaching," 20.

the door to subjectivism and uncontrolled speculation, for it prompts a preacher to read into texts anything he prefers, rather than to endeavor to appreciate the text as the author originally intended.

Moralizing, in the criticisms of the exemplary approach, means paying undue attention to the virtues or vices of people in historical texts, emphasizing ethical models. For example, Joseph's refusal to give in to the temptation to adultery would be viewed as a good model for Christian conduct, and Abraham's lies in Gen 12 and 20, concerning his wife, would be considered as white lies. Van Dijk wrote,

> At best one may say that a few good, scriptural remarks were occasioned by the text, but that is, strictly speaking, no longer the Ministry of the Word . . . For then the content of the sermon is determined not by the text itself but by the preacher's ingenuity.[133]

In this way, Scripture becomes no longer God's Word but a collection of ancient biographies and stories, though still beneficial to people. Redemptive history advocates therefore objected to the exemplary approach in various ways, describing it as psychologizing, spiritualizing, and moralizing, and resulting in dehistoricizing the texts. In addition, exemplary preaching was criticized as forcing scriptural texts into the explication-application dualism, in which the Word of God is seen as just an objective factor, so that the preacher must add an application with appropriate subjective matter for the people in the pew.[134] For the exemplary preachers, various kinds of application needed to be added to explication of the historical text to make it relevant to members of the congregation with their differing needs.

According to Greidanus, the most fundamental objection against exemplary-subjective preaching is that it fails to overcome the objective-subjective dilemma and leads to the explication-application scheme.[135] Objective preaching presents the external truth to hearers, such as God's redemptive acts in history, while subjective preaching highlights one's inner experience of that salvation. Holwerda rejected this dualistic scheme because it disregards the nature of God's Word and the nature of preaching. He said, "The whole sermon is then from A to Z explication, but also beginning with the first full sentence directed toward application, and

---

133. Dijk, "Tot onze leering," 279, quoted in Greidanus, *Sola Scriptura*, 82.
134. Greidanus, *Sola Scriptura*, 91–93.
135. Ibid., 88.

remains hereby Ministry of the Word."[136] According to Trimp, Holwerda obviously disliked choosing either objectivism or subjectivism in connection to preaching, because Scripture itself has both.[137] The objection against the explication-application scheme was thus actually against the objective-subjective dualism, which always existed in the history of preaching, swinging from objective to subjective preaching. Thereby the objection to exemplary preaching was considered, by exemplary advocates like Bavinck, as a reaction against pietism and subjectivism, which emphasized personal experience of salvation or self-examination, and which permeated traditional preaching.[138] The criticisms of exemplary preaching were thought to be reviving the objective-subjective or explication-application dilemma again.

However, the Dutch controversy did not deal specifically only with the objective-subjective dilemma but more broadly with the concept of Scripture itself, while the corresponding American debate focuses on the explication-application dilemma. We discuss the latter in more detail later in this chapter and also in chapter 4.

We have now examined major aspects of criticisms of exemplary preaching in terms of theological, hermeneutical and homiletical objections. These criticisms converge into one central theme—how to view historical texts. In the following sections we shall now explore the defense of the exemplary approach and its criticisms against the redemptive-historical approach.

Defense of the Exemplary Approach

This defense was presented mostly in the form that the traditional exemplary method continued because historical precedent and Scripture justified it. The exemplary group primarily appealed to Reformed Fathers, like Calvin, to vindicate their approach. For example, J. Douma (1881–1941)[139] showed that exemplary preaching, rejected by redemptive-historical proponents like Schilder, was Calvin's normal method

---

136. Holwerda, *Begonnen hebbende van Mozes*, 108, quoted in Renninger, "New Testament Use of the Old Testament Historical Narrative," 37.

137. Trimp, *Preaching and the History of Salvation*, 91.

138. Greidanus, *Sola Scriptura*, 87.

139. Douma, an advocate of the exemplary approach, wrote a number of articles in *De Heraut* on "Calvin's Preaching on Historical Material" (2 March to 27 April 1941 and 14 December 1941 to 5 April 1942).

of preaching.[140] By presenting evidence from Calvin's sermons, Douma maintained that Calvin stood in the tradition that called history "the teacher of life," as in his commentary on Rom 4:23:[141]

> We are, by this passage, reminded of the duty of seeking profit from the examples recorded in Scripture . . . If then we would make a right and proper use of sacred histories, we must remember so to use them as to draw from them sound doctrine. They instruct us, in some part, how to frame our life; in others, how to strengthen faith; and then, how we are to be stirred up to serve the Lord. In forming our life, the example of the saint may be useful; and we may learn from them sobriety, chastity, love, patience, moderation, contempt of the world, and other virtues.[142]

Calvin here suggests that a preacher should use biblical histories properly, by drawing clear biblical doctrine from them and taking examples from them for the spiritual benefit of the congregation. Clearly, Calvin had approved the exemplary use of redemptive history for preaching, considering it as a preacher's duty. Douma therefore affirmed confidently that Reformed Fathers, like Luther and Calvin, recognized redemptive history in Scripture, but freely used biblical persons and events as examples of Christian virtues to be followed, or as warnings of vices to be avoided.[143] Huyser also claimed that all Reformed preachers who followed Luther and Calvin saw it as their duty to interpret and apply biblical history in an exemplary way, and thus draw the line from the past to the present.[144] In addition, Douma claims that Kuyper supported the exclusive redemptive-historical approach to historical texts, but in practice held a synthesis of the redemptive-historical and exemplary approaches.[145]

140. Trimp, *Preaching and the History of Salvation*, 108.

141. Rom 4:23 "Now, it was not written for his sake alone, that it was imputed to him" (AV).

142. Calvin, *Commentaries on the Epistles of Paul the Apostle to the Romans*, 182–83.

143. Douma, "Calvijn over Historische Stoffen."

144. Huyser, "Exemplarische prediking," 211, quoted in Greidanus, *Sola Scriptura*, 10.

145. Douma, "Calvijn over historische stoffen." Kuyper wrote a series of articles in 1895 and the May 1938 front page of *De Reformatie* quoted several extracts which gave the impression that Kuyper supported the exclusive redemptive-historical approach of Schilder. However, Douma analyzed them in detail and conclusively said that Kuyper held to both the redemptive-historical and the exemplary approach. Quoted

Hoekstra, author of *Gereformeerde homiletiek* (1926), also emphasized the faith and life of biblical characters as being necessary for stimulating believers.[146] Redemptive history advocates, like Schilder and Van't Veer, had often quoted Hoekstra to defend their approach, but he had more encouraged the exemplary approach, using a psychological analysis of the human soul in historical texts.[147] The exemplary group thus appealed to these historical precedents, as they supported both the redemptive-historical approach and the exemplary method.

Biblical preachers, like Paul, James, and the author of Hebrews, were taken as unquestionably legitimating examples in the exemplary approach to historical texts. Huyser said his chief reason for defending exemplary preaching was not the practice of the Christian church but Scripture itself, which provides its basis.[148] For him, scriptural passages, especially Rom 4:23–24; 1 Cor 10:1–13; Heb. 11:1–40; and Jas 5:10, 13–18, supported the exemplary approach, which thus may be extended to all biblical texts. Douma also assumed that those examples in the NT were adequate for justifying the exemplary method.[149] J. L. Koole stated later, in 1965, that exemplary preaching is "clearly enough legitimated in 1 Cor. 10" and thus can appeal to the whole of the NT.[150] Grosheide particularly provided a hermeneutic rule for the exemplary approach based on 1 Cor. 10, claiming that the passage expresses the history of Israel in the desert, with examples and warnings for us, for whom they were written, and thus it can be a model for sermons from historical texts.[151]

---

in Renninger, "New Testament Use of Old Testament Historical Narrative," 40.

146. Hoekstra, *Gerefomeerde homiletiek*, 264, 268. Hoekstra says, "One may never forget that Christ must be central and that the ministry of the Word may never degenerate into a character analysis of Mary, Thomas, or Peter." He adds later that a look at the height and the depth in the lives of the Bible saints is stimulating for the faith life of God's children. Quoted in Greidanus, *Sola Scriptura*, 66.

147. Renninger, "New Testament Use of Old Testament Historical Narrative," 40.

148. Huyser, "Exemplarische prediking," 17–18, quoted in Renninger, "New Testament Use of Old Testament Historical Narrative," 42.

149. Douma, "Exemplarische prediking," quoted in Greidanus, *Sola Scriptura*, 113. Douma said, "Laten we dan nu nagaan, wat de Schrift zelf ons inzake exemplarische prediking leert. Bij de Schrift als het onfeilbare Woord Gods ligt toch de beslissing," which translates as, "Let us now consider what Scripture itself teaches us on exemplary preaching. Because Scripture is the infallible Word of God for the right decision." By this Douma is implying that Scripture suppports the exemplary function of the Word.

150. Koole, "Het soortelijk gewicht van de historische stoffen van het Oude Testament," 101, quoted in Greidanus, *Sola Scriptura*, 110.

151. Grosheide, *Hermeneutiek*, 189, quoted in Greidanus, *Sola Scriptura*, 114.

However, the redemptive history group raised questions about the word *examples* (*tupoi*) in the 1 Cor 10:6 passage. Holwerda and Van't Veer understood the word *tupoi* here as "types," which means historical events foreshadowing events in the NT, depending on Goppelt (1911–1973) in his book *Typos: die typologische Deutung des Alten Testaments im Neuen* (1939).[152] Van' t Veer asserted that a typological interpretation is based on salvation history in the OT, and thus only the redemptive-historical approach provides the proper interpretation of these examples or types.[153] He subsequently objected to understanding 1 Cor 10 as referring to general examples, such as man's immorality or grumbling, without a redemptive-historical context. Paul's intention was to give a warning that NT people should not commit similar sins to OT people against God's special redemption. Van Dijk strengthened the argument that the meaning of types in 1 Cor 10 is entirely different to the exemplary side's contention, as it expresses individual actions in revelation history and so becomes an example for us.[154] In spite of these criticisms, exemplary preaching advocates did not shrink from proclaiming that every preacher should follow the methodological example of the prophets and apostles, shown in Scriptures like the whole of Deuteronomy; Ps 78; Hos 12:4–7; John 8:37–40; Rom 4:23–24; 1 Cor 10; Heb 11; and Jas 5. The debate found its essential dilemma in how to view and interpret the Scriptures, especially passages with alleged examples of the exemplary approach. We will discuss this in more detail later in this chapter.

We now examine the basic common conceptions and inferences of the redemptive-historical approach and then objections to that approach.

Redemptive-Historical Approach

The understanding of redemptive history by the redemptive history group was basically expressed in three propositions. Trimp describes them as "facts," "unity," and "continuing story."[155] Greidanus explains them as three postulates. These are identified as "redemptive history is history;" "redemptive history is a unity;" and "redemptive history means

---

152. Renninger, "New Testament Use of Old Testament Historical Narrative," 34; cf. Goppelt, *Typos*, 4–6.

153. Veer, "Christologische prediking," 164.

154. Dijk, *PE* 6 (1941), 307; quoted in Greidanus, *Sola Scriptura*, 115.

155. Trimp, *Preaching and the History of Salvation*, 51–54.

progression."[156] The first postulate emphasizes the reality of redemptive history in human history; the second concerns the oneness of redemptive history through the whole Scriptures, consisting of the history of God's redemption for his people; the third highlights the gradual development of redemptive history from the beginning to the end of human history. These concepts were originally presented in Vos's inaugural address on 8 May 1894 in Princeton Theological Seminary, as we have discussed in chapter 2.[157]

Schilder, who was twenty-eight years younger than Vos, became the European pioneer of the redemptive-historical approach, while Vos was its American leader.[158] As he had recognized the danger of Barthian theology and was determined to defend the historicity of biblical narratives, for example Gen 3, Schilder recapitulated the basic postulations of redemptive history. He defined redemptive history as "the successive realization in time of God's thoughts of peace for us according to his fixed plan, and the fulfilment in time of this work-program which Father, Son, and Spirit decided upon before time."[159] Here, "successive realization in time" means actual progressive fulfilment of God's redemptive plan. This definition of redemptive history includes three basic components, "reality," "unity," and "progression," which Schilder first outlined. He stated in 1935, "God's redemptive work does not make a separate (fancy) history, detached from 'secular,' but it enters history and comes about with and through (real) human history."[160] Barth's dialectical theology, however, separates redemptive history in the Bible from ordinary history and places it into supra-history, so that history becomes a dualism with two historical realms: history and supra-history. Schilder's first postulation of redemptive history thus objects to this dualism, as he claimed in 1931 that "History is a unity and this unity is apparent in Scripture, thus we need to be acquainted with the central thrust of its development and its factual turning points in the whole history."[161] This saying covers the second and third components. In the final analysis, these three components characterize redemptive history as being "one progressing history."

---

156. Greidanus, *Sola Scriptura*, 122–24.
157. Vos, "Idea of Biblical Theology," 3–24.
158. Thomas, "Learning from the Life of Dr. Klaas Schilder," part 3.
159. Schilder, *Ref* 21 (1946), 225.
160. Schilder, *Wat is de hemel?* 68.
161. Schilder, *Ref* 11 (1931), 365.

According to Greidanus, these three components became the actual foundation for the hermeneutical principles of the redemptive-historical approach and, surprisingly, the exemplary group also held them in common. Both groups opposed dialectical theology's disparaging of the history of God's redemption. They also agreed that redemptive history is so important, and directly related to God's revelation, that it should not be slighted.[162] Why did the conflict over these common principles occur? According to Greidanus, it concerned inferences drawn from these principles.[163]

The exemplary side claimed that the inferences of the redemptive-historical side went too far from the basic components of redemptive history, becoming excessive, and they accordingly opposed them. For example, Schilder articulated:

> A sermon dealing with 'historical material' is a real sermon if it pointed out God's work of self-revelation unto salvation in Christ, *as that work has advance to that temporal 'juncture' into which the text introduces us* and only if it connects this particular 'point' of God's work with the whole 'line' of God's progressing work.[164]

This means a sermon on an historical text set forth, without designating the specific juncture in the temporal line, does not minister God's Word. However, to determine the exact time of the historical text, with respect to the whole timeline of redemptive history, is so difficult that even specialized historians, like W. Ramsay,[165] have difficulty in dating some biblical texts. The date of many biblical events, such as Christ's feeding of the five thousand and Paul's writing of the Epistle to the Galatians, cannot be precisely determined. Those historical texts which cannot be exactly dated thus become disqualified, in Schilder's prescription, for

---

162. The proponents of the exemplary side, as well as the redemptive-historical side, emphasize the importance of redemptive history. For example, Hoekstra says in *Homiletiek*, 353, "The history of redemption is so extremely important because God realizes his counsel and reveals his thoughts in the historical facts." Dijk, another exponent of the exemplary approach, also remarks in *Dienst der prediking*, 199, "The history is of such vital importance because God's revelation in this world . . . is neither a-historical nor suprahistorical but . . . enters history and works out God's plan in the facts of history." Quoted in Greidanus, *Sola Scriptura*, 121.

163. Greidanus, *Sola Scriptura*, 125.

164. Schilder, *Ref* 11 (1931), 375, quoted in Trimp, *Preaching and the History of Salvation*, 83–84.

165. Ramsay, *St. Paul*, 22–38.

use as "a real sermon." For this reason, the exemplary side opposed their opponents' extreme inferences from the basic postulates of redemptive history.

The redemptive-historical side inferred that to describe the progression of redemptive history properly should be a supremely important task for the interpretation of historical texts, whereas the exemplary side thought differently. For example, Schelhaas opposes this position in that the progression of redemptive history cannot be rectilinear because "there are times of scarcity of revelation and of general relapse of faith."[166] He affirmed that God's revelation never presents a straight-line progression, but rather an "organic progression." In response, Schilder argued that the "progression of revelation" does not depend on man's reaction, and thus the failure of man's faith does not necessarily mean a regression of revelation.[167] For Schilder, God does not speak, but acts rectilinearly, thereby moving closer to His final goal.

I strongly disagree that the redemptive-historical side understood the progression of redemptive history as a rectilinear process. There is a misconception of progression on the exemplary side, especially by Schelhaas. In addition, Dijk states,

> He who supposes that in preaching historical texts he can date every moment exactly and that he can plot the precise curve of the line of progression in God's revelation, leaves the area of God's Word and becomes entangled in his own constructions and conclusions.[168]

Afterwards, the inferences showing the progression of redemptive history revelation as the most important factor in interpreting a historical text became a central issue between both sides in the Dutch debate. Here, progression means that the revelation of God's redemption passes through a gradual development from its initial stage to the final stage of its fulfilment in history. This basic concept was acceptable to both parties of the Dutch debate, however, showing that the manner of the progression of redemptive history became a major issue of contention.

Concerning progression, Greidanus vindicates the redemptive-historical side in three ways. Firstly, no one claims they can identify the precise point of the progression line in redemptive history. Secondly,

---

166. Schelhaas, *GTT* 42 (1939), 123, quoted in Greidanus, *Sola Scriptura*, 127.
167. Schilder, *Ref* 20 (1939), 96, quoted in Greidanus, *Sola Scriptura*, 127.
168. Dijk, *Dienst der prediking*, 110, quoted in Greidanus, *Sola Scriptura*, 129.

Schilder's excessive view in relation to the progression of revelation was not unsupported by other redemptive-historical scholars like Holwerda and Veenhof, and thus cannot be regarded as a specific problem in the redemptive-historical approach. According to Greidanus, the redemptive-historical approach generally places more emphasis on the progression of revelation as the difference between the "then" and "now," rather than on the exact dating of progression as a minute by minute advance. Thirdly, to date a text within redemptive history is necessary for an appropriate interpretation, because a preacher should designate the timeline of the text "before and after,"[169] otherwise we cannot locate the text rightly in the line of redemptive history and then interpret it according to redemptive-historical principles. The issues actually converge into the difference over how to approach historical texts. We now need to explore the methods of interpreting historical texts.

Interpreting Historical Texts

An historical text is understood as a scriptural text in which the factual history concerning God's redemptive history has been recorded.[170] Thus the nature of this historical text should be found in the aforementioned characteristics of redemptive history—historicity, unity, and progression. The parties in the Dutch debate did not differ at all about these basic components, despite others like Bultmann and D. Gowan who differed in insisting that historical texts like Exodus have nothing to do with real history, but may embrace saga, legend, and short story.[171] Both the redemptive-historical and exemplary sides agreed in principle that a preacher should do justice to the nature of the historical text as the preaching text, but in practice differed as to how to do this.

As for interpreting historical texts acceptably, the redemptive-historical side primarily emphasized the "foundational function of RH." Historical texts like the gospels, which tell of God's saving acts through Christ in history, lay the foundation for doctrinal or ethical texts, as in the Pauline epistles which indicate how to receive God's grace and live according to His purpose. Thus dogmatic texts presuppose the redemptive history of historical texts, and not vice versa. Holwerda contends, "If one

---

169. Greidanus, *Sola Scriptura*, 129–30.
170. Ibid., 131.
171. Gowan, *Reclaiming the Old Testament*, 15–17.

concedes that history lays the foundation for dogma and ethics, he cannot view historical material as illustrative matter: the foundational function of RH for dogma excludes an illustrative function."[172] He considers that if historical texts were taken as illustrative material for doctrines and ethics, then these would be supposed as prior to redemptive history; eventually this would not do justice to those texts. However, it is not logical to argue that the foundational function of an historical text prohibits an illustrative function for doctrines or ethics for, if so, we should not then take any illustration, like Christ's humbleness and obedience to death (Phil 2:8), from any of the historical texts in the gospels. Such an argument is invalid and has no appeal for the exemplary side. We will discuss this in the following section.

In addition, the redemptive-historical group suggested two hermeneutical methods for doing justice to historical texts in preaching: "organic interpretation" and "synthetic interpretation." Organic interpretation handled a text as part of an organic body, viewing the text in relation to the whole scheme, namely, the unity of redemptive history, thus frustrating the fragmentary approach. This method is valuable in discovering the unity of redemptive history, especially christological elements, but also tends to pay little attention to what God says about people in the text.[173] The unity of redemptive history regulates the progression of redemptive-historical revelation and the continuity between the past and present in the text. The organic interpretation, vouching for the unity of redemptive history, may lead to a synthetic interpretation.

Synthetic interpretation integrates elements of a text into a whole and makes every text unique along the progression of redemptive history. The term *synthetic* was specifically designated here as an antonym of the atomistic interpretation encountered in exemplary preaching. For the redemptive-historical side, atomistic interpretation, in which a favorite element is selected among other elements of a text and made a general religious instruction, like patience and prayer, should be dispelled by this synthetic method. An interpreter should keep his eyes on the specific relationship of the elements within the text. Synthetic interpretation thus brings out the text's uniqueness by synthesis of its elements at that particular time and place, even though the same elements can be found in other texts. For example, the prayer of Christ in Gethsemane is unique

---

172. Holwerda, *Begonnen*, 88, quoted in Renninger, "New Testament Use of Old Testament Historical Narrative," 28; Greidanus, *Sola Scriptura*, 131.

173. Greidanus, *Sola Scriptura*, 136.

because it relates to His submission to God's will and His specific task as redeemer. If one only says here that prayer is an example for believers, this would violate the nature of the text for redemptive-historical proponents. However, the exemplary side insists on the general applicability of the text and criticizes the one-sidedness of the redemptive-historical method as being irrelevant to Christian life today. We will examine this criticism in detail later.

In summary, the organic and synthetic interpretations suggested by the redemptive-historical side indicate the text's relatedness to Christ, and only then can it be treated as a text for preaching. We now examine the features of redemptive-historical preaching.

The Features of Redemptive-Historical Preaching

Redemptive-historical preaching was characterized as "christocentric preaching," "*sola scriptura*," and "historical preaching" by Greidanus.[174]

Firstly, christocentric preaching engages the unity of redemptive history because each historical text by nature relates to the work of Christ. The exemplary side also accepted this basic rule. Dijk says: "We are dealing with the history of revelation which leads to Bethlehem and Golgotha and finds its 'centre' in the Christ of God."[175] They actually see the coming of Christ in that history and are not reluctant to draw a line from the OT historical text to Christ. However, for the redemptive-historical side, christocentric preaching does not simply draw a line from every text to Christ. On the contrary, such a way of preaching has the potential to become a Barthian type sermon, viewing two different historical events within the same horizontal line, and would then err by dehistoricizing historical texts. The redemptive-historical side opposed this way of schematized parallelism. Christocentric preaching, in Holwerda's view, signifies rather the fullness of God's revelation in Christ from a specific point of redemptive history.[176]

Thus one can preach a christocentric sermon without directly pointing to Christ. Bryan Chapell agrees with this by affirming: "... even if a preacher does not specifically mention an aspect of Christ's earthly

---

174. Ibid., 140–52.
175. Dijk, *Dienst der prediking*, 82, 201; quoted in Greidanus, *Sola Scriptura*, 141.
176. Greidanus, *Sola Scriptura*, 144.

ministry in a sermon, it can still be Christ-centered."[177] For Schilder, christocentric preaching is based on properly perceiving Christ, who had moved through the OT, preparing the way for His own coming in the flesh, and reaching a certain point of God's whole salvation plan.[178] Christocentric preaching should therefore also be called theocentric preaching, because the latter proclaims God as He has revealed Himself in Christ.[179] For the redemptive-historical side, to extract human examples is adverse to the nature of historical texts, which are of innate theocentric-christocentric historicity.

Secondly, the preaching of *sola scriptura* relates to the uniqueness of the Bible, differentiating it from other religious texts. The uniqueness of the Christian Bible lies in God's redemptive acts through Jesus Christ; otherwise people like Abraham, Elijah, and even Christ, would not be special for us because other religious texts like the Koran also provide similar people as good examples. However, the Bible proclaims exclusively and consistently "one redemptive history"—that God has saved His people through His only Son Jesus Christ.[180]

Preaching *sola scriptura* means, for the redemptive-historical group, that people in the Bible should not be overly emphasized, but only presented in the context of God's unique redemptive history. For example, when God and man appear in a historical text as two factors requiring explication and application, the text should be understood in such a way as to show that God freely proceeds by His acts to redeem His people through Christ, and that man encounters this saving God in His redemptive acts in Christ.[181] For the redemptive-historical side, theocentric-christocentric preaching was therefore recognized as the preaching of *sola scriptura*.

Thirdly, historical preaching focuses on the progression of redemptive history, which appears to locate an historical text within the whole context of redemptive history. The dating of historical texts is required for understanding the historical gap between then and now. Were it not for this time-designation process, historical events like Christ's crucifixion and resurrection would be timeless and considered to repeatedly

---

177. Chapell, *Christ-Centered Preaching*, 303.
178. Greidanus, *Sola Scriptura*, 143.
179. Chapell, *Christ-Centered Preaching*, 304.
180. Goldsworthy, *Preaching the Whole Bible as Christian Scripture*, 11–21.
181. Greidanus, *Sola Scriptura*, 147.

happen at any time.[182] Objecting to such preaching from an historical text, the redemptive-historical advocate Schilder wrote: "Let there be no anachronism, especially not in the history of salvation, which is always progressive, which always wants to advance from the potential to the deed, from latent to patent development, from bud to flower, from morning to day."[183] For this reason, redemptive history with its historical preaching refused to encourage or allow psychologizing, spiritualizing, or moralizing.

We now need to examine in detail criticisms of the redemptive-historical approach.

Criticisms of Redemptive-Historical Interpretation and Preaching

The exemplary side objected to the exclusive redemptive-historical approach to historical texts as being irrelevant to the congregation. For example, Douma expressed his objection that previously it had been normal for historical texts to be presented relevantly, but in his day such sermons would merely describe a moment in the process of redemptive history and become irrelevant.[184] Krabbendam presents a similar criticism by comparing redemptive-historical preaching to a Boeing 747 flying over beautiful landscapes but never touching down. In like manner, redemptive-historical preaching does not touch the real life of the Christian on the ground.[185] Bavinck, one exponent of exemplary preaching, highlights his complaints about the exclusive redemptive-historical approach: "Many sermons in our time are splendid discourses, profound lectures about some redemptive-historical thought, but they are not sermons in the true sense of the word . . . These preachers have forgotten the man in the pew."[186] These objections were mainly about the accompanying irrelevancy of the exclusive redemptive-historical approach, due to its unilateral explication.

---

182. Bultmann, *Theology of the New Testament*, vol. 1, 303.

183. Greidanus, *Sola Scriptura*, 148.

184. Douma, "Calvijn over historische stoffen," nos. 3292 and 3300, quoted in Greidanus, *Sola Scriptura*, 152-53.

185. Krabbendam, "Hermeneutics in Preaching," 235-36.

186. Greidanus, *Sola Scriptura*, 153; cf. Bavinck, *De toekomst van onze kerken*, 20.

The redemptive-historical side defended its position, as in Holwerda's declaration: "We can overcome the defect of the objective-subjective scheme only when we fully recognize that preaching is a moment of living intercourse between the Lord and his people."[187] He appealed to the living power of God's Word. Spier elucidated this point: "The Bible is neither objective nor subjective . . . The Gospel is the power of God unto salvation (1 Cor 1:18) . . . Thus the Word of God is the dominating norm for our lives."[188] For Spier, a preacher should proclaim only that Word, without adding any application, because that Word already has relevance for people due to its own living power. Veenhof confidently claims: "The only application of which the minister of the Word would take responsibility is *the choice of the text.*"[189] The text, therefore, has its own unique explicatory-applicatory function. The redemptive-historical side eventually proposed a strict guideline for textual, expository preaching, in order to escape from both the objective-subjective dilemma and the charge of irrelevance.

There remains a problem, however, because the redemptive-historical approach excludes the exemplary application of the text. In contrast, for H. Robinson expository preaching by definition is "the communication of a biblical concept, derived from and transmitted through an historical, grammatical, and literary study of a passage in its context, which the Holy Spirit first applies to the personality and experience of the preacher, then through him to his hearers."[190] Here, the phrase "through the preacher to his hearers," means application of the biblical truth to the congregation through the preacher's own words, which becomes an essential part of expository preaching. The exclusion of application from expository preaching is thus unacceptable for general homiletical scholars like Robinson.

---

187. Ibid., 157; cf. Holwerda, *Populair-wetenschappelijke bijdragen*, 9–33.

188. Ibid., 154; cf. Spier, "Wijsbegeerte en predkiking," 57.

189. Gootjes, "Book Introduction," 15; cf. Greidanus, *Sola Scriptura*, 168. Gootjes pointed out that Greidanus translates this sentence into a somewhat unclear meaning: "The only application which the minister of the Word must make is *the choice of the text.*" Does this mean that he cannot apply the text to the congregation except by choosing it? However, the Dutch original sentence renders the clear meaning that the preacher should consider the context of his congregation first and select the appropriate text for it, and then only explain the text with application in it. Therefore the responsibility of applying application is for the text itself not for the preacher.

190. Robinson, *Expository Preaching*, 20.

In addition, the exemplary side criticized the one-sidedness of handling historical texts in the exclusive redemptive-historical approach. For example, Holwerda's claim, that the foundational function of salvation history excludes an illustrative function of the texts, was rejected by the exemplary side by appealing to examples of illustration in, for example, Ps 78 and Rom 4:23–24, in which history is evidently functioning as illustration. In the latter, Abraham's justification, originally recorded in the OT historical text, functions as both a foundation for the doctrine of justification and as an illustration for individual believers.[191] The Bible explicitly says that it was written not for his sake alone "but also for us," and this signifies that an historical text can be selected for illustration and application applied to us. Ps 78 also restates the history of Israel for instruction or examples which should not be followed by descendants. The historical-theological fact of Christ's incarnation and ministry are also given in Phil 2:5 for doctrine and as an example for believers. These biblical examples challenge Holwerda's position.

Huyser also charged Holwerda with being contradictory in prescribing that the foundational function of redemptive history excludes an illustrative function, yet suggesting that a doctrine may be illustrated with an historical event, apart from historical texts.[192] Greidanus judges Huyser's charge as a misconception of the redemptive-historical approach:

> Unfortunately, Huyser somehow misses the point Holwerda is making, for there is no question of a contradiction here. Having argued that the foundational function of redemptive history excludes an illustrative function, Holwerda continues: "One may, naturally, illustrate a certain 'truth' with an historical text when one is preaching on a text from the epistles or on one of the commandments . . . But when one has chosen an historical text as a preaching-text, that text must be taken in accordance with its own nature and no longer as illustrative."[193]

However Huyser is, in Renninger's opinion, correct to criticize the redemptive-historical side in that if history can be used for illustrating doctrine in the epistles, why cannot the OT historical text be used illustratively?[194] Trimp supports Renninger by saying that Holwerda's

---

191. Renninger, "New Testament Use of Old Testament Historical Narrative," 43.
192. Greidanus, *Sola Scriptura*, 132.
193. Ibid., 132.
194. Renninger, "New Testament Use of Old Testament Historical Narrative," 43.

argument on the foundational function cannot be defended because it is possible that redemptive history also exerts an illustrative-pedagogical function in the context of the work of the Holy Spirit.[195]

These criticisms were mostly attributed to the exclusive way of the redemptive-historical approach and its resultant irrelevancy for contemporary believers. The exemplary side appealed to several NT texts, like Rom 4:23–24; 1 Cor 10; Heb 11; and Jas 5, which adopt OT historical texts for illustration. Undoubtedly the redemptive history side did not acknowledge these NT texts as supporting the exemplary side's claim, but the NT's use of OT historical material became the final issue, and recognized as relevant to the Dutch debate.

It will now be helpful to examine the discussions over related NT passages, in order to further understand the Dutch debate.

New Testament Use of Historical Texts

Three passages from the NT—1 Cor 10; Heb 11; and Jas 5—specifically require our attention because they are most often referred to in the Dutch discussion. Huyser criticized the exclusive redemptive-historical approach, largely based on those passages, and Van't Veer and Holwerda have mainly mentioned them in defending their position. Moreover, the discussion concerning these passages is one of the essential parts in the dealings of Greidanus, Trimp, and Renninger with the Dutch debate. For convenience's sake, we begin with Jas 5:13–18, then consider Heb 11 and, finally, 1 Cor 10.

James 5:13–18

These verses recount the powerful prayers of Elijah from 1 Kgs 18 and appear to validate the exemplary approach to historical texts in the OT. Van Dijk, however, claimed that James's usage cannot possibly be normative for our preaching of this OT text, because his use of Elijah as an illustration and our textual preaching on 1 Kgs are different.[196] While James may use history, preaching on an historical text like this is very different as the preacher must primarily do justice to the nature of the text. According to Van Dijk, James did not preach on 1 Kgs 18 but merely extracted an

---

195. Trimp, *Preaching and the History of Salvation*, 131–33.
196. Greidanus, *Sola Scriptura*, 118.

example from the history in that passage. It is not clear what Van Dijk intended to affirm by this argument.

On the other hand, the exemplary side viewed this passage as irrefutable validity for taking an example from the historical text for contemporary believers. Huyser claimed that if James derived an example from 1 Kgs, a preacher must bring out this example when he preaches on that text.[197] For Huyser, following James's example is the duty of biblical preachers, otherwise they would violate a scriptural principle.

In contrast, Van't Veer asserted that James did not preach on 1 Kgs 18, but mentioned Elijah's prayer in an exposition on prayer. He concluded that the text did not support the exemplary method.[198] In my view Huyser is correct in that, as an inspired writer of Scripture, James is taking an example from OT history, and thus providing preachers with a warrant to take illustrations from OT history. However, whether this method does justice to the nature of historical texts is not yet clear.

Hebrews 11

This passage speaks about the faith of believers, like Abel, Noah, Abraham, and David, whom we should take as our models, to follow in their faith and obedience. Huyser claimed that a preacher receives the right to treat analogous incidents in OT historical texts as an extension of Heb 11:3–31.[199] Holwerda disagreed, because there is no objection to choosing illustrative material from redemptive history in dogmatic texts like Heb 11,[200] but preached according to the redemptive-historical method. Van't Veer holds a similar view that all these examples of faith in Hebrews 11 show the way to read OT history as redemptive history, so the example can be understood in context biblically. He says, "It is truly unnecessary that we place next to the RH method another element: the exemplary element... Indeed it is so that this 'exemplary element' can be discovered only in the RH method, therefore Christologically."[201] In other words, if a preacher selects examples from OT history consistent with redemptive

---

197. Ibid., 118.
198. Veer, "Christological Preaching," 27.
199. Greidanus, *Sola Scriptura*, 116.
200. Holwerda, "History of Redemption," 14.
201. Veer, "Christological Preaching," 32.

history for application to contemporary believers, it is not objectionable to redemptive-historical advocates.

By then the disagreement was not just about using examples from historical texts, but using them without regard to "the scriptural sense of the texts." By this, Van't Veer means relating the OT history to Christ, as in verse 26, where it says that "he esteemed the reproach of Christ greater riches than the treasures in Egypt; for he looked to the reward." However, is it right to say that Scripture provides only the christological sense in its historical texts? Is it not legitimate to speak of human examples, without relating to Christ, when one preaches on historical texts? In the next chapter we shall suggest answers.

1 Corinthians 10:1–11

We considered these verses briefly earlier in this chapter, but now examine them in more detail regarding the scriptural sense of speaking on examples from the historical text. The disputed word was *examples* (*tupoi*) in verses 6 and 11, where Paul provides reasons why the historical texts were written: "Now these things occurred as examples to keep us from setting our hearts on evil things as they did" (v. 6); "These things happened to them as examples and were written down as warnings for us, on whom the fulfilment of the ages has come" (v. 11). The exemplary side viewed the word *tupoi* as examples to be followed, or avoided, by us, while the redemptive historical side interpreted it as types, which must be interpreted typologically. Van't Veer articulated that the specific sense of *type* means the reality that something that is to come is previously determined, pictured in the framework of a history that occurred previously.[202] If we take this definition and its corresponding typological interpretation, we should expect that the whole NT church would fall into sin and be destroyed by God's judgment, because this was predestined in the type.[203] However, it is not the intention of this text to prophesy such a fate.

The Greek word *tupos* has diverse usages, like example, pattern, proof, and sample, throughout Scripture.[204] Care should be exercised in

---

202. Ibid., 30.

203. Greidanus, *Sola Scriptura*, 115.

204. The Greek word *tupos* was also used with the meaning of "form" in Rom 5:14, 6:17; Phil 3:17; 1 Thess 1:7; 2 Thess 3:9; 2 Tim 1:13; 1 Pet 5:3. Cf. Trimp, *Preaching and the History of Salvation*, 99.

deciding the meaning of a word in historical texts, because of various semantic and cultural gaps between then and now. The intended meaning of an historical word in an ancient text would be the "field-orientated (contextual) sense" rather than the "conceptual sense," which is usually decided by arbitrarily selecting one from among the various lexical concepts.[205] In 1 Cor 10, Paul related the word *examples* to the intention of this OT historical text. Thus its meaning would be identified by the intention of the text. There is another problem, however, for when we investigate how OT texts are used in the NT, there is a suspicion that the NT writer might have imposed his own ideas into the OT text when incorporating it into his own text.

James Aageson has surveyed this subject extensively and concluded that Paul worked with his biblical texts, interpreting them from the perspective of his christological context.[206] Paul's christological context was formed by his radical conversion experience in encountering Christ, and this then became the theological perspective through which he read OT texts. For example, the identification of the rock in 1 Cor 10:4 with Christ is, in fact, an important hermeneutical key to the whole text of 10:1–33. For Paul, OT historical texts, his christological perspective, and the context of his congregation were always woven into his texts.[207] Thus it is correct for Van't Veer to say that Pauline texts, at least in the case of 1 Cor 10, should be interpreted christologically.

However, whether christological hermeneutics excludes the exemplary approach is another matter. I disagree with Van't Veer's allusion that this christological approach in 1 Cor 10 removes the right to use examples from historical texts.[208] One reason is that the word *tupoi* implies not types foreshadowing the NT church, but rather examples warning us not to follow Israel who perished, because verse 6 says " . . . as examples to keep us from setting our hearts on evil things as they did," while verse 11 also says " . . . as examples and were written down as warnings for us . . . "

The intention of the historical text is thus, for Paul, not types, but examples of warning and admonition for the NT church. This scriptural intention can be fulfilled only through the christological connection

---

205. Cotterell and Turner, *Linguistics & Biblical Interpretation*, 146–55.

206. Aageson, *Written Also for Our Sake: Paul and the Art of Biblical Interpretation*, 16.

207. Aageson, "Written Also for Our Sake: Paul's Use of Scripture in the Four Major Epistles," 179–81.

208. Veer, "Christological Preaching," 31.

between the exodus community and the NT Corinthian church. Van't Veer and Holwerda,[209] as well as Chapell, also admitted this, being in agreement that a preaching text can be Christ-centered without directly mentioning Christ.[210] We can therefore safely affirm that the christological interpretation never excludes the exemplary approach. If that is so, there should have been no dispute between the exemplary and redemptive-historical sides, for the issue was that of respecting the nature of historical texts. The latter did it by explicitly drawing a direct line to Christ, whereas the former did it implicitly, by using examples for the benefit of hearers. Either way, a sermon can be said to be doing justice to the text when the preacher fully recognizes the intention of the text and locates it within the scope of God's redemptive work through Christ.

Dilemma and Schism of the Church

As we have seen, the essential difference between the two debating parties lay in how to view and preach an historical text. The question of the intention of OT historical texts in the NT became a major issue and it was agreed that they never exclude an exemplary function. Renninger, who has extensively explored the exemplary use of OT historical texts in the NT, concludes, as a corollary, that the NT writers were undoubtedly aware that OT historical texts may have an exemplary function.[211] The conflict might have been solved at this point.

It is necessary to look elsewhere for the fundamental cause of the division between the two parties. Greidanus felt there was no way out of this dilemma, because there is no third possibility.[212] He thus proposes his own modification of those presuppositions in hermeneutics and homiletics, because he believes it would open the way to another choice. However, this solution also has a crucial problem, which we discuss in the next section.

I submit that the fundamental root cause in the unresolved dispute between the two parties should be sought in the age-old disharmony within the GKN, which was formed in 1892 by an amalgamation of

---

209. Ibid.; Holwerda, "History of Redemption," 14–15.

210. Chapell, *Christ-Centered Preaching*, 209–20, 301–5.

211. Renninger, "New Testament Use of Old Testament Historical Narrative," 33–38, 46–49, 299.

212. Ibid., 49.

groups with different theological tendencies. Among them, as mentioned previously, the Old Calvinists were inclined to the more experiential and inward side of religion, rooted in Dutch Pietism, whereas the Neo-Calvinists expressed a strong aversion to pietistic features, such as subjectivism, individualism, and spiritualism, and accordingly strove to remove them from the church.

According to Pronk, Dutch Pietism had been greatly influenced by Puritanism and was characteristically concerned with personal salvation and sanctification.[213] The Puritan-minded Calvinists emphasized the holy life of individual believers, differentiating true converts from hypocrites in their preaching. For Neo-Calvinists, mostly involved in the Dooyeweerdian New Direction philosophical movement, the externals of religion, like culture and education, were emphasized more than the internal or moral aspects. The latent conflict between the two different Calvinist groupings subsequently developed into an explosive confrontation over preaching but, in addition, the advent of Barth's neo-orthodoxy had its own influence on theological thought and even widened the cleavage between the two groups. Neo-Calvinists, like Schilder and Van't Veer, recognized the danger of Barth's theology and its dehistoricizing characteristics and aligned it with pietistic subjectivism and spiritualism. The Old Calvinists would by no means identify themselves with Barth's dialectical theology, but their opponents viewed them as opening the door to dehistoricizing theology through their exemplary preaching. As a result the Neo-Calvinists began to criticize more fiercely the alleged dehistoricizing approach, even though the exemplary side denied the charge. The two parties were eventually even more widely divided in confronting Barthian theology.

The dilemma, which the two parties had difficulty in resolving, resulted in the separation of the redemptive-historical group from the church. According to Geoff Thomas, the schism was in fact initiated by the ecclesiastical hierarchy who excommunicated Schilder from the General Assembly in 1944.[214] De Jong describes this:

213. Pronk, "Preaching in the Dutch Calvinist Tradition."
214. Thomas, "Learning from the Life of Dr. Klaas Schilder," part 3. The church synod had dealt with allegedly suspect theology, which Schilder might have taught in school through the period of Nazi occupation during the Second World War, and eventually, in 1944, ousted Schilder and many others, including Greidanus, from the GKN denomination. Dooyeweerd, a leader of the New Direction and once a colleague of Schilder, was not included with those expelled. The proponents of redemptive history were thus later discontented with Dooyeweerd. However, Dooyeweerd strived to

> What first had offered so much inspiration and encouragement to many was marred by the rise of a vicious party-spirit; personalities and periodicals and even institutions of theological learning came to stand in strong opposition to each other in consequence of which a breach was forced upon the congregation throughout the land by the synod of 1944.[215]

Here "a vicious party-spirit" speaks of factionalism in the church, which caused the synod of 1944 to make the fateful decision to excommunicate Schilder and his colleague, the elderly Greidanus, from the church. This factional decision tore the heart out of the church, because ministers, elders, families, and whole congregations all over the country, amounting to 216 churches, 152 ministers and 77,000 members, left the church in 1946 to follow the excommunicated leader and form a new denomination of Liberated Churches.[216] This church schism terminated not only ecclesiastical fellowship but also further discussion over exemplary preaching. Huyser attributed the termination of discussion to the split in the GKN, since the most anti-exemplary proponents like Schilder left the church.[217]

The schism, nevertheless, had a significant effect on preachers and theologians in Holland and in other countries, although the Dutch debate had proceeded for about two decades during the 1930s and 1940s. We will discuss this in more detail in the following chapters. Before that, we need to outline and assess briefly the evaluations made by the theologians involved in the debate.

Assessment and Suggestions

Greidanus provides his own evaluation of the Dutch debate in two ways: firstly, the hermeneutical use of progression in redemptive history and, secondly, the characteristics of historical texts. Firstly, Greidanus considers that the "progression of RH," in the exclusive redemptive-historical approach, led to "schematism, speculation, and objectivism."[218] For Greidanus, Schilder superimposed his rigid scheme of redemptive-historical

---

defend Schilder, not because Schilder was right in his theology, but because he thought the church order was being violated. Cf. Plantinga, "Understanding Dooyeweerd Better than He Understood Himself," 111.

215. De Jong, "Introduction," 2.
216. Thomas, "Learning from the Life of Dr. Klaas Schilder," part 3.
217. Renninger, "New Testament Use of Old Testament Historical Narrative," 23.
218. Greidanus, *Sola Scriptura*, 174.

progression on historical texts in such a way that the texts no longer say what they were intended to say.[219] The obsession that every text must fit into this scheme leads into the trap of speculation. Moreover, Schilder's primary focus on describing redemptive-historical progression, with his aversion to subjectivism and mysticism, makes his sermons predominantly intellectual and objective, like a lecture.[220] In Greidanus's thinking, Schilder's presupposed redemptive-historical framework makes it more difficult to achieve relevancy.

Secondly, Greidanus assesses that the debate fell into an impossible dilemma because the two sides failed to pay full attention to the nature of historical texts.[221] The redemptive-historical side, in particular Holwerda and Schilder, identified historical texts with historical facts, and thus tried to find the original facts behind the texts. Here, the phrase "original facts" means God's original revelation of His words and acts, constituting redemptive history. Greidanus describes this redemptive-historical method as *sub scriptura*, insomuch as it goes down to the fact-level below the texts.[222] According to Greidanus, the exemplary side also failed to point out the crucial fallacy of this redemptive-historical approach, inadvertently accepting the basic postulations, especially the factuality, of redemptive history for interpreting historical texts. Thereby they also sought the original facts behind the texts and appended exemplary elements to them. Both sides were deficient, in Greidanus's judgment, in giving sufficient attention to the nature of historical texts.

Greidanus gives a lengthy explanation for the features of the historical texts. To be brief, the historical texts are just the proclamation, that is, the *kerygma*, of the past facts of God's redemption at various stages of redemptive history.[223] Thus he suggests some guidelines for preaching on historical texts:

> Though the historical texts witness to God's acts in history, the nature of their witness is not objective description but proclamation: their aim is kerygmatic. A comparison of parallel historical texts shows that the biblical preachers (writers) have a liberty similar to that of painters: the authors of Scripture do not present precise photographic accounts (an impossibility

---

219. Ibid., 176.
220. Ibid., 180.
221. Ibid., 192–194, 199.
222. Ibid., 193.
223. Ibid., 212.

for any historiographer, certainly for one who proclaims God's acts in history) but compositions, word-paintings ... We would therefore, take as our starting point not redemptive history but the historical text.[224]

Here Greidanus affirms that the nature of historical texts is the proclamation of God's acts in history, providing us not with precise photographic accounts but with composite word-paintings. By this he means one's free interpretation and remake of God's acts in history, which is not history itself. This implies that the proclamations are not necessarily historical facts which require to be precisely dated in history. The preacher, therefore, need not be concerned about the factuality of the historical texts, but instead focus on the proclamation of the texts. Greidanus considers this approach the best solution to the Dutch dilemma about preaching on historical texts, for an emphasis on historical texts as historical proclamation leads to a different approach and will do more justice to *sola scriptura* than the redemptive-historical or exemplary approaches.[225]

However, Greidanus's suggestion is, in my opinion, invalid regarding the essential issues in the Dutch debate. Both the redemptive-historical and exemplary sides accepted the historical factuality and, thus, historicity of the redemption of Christ as being foundational for interpreting the whole of Scripture, but differed in how to apply them to historical texts. Thus Greidanus's suggestion of disregarding the factuality of historical texts would be totally unacceptable to both parties in the debate.

Moreover, the Dutch redemptive-historical approach originally appeared as a reaction against the dehistoricizing dialectic theology which disregards the factuality of God's redemptive events in history. For Reformed scholars like Schilder, Barth's theology and its concept of history as *supra-history* ultimately undermines the foundation of Christianity as in 1 Cor 15:14. Greidanus's suggestion is not very different from Barth's methodology of interpreting historical texts and so his suggestion would be unacceptable to the redemptive-historical group who opposed Barthian dialectical theology.

Notwithstanding, the Old Calvinist advocates of exemplary preaching adopted the methods of psychologizing, spiritualizing, and moralizing, which were essential characteristics of the dialectic theology. For them, this was only in order to deliver relevant preaching to the congregation,

---

224. Ibid., 214.
225. Ibid., 212.

in contrast to the more irrelevant preaching of the redemptive-historical approach. Greidanus's suggested methodology, which is only a modification of the original redemptive-historical approach, excludes the exemplary approach and might not appeal to the redemptive-historical group who desired relevance.

Greidanus's suggestion does not help resolve the dilemma. On the one hand, his method does not comply with the basic conception of historical texts in both parties, and his approach is found in Bultmann's demythologizing methodology which seeks to reach the kernel of existential *kerygma* beyond the husk of objective history.[226] Nor do Greidanus's guidelines for interpreting historical texts appease the exemplary side, because they only appeal to the *kerygma* of texts and have nothing to do with the examples which the exemplary side expected.

Trimp examined this Dutch debate in 1983 and provided his own evaluation.[227] He began with the commendation that the redemptive-historical approach stimulated preachers to respect the Bible as the revelation of the living God. For Trimp, it was much appreciated that Schilder had to fight for "the history of salvation (RH)" against other ways of thinking that subordinated the Bible to human ideals, or theology to experience, as in the charismatic movement. In addition, the concept of redemptive history is still more important to Trimp, because it brought a welcome fresh breeze into the church in his country, which had suffered from unwelcome influences, such as Dutch Pietism and traditionalism, which stifled religious life into a scholastic category, and even from the threat of biblical criticism, which attempted to destroy biblical history. Trimp concluded that the refined insight into the nature of God's revelation and redemption should be received with gratitude to those leaders of 1920 to 1945.[228]

However, Trimp criticized the redemptive-historical approach as having created a false dilemma. According to him, the redemptive-historical approach started deficiently with vague definitions of both example and salvation history. The subsequent discussion thus led to a disastrous consequence. However, as we examined earlier, the discussion, and its subsequent dilemma, was connected to differences in viewing historical

---

226. Bultmann, "Hermeneutics and Theology," 241–255.
227. Trimp, *Preaching and the History of Salvation*, 93–134.
228. Ibid., 95.

texts, and not to the vague semantic definitions of those words.[229] For Trimp, history contains examples in itself and thus it is natural that salvation history in Scripture allows the use of examples.[230] But, again, this argument does not deal with the issue in the debate, which was not history versus example, but rather the exclusive redemptive-historical view versus the inclusive exemplary view on historical texts.

In addition, Trimp objects to the contrast that Holwerda posited between the "history of salvation (RH)" and the "order of salvation."[231] I agree that the latter is an integral part of the former because a history of salvation in Christ relates to each individual. Holwerda had wanted to warn against transposing redemptive history into the order of salvation by highlighting "our own Gethsemane," "our own Golgotha," and "our own Pentecost" in historical texts in the gospels instead of preaching the redemption of Christ for us. He accordingly stressed the distinction between the history of salvation and the order of salvation. Therefore I do not regard Holwerda's differentiation of the history of salvation from the order of salvation as being at fault, because otherwise redemptive history would be mixed with the psychology of Barthian supra-history.

On the other hand, some of Trimp's criticisms of the redemptive-historical approach are correct and helpful. For example, he says that to put historical texts into the hermeneutical question, "How is Christ revealing Himself in His coming in that particular moment?" is a "revelation-historical reduction" of the history of salvation.[232] I agree fully with his criticism. Moreover, he maintains that God is involved in history with people in the OT, communicating His love in Christ and through the Spirit of Christ, and so we cannot view OT history as only a foreshadowing of Christ's coming. Because the history of salvation is to be viewed as God's saving event on behalf of His people in Christ, we cannot disregard God's people and their experiences.[233] In my judgment, Trimp is correct

---

229. In relation to the definition of "example," refer to the section "Exemplary Preaching: General Survey." Holwerda selected the word "exemplaric" because it finds a solution by treating biblical history as a number of independent happenings, which are examples for us. Concerning the definition of "history of salvation," I have explained that it is a complicated phrase to define, but Schilder defined it well with three postulates which are in principle coincident to Vos's definition of it. Thus, Trimp's criticism of the vague definition of "salvation history" is, in my view, not correct.

230. Trimp, *Preaching and the History of Salvation*, 96–101.

231. Ibid., 118.

232. Ibid., 125.

233. Ibid., 127.

to emphasize the place of God's people in the scope of redemptive history, while criticizing the exclusive redemptive-historical approach as being mistaken in always putting historical texts into the scheme of Christ. Otherwise, God's people on their pilgrim path to heaven would not be mentioned in redemptive history, and this would be a huge loss to our spiritual knowledge and encouragement.

Nonetheless Trimp partly praises this redemptive-historical approach as having done a pioneer work, even with its inevitable mistakes, though being in need of further development for proper redemptive-historical preaching. He proposes that redemptive-historical preaching should be preaching about the living God within His trinitarian-historical self-revelation.[234] This proposition seems rather abstract, but it is a suggestion as to how to distinguish scriptural examples from illegitimate examples by paying more attention to the work of the Holy Spirit in relation to God's elect people, like Abraham and Elijah. I regard Trimp's suggestion as constructive and helpful for those who wish to develop the redemptive-historical approach further, because the exclusive redemptive-historical approach was deficient in viewing God's people (the church) and pneumatology in the history of God's redemptive action through Christ.

Finally, Trimp identifies the core of the Dutch dilemma by pointing to the ecclesiastical context within which the homiletical debate took place. The dilemma was deeply rooted in the differences of theological perspective in the GKN and the struggle took place, to a large extent, between Dutch Pietism and its residual subjectivism such as self-examination, and Kuyperian dogmatic theology, such as presumptive regeneration and infant baptism.[235] The Kuyperian Neo-Calvinists intended to counter the subjectivism, whereas the pietistic Old Calvinists clung to the traditional method. Trimp thus evaluates that the issue of "example" in preaching could not be discussed exclusively on its own because the discussion was occasionally overshadowed by controversy over the difference of

---

234. Ibid., 138.

235. Ibid., 85–86. Trimp says, "On the one hand, this controversy had a negative effect on the purity and peacefulness of the dialogue. On the other hand, the subject itself was directly related to the entire controversy, which at its core involved the struggle against subjectivism and individualism, and the attempt to liberate people from the mistaken formulation inherited from the Dutch Second Reformation and Kuyperian dogmatics."

theological perspectives in the church.[236] In my view, this assessment is especially helpful in that it contrasts causes of the Dutch dilemma, and indicates that the dilemma between exemplary and redemptive-historical preaching would only be resolved if theological factionalism is removed.

Conclusion

The central issue, we have seen, in the Dutch homiletical debate, was how to view and handle historical texts as preaching texts. While both the redemptive-historical and exemplary sides claimed to do justice to the biblical texts, the discussion was clouded by the factionalism deeply rooted in the different theological perspectives of the Dutch Pietism of the Old Calvinists and Neo-Calvinism. The pietistic Old Calvinists believed strongly in experiential theology, emphasizing conversion, inwardness, prayer, spirituality, even mysticism and so on.[237] The Neo-Calvinists accentuated the Christian's cultural mandate and social involvement, preferably with the externalization of the doctrines of grace, especially justification and regeneration.[238] This tension between the two groups came to prominence during the homiletic debate, and led to fierce controversy, with no prospect of reaching a peaceful agreement.

The Dutch debate should not, therefore, be viewed as an entirely theological discussion seeking to realize the reformation principle of *sola scriptura*. Even though the Dutch debate has ended, it has affected Reformed theologians beyond the Netherlands, and given rise to another debate in America, and to that I now turn in the next chapter.

---

236. Ibid., 139.

237. Beeke, *Quest for Full Assurance*, 307. According to Beeke, the experiential theology of Dutch Pietism sought a healthy balance between mysticism and precisionism.

238. Pronk, "Neo-Calvinism."

4

The American Debate
Homiletics and Redemptive History

THE DUTCH DEBATE INFLUENCED Reformed churches in America and stimulated, as well as fuelled, new homiletical redemptive-historical debates, which are closely related to the Korean debate on redemptive history. In order to analyze competently the Korean redemptive-historical debate in all its theological complexity, it is also necessary to understand adequately the American debate. In this chapter, I intend to discuss the origin, progress, result, and influences of the American redemptive-historical debate.

American Homiletical Debate

On 12–14 March 2002, in a conference at Greenville Presbyterian Theological Seminary, William Dennison introduced the debate on redemptive history in America. This debate is similar to the Dutch one, but only in the sense that it deals with the redemptive-historical homiletical issue. However, it is also different because it tends to characterize the principles of biblical theology, especially Vos's legacy. Dennison describes the debate as emerging from a "cloud of suspicion" regarding the soundness of biblical theology and its aligned sermons that appeared within Reformed confessional churches and seminaries in America.[1]

---

1. Dennison, "Biblical Theology and the Issue of Application in Preaching," 119.

Gaffin also confirms the fact that some Reformed circles in America have been sceptical of the biblical theology of Vos's tradition.[2] According to Dennison, the suspicion was increasing to the extent that candidates for the church ministry had been privately told in some denominations, which cannot be specifically identified by Dennison himself, that in order to be ordained they should not use biblical theology exegesis. Against this background, a homiletical debate relating to Reformed biblical theology was inevitable. To understand the situation, it is necessary first to examine the criticism of Reformed biblical theology.

Criticism of Reformed Biblical Theology

William Dennison testified that although it was not clear what specific matters contributed to the current cloud of suspicion of biblical theology, it had been intensified in three areas in Reformed churches in America.[3] Firstly, biblical theology had its origin in the critical-liberal theological tradition of the German Enlightenment and was likely to undermine theological orthodoxy within the Reformed tradition. Secondly, the redemptive-historical understanding of biblical theology is one of many perspectives on biblical literature and should not be considered as the indispensible interpretive key to Scripture. Thirdly, biblical theology is inappropriate for applying biblical text to the lives of believers because it focuses only on the explication of the given text without touching hearers' urgent needs. Furthermore, proponents of biblical theology, like James Dennison, appear to dislike application because they see that as the task of the Holy Spirit alone, not the preacher.[4] These criticisms require examination in more detail.

Firstly, the origin of modern biblical theology is found in German critical-liberal theology. Vos agrees, affirming that it was born in Germany under the spirit of rationalism, which led on to the questioning, and then the denial, of supernatural and propositional revelation.[5] Examples

2. Gaffin, "Biblical Theology and the Westminster Standards," 165.
3. Dennison, "Biblical Theology and the Issue of Application in Preaching," 120.
4. Dennsion, "What is Biblical Theology?" 36–37.
5. Vos, "The Idea of Biblical Theology," 15–17. Vos stated that in the biblical theology of rationalism, the historical principle merely served to eliminate, or neutralize, the revelation principle. According to Vos, revelation as an act of God, theistically conceived of, has the character of supernatural redemption and thus can in no wise be associated with anything imperfect or impure or below the standard of absolute truth.

can be seen in the works of Baur, Wrede, and Räisänen.[6] What Vos did was to provide a different foundation for biblical theology, consisting of the traditional principles of revelation, supernaturalism, historical progress, practicality, and unity, with multiformity of God's self-revelation; for Vos, biblical and theological study should be based on such principles.[7] Vos's methodology in biblical theology is fundamentally different from that of the rationalist tradition, emphasizing both historical progress and theological unity in the Bible.[8] I emphasize Vos's distinctive understanding and approach to biblical theology to show that it is unfair to claim that his biblical theology, or what is often referred to as Reformed biblical theology, would be harmful to Reformed pulpits, on the false charge that it came from a critical-liberal stable.

Secondly, there are many genres in Scripture, so a specific methodology cannot be all-embracive. However, whether the redemptive-historical approach is just a specific methodology, or a comprehensive perspective concerning how to view the whole of Scripture, is a crucial matter in the debate on biblical theology. For example, scholars of the history of religions school, like Baur and Wrede, view the Bible as a human work like any other ancient text, while Reformed scholars, like Vos and Ridderbos, conceive it as the product of God's supernatural acts of redemption in history. The former thus develop various critical approaches to interpreting Scripture. Hasel describes four different approaches[9] to the NT, while Childs prefers to highlight eight current models for biblical theology[10] and H. Mead lists as many as nine.[11] For these scholars, the redemptive-historical perspective is reckoned as just one of many ap-

---

6. Yarbrough, *Salvation Historical Fallacy?* 63.

7. Vos, *Biblical Theology*, 11–14.

8. Vos, "Idea of Biblical Theology," 22.

9. Hasel, *New Testament Theology*, 72–139. They are: "Thematic," "Existentialist," "Historical," and "Salvation history."

10. Childs, *Biblical Theology of the Old and New Testaments*, 11–29. They are: "Dogmatic," "Allegorical or Typological," "Great Ideas or Themes," "Heilsgeschichte or History of Salvation," "Literary Approaches," "Cultural-Linguistic Method," "Sociological Perspectives," and "Jewish Biblical Theology."

11. Mead, *Biblical Theology*, 123–24. They are arranged into three groups according to whether the focus is on the content (systematic/doctrinal, cross-section or central themes, story/narrative); on the shape of the material (tradition history, canonical authority, witness/testimony); or on the perspective of the interpreter (existential, experiential, social/communal). All these methods directly relate to how to view Scripture and how to conceive what task is to be done through biblical theology.

proaches to the Scriptures. However, for proponents of Reformed biblical theology, like Clowney,[12] Gaffin,[13] and James Dennison,[14] interpreting the Bible correctly involved accepting that Scripture was divinely structured in recording and teaching the history of God's redemption. The redemptive-historical perspective, accordingly, is accepted as the overarching rule for interpreting Scripture in some Reformed groups in America. Thus, it is unacceptable for Reformed groups to hold to the second charge that the redemptive-historical approach is wrongly considered as being crucial to interpreting Scripture.

Thirdly, to claim that biblical theology opposes application in preaching is an arguable point, which in turn occasions a fierce debate in America. According to William Dennison, biblical theology advocates are said to have stated that they are against application, as they regard that role to be the task of the Holy Spirit.[15] Jay Adams, for example, claims that conservative biblical theology preachers, sailing in the wake of Vos, tend to ignore or even oppose the use of application in a sermon.[16] This criticism is not entirely valid, because most of its proponents, like Clowney, John Murray, and Gaffin, regard application as an essential element of sound preaching. On the other hand, some biblical theology advocates, like William Dennison and his brother James, insist that the Holy Spirit directly effects God's salvation in Christ to God's children with divine power, so a preacher should not try to add his own application to the preaching.[17] This group objects to application, in order to highlight the theme of redemptive history—the person and work of Christ in history through all of Scripture. Lindblad designates this group as proponents of "exclusive Vosian RH preaching,"[18] while Carrick calls them an "extreme wing of the RH school."[19] John Frame implies that some redemptive-historical preachers, such as the Dennison brothers, have an antipathy to the very idea of application.[20] I argue, therefore, that the criticism of

12. Clowney, *Preaching and Biblical Theology*, 16–19.
13. Gaffin, "Redemption and Resurrection," 229–30.
14. Dennison, "What is Biblical Theology?" 36–37.
15. Dennison, "Biblical Theology and the Issue of Application," 120.
16. Adams, *Truth Applied*, 20–21.
17. Dennison, "Redemptive-Historical Hermeneutic and Preaching," 26.
18. Lindblad, "Redemptive History and the Preached Word," part 1: Introduction, 22.
19. Carrick, Imperative of Preaching, 135.
20. Frame, *Ethics, Preaching, and Biblical Theology*.

Reformed biblical preaching in regard to application should be directed only to a specific group of biblical theology scholars, the so-called "extreme wing of RH preaching," but not to all advocates of biblical theology.

According to Professor R. J. Cara of the Reformed Theological Seminary in Charlotte, there are four distinct groups regarding the redemptive-historical issue in contemporary Reformed circles: (1) RH only, (2) RH primary, (3) RH important, and (4) RH unimportant.[21] I will now explain these different groups.

The first group excludes any approaches other than the redemptive-historical perspective.[22] The second group sees redemptive history as the primary consideration for the right understanding of Scripture.[23] The third group considers redemptive-historical themes important, but not necessarily the primary, or only, themes in the Bible, and not the only method of preaching.[24] The fourth group does not, in theory, exist in Reformed circles, because their theology always emphasizes redemptive history to some degree. However, Cara maintains that many in, practice, rarely discuss the topic with regard to the redemptive history timeline, except for referring to traditional systematic theology.[25] Even though

---

21. Cara, "Redemptive-Historical Themes in the Westminster Larger Catechism." Cara explains the redemptive-historical themes using three foci: the first is a focus on the redemptive-historical events of history, as in Spykman, *Reformational Theology* and VanGemeren, *Progress of Redemption*; the second is a focus on any subject, like "land," "temple," and "worship," coming directly from the biblical text viewed through the timeline of biblical history; the third is a focus on a redemptive message that every section of the Bible is supposed to have for God's people, centered on Christ. There is disagreement within Reformed circles as to the extent to which redemptive-historical themes are considered as the main themes in the Bible.

22. Ibid., 59. Cara puts into the first redemptive-historical only group those who are favorable to N. T. Wright's views of justification and the "new perspective" and in addition to the exclusive redemptive-historical preaching group in the Dutch debate.

23. Ibid., 59–60. Cara places Ridderbos and G. E. Ladd, in this group. Cf. Ridderbos, *Paul*; Ladd, *Theology of the New Testament*. Cara also identifies R. Gaffin and T. Longman with this group. Cf. Longman, *Literary Approaches to Biblical Interpretation*, 68–69. For example, Gaffin says the essence of theology is interpretation of the history of redemption, but he does not insist on redemptive-historical only in *Resurrection and Redemption*, 24.

24. Ibid., 60. Cara identifies John Frame, Hasel, and even himself with this group. Cf. Frame, *Doctrine of the Kingdom of God*, 207–12; Frame, *Doctrine of God*, 7–9. Hasel emphasizes redemptive history but concludes that no center can be sufficiently broad in *New Testament Theology*, 163. Cara himself and Meredith Kline see covenant theology, which has many redemptive-historical aspects, as the best organizing principle of Scripture, while others find yet another center to the Bible.

25. Ibid.

Reformed scholars agree that God's redemption of His people through Christ is the center and theme of all of Scripture, there are disagreements among them concerning the degree to which redemptive-historical principles are applied to interpretation and preaching. For instance, Gaffin claims redemptive history as the primary control on a given biblical text, but Cara considers that many other principles, like the Trinity, covenants, literary context, and analogy of Scripture, can be equally important controls.[26] Such differences between the four groups contribute to the complexity so that it would be simplistic to reduce the tension to merely one group or dimension. While acknowledging that, the theological tension over redemptive-historical themes appears more acute between the redemptive history only group and the others. From the homiletical aspect, this tension appears especially between the "extreme wing" and the "more moderate wing of RH preaching."

I now intend to explore the formation of redemptive-historical preaching in America, as this forms the direct background to the American homiletical debate.

Background: Westminster Theological Seminary and Edmund Clowney

It is not incidental that the major participants in the debate over redemptive-historical preaching in America have a connection with WTS[27] and especially with Clowney's teaching. For example, William Dennison attended WTS from 1973 to 1980 and was taught redemptive-historical preaching by Clowney. James Dennison had worked as a librarian and a lecturer in church history in WTS California from 1980 to 2000. John Frame, one of the critics of redemptive-historical preaching, also graduated from WTS and was influenced by many professors, including Clowney.[28] Those who had an interest in, and participated in, the

---

26. Gaffin, "Systematic Theology and Biblical Theology," 294; Cara, "Redemptive-Historical Themes," 60.

27. WTS Philadelphia was founded in 1929 by the private funding of J. Gresham Machen. WTS California was founded in 1979 as a branch of WTS Philadelphia, becoming an independent institution in 1982. Its name was then changed to Westminster Seminary California (WSC). However, people still refer to it as WTS California and I will also refer to it by that name.

28. Frame, "Ethics, Preaching, and Biblical Theology." Frame says, "at Westminster Seminary, one of the most exciting discoveries students make is the history of

debate on redemptive history, for example, Adams, Krabbendam, Gaffin, Pipa, and even John Carrick, have strong connections with either WTS Philadelphia or WTS California. Carrick, Professor of Homiletics in Greenville Presbyterian Theological Seminary (GPTS), strongly supports this point, claiming that the WTS tradition in the United States has been powerfully influenced by, and has itself powerfully influenced, Reformed biblical theology and redemptive-historical preaching and the intertwining of them.[29] According to Carrick, the original debate over exclusive redemptive-historical preaching faded in the Netherlands, but continued in North America by way of significant Dutch immigration in the mid-twentieth century and also through the strong influence of WTS.[30]

The specific influence of WTS on redemptive-historical preaching has undeniably been through Clowney (1917–2005) who taught practical theology and church doctrine, with special emphasis on redemptive-historical preaching, at WTS Philadelphia from 1952 to 1984 and at WTS California from 1980 to 1999. Geoff Thomas, a Welsh Baptist pastor, graduated from WTS in 1965 and remembers Clowney emphasizing the value of the insights of redemptive history and applying them to the text under consideration.[31] J. Peter Vosteen, a graduate of WTS in 1956 and now principal of NWTS, acknowledges that Clowney had a profound effect on his own thinking as he came to a Reformed position.[32] Vosteen has recently appeared as a leading figure in the extreme wing of redemptive-historical preaching. Lindblad states that Vosian biblical theology came to wield a tremendous influence upon Reformed pulpits through Clowney's teaching and works, especially, his *Preaching and Biblical Theology* (1961).[33] Whereas Vos's biblical theology was developed through WTS faculty members such as John Murray, Meredith Kline, and Richard Gaffin, the adaption of it to a redemptive-historical model of preaching was achieved by Clowney. Vos's tradition, and Clowney's

---

redemption or biblical theology . . . And biblical theology opens up to us the wonderful vision of the eschatology of redemption: that in Christ the last days are here, and we are dwelling with him in the heavenly places."

29. John Carrick, *Imperative of Preaching*, 115.
30. Ibid., 114.
31. Thomas, "Edmund P. Clowney 1917–2005."
32. Vosteen, Review of *Preaching Christ in All of Scripture*, 49–51.
33. Lindblad, "Redemptive History and the Preached Word," part 1: Introduction, 20–21.

appropriation of it to redemptive-historical preaching, became the background of the debate over redemptive-historical preaching.

Clowney's formulation of redemptive-historical preaching is found in his *Preaching and Biblical Theology*, which presents how Vos's biblical theology relates to preaching and suggests methods of making sermons based on that discipline.[34] I shall now briefly describe Clowney's major points in that work:

1. The right understanding of biblical theology as a distinct and fruitful study of both historical progression and the theological unity of God's self-revelation in the Bible, provides the full context for the exegesis of particular passages of Scripture.[35]

2. For a genuine renewal of authority in preaching, a preacher should study biblical theology itself, which reveals the grandeur of God's sovereign power manifested in redemptive history.[36]

3. Characteristics of biblical theology preaching are: firstly, recognizing its proper place eschatologically in the church and the world; secondly, bringing to the foreground the richness as well as the authority of preaching; thirdly, centering preaching on its essential message of Scripture, Jesus Christ, then unlocking the objective significance of redemptive history, focusing on, or linking to, Jesus Christ as the core of redemptive history.[37]

4. In this way, a clearer understanding of biblical theology and a sharper discernment of the redemptive-historical perspective will aid us in appreciating the symbolism and the typology of Scripture, the principle of organic connection between promise and fulfilment, so we will be able to work in confidence and honor the Word of God.[38]

In this work of Clowney, the overarching theme is that Vos's biblical theology best helps a preacher to prepare for redemptive-historical preaching, with its divine authority, eschatological urgency, unexpected richness, and ecclesiastical relevancy in preaching Christ from Scripture. In this way the preacher can enter a new dimension of preaching, which

---

34. Clowney, *Preaching and Biblical Theology*, 5–6.
35. Ibid., 9–19.
36. Ibid., 20–62.
37. Ibid., 63–86.
38. Ibid., 87–121.

respects the fullness of God's revelation. This brief but effective guidance to Vosian biblical theology set a firm foundation for a specific style of preaching, the so-called Christ-centered redemptive-historical preaching, which had great influence in Reformed pulpits in America.

The Extreme Wing of Redemptive-Historical Preaching: Kerux and NWTS

Some of Clowney's students, however, who were enthusiastic advocates for Vos's biblical theology, went far beyond what their teacher originally intended. Geoff Thomas testifies that Clowney's approach tended to be absolutized by some of his students,[39] but he does not explain why, or how, that happened. I assume it was because so much emphasis was placed on redemptive-historical preaching, in that it opens up a new rich world of revelation, that its proponents are likely to magnify its importance. Gaffin states that it would be misleading, as is often done by its more enthusiastic advocates, to create the impression that biblical theology brings something totally new into the life of the church.[40] Frame also acknowledges that it is possible to go too far in emphasizing redemptive history, because one learns to view Scripture from the redemptive-historical perspective and then, through biblical theology, is opened up to the wonderful vision of eschatological redemption in Scripture.[41] On this account, there emerged a group which became extreme in favoring biblical theology or redemptive-historical preaching in America. These extremists insisted that the redemptive-historical perspective alone, with its special emphasis on the eschatological aspects, was essential in Reformed sermons, thus repudiating application.[42] However, Clowney, and even Vos, never sanctioned the eradication of application in biblical theology or redemptive-historical preaching. Clowney accuses the extremists by saying that the redemptive-historical approach necessarily yields ethical application, which is an essential part of preaching God's Word.[43] Vos also intended to harmonize the antithesis between this world and the

---

39. Thomas, "Edmund P. Clowney 1917–2005."
40. Gaffin, "Systematic Theology and Biblical Theology," 292.
41. Frame, "Ethics, Preaching, and Biblical Theology."
42. Kerux, "Biblical Theology Primer." Cf. Dennison, "Biblical Theology and the Issue of Application in Preaching," 149.
43. Clowney, *Preaching and Biblical Theology*, 80.

world-to-come through his eschatological concept, rather than to hold to an exclusively heavenly arena. He stated that all eschatological interpretations of history, when united to a strong religious mentality, cannot but produce the finest practical theological fruit.[44] These are reasons for affirming that the extreme wing of redemptive-historical preaching went too far, beyond the original themes of Vos's biblical theology and Clowney's redemptive-historical preaching.

This group's view of redemptive-historical preaching has been propagated through *Kerux* and NWTS. The journal *Kerux*, founded in 1986 by James Dennison and published three times a year, has become a major platform for the exclusive redemptive-historical position. In its first issue, Dennison explained the idea of *Kerux* as "the herald" of Vos's biblical theology and the Christ-centered redemptive-historical preaching originated by it. In his introduction to *Kerux* in this first issue, Dennison acknowledges that he, as editor, owed a debt to Vos which is reflected in the desire to "evangelize" others with the insights Vos had mined from the biblical text.[45] Dennison claims he discovered the biblical theology of Vos, and consequently his love of the Christ-centered approach was greatly heightened, when he was preaching through the Gospel of John in 1972.[46] His brothers, Charles and William, share his convictions and zeal. Charles Dennison (1944–1999) attended WTS in the early 1970s and thus was probably influenced by the WTS tradition, as evidenced by his saying, "In 1970, when Sidney Greidanus's *Sola Scriptura* appeared, an electric shock went through a number of us at Westminster Seminary."[47] He afterwards became a strong exponent of redemptive-historical preaching, due to his teachers, and regularly contributed sermons or essays relating to Vosian biblical theology to *Kerux*, while ministering in Grace Church,

---

44. Vos, *Pauline Eschatology*, 61.

45. Dennison, "Introduction," 2–3.

46. Northwest Theological Seminary, "Faculty, Staff and Board of Directors." James Dennison's profile: Now Professor of Church History and Biblical Theology, Academic Dean of NWTS, Lynwood, WA; B.S., Geneva College, 1961; B.D./M.Div., Pittsburgh Theological Seminary, 1968; ThM., Pittsburgh Theological Seminary, 1973. Ordained by the United Presbyterian Church in the United States of America (UPCUSA), 1970; Presbyterian Church in America (PCA), 1979; OPC, Presbytery of the Northwest, 2001-present. Pastor, Pioneer and Pleasant Grove (UPCUSA) Ligionier, PA, 1970–79; Librarian and Lecturer in Church History, Westminster Theological Seminary in California, 1980–2000.

47. Dennison, "Preaching and Application," 44–52. This is a review of Greidanus, *Modern Preacher and the Ancient Text*.

Sewickley, Pennsylvania, in the Orthodox Presbyterian Church (OPC) denomination, from 1976 until his death.[48] His sermons, with their exclusive redemptive-historical character, are found in *Kerux*.[49] William Dennison also seems to have been influenced by Vos and Clowney during his study at WTS from 1973 to 1980. He is now the most able spokesman in the extreme wing of redemptive-historical preaching and one of the most effective contributors to *Kerux*.

NWTS is linked to *Kerux*, and also appears as the new headquarters of the extreme wing of redemptive-historical preaching. J. Peter Vosteen is principal and also pastor of Lynwood OPC, where NWTS opened its doors on 4 September 2001.[50] The conviction of the seminary is clear: "The specific emphasis of NWTS would be Biblical Theology in the tradition of Geerhardus Vos, presuppositional apologetics in the tradition of Cornelius Van Til, and orthodox confessionalism in the classic Calvinistic tradition."[51] We also find *Kerux* appears as its official journal.[52] In fact, faculty membersof NWTS show themselves to be enthusiastic advocates of biblical theology preaching. For example, Vosteen[53] had once respected Clowney and expected him to develop redemptive-historical preaching

---

48. Grace Orthodox Presbyterian Church, "Our History." Charles Dennison was well respected as a preacher, presbyter, and denominational church historian during his service within the OPC.

49. For example, "What is the Gospel?"(Matt 11:2–6); "Eschatology and Office" (Isa 24:23); "August Son" (Jer 8:20); "Jesus, the Multitudes and Us" (Matt 7:7–29); "The Law from the New Mount" (Luke 5:17–26); "Rabboni" (John 20:16); "The New Heavens and the New Earth" (Heb 12:26–29). These sermons are very similar in tone to Vos's sermons in *Grace and Glory*.

50. The seminary was formally organized on 15 September 2000 when the organization decided to bring a new Reformed theological seminary to the Pacific Northwest in order to educate laypersons and ministerial candidates in the effective analysis and use of the Scriptures.

51. Northwest Theological Seminary, "Mission Statement."

52. It seems that the private journal of James Dennison came to be supported by, and merged with, NWTS, when he moved from WTS California to the newly established NWTS.

53. Vosteen founded NWTS in his church. He is the author of "Pastoral Preaching" in *The Preacher and Preaching*, edited bySamuel T. Logan. It is ironic that he only recalled Van Til, Stonehouse, John Murray and Kline as his teachers, whereas he confessed elsewhere that he had Clowney, who had a profound effect on his thinking, as his teacher for all his courses.

further, but he has since expressed disappointment that Clowney had no longer seemed favorable to extreme biblical theology preaching.[54]

Kerux readers and NWTS tend to hold fiercely to Vos's eschatological perspective over that of Clowney's formulation of redemptive-historical preaching, even to the extent that they place all other elements of Scripture into that frame. For example, James Dennison writes:

> It is this eschatological perspective which is so peculiar to Reformed biblical theology. We want to ask . . . about the eschatological dynamic. We are not merely devoted students of redemptive-historical relationships, these retrospective and prospective connections . . . In fact for the whole of the New Testament, he [G. Vos] describes the relationship between those two ages as one of an overlap. The age to come moves forward to invade or overlap this present age. I would like to take Vos a step further . . . to suggest . . . that the age to come, eschatologically, overlaps even the whole Old Testament period.[55]

Here Dennison overrates Vos's eschatological perspective and tries to advance the perspective to the point that it should be applied to every OT text. For example, David's confession that the Lord was his shepherd (Ps 23:1) is eschatologically interpreted so Christ becomes our "eschatological shepherd" and we are His "eschatological lambs."[56] Dennison identifies the shepherd directly with Christ, and the lambs with modern believers, without proper historical ground, and so disregards temporal distance between then and now. On the other hand, Clowney may first describe the meaning of shepherd and lambs in the OT context and then explain how they link to Christ's redemption in the NT era through redemptive history. We can find such typological interpretation in Clowney's diagram.[57]

---

54. Vosteen, "Review," 49–51.

55. Dennison, "Building the Biblical Theological Sermon," part 1: Perspective, 30–43.

56. Dennison, "Shepherd-Lord," 50–55. The term "eschatological" is unnecessarily confusing, because it generally refers to the things of the last days, which begin with Christ's first advent and end with His second coming.

57. Clowney, *Preaching Christ in All of Scripture*, 32. Cf. Clowney, *Preaching and Biblical Theology*, 110. According to Clowney, an OT event symbolizes a truth of God's revelation in the first level (T1); this truth progress through redemptive history and finally arrives at its fulfilment in Christ (Tn). Symbolism means referring to revealed truth as it is manifested in a particular horizon of redemptive history; typology means the prospective reference to the same truth as it is manifested in the period of the

For Vos, eschatology means that the end of history—"the last days" which the OT had prophesied—has come already in the person and work of Jesus Christ, but its consummation, that is, "the last day," lies in the future with Christ's second coming.[58] Vos emphasized that Paul's concept of eschatology informs us that the endowment of Christ with the Spirit and its heavenly blessedness is to be enjoyed in principle by believers here and now.[59] James Dennison emphasizes the eschatological aspect from all of Scripture, but he goes too far in applying it to the whole of the OT. His approach is open to criticism. Firstly, it does not do justice to the OT texts, because it searches exclusively for an eschatological and christological analogy rather than for what the text originally meant. Secondly, it violates the time span of "the last days" by expanding the eschatological era even to Genesis. Thirdly, it usually minimizes the essential aspect of Reformed eschatology, which is the so-called "not yet," in the course of emphasizing only the "already" aspect of eschatology. However, Vos emphasized that the idea of the future by no means recedes into the background.[60] His eschatological perspective always presupposes the consummation of God's redemption in the future, but also its incipient realization in the present, and so he calls the present status "semi-eschatological." Dennison's approach, in disregarding the future aspect of eschatology, does not accord with Vos's view of eschatology. Nevertheless, Dennison considers that his eschatological approach makes an advance on that of Vos and is the best for preaching. He affirms:

> . . . I believe it is the cure for the topical drivel that flows from more and more Reformed pulpits. It is the remedy for the increasing misapplication of Scripture in so called "practical" Christian sermons. And it is the solution to dull, boring and trivial doctrinal or catechetical preaching. In sum, if biblical-theological preaching is the method of correctly exegeting the plan of God, both historically and eschatologically conceived, then biblical-theological preaching is the most biblical, the most theological and the most exciting preaching of all.[61]

---

fullness of truth, namely, of eschatological realization, which is the time of Jesus Christ.

58. Vos, "Eschatology of the New Testament," 26.

59. Vos, "Paul's Eschatological Concept of the Spirit," 124.

60. Vos, *Pauline Eschatology*, 40.

61. Dennison, "Building the Biblical Theological Sermon," part 1: Perspective, 30–43.

For this extreme wing of eschatological redemptive-historical preaching, any other Reformed preaching is wrong unless this Vosian biblical theology approach is followed.[62] This exclusive approach is more evident in the matter of application. Charles Dennison considers that insistence on application is theologically wrong because it regards the Word as deficient, needing to be supplemented by man-centered methods for bridging the "then" of Scripture and the "now" of the modern world.[63] He says, "Over against the seeming monolithic consensus about the program of application stands Geerhardus Vos."[64] He believes that Vos opposes application, but I underline the fact that Dennison's claim is based only on one brief statement by Vos, namely, " . . . we know full well that we ourselves live just as much in the New Testament as did Peter and Paul and John."[65] However, this is an isolated quotation from Vos and furthermore it is at best ambiguous with regard to opposing application.[66] Nevertheless, Charles Dennison wrongly assumes Vos's position, observing that few understand Vos's teaching on this aspect of the subject and are thus capable of using it.[67]

What Charles Dennison implies is that no human preacher can, or should, seek to provide application of the Word as that is the task of the divine text itself. His belief is that we live in the period of the "now,"

62. Dennison, "What is Biblical Theology?" 41. Dennison says, "Preaching which does any less is bankrupt. For anything less is not an exaltation of God in his glory or the Son of God in his mercy . . . but is the promotion of the earthy agenda of the preacher."

63. Dennison, "Preaching and Application," 49–50.

64. Ibid., 52.

65. Vos, *Biblical Theology*, 303.

66. Ibid., 299–304. Vos intends to describe "the structure of New Testament revelation," which should be determined from within Scripture itself. He explains the seeming disproportion in chronological extent between the OT and the NT by considering the NT era as extending until the consummation. It can be said, as a corollary, that we all live in the period of the NT canon. This is the point of Vos's assertion in the section Dennison quoted and it gives no clue that he opposes application.

67. Dennison, "Preaching and Application," 52. Dennison says, "Unfortunately, this fact does not appear to be known 'full well.' Few, if any, seem to work out of a hermeneutic that gives any evidence of having grasped it. And what a shame, since the Bible's point of view is so magnificently sublime. The only real 'then and now' is the 'then' of the old and the 'now' of the new. We live now in the glorious day of salvation that spans the time from our Savior's first advent to his second, or more specifically from his resurrection to ours. There are no 'modern' preachers; there are only preachers."

which is the eschatological period of the NT, while the prophecies and promises for God's kingdom were given in the "then" of the OT. And all things in the "then," that is, the OT, are actually and thoroughly accomplished through Christ in the eschatological "now" of the NT. This means that we live in the period of real application. Thus, no more application is required beyond the Scriptures. While his claim regarding the exclusive role of Scripture appears superficially to be most respectful of Scripture, there is here a crucial fallacy that negates temporal distance between the biblical period "then" and our contemporary "now." It also implies the possibility of the historicity of biblical events evaporating into unhistorical text. Consequently, the most important character of redemptive-historical preaching would then be lost.

At this point I refer to numerous weaknesses in the reasoning of the material which has appeared in *Kerux*. For example, Charles Dennison asserts:

> Good preaching doesn't pull the Word into our world as if the Word were deficient in itself and in need of our applicatory skills. Instead, good preaching testifies and declares to us that we have been pulled into that Word which has its own marvellous sufficiency.[68]

Interestingly, Dennison here does not define the term "preaching" prior to referring to "good preaching," so what turns "preaching" into "good preaching"? Terms are being used loosely here by Dennison. Furthermore, there is no logical relation between people being pulled into the Word and accepting the principle of the sufficiency of God's Word. I question, too, whether Dennison fully appreciates the technical term the "self-sufficiency of Scripture," which I accept as signifying in the Reformed tradition that

> The whole counsel of God, concerning all things necessary for his own glory, man's salvation, faith, and life, is either expressly set down in Scripture, or by good and necessary consequence may be deduced from Scripture: unto which nothing at any time is to be added, whether by new revelations of the Spirit, or traditions of men."[69]

I suggest that Dennison is here confusing two separate ideas, namely, the adding of new revelation or church tradition to Scripture, which would

---

68. Dennison, "Some Thoughts on Preaching."
69. Westminster Assembly, *Westminster Confession of Faith*, 1:6.

violate the Reformation rule of *sola scriptura*, with the separate idea of seeking to apply God's sufficient Word to people in their situations.[70] These two ideas are distinct but are confused in Dennison's reasoning.

One contributor to *Kerux* expresses the kind of exclusivism we have been describing and does so in a critical review of Bryan Chapell's position. The critic concludes: "While Chapell remains forever busy looking for a bridge with which to apply ancient principles to the modern world, Vos finds the ladder that connects heaven to earth, God to His people. Christ is that ladder."[71] But in response to the issue of bridging the text and the people, I question whether there is a major difference between Chapell and Vos. Admittedly, Chapell seeks the bridge from outside the text, while Vos finds it in Christ through the text, but there is no essential conflict necessitating the selection of one option against the other. Chapell is employing a legitimate and primary hermeneutical process in order to bridge "two horizons," namely, the temporal distance between the text and ourselves in the contemporary world. Vos's concern is to identify the redemptive-historical significance of the text which he believed had been supernaturally and organically weaved into the whole of Scripture. The two approaches are equally essential for responsible hermeneutics and also homiletics, and so the *Kerux* contributor is arguing on an improper basis.

We now need to examine in more detail the criticisms of the method of the extreme wing of redemptive-historical preaching.

Opponents of Exclusive Redemptive-Historical Preaching

There have been many renowned critics of the extreme wing of redemptive-historical preaching. Carrick has named several scholars, including Hendrik Krabbendam, Jay Adams, John R. De Witt, and John Frame, who have links with WTS.[72] There are others, like Roy Taylor and David Murray, who are also well known. The criticisms of these differ one from another, and so we need to examine each one briefly in order to understand the criticisms relating to the exclusive redemptive-historical approach.

---

70. MacArthur, "The Sufficiency of the Written Word," 151–83.
71. Findley, Review of *Christ-Centered Preaching*, 37–41.
72. Carrick, *Imperative of Preaching*, 117–119.

Firstly, Hendrik Krabbendam criticized the redemptive-historical method of preaching of both the Dutch and American proponents for not focusing primarily on the given text; they impose their preferred redemptive-historical scheme on the text. Krabbendam wrote, "What is the function of the text in the RH method? It has been astutely observed that the focus of this method is not first and foremost the text, but rather the various facts and stages of unfolding RH."[73] The claim, then, is that the text in this method is often violated to comply with a narrow understanding of redemptive history. However, a Christians needs help from the biblical text in his daily life.[74]

Krabbendam distinguishes the meaning of the text from its significance. For him, the biblical text has only one unchangeable meaning, which is the authorial intent, but the significance of the text is manifold because the persons, situations, and predicaments to which the text should be related are manifold.[75] Thus preaching, as delivering the message or meaning of the biblical text to people in the world, requires not only thorough exegesis of the text but also understanding of its relevant significance for the different situations of the hearers. The latter definitely depends on the former and subsequently bears upon the life of the hearer. Krabbendam therefore criticized the redemptive-historical method as missing the full meaning of the text and its corresponding significance.[76] I regard his criticism as valid, at least regarding *Kerux* advocates, in that for them redemptive-historical preaching is only interested in the eschatological meaning rather than the authorial intent of the text.

Secondly, Adams thinks some biblical theology preachers have been influenced by neo-orthodoxy and so consequently tend to oppose the use of application in sermons. According to Adams, Barth, the father of neo-orthodoxy, thinks it is impossible for humans to apply Scripture, for this task belongs to God alone. For Barth, the application is made through a "direct encounter between man and God," which is the critical, existential and revelatory moment in which he can make a decision and respond, and the preacher has no part to play in that sacred moment of encounter where the Bible "becomes" the Word of God to that individual.[77] It is pos-

---

73. Krabbendam, "Hermeneutics and Preaching," 235.
74. Ibid., 236.
75. Ibid., 229–30.
76. Ibid., 236.
77. Adams, *Truth Applied*, 19–20.

sible that elements or perceptions of Barth's teaching may have affected some biblical theology preachers in this subtle manner. Adams adds at this point:

> Conservative biblical-theological preachers, sailing in the wake of Geerhardus Vos, tend to ignore (or even oppose) the use of application in a sermon. They expect the listener to make his own application (if any) of the sweeping truth they set forth on their excursions from Genesis to Revelation as they chase down a figure or a theme. Or, like Barth, they leave the application to God. The two major differences between some present-day preachers and Barth is that the former (1) do not hold to the Neoorthodox 'encounter,' and (2) are less concerned about the contemporary scene than Barth.[78]

Here Adams contends that to oppose the use of direct application and to leave application to the listener or God's arena makes the biblical theology preachers stand on the same ground with Barth, even though they disagree theologically. However Adams did not provide proper reasons for his identifying conservative biblical theology preaching with Barth's, other than that of application. Thus, I am not impressed by his criticism, for Adams does not argue or support his case well and his criticism is invalid.

For Adams, application is an indispensable task for the preacher, because preaching is heralding rather than mere exposition, lecturing or sharing. I note that *Kerux* contributors also claim to be heralds (*kerux*), so Adams suggests they are not fulfilling that task without applying the text. Another consideration is that the original Greek term *kerux* implies not only proclaiming God's truth but also accomplishing the divine purpose in His people.[79]

---

78. Ibid., 21. Adams commented in a footnote, "For a good example of the sort of biblical-theological sermon about which I am speaking, see Geerhardus Vos, *Grace and Glory* (Grand Rapids: Reformed Press, 1922). Although these sermons are beautifully written and full of instructive matter, there is no application in them."

79. Adams, *Preaching with Purpose*, 6–15.

Thirdly, De Witt, Emeritus Professor of Church History in RTS from 1975 to 1982,[80] joined in criticizing the redemptive-historical approach.[81] While De Witt intended to describe the main failing in evangelical preaching, and in doing so referred to the insight of the redemptive-historical method as valid, yet he regarded warm, pointed, applicatory preaching as essential. He stated, however, that he had not seen the two conflicting methods of evangelical and redemptive-historical preaching harmonized until 1980, so there was need of more work. "If the RH interpretative principle robs men of power in the pulpit," he writes, "there is something radically wrong with it. And I fear that it has done just this in not a few instances."[82] He viewed redemptive-historical preaching as powerless and requiring radical improvement, though he provides no details or reasons. However, one statement he makes throws light on the matter. Essentially he criticizes younger Reformed ministers who are indifferent to the careful crafting and preparation of sermons, claiming that God is sovereign in accomplishing His purpose whatever the sermon is like. That is a form of fatalism by which these preachers excuse themselves of the responsibility of preparing well for preaching. De Witt describes this attitude as "disastrous and intolerable." He views "dullness" and a "boring" approach in preaching as inexcusable, and I agree.[83]

Fourthly, Frame criticizes redemptive-historical preaching in a similar way to De Witt: "Young preachers who try to preach RH sermons often spend so much time preparing the theology of their message that they completely neglect rhetorical consideration, i.e. communication."[84] He advises young preachers to preach the gospel of grace clearly, and its proper relationship with regard to works.

According to Frame, there are eight "major dangers" in preaching exclusively on redemptive-historical themes:

---

80. De Witt graduated from WTS (BD) and received a DD from Rhodes College. He has over fifty years' experience of pastoral ministry. He was Professor of Church History and Systematic Theology in Reformed Theological Seminary, Jackson (1975–1982), Senior Pastor of Second Presbyterian Church in Columbia, SC (1983–1992), and Moderator of the General Synod of the Associate Reformed Presbyterian Church (2009). He is also the translator of Ridderbos, *Paul*.

81. De Witt, "Contemporary Failure in the Pulpit," 19–24. This is a personal letter sent to Samuel T. Logan in 1980, in response to a request which Logan sent to several ministerial brethren asking for their views on the subject of preaching.

82. Ibid., 20.

83. Ibid., 22.

84. Frame, "Ethics, Preaching, and Biblical Theology."

1. Biblical truth can be de-emphasized as, for example, when a preacher disregards the specifics of Rom 12 because of an exclusive focus on redemptive-historical themes in Rom 1–11.
2. Application would be ignored or limited.
3. Refusal to make practical, ethical application signifies a failure to preach the whole counsel of God, and not adequately edify believers.
4. A preacher would be obsessed with a jargon-laden vocabulary, like "eschatological."
5. An exclusive emphasis on redemptive history can become repetitive and boring.
6. Zeal for redemptive-historical preaching often leads to a critical attitude towards those who do not share the same emphasis.
7. An excessive emphasis on redemptive history exposes preachers to the danger of illogical dogmatism.
8. For young preachers especially, the redemptive-historical method requires considerable time preparing the theology for the sermon, which often fails to communicate with the people.[85]

Frame strongly recommends young preachers to keep to the normative aspects of biblical ethics, as well as the redemptive-historical contexts in Scripture, yet he commends Clowney and, surprisingly, Dennison.[86]

Taylor, Professor of Homiletics at RTS,[87] pointed out a threefold problem with regard to preaching without application.[88] He considers such preaching unbiblical and ineffective because it deviates from mainstream Protestant preaching. He referred to English Puritans, like William Perkins, who emphasized that preaching should explain the biblical text clearly and apply it to the situations of its hearers.[89] Taylor's criticism

---

85. Ibid.

86. Ibid. Frame says, "The best RH preachers understand this [application is necessary for good preaching]. Some of the most powerful ethical preaching I have heard has come from Ed. Clowney and Jim Dennison." After describing the dangers of exclusive redemptive-historical preaching, he adds at the end, "I think it is usually counter-productive for young preachers to try to emulate the profundity of Clowney or Dennison."

87. Taylor served as Professor of Practical Theology at RTS, Jackson, for ten years and has served as adjunct professor at RTS, Atlanta, since 1998.

88. Taylor, "So What?" 109–14.

89. Ibid., 110;. cf. Lewis, *Genius of Puritanism*, 144.

of redemptive-historical preaching differs from others in that he provides more simple grounds for criticizing the redemptive-historical method in terms of the Bible, the Reformed tradition, and contemporary relevance.[90]

Murray, Professor of Old Testament and Practical Theology at Puritan Reformed Theological Seminary since 2007,[91] enumerates ten weaknesses of exclusive redemptive-historical preaching:[92]

1. Lack of application.
2. Confusion of one meaning with multiple application.[93]
3. Limiting preaching to one style.
4. The exclusion of biblical examples.
5. An overemphasis on definitive sanctification.
6. Preoccupation with eschatology.
7. A more mystical view of the Christian life.[94]
8. Dehumanizing the Bible.
9. A failure to distinguish between morality and moralism.
10. The danger of Christomonism.

Murray's analysis repeats previous criticisms and differs only slightly from that of Frame's in suggesting that redemptive-historical preaching should be encouraged provided it avoids the dangers identified, whereas Frame recommends not engaging in redemptive-historical preaching in the early years of ministry.[95] Murray commends Jonathan Edwards's sermons as a good example of Puritan redemptive-historical preaching.

---

90. Ibid., 114. This deduction was made due to his wife's evaluation of his own past preaching in that manner.

91. PRTS, Grand Rapids, MI, was opened by Dr. Joel R. Beeke in 1995 with the acceptance of four seminary students from the Heritage Reformed Congregations. Its goal is to prepare ministers who will faithfully endeavor to propagate and defend Reformed theology. There are four full time professors including Murray and thirty visiting lecturers.

92. Murray, "Dangers of Redemptive-Historical Preaching."

93. Krabbendam discussed this matter and concluded that the redemptive-historical approach failed in arriving at the original meaning of the text and its various significances. Murray makes the same point in different words.

94. Jay Adams criticized this problem as the common ground with Barthian theology.

95. Frame, "Ethics, Preaching, and Biblical Theology."

GPTS recently emerged as the leading opponent of redemptive-historical preaching among American theological schools, partly due to the fact that the recent theological debate on the subject took place in GPTS's Spring Conference in 2002 and John Carrick, a professor at GPTS, emerged as an excellent debater against the redemptive-historical method. One purpose of GPTS is " . . . to provide for the Church an adequate supply and succession of able and faithful New Covenant ministers of the Word and sacraments . . . accurately handling the Word of truth; reproving, rebuking, and exhorting by means of expository, experimental, and application preaching."[96] Its website also claims that GPTS seeks "experimental Calvinism."[97] This goal of GPTS is diametrically opposed to that of *Kerux* and NWTS and their basic allegiance to Vos's biblical theology, Van Til's presuppositionalism, and the confessionalism of classic Calvinism. This 2002 Conference has the most confrontational debate between the two parties conducted by reputable scholars, and we will discuss it in the following section.

There are many more opponents and criticisms of the exclusive redemptive-historical approach to preaching than we have examined, but I have identified a fair and comprehensive cross-section of these criticisms. For example, when criticizing redemptive-historical preaching, Krabbendam speaks of a hermeneutical fallacy, while Adams suspects that the redemptive-historical approach is linked to Barth. De Witt refers to the hermeneutical problem of powerlessness, Frame and David Murray warn comprehensively of the dangers of redemptive-historical preaching and, in a complementary manner, Roy Taylor identifies a threefold problem in that preaching. However all these criticisms converge into one basic principle—that application is essential in preaching. I submit that the question of application in Reformed preaching has become the essential issue in the American debate.

We now need to examine the ground motives of each debating party in order to understand more clearly their respective campaigns for or against application.

---

96. Greenville Presbyterian Theological Seminary, *2010–2013 Academic Catalog*, 8.
97. Greenville Presbyterian Theological Seminary, "Faculty," line 2.

Dilemma: Explication versus Application / Indicative versus Imperative

William Dennison, in the 2002 GPTS Conference, attempted to resolve the deadlock in the debate concerning redemptive-historical preaching. For him, the major criticism focused on the issue of application, concerning which there is a dilemma in Reformed circles. He writes: "Over the past fifteen years I have come to believe that the application debate regarding biblical theology is an issue of one's presupposition."[98] In other words, he suggests that each party approaches the issue of application in the grid of their own thought system. Although most advocates on both sides accept progressive biblical revelation and acknowledge application as being essential in Christianity, they cannot reach agreement on application.

Employing Van Til's presuppositional theory, Dennison tries to dismantle the criticisms of redemptive-historical preaching. Quoting Roland N. Stromberg,[99] he claims that the Greek and Judeo-Christian traditions have contributed to two essential elements in Western historiography: the meaningfulness of time, namely, the self-determination of man as he is placed in different life situations (Greek), and, by contrast, God governing all events in history as it moves towards its final goal (Judeo-Christian).[100] Consequently, for ancient historians, like Herodotus (484–435 BC) and Tacitus (59–120 AD), history is subordinate to ethics, that is, moral principles, for the self-determination of people. In medieval education, history was a subtopic of grammar and rhetoric, which were also used for ethical lessons. For William Dennison, this subservient rhetoric in the medieval period had influenced church homiletics, so the concept that preaching intends to shape human belief and morality, or that biblical history may serve ethics and faith, must be the result of the influence of classical rhetoric.[101]

---

98. Dennison, "Biblical Theology and the Issue of Application," 121.

99. Stromberg (1916–2004) was an American historian who taught in several universities in America: University of Maryland (1947–66); Southern Illinois University (1966–67); University of Wisconsin (1967–87). Cf. Merrick, "Roland Stromberg."

100. Conkin and Stromberg, *Heritage and Challenge of History*, 16; quoted in Dennison, "Biblical Theology and the Issue of Application," 123.

101. Dennison, "Biblical Theology and the Issue of Application," 129.

This trait, he argues, is still found widely in Reformed pulpits, as exemplified by William Shedd,[102] Robert L. Dabney,[103] and Martyn Lloyd-Jones. For example, when Lloyd-Jones maintains in his *Preaching and Preachers* that all preaching must be expository and identify a particular doctrine which has been derived from the text,[104] that is, in Dennison's judgment, evidence of his homiletics being influenced by the classical rhetoric in which history serves ethics. Dennison proceeds to claim: "Herein, the essential pattern of the classical model raises its head once again; history has a subordinate position in the enterprise."[105]

For Dennison, there are others, such as Geoff Thomas, Jay Adams, John Frame, Bryan Chappell, and Hendrik Krabbendam, who are involved in this kind of expository preaching, which distinguishes between the "indicative and imperative" structure of biblical revelation. The "indicative" serves to explain from the given text the historical facts and their significance in God's redemption for His people, whereas the "imperative" speaks out the commands of necessary response to the Word. The traditional balance exists between interpreting the historical character of the text and applying it to our lives. Dennison considers this balance a synthesis of the classical rhetoric with biblical revelation, as Western culture consists of both the Greek tradition and the Judeo-Christian. He concludes: "In this context, it seems to me, the synthesis of classical rhetoric with 'revealed Biblical religion' is fundamental to the structure of the traditional expository and exemplary sermon: it has not overcome that synthesis."[106] Moreover, he reckons that this synthesis is the root problem of the application issue. Thus traditional expository preaching, which maintains balance between the indicative and the imperative is, for Dennison, synthetic rather than thoroughly biblical. To put it in a Van Til context, the starting point of traditional preaching is in the rational-empirical world of antiquity.[107]

In response, I question Dennison's claim that the indicative and imperative in traditional preaching is deduced from classical rhetoric. He assumes, merely on the ground that the Greek tradition has a

---

102. Shedd, *Homiletics and Pastoral Theology*, 33.
103. Dabney, *Sacred Rhetoric*, 30–48.
104. Lloyd-Jones, *Preaching and Preachers*, 75.
105. Dennison, "Biblical Theology and the Issue of Application," 134.
106. Ibid., 136.
107. Ibid.

characteristic of emphasizing the self-determination of man in history, that to add the ethical imperative is due to the influence of classical rhetoric. However, it is clear that there are also many ethical imperatives in the Judeo-Christian tradition, especially in the Scriptures. We discuss this matter in more detail later on in this chapter. I submit that Dennison's suspicion that all preaching with the indicative and imperative balance is tainted by undesirable classical rhetoric is based on his own assumption, which is invalid.

Nor is Dennison justified in asserting that the advocates of biblical theology preaching are not tainted by the classical worldview because they never make biblical history and events an instrument for ethical instruction. For Dennison, even the Reformers, like Luther and Calvin, could not overcome the Greek influence, since grammar was prior to history in their hermeneutics, namely, the grammatical-historical principle. On the other hand, Vos broke out of that influence, and so his followers are free from it. Dennison writes:

> Standing on the back of the Reformers, Vos provides the weapon to demolish the classical world-view; he moves the discipline of history or, more specifically, the self-disclosure of God in history, to the front of the paradigm . . . Perhaps the paradigm shift (from the Reformers to Vos) can best be described in light of hermeneutics: the grammatical-historical method of interpretation became the historical-grammatical method of interpretation.[108]

Dennison is here claiming that in Vos's historical-grammatical paradigm, grammar (language), rhetoric, logic, and ethics are now subordinate to the Triune God of the Bible and the revelation of Himself in history. However, it is unclear how the grammatical-historical method became different from the historical-grammatical method. There is no essential difference between the Reformers and Vos in hermeneutics. Dennison's assertion that advocates of Vos's biblical theology keep themselves from classical influence is thus invalid.

Dennison then offers a biblical example for that method from the apostle Paul, who did not approach the Corinthians with "eloquence" or "persuasive words" (the classic rhetoric) but instead with preaching Christ and Him crucified (history of redemption) "with a demonstration of the Spirit's power" (1 Cor 2:1, 4). Dennison comments, "Good

---

108. Ibid., 146.

Biblical preaching draws the congregation into the event ... in Paul the Holy Spirit infallibly interprets the actual death and resurrection of Jesus Christ in history."[109] He then provides another example for ethical application from the biblical text: when God gave the Ten Commandments to Israel. God's great salvation of His people from Egypt set the context for faithful obedience (Exod 20:3). He also adds Paul's confession in Gal 2:20–21 to these examples. Dennison affirms there is no moral Christian life without Christ, and the imperative for ethics is grounded in the indicative of Christ's death and resurrection.[110] This is agreed to by his opponents, like Frame and Carrick, who would support Dennison here.

But Dennison goes further to emphasize the nature of biblical application at this point: "The preacher does not take the word and apply it to you, but the preacher takes you and applies you to the word."[111] Dennison means that biblical application is "assimilation" of oneself with the text, so that the believer participates in, or merges into, the events or the characters of the biblical text.[112] Conversely, the critics of biblical theology use the text as an instrument of "aspiration," where application is made with ethical principles extracted from biblical examples, such as Abraham's act of faith in offering Isaac, Moses's strength before Pharaoh, David's defiance before Goliath, and Christ quoting Scripture to resist Satan.[113] A preacher therefore urges the congregation to emulate these biblical examples. Here the classical "self-determination" seems to be revived, so that Dennison claims from Van Til's presuppositional perspective that "the critic of BT is tainted by the rational-empirical classical worldview."[114]

Now the dilemma of application (application versus explication, or imperative versus indicative) becomes, for Dennison, apparent between two different presuppositions. One is allegedly influenced by the classical-rational worldview, and the other by Vos's biblical theology. The former seeks allegedly a hearer's "self-determination," but the latter drives him to "union with the text." Thus it becomes the struggle between application "from text to you" and "from you to text," or "aspiration" and "assimilation." Dennison concludes: "Specifically, the critic of BT understands

---

109. Ibid., 147.
110. Ibid., 149.
111. Ibid.
112. Dennison, "Redemptive-Historical Hermeneutic,'" 27.
113. Ibid.
114. Dennison, "Biblical Theology and the Issue of Application," 150.

application as a moral concept in distinction from the historical events in the biblical text, whereas the biblical theologian understands application as a moral concept in union with the historical events of the biblical text."[115] Here Dennison does not deny in theory the necessity of application, but rejects in practice the traditional application pattern.

John Carrick, responding to Dennison's argument in the 2002 Conference, gives his own analysis on the issue of application: "Preaching that lacks application is the bane of the modern Reformed pulpit."[116] He also concurs with Robert Dabney's aphorism, that the great aim of the preaching of the Word is "to produce a definite practical volition in the hearer." For Carrick, the homiletical ideal of the balance between explication and application of the Word is one which accords with the analogy of Scripture.[117] After reviewing the Dutch "exemplary versus redemptive-historical" debate, and examining several criticisms of redemptive-historical preaching, Carrick assesses that preaching as having gone astray through its failure to note and to implement the indicative-imperative pattern or structure of New Testament Christianity. Here Carrick disagrees with Dennison.[118] What is the difference between them?

Carrick appeals to several Reformed theologians like J. Gresham Machen[119] and Sinclair B. Ferguson[120] in support of the indicative-imperative pattern in preaching. Carrick affirms that Christianity begins with an indicative whereas liberalism always moves to the imperative.[121] For John Murray, in the context of sanctification of the saints, "the interweaving of the indicative and the imperative" is heightened.[122] Gaffin emphasizes the indicative-imperative structure, especially the principle

---

115. Ibid.

116. Thomas, "Powerful Preaching," 380, quoted in Carrick, "Redemptive-Historical Preaching," 119.

117. Carrick, "Redemptive-Historical Preaching," 155.

118. Dennison, "Redemptive-Historical Hermeneutic," 37.

119. Machen, *Christianity and Liberalism*, 47: "Christianity is a religion founded not on aspiration, but on facts. Here is found the most fundamental difference between liberalism and Christianity—liberalism is altogether in the imperative mood, while Christianity begins with a triumphant indicative." Although Machen specifically emphasized the indicative mood, he did so in order to highlight the fundamental difference between the two systems.

120. Ferguson, "Exegesis," 193.

121. Carrick, "Redemptive-Historical Preaching," 157.

122. Murray, *Collected Writings*, vol. 2, 280–81, quoted in Carrick, "Redemptive-Historical Preaching," 158.

of "irreversibility" and "inseparability" between the two moods. The "irreversibility" means that the indicative always precedes and the order is never transposed. The "inseparability" means the two moods always go together in the theology and preaching of the NT, as in Paul's writing.[123] For Carrick, the validity of the indicative-imperative pattern is abundantly endorsed in these authoritative Reformed scholars, but also in Scripture.

Carrick searches the Bible for irrefutable evidences of the validity of the indicative-imperative pattern, firstly, by using 1 Cor 10:5–11 where he contends that when Paul draws a straight line from the Israelites in the wilderness to the Corinthians in the first century, he has turned the indicative into the imperative.[124] Then Carrick insists that Heb 11 is both powerfully christocentric and also exemplaristic. Referring to the Epistle of James, he asks: "Does the RH school regard James's reference to Elijah as atomistic and moralistic, or not?"[125] He alludes to Christ's instruction in John 13:15 as possibly Himself being our example, and to Peter's description of Christ's suffering as our model to follow. From these passages endorsing the validity of scriptural example, Carrick affirms that the christocentric aspect does not, and must not, exclude the exemplary; likewise the indicatives of history must not exclude the imperatives of ethics.[126]

Carrick then claims that "*Kerux* reveals a striking emphasis upon the centrality of Christ and upon the believer's union with Christ . . . *Kerux* reveals a striking lack of emphasis upon the need for repentance and sanctification."[127] For example, the phrases appearing in *Kerux* such as "you are part of a cosmic drama . . . the Logos is yours!,"[128] "I leave you today participating in the story—the story of the birth of Immanuel,"[129]

---

123. Gaffin, "Reformed Hermeneutics," part 3. This is a series of lectures delivered at the Annual OPC Home Missions Training Conference at Camp Geneva in Holland, Michigan, 16–19 May 1998. Quoted in Carrick, "Redemptive-Historical Preaching," 158–159.

124. Carrick, "Redemptive Historical Preaching,"160.

125. Ibid., 162. Gaffin comments on this part: "A minor point of the text may on occasion legitimately be a major emphasis of the sermon." He means that a seemingly trivial thing in the text of 1 Kgs 18, that is, Elijah's faithful prayer, becomes a very important message in James's epistle. Cf. Gaffin, "Reformed Hermeneutics," part 2.

126. Ibid., 163.

127. Ibid.

128. Dennison, "Life, Light, Lamb and the Logos," 36.

129. Dennison, "Born of the Virgin Mary," 25.

"find your story within the structure of John's story of Jesus,"[130] and "find your life in the text of the word of God"[131] are at best quasi-application.

In addition, Carrick refers to a maxim of the *Kerux* contributors as expressed by Charles Dennison: "Good preaching is God-centered, not man-centered . . . Good preaching does not make the text meaningful for us and our contemporary situation meaningful; rather good preaching makes us and our contemporary situation meaningful in the text."[132] Here, he finds a faulty dichotomy between God-centered and man-centered preaching. But there can be good God-centered preaching, other than the exclusive redemptive-historical model, whilst making the text meaningful for hearers. For example, Calvin as a preacher strove to bridge the gap from the text to everyday life by showing its practical relevance, while he believed in the relevancy of the Bible itself, and fulfilled the task through divinely prescribed means, such as encouragement, rebuke, reproof, correction, consolation, and challenge.[133] Calvin made the text meaningful to people in the pew, so why have *Kerux* writers raised an arbitrary tension between traditional preaching and their method?

Carrick traces the root of the problem back to Vos's biblical theology, referring to James Dennison's article, "What is Biblical Theology?" He identified four fallacies in the extreme wing of redemptive-historical preaching. Firstly, proponents are obsessed with Vos's biblical theology, regarding it as the only hermeneutical methodology available to, or legitimate for, the theologian or preacher to use.[134] However, this was not Vos's intention, because in his inaugural address he warned specifically against attempts to supplant systematic theology.[135] Secondly, they show an excessive emphasis on the one-sided eschatological aspect of Vos's es-

---

130. Dennison, "John 2," 12.

131. Dennison, "Paul on the Damascus Road," 27.

132. Dennison, "Some Thought on Preaching," 6, quoted in Carrick, "Redemptive-Historical Preaching," 164.

133. Lawson, *Expository Genius of John Calvin*, 104.

134. Carrick, "Redemptive-Historical Preaching," 166.

135. Vos, "Idea of Biblical Theology," 23–24. Vos said, "The very name Biblical Theology is frequently vaunted so as to imply a protest against the alleged un-Biblical character of Dogmatics. I desire to state most emphatically here, that there is nothing in the nature and aims of Biblical Theology to justify such an implication. For anything pretending to supplant Dogmatics is the crown which grows out of all the work that Biblical Theology can accomplish." In this respect, Lloyd-Jones's emphasis on doctrinal preaching is not in discordance with that of Vos. Cf. Lloyd-Jones, *Preaching and Preachers*, 75.

chatology. However, Vos's eschatology is more full-orbed, not restricted to semi-eschatological aspects, but also placing emphasis on the second coming of Christ.[136] Thirdly, they excessively under-emphasize the ethical aspects of Christianity in the course of over-emphasizing the one-sided eschatological aspect; this is intensified by their own phrase: "eschatology is prior to soteriology!"[137] However, according to Carrick, Vos never mentioned that eschatology is always superior to soteriology. Fourthly, they demonstrate an idealization, or an idolizing, of Vos as a preacher, which must be challenged.[138] Vos's preaching is far from being ideal, and Carrick rightly judges that his sermons savor too much of theological essays which can only be appreciated by those who are well educated; his sermons show a minimal level of application.[139] Adams and Machen also support this point.[140]

Finally, Carrick affirms that true preaching involves a balance between the indicative and imperative moods. Adhering to the definition of preaching—*explicatio et applicatio verbi Dei*: the explication and application of the Word of God—he maintains that true preaching is not mere explication or exhortation. Carrick quotes Gaffin again:

> A proper grasp, a proper maintenance of the relationship between the indicative and the imperative get us right to the heart of the Christian life, whereas where that relationship is not properly maintained, deviations—distortions of a more or less serious character—are going to enter the picture.[141]

Nevertheless, the tension between the two debating parties has not yet been resolved. William Dennison, in his reply to Carrick, insists he does not recognize himself in the criticisms of redemptive-historical preaching, especially with regard to the lack of application.[142] He maintains he agrees with the indicative-imperative paradigm, referring to his article in the *Calvin Theological Journal* in 1979. For Dennison, the contempo-

136. Carrick, "Redemptive-Historical Preaching," 166–67.
137. Ibid., 167–68.
138. Ibid., 168–69.
139. Ibid., 169.
140. Cf. Adams, *Truth Applied*, 20: see especially footnote no. 4; and Stonehouse, *J. Gresham Machen*, 72. Machen said, "He is usually rather too severely theological for Sunday morning." Quoted also in Ferguson, "Introduction," viii.
141. Gaffin, "Reformed Hermeneutics," part 3, quoted in Carrick, *Imperative of Preaching*, 146.
142. Hamilton, "Wherein Consists Reformed Spirituality?" 12.

rary controversy came from two different presuppositions, but Carrick disagreed as he felt it to be a matter of balance between the two moods, not an issue of presuppositions. Dennison replied that he was not interested in "balance," which he regarded as an Aristotelian golden-mean concept, but rather in intimate or existential union.[143] The discussion seems endless, and I will discuss in chapter 6 the possibility of a commonly accepted criterion which may contribute to resolving or reducing the tension.

I now intend to evaluate the discussion between Dennison and Carrick.

Evaluation and Suggestions

In evaluating the above debate, several criticisms can be made regarding the respective approaches of both William Dennison and Carrick.

Firstly, I judged that Dennison's approach was inappropriate for fruitful discussion. Embracing Van Til's presuppositional theory, his major thesis was that critics of biblical theology were influenced in some degree by the old rational-empirical worldview, whereas the exponents of biblical theology, like himself, were free from such influence.[144] This approach was originally oriented as antithetical to catholicism's synthetic approach.[145] It emphasizes that God is all-sufficient, self-explanatory, and speaks with absolute authority through the Scriptures, which therefore do not require an appeal to human reason for their ultimate justification.[146] This approach has provided not only a powerful impetus for reform in Christian thinking,[147] but also great help in defending the Reformed faith from temptation to compromise with the secularization of the church.[148] Further, sadly, this censorious approach entails a "them versus us" attitude and expresses strong antagonism to other Reformed colleagues.[149] Frame

---

143. Ibid., 13.
144. Dennison, "Biblical Theology and the Issue of Application," 150.
145. Van Til, *Defense of the Faith*, 3–6.
146. Van Til, *Christian Theory of Knowledge*, 13–15.
147. Bahnsen, *Van Til's Apologetic*, 12–13.
148. Hart and Muether, "Why Machen Hired Van Til."
149. Rushdoony, "Foreword," viii. Rushdoony states, "His [Van Til's] critique is directed to the presuppositions of thought with a radical thoroughness. This fact accounts for the nature of Van Til's influence: he either reshapes the thinking of those who come within his orbit or incurs their consistent opposition."

reports there were partisan battles, though he does not give concrete references, over Van Til's apologetics in recent Reformed history, which resulted in schism within a Reformed school.[150] Even Dennison acknowledged, "I have become convinced that this is not a fruitful discussion."[151]

Secondly, Carrick cannot escape criticism either, for he misunderstood the nature of the American homiletical controversy by identifying it with the Dutch homiletical debate. Such an approach was unhelpful because the *Kerux* writers themselves had not aligned themselves with the redemptive-historical school within the Dutch debate, and so Dennison could rightly protest, "I don't see myself in terms of the Netherlands discussion."[152] Nevertheless, Carrick confused the two debates and identified Dennison with them, assuming that the extreme wing of redemptive-historical preaching, especially the *Kerux* writers, maintained fundamentally the same points, such as eliminating the exemplary use of the text, as the redemptive-historical school in the Dutch debate. For example, Carrick states, "Historically, this tendency on the part of the redemptive-historical school to supress, or even to eliminate, the note of exhortation in preaching emerged . . . "[153] He then links this to the contemporary situation: "This tendency to suppress or to eliminate the imperative mood is evident more recently both in the homiletical philosophy and the published expositions of *Kerux*."[154] Carrick also attributes the principles of redemptive-historical preaching to both "the extreme wing of the RH school," that is, the *Kerux* supporters, and "the RH school in the Netherlands," thus making no distinction between the two schools. He says:

> Indeed, we believe that the RH school has yet to provide a satisfactory refutation of the position that the writer to the Hebrews in chapter eleven, the Apostle Paul in 1 Corinthians 10, James in chapter five, and the Lord Jesus Christ in Luke 17 ('Remember Lot's wife') all endorse the validity and the spiritual value of scriptural examples . . . The Christocentric does not and must not exclude the exemplary; the indicatives of history do not and must not exclude the imperatives of ethics.[155]

---

150. Frame, "Ethics, Preaching, and Biblical Theology." Frame did not specifically name the school in which the schism happened.
151. Hamilton, "Wherein Consists Reformed Spirituality?" 13.
152. Ibid., 12.
153. Carrick, "Redemptive-Historical Preaching," 154.
154. Ibid., 163.
155. Ibid.

It is clear, here, that for Carrick the redemptive-historical school in the Dutch debate overlaps the extreme wing of the redemptive-historical school in the American debate. However, I must point out that there are explicit and crucial distinctions to be made between these two schools, even if there was also a considerable similarity between them. The differences need to be identified and I will do this in more detail in the next section.

Thirdly, Carrick and Dennison fail to address their respective arguments. For example, Dennison is concerned that traditional preaching is being influenced by classical rhetoric, which focuses only on "man's self-determination," and so claims that Reformed preaching should change its "indicative and imperative" aspect to the "imperative within indicative," which is allegedly purely biblical. Dennison maintains that " . . . the biblical theologian understands application as a moral concept in union with the historical events of the biblical text."[156] In response, I suggest Carrick should have explained clearly that the indicative and imperative structure is not rooted in the classical worldview, and especially that the imperative mood has nothing to do with the classically tainted self-determination. But Carrick focuses only on the legitimacy of a "balance" in using the indicative-imperative, as he criticized the extreme redemptive-historical denial of application. Dennison's response, "I'm not interested in balance!" only confirms Carrick's misunderstanding. Carrick insists that Vos's eschatology does not support the exclusivism of the extreme wing, specifically in excluding the ethical aspects of the Christian's life, which means the imperative mood in Scripture. In his response, Dennison should have argued that their exclusive approach is thoroughly consistent with Vos's biblical theology and eschatology, but instead he only emphasizes the antithesis between Vos's biblical theology and its critics, implying that opponents of the extreme wing must be opponents of Vos's biblical theology. Even though he appeals to the validity of the "exclusive indicative mood," this is irrelevant and fails to provide an adequate explanation for the basis of his exclusive approach. I submit that both Carrick and Dennison fail to engage with each other's position.

Notwithstanding, there are benefits which arise from the debate. It challenges us to reconsider Vos's biblical theology with its redemptive-historical principles, then to exercise more caution concerning a possible rationalist approach, with its more human-centeredness, affecting

---

156. Dennison, "Biblical Theology and the Issue of Application," 150.

exemplary preaching in Reformed churches. There is also a warning from the debate regarding the danger of overemphasizing certain aspects and implications of Vos's biblical theology.

I submit further that the American debate still leaves critical issues untouched. Participants in the debate, at least Carrick and Dennison, appear too preoccupied with criticizing their opponents rather than in attempting to reach the heart of the debate. From my research I identify several themes requiring more careful in-depth analysis and evaluation. These themes include the following: Does Vos's biblical theology really reject or neglect the imperative mood? Is it correct to maintain that Vos's eschatology actually excludes the ethical aspects relating to the lives of believers? Can the principle of "union with Christ" be compatible with "self-determination"? Furthermore, I am intrigued as to why Vos's sermons use so little application or the imperative. Are there theological reasons restraining Vos in this respect? All these questions can be reduced to one major comprehensive question, namely, how should we perceive and interpret Vos's biblical theology with regard to the imperative mood or application? Dennison and Carrick both fail to investigate this major question with its various aspects.

I acknowledge that Dennison quotes Vos many times in order to justify his method, but in most cases the quotations are unclear and even incorrect. For example, Dennison claims that Vos supports him in maintaining that "the imperative is implied in the indicative," by saying, "Vos put it this way: the indicative effects or is the source of the imperative."[157] Here, however, it is definitely far from clear that Vos endorses a hiding of the imperative mood within the indicative. The statement could be understood as confirming the position of his opponent. In addition, this quotation is incorrectly referenced by Dennison in the footnote[158] and this carelessness does not engender confidence in his scholarship. Carrick is equally as guilty as Dennison. He claims dogmatically that "Vos's own treatment of eschatology is not restricted to this aspect of eschatology (as in Dennison's approach); it is much more full-orbed and includes, for instance, a strong emphasis upon the

---

157. Ibid., 144.

158. Dennison states that he is citing Vos, "The Eschatological Aspect of the Pauline Conception of the Spirit," 237, but that essay is, in fact, placed in pages 91–125; in addition, the article titled "The Doctrine of the Covenant in Reformed Theology," 234–67, on the page 237 that Dennison refers to, has nothing to do with Dennison's intention to get support from Vos. Neither passage matches Dennison's citation.

second coming of Christ."¹⁵⁹ This statement appears to be a refutation of his opponent, but Carrick fails to refer to Vos. The critical issues, therefore, regarding Vos's biblical theology and the imperative mood are left unresolved in the American debate.

I deem it necessary, therefore, that the alleged link between Vos's biblical theology and the "exclusion of the imperative," as with the "extreme wing," needs to be examined more closely. I submit that the American homiletical debate centers on the tension between "the both" of the indicative and imperative moods and "the only" indicative, in which the imperative is implied. Dennison holds to the "only" position whereas Carrick embraces "the both," but with a careful balance. Carrick is oriented towards the structure of biblical narration, as in the Pauline epistles, while Dennison is firmly aligned with Vos's biblical theology. My judgment is that the key to resolving the tension between the two sides can be found in neutral ground, in Vos's view on Pauline ethics, especially on the significance and relationship of the indicative and the imperative.

My judgment is confirmed by the fact that the relationship between the indicative and the imperative has been widely recognized in biblical theology as a key to understanding Paul's ethics. For example, Bultmann identified the "indicative and imperative" as the basic formula of Pauline ethics in his essay "The Problem of Ethics in Paul"(1924),¹⁶⁰ refuting previous theories that the two moods in Paul are a contradiction, or antinomy, because the "indicative" proclaims "the justified person" freed from sin, which connects with the "imperative" commanding the same person to fight against sin.¹⁶¹ He affirmed that the indicative of God's redemption was meaningful, or gained real existence, in the moment of our obeying the imperative, namely, our decision-making by faith.¹⁶² V. P. Furnish, Emeritus Professor of New Testament at Perkins School of Theology, Dallas, described the relation of the indicative and imperative as crucial to Pauline

---

159. Carrick, "Redemptive-Historical Preaching," 154.

160. This essay was a turning point in the study of Pauline ethics because the indicative and the imperative no longer became a mere part of Paul's ethics but were considered the key to understanding the full scope of Pauline ethics. Thenceforth scholars of Pauline study would need to respond to Bultmann's proposition relating to Pauline ethics. Cf. Dennison, "Indicative and Imperative," 59.

161. Bultmann, "Problem of Ethics in Paul," 195–96. Bultmann refuted Wernle, who pointed out that Paul's statements seemed to be self-contradictory but appeared side by side, that is, the indicative and the imperative.

162. Ibid., 212.

ethics.¹⁶³ However, he differed from Bultmann in considering that the connection of the two moods is in "Christ's love," not in existential decision.¹⁶⁴ Recently Richard B. Hays has defined NT ethics as having a fourfold task: firstly, reading the text carefully; secondly, placing the text in canonical context; thirdly, relating the text to our situation; and, fourthly, living the text out in our lives. For Hays, the indicative and the imperative are organically connected to each other as a tree to its fruit (Matt 7:18, 20); there can be no true understanding of God's redemption (indicative) apart from lived out obedience (imperative).¹⁶⁵ More lately B. Rosner has added that the close relation of the indicative (what God has done) to the imperative (what believers must do) provides the overall orientation of Paul's ethics, as can be seen clearly even within the compass of a single verse like 1 Cor 5:7, Gal 5:1, and Gal 5:35.¹⁶⁶ Besides these, others, like O. O'Donovan¹⁶⁷ and M. Hill,¹⁶⁸ see the indicative and imperative as being connected by God's goal for the universe: the imperative is given to us for the purpose of reorientation of our being in Christ, that is, to live for God's glory, not for ourselves.¹⁶⁹ All these scholars agree that the indicative and the imperative have a close, inseparable connection with each other, which thus forms the basic tool to understanding Paul's ethics.

The issue, however, is not that of recognizing the close relationship between the two moods, but rather of understanding how the indicative activates the imperative. Carrick maintains only that we should follow the basic structure of the balance between the indicative and the imperative, but he does not indicate how this is to be achieved.¹⁷⁰ Ironically, Dennison also claimed a "balanced, unified, and intimated" structure of

---

163. Furnish, *Theology and Ethics in Paul*, 208–26.

164. Furnish, *Love Command in the New Testament*, 94–95.

165. Hays, *Moral Vision of the New Testament*, 7.

166. Rosner, "Paul's Ethics," 217.

167. O'Donovan, *Resurrection and Moral Order*.

168. Hill, "Theology and Ethics in the Letter to the Romans."

169. Windsor, "Indicative and Imperative in the Letters of Paul." Windsor is undertaking PhD studies at the Department of Theology and Religion, Durham University in North-East England. He formerly served as a minister at St Michaels Anglican Cathedral in Wollongong, NSW, Australia.

170. Carrick, "Redemptive-Historical Preaching," 174. Carrick says, "The doctrinal must be balanced by the ethical; *historia salutis* must be balanced by *ordo salutis*; the work of Christ must be balanced by the work of the Spirit. It is absolutely essential that *the great indicatives of Christ's accomplishment of redemption* be balanced by *the great imperative of the Spirit's application of redemption.*"

the indicative and the imperative for Christian ethics, but considered that the "how" should be different from that of Bultmann and others who lead us to moralizing legalism. Dennison emphasizes, "It is absolutely necessary for us to discover, understand, and expand upon Paul's dynamic for ethics—the indicative and the imperative grounded completely in Jesus Christ and made effectual in the new covenant community by the work of the Holy Spirit!"[171] He proposes Vos's redemptive-historical approach for discovering Paul's ethics: "The question is whether we are going to probe the ethical structure of Paul's thought and realize, as Vos did, that a redemptive-historical hermeneutical methodology exposes Paul's structure without abstracting the basic character of the Scripture."[172] The question of how Vos's biblical theology perceives Paul's ethics in relation to the two moods thus becomes the key to solving the dilemma of the American debate. It requires a closer examination of Vos's biblical theology and eschatology in relation to Pauline ethics. However, this is a huge and long-term task and beyond the scope of this work, so I leave it to those who wish to develop further discussion on this subject. But before concluding this chapter, I intend to compare the American debate with the previous Dutch debate.

Comparison with the Dutch Debate

The American homiletical debate over redemptive history was affected by the preceding Dutch debate in two ways: through the emigration of Dutch people to North America in the mid-twentieth century and then through WTS, especially through Clowney's introduction of redemptive-historical preaching based on Reformed biblical theology, that is, Vos's biblical theology. When the Dutch people emigrated they took with them their theological convictions from their home churches in the Netherlands. I note here that there have been differences regarding redemptive-historical preaching between the Dutch communities in America, but they do not have any significant influence on the American debate. As I have shown, the real origin of the American debate over redemptive history is found rather in Clowney's formulation of biblical theology preaching.

Nevertheless, the Dutch debate has a connection to the American debate. The Americans had heard of, and read about, the Dutch debate

---

171. Dennison, "Indicative and Imperative," 78.
172. Ibid.

and knew about the issues in the Netherlands. When Clowney introduced a method of redemptive-historical preaching in his *Preaching and Biblical Theology*, he criticized the original redemptive-historical school and suggested instead a more balanced way of redemptive-historical preaching, based on Vos's biblical theology, in which he recommended ethical application be included in a redemptive-historical sermon to ensure a more biblical method of preaching. Clowney's followers have been divided into two groups: those who focus on the redemptive-historical method based on Vos's biblical theology, and those who emphasize a balance. For this reason, the former have been confused with the redemptive-historical school in the original Dutch debate, but they deny being aligned with the Dutch debate and prefer to call their method biblical theology preaching rather than redemptive-historical. Despite their aspiration, most critics like Carrick and Krabbendam consider the extreme wing of redemptive-historical preaching as falling into the same mistakes as the original redemptive-historical school. Whether they want it or not, the participants of the American debate are classified according to the Dutch debate.

When we compare the two debates, it can be seen that the Dutch debate focuses only on the historical text, whereas the American debate discusses Vos's biblical theology and its aligned preaching. The former starts with Schilder, but its context or background is the movement of Dooyeweerdian philosophy, referred to as the New Direction; the latter starts with Clowney, but its theological background is Vos's biblical theology. The former's emphasis was on "doing justice to the nature of historical text" and determining which approach is most valid for the goal of *sola scriptura*. The American debate has the same ultimate goal, but its primary question concerns who keeps most closely to the basic structure of Scripture, especially Pauline ethics, in faithfully following Vos's biblical theology or eschatology.

The major similarity is found in the antithesis between "exclusivism" and "inclusivism." The former claims the "only" redemptive-historical approach, while the latter wants "both" redemptive-historical and exemplary. The essential distinction between the two debates is in its different focus; the Dutch debate centered around "exemplary" preaching while the American debate focuses on "application," especially the "imperative mood." The table below compares the two debates.

Debate	The Dutch Debate (1930s–40s)	The American Debate (1980s–Present)
Participants	Redemptive-historical versus exemplary preaching	"Extreme" wing versus "Traditional"
Origin	New Direction and Schilder	Vos and Clowney
Central Issue	What is the right approach to historical text: exemplary or redemptive-historical?	Is it valid to exclude application or "the imperative" from redemptive-historical preaching?
Root	Kuyper's Neo-Calvinism and Dutch-Pietism (experientialism)	Hyper-Vosian and experiential Calvinism
Institutions	GKN, later split into Liberated Churches (31st section)	NWTS (*Kerux*), WTS, GPTS
Progress	"exclusivism" versus "inclusivism"	the "only" indicative versus the "both" of the indicative and the imperative
Result	Church schism	On-going
Strengths	Significant concepts such as principles of the redemptive-historical approach	Providing new insight on Vos's biblical theology and warning to the exclusivists
Weaknesses	Not overcoming factionalism	The essential issues untouched

Conclusion

The American homiletical debate is distinct and different from the Dutch debate, even though most critics confuse them and even identify them as one and the same. The Dutch debate centers around the issue of the exemplary method, while the American debate majors on application or the imperative mood. The relation of the indicative and imperative in Pauline ethics, especially the question of how Vos's biblical theology perceives Paul's approach to the two moods, becomes the key to solving the American redemptive-historical debate. This requires more research and I suggest an expert on Vos's biblical theology should handle this matter.

In the next chapter I discuss more of the background to this debate, particularly in relation to Protestant churches in Korea.

5

Confusion and Definitions
Homiletics and Redemptive History

HAVING BRIEFLY EXAMINED THE background to the concept of redemptive history, we now need to look in more detail at the historical understanding of it, especially in terms of its beginning, progress, and present status in Korean Protestant churches. The understanding of Korean Christians concerning redemptive history is significantly affected by the works of Western theologians like Cullmann, Bultmann, and Barth initially, then Vos and Ridderbos, and, more recently, also by Greidanus and Trimp. A careful survey, therefore, of Korean literature dealing with redemptive history is necessary in order to understand how redemptive history has been differently accepted and how confusion has gathered around this subject.

Perspective on Redemptive History in Korea

The import of the redemptive-historical perspective, at different periods and through different theological perspectives, has stimulated Korean Protestant churches, but at the same time it has also brought confusion in its wake. Many Korean scholars, for example, Sung-Kuh Chung and Jee-Chan Kim, consider that the redemptive-historical method had its origin in Holland, especially with Schilder, who initiated the Dutch homiletical debate in the 1930s.[1] Theologians like Gwang-Shik Kim claimed

---

1. Kim, "To answer Hae-Moo Yoo's Refutation."

that Oscar Cullmann was its originator, but still others like Rak-Jae Choi strongly affirmed that Vos must be recognized as its founder. There have been different opinions, therefore, about the origin and development of redemptive history, which adds to the confusion on the subject in Korea.

In this context, I now intend to survey first the import of the idea of redemptive history into the literature of Korean scholars before relating this to Western theologians like Cullmann, Barth, and Vos. Finally, we will compare the concepts of Western theologians advocating redemptive-historical preaching with each other in order to explore a definition and understanding of the method.

The Early Korean Presbyterian Church

Protestantism initially challenged the Korean people through the distribution of Bibles from the 1830s to the 1870s by Western missionaries like Carl Gutzlaff,[2] Robert Thomas,[3] John Ross, and John McIntire,[4] when Korea at the time remained closed to foreigners. Soon other missionaries began to enter "the quiet hermit country" after its official policy involved opening its doors gradually to the West. Churches were then planted through the efforts of early residential missionaries like Horace

---

2. Moffett, *Christians of Korea*, 34; Gutzlaff was originally sent as an interpreter with the British ship *Lord Amherst* by the East India Company when it was opening the northern ports of China for British trade. After visiting Chinese ports, the ship crossed the Yellow Sea to Korea and sailed along the west coast of the Korean peninsula, Whang-Hoi Do, and Chung-Cheong Do for a month in 1832, distributing Chinese Bibles and tracts. Even though there was no direct response, Gutzlaff expected it in later days: "Let us hope that better days will dawn soon for Korea."

3. Davies, "Korea's Debt to a Welshman," 12. Thomas was ordained by the Welsh Congregational Church in Hanover Chapel, Abergavenny, South Wales, and sent by the London Missionary Society to Shanghai, China in 1863. He spent ten weeks in 1865 on the coast of Whang-Hoi Do in Korea, studying the Korean language and distributing Bibles to the people he met. He returned to Korea in August 1866 with the American vessel *General Sherman*, but became the first martyr of Protestantism in the Korean church while distributing Bibles.

4. Clark, *History of the Church in Korea*, 65. John Ross and his brother-in-law, John McIntyre, were missionaries of the Presbyterian Church of Scotland, and baptized the first Korean Christian in Manchuria, the northern border area between China and Korea, in 1876. They have been called the "Wycliffes of Korea," because they prepared the first Korean Bible before any missionary entered Korea.

G. Underwood[5] and Henry G. Appenzeller.[6] As a result of their work, the Korean Protestant church was established and experienced steady growth from the beginning,[7] expanding from a handful of believers in 1885 to a total community of some fifty thousand by 1905, two hundred thousand in 1909, soaring to three million in 1960.[8] In this remarkable growth, the Presbyterian Church became the strongest denomination.[9] In 1960 Presbyterians numbered 775,000, Methodists 235,000, and other denominations were very small in comparison.[10] The total Christian community had reached more than 12,900,000 by 2003.[11] In understanding

---

5. Moffett, *Christians of Korea*, 37–38. Underwood was a missionary of the Northern Presbyterian Church of the United States. He arrived in Korea on Easter morning 1885 as the first official Presbyterian pastor. He started his mission in medical care and educational work, but soon learned the Korean language and preached the gospel in the streets rather than working in the hospital. In time people gathered around Underwood asking questions about the Bible, so the first Presbyterian church was born in this context. On 12 September 1887, the Sae-Moon-An Church was organized with fourteen members at Underwood's home in Cheong-Dong, Seoul. This became the first organized Protestant church.

6. Shearer, *Wildfire*, 33–41. Appenzeller, the first Methodist missionary, arrived in Korea and cooperated with Underwood in evangelizing the Korean people by means of medical care, education, business, and planting churches. He founded the first Methodist church in Korea, named Cheong-Dong Methodist Church. Other missionaries, from the Australian Presbyterian Mission in 1889, the Church of England in 1890, the American Southern Presbyterian Mission in 1892, and the Canadian Presbyterian Church in 1898, came to Korea and worked very hard. Some of them travelled a thousand miles a year on foot.

7. Ibid., 49. The annual report from Pyeong-Yang in 1895 said: "Work in Pyongyang has passed the initiatory stage. The Church is beginning to develop, to expand and to make itself as a factor in the life of the city and surrounding rural areas." The missionaries there took on a full load of follow-up work, teaching and examining candidates for baptism, and training those won to Christ in the rudiments of the faith.

8. Moffett, *Christians of Korea*, 49–50. There were unquestionably several advances and recessions along the growth line, and Moffett divided those into eight periods. Scholars suggest many reasons for the remarkable growth.

9. Han-Mee-Joon and Gallup Korea. *Research Report*, 153. According to this report, Protestant Christians comprise over 20 percent of the more than forty-six million population of South Korea; among them Presbyterians comprise more than 70 percent.

10. Moffett, *Christians of Korea*, 26.

11. Han-Mee-Joon, *Report for the Future of the Korean Church*, 305. Here Han-Mee-Joon stands for "The meeting of the people preparing for the future of the Korean Church." This statistic was produced by research with Gallup Korea; the total community of Protestants is given as 12,952,367.

Korean Protestantism, therefore, I give priority to examining the Korean Presbyterian Church.

The theology of the early Korean Presbyterian Church was provided and taught by the early missionaries,[12] and it was early Presbyterian missionaries who organized the Presbyterian Council in 1893,[13] with its purpose being "the uniform organization in Korea of one native Church holding to the Reformed faith and a Presbyterian form of Government." As an essential part of accomplishing its purpose, the Council established a theological school in 1900, which educated and trained capable leaders with a Bible-centered faith for the Presbyterian Church.[14] With the growth of churches, the first independent presbytery (1907) and the General Assembly (1912) were formed. For the statutes of those associations, the Creed of Twelve Articles and the Larger and Shorter Catechisms were accepted by the early Presbyterian Church in Korea and so it embraced classical Calvinism.[15] Hyung-Ryong Park, the first principal of Chong-Shin Theological Seminary, testified that for the first fifty years, from 1885 to 1935, the Korean church had progressed by means of teaching Calvinism, a legacy of the early missionaries. The faith and theology of early Presbyterianism in Korea was Reformed.[16]

---

12. Conn, "Studies in the Theology of the Korean Presbyterian Church," 26. Conn attested, quoting A. J. Brown, who was a director of the Northern American Presbyterian Mission Board in the 1910s, that the early missionaries in Korea were the true successors of the American Puritans. This showed in their lives, as they kept the Lord's Day holy, and abstained from dancing, smoking, and other pleasures. Their theological tendency was strongly conservative, especially in rejecting biblical criticism. They deemed liberal theology and higher criticism to be dangerous heresies.

13. Clark, *History of the Church in Korea*, 111. As the number of missions working in such a small country as Korea increased, they needed to cooperate with each other to avoid unnecessary duplication of effort and competition. The Council was composed of four missions in Korea: the Northern Presbyterian Mission (American), the Australian (Victorian) Mission, the Southern Presbyterian Mission, and the Canadian Presbyterian Mission. The Council divided the mission fields in Korea according to these four missions.

14. Ibid., 133. This school became the womb of theological leaders and is the first Protestant theological educational institution in Korea. It produced very capable church leaders, such as Kyung-Jo Suh, Suk-Jin Han, Nin-Soo Song, Chun-Paik Yang, Kee-Chang Bang, Sun-Joo Kil, and Kee-Poong Lee, who are all major figures of the great revival of the Korean Church in 1907.

15. Conn, "Studies in the Literary Criticism of the New Testament Presbyterian Church," 31.

16. Rhodes, *History of the Korea Mission*, vol 1, 404–5.

The concept of redemptive history was not explicitly discussed at this early stage, but it was implied in articles written by early missionaries in this period. *Shin-Hak-Jee-Nam*, the first theological journal of Korea, published by the Presbyterian Theological Seminary in Pyeong-Yang, confirms this.[17] The theological articles and essays in this journal were mostly about sermon plans, basic doctrines, illustrative preaching anecdotes, and brief introductions to the Bible. Thus the term redemptive history, possibly controversial and perceived as being rooted in liberal theology, may have been prevented from being discussed, but some articles dealt with the essential concept of redemptive history indirectly in themes such as "Time and History," "God's Providence," and the "Economy of God." For example, W. C. Eerdman, principal of Pyeong-Yang Theological Seminary, discussed God's ultimate goal of controlling the world, saying that God's economy is essentially to let this world fully know His glory,[18] and he mentioned some aspects of the redemptive-historical concept. H. E. Blair, professor in the same seminary, talked about Christ's recognition of time for the fulfilment of God's redemption.[19] He was expressing the idea of redemptive history, but without using the actual term. Although the comprehensive concept of redemptive history was not present in this period, there must have been a perception of the loci of redemptive history.

Theological Turbulence and Schism

From the 1930s to the early 1960s there was theological turbulence in Korean Protestant churches, which started with the introduction of theological liberalism. In the late 1920s, some Korean Christian leaders, like Pil-Geun Chae, Chang-Geun Song, and Jae-Joon Kim, returned home from their studies in Japan, America, and Canada with critical views of the Bible and gradually introduced these ideas into Korean churches.

---

17. "Index of *Shin-Hak-Jee-Nam* from 1918 to 1971," 311–73. This journal was first published in 1918, eighteen years after the Presbyterian Theological Seminary first opened in 1901, and continued until it closed on 25 October 1940 due to Japanese religious persecution. Fourteen years after, through national deliverance from the Japanese and also the Korean Civil War, the newly organized Presbyterian General Assembly Theological Seminary restarted the journal in 1954. It continues until now through Chong-Shin University.

18. Eerdman, "God's Great Economy," 5–12.

19. Blair, "Time and the Event," 36–44.

This created conflict with the traditional system of theology, but the new theology was unsuccessful in the initial stages because missionaries and conservative leaders opposed it.[20] However, the situation soon changed due to Japanese persecution. The Japanese colonial government oppressed church leaders by imposing on them the worship of the Japanese Shinto gods, while compelling them to regard their emperor as a living god. Most conservative Christian leaders declined to pay obeisance at the Shinto shrines and were imprisoned or killed. Consequently some vacancies in church leadership were filled by those who embraced a more liberal theology and who were more cooperative with the Japanese policy.[21] This led to the spread of liberal theology without opposition from the Reformed missionaries, who had left Korea during the last ten years of Japanese oppression.

In 1945 national independence from Japan was obtained, but theological struggles between liberals and traditionalists became even more intense than formerly. Conservative leaders, released from prison and imminent execution by the national liberation, were deeply troubled about the theological and administrative compromise which church leaders had indulged in during the Japanese annexation. They now demanded genuine, public repentance, and the resignation of all compromising church leaders, for the purpose of rebuilding the Korean church in a more spiritual way. Some leaders continued to hold ecclesiastical power and rejected their appeal, and so the conflict between them increased.[22]

The Korean Civil War (1950–1953), which occurred five years after liberation, contributed to making the disharmony and cleavage in the church more severe. Eventually the Korean Presbyterian Church divided, firstly into two, then three, and later four denominations during the 1950s; this involved the division of the Goryo Group (now Koshin) in 1952, the Kijang Group in 1953, and the Hapdong and Tonghap in 1959.

---

20. Huh, *History of the Korean Presbyterian Church in Korea*, 214–15.

21. After deliverance from Japanese rule, the idol worshippers claimed that they had had to make a hard choice, to preserve the Korean church from the risk of annihilation, despite the disgrace and contempt levelled against them. We cannot say most leaders helping Japanese policy were all liberal theologians, but it can be said that the enforced Shinto worship or the lethal resistance against it were respectively backed by the two theological positions: liberal theology or conservative theology. Cf. Huh, *History of the Korean Presbyterian Church in Korea*, 253.

22. Kim, *History of the Korean Church in the Ten Years Since Liberation*, 556.

These initial schisms were followed by numerous other church divisions in the Korean Presbyterian Church.[23]

The actual term and concept of redemptive history appeared in Korea at this time of struggle and schism in the Korean Presbyterian Church during the 1950s. Hyung-Ryong Park, the first principal of Chong-Hoi Theological Seminary from 1948,[24] attempted to interpret historical events like the Second World War in an article, "Providence and History" in 1954. Presupposing that it is important to find a way of interpreting God's providence in history, he emphasized that there could be a wilful misinterpretation of events, as with one group of German theologians, especially Gerhard Kittel, who claimed that Hitler was the great leader whom God raised up. Kittel added that the church, which had the Holy Spirit and the Word, was able to say whether the political activities of Hitler were of God or not. Some theologians thus consequently supported the idea that Hitler was raised up by God, and allowed to impose such a disaster in world history, as an expression of divine judgment. Park disagreed with the opinion that the national calamity of the Korean Civil War was God's judgment on the Korean church because of disunity, yet the idea permeated Christian churches in Korea at the time. Park thought differently, saying, "Only God's revelation interprets rightly the providence of God which appeared in world history,"[25] meaning that the national disaster could not be explained by artificial causes and effects. In a later complementary article, Park claimed that the interpretation of history should find its right direction in considering the kingdom of God, in which context human history moves, but centering in the consummation of the redemption of God's chosen people.[26] This is the first concept of redemptive history which appeared in the articles of the Korean Protestant church, but still without using the actual term.

The first use of the term *redemptive history* appeared in 1959 in an article by Nam-Dong Seo, a professor of Han-Shin Theological

---

23. Song, "Historical and Theological Analysis of Schism," 13–29, 305–16. There are now more than one hundred Presbyterian denominations in Korea. According to Song, the schisms resulted from many complex causes, including historical, political, sociological, and theological factors, but I consider all these schisms are rooted in the early struggle in the 1950s.

24. The official English name of this school is the Korean Presbyterian Assembly Theological Seminary.

25. Park, "Providence and History." (1954).

26. Park, "Providence and History." (1964).

Seminary,[27] titled "The End and History." This short article follows Bultmann's main ideas in his *History and Eschatology*.[28] Seo used the term as he explained the perception of the end of history in the primitive church. According to Seo, Christ proclaimed the end of redemptive history as the final day of "salvation and judgment," which would come very soon. The primitive Christian community lived in this recognition of eschatological immanency. However, their anticipation of the end had been gradually modified with the prospect of its delay. Afterwards the eschatological consciousness of primitive Christianity dissolved into general history, natural history, and, finally, existential history of the individual human being. This explanation of history was a recycling of Bultmann's ideas.

Seung-Eun Yoon, a graduate from the Korean Methodist Theological Seminary in 1959, published his graduating thesis, titled "Christ's Redemptive Historical Once-For-Allness."[29] He discussed Christ's acts in redemptive history, claiming that Christ's business was unique because his sacrificial death is once-for-all, never to be repeated. He mentioned Christ's redemption as "the midpoint of RH," and defined the characteristics of redemption as being complete, non-repeatable, and everlasting. He then described the meaning and function of the Christ event in the present and in the future of redemptive history, concluding that Christians have hope in God to revive their dead bodies in the future because they believe in the Christ event of Christ's resurrection in the present.[30] This logic depended on Cullmann's corollary in *Christ and Time*. These early theses are little more than book reviews of earlier Western works. The understanding of redemptive history in this period was still elementary, except when introducing some theories of Western theologians.

1960s to 1980s: Church Explosion

The Korean Protestant church increased more rapidly during the 1960s to 1980s than in any other period in its history. For instance, six new churches were planted daily in the 1970s.[31] There are various explanations

27. Seo, "End and History."

28. Bultmann, *History and Eschatology*. Cf. Seo, *Review of History and Eschatology*.

29. Yoon, "Christ's Redemptive-Historical Once-For-Allness," part 1, 108–17. This thesis received the "honourable thesis prize" from the Christian Literature Society of Korea.

30. Yoon, "Christ's Redemptive-Historical Once-For-Allness," part 2, 70–77.

31. Ro, "South Korea," 545.

for this remarkable church growth. Historically, the Japanese annexation (1910–1945) and the Korean Civil War (1950–1953), which undermined and devastated all aspects of Korean society, may have encouraged people to find their comfort and spiritual liberation in Christianity. Politically, the constant threat from communist North Korea and, economically, the extreme poverty during the 1950s, may also have encouraged people to turn to Christianity rather than remain in traditional religions like Buddhism or Confucianism.[32] Cho-Joon Park, retired pastor of Calvary Presbyterian Church in Seoul, found reasons for this church growth in Korean Christians' commitment, specifically in aspects such as "the seed of martyrs' blood," "enthusiastic evangelism,"[33] and "the dawn prayer meeting."[34] During this period of rapid growth, many new theological ideas were imported, especially from the West, which brought considerable confusion, as well as stimulation, to the churches.

During this period of church growth, Korean biblical scholars began to translate some Western literature on redemptive history and to discuss its application to the Korean situation. Dong-Shik Chi (1910–1977), a professor at Yon-Sei University from 1947 to 1975, introduced the concept of redemptive history as a trend in modern theology in 1962. He commenced his article by saying that the two distinctive German terms *Historie* and *Geschichte*,[35] both of which are combined in the Korean word *Yuk-Sa* (history), are like a "column and its center."[36] He said the meaning, or core, of history is found in the redemption of Christ.[37] This concept of *Heilsgeschichte* was, according to Chi, first advanced from eighteenth century German Pietism, specifically from Bengel.[38]

---

32. Ro, "Non-Spiritual Factors in Church Growth," 159–170.

33. Song, "Historical and Theological Analysis of Schism," 69. For example, there were five massive evangelical movements from 1965 to 1980: the Thirty Million to Christ Movement of 1965; the Billy Graham Crusade of 1973; Explo '74 in 1974; the '77 Evangelization in 1977; the '80 World Evangelical Crusade in 1980.

34. Park, "The Dynamics of Young Nak Presbyterian Church Growth."

35. The distinction between these two words has already been explained in "Definitions" in chapter 1.

36. *Historie* renders the scientific, but provisional, answers to human life, but *Geschichte* provides the ultimate and everlasting meaning of it as the core of history. The meaning and core of history is found at the redemption of Christ, because God's "question and answer" is believed to be given in Jesus Christ.

37. Chi, "Modern Theology and the Concept of Redemptive History," 197–210.

38. Bengel sought the meaning of history through this concept, considering that the recognition of God's goal of redemption, which has been gradually accomplished

Hofmann and Beck, representatives of the "school of *Heilsgeschichte*," developed the basics of Bengel's concept in the nineteenth century and modified it in connection with Hegel's dialectical philosophy of history. Thus, Hofmann proposed an allegedly comprehensive interpretation of history in the Bible, which was different from the previous teleological understanding of *Heilsgeschichte* as salvation history.[39] Among moderns, A. M. Hunter, a Scottish New Testament scholar, was recognized by Chi as an important proponent of salvation history, because Hunter considers that *Heilsgeschichte* presents the whole content of the New Testament.[40] E. Stauffer, a German theologian, was also identified as affirming that the "Jesus event" is the center of God's predetermined design of history and also of God's mysterious wisdom and economy for the kingdom of God.[41]

Chi also recognized Cullmann and Bultmann as being preeminent writers on this subject. According to Chi, Cullmann developed the traditional theology of salvation history through contending for the linear shape of time, with Jesus Christ as its center. Bultmann differed from Cullmann, saying "How come the time factor could be the matter for the eschatological being, Jesus?" The history which Cullmann discussed did not, in Bultmann's opinion, seem to be different from human world history, but the history in the Bible is admittedly distinct from world history. For Bultmann, the Christ event in the New Testament is timelessly eschatological.

In Chi's understanding, Bultmann's eschatological event fulfils the "here and now" in Christ's church. Christians must be changed by this eschatological event, which repeats itself in preaching and in the decision of believers. According to Chi, Bultmann affirmed that the first advent of Christ, as the eschatological event, was achieved not in chronological time, but in the eternal frame of redemption. Thus, for Bultmann,

---

through history, is primarily required to understand the history of the Bible.

39. Chi, "Modern Theology and the Concept of Redemptive History," 199.

40. Hunter, *Message of the New Testament*, 11, quoted in Chi, "Modern Theology and the Concept of Redemptive History," 200. Hunter defined *Heilsgeschichte*, or salvation history, as "the consistent story of salvation" by which God accomplished His aspiration of saving His people through sending His Son, the Christ, to fulfil His plan of redemption.

41. Chi, "Modern Theology and the Concept of Redemptive History," 201. According to Chi's understanding of Stauffer, human history not only progresses through and in Christ in the present, but also the coming kingdom of God will be fulfilled centering on Jesus Christ.

real time and history have nothing to do with the religious experience of believers in Christ.

In Chi's understanding, however, Karl Barth acknowledges "special history," as does the school of *Heilsgeschichte*, as the story of Jesus Christ. But history, for Barth, is "supra-temporal history,"[42] which means that the saving events of Christ do not need to have actually happened in the real world. Chi appraised Barth's view as a "more developed perspective" of redemptive history, which progressed from the school of *Heilsgeschichte*. Chi thought that the old school of redemptive history lacked in objectifying the special history of Christ, but Barth had found a way through the concept of *Urgeschichte* (original history).[43] Chi shows in this way that Barthian theology affected Korean churches at this time.

Chang-Kyu Lee, a professor of the Korean Methodist Theological Seminary, gave helpful insight into *Heilsgeschichte* in a theological article in 1966.[44] He started by limiting the area of salvation history,[45] and described briefly the development of the concept. According to Lee, in the late 1950s Von Rad advocated the salvation-historical approach to the Old Testament,[46] and G. E. Wright, supplementing this, added that biblical theology means the confession and reappearance of God's saving actions in specific history.[47] Lee also mentioned Stauffer's[48] and Piper's[49]

---

42. Barth, *Church Dogmatics* II/2, 6.

43. Chi, "Modern Theology and the Concept of Redemptive History," 208–09.

44. Lee, "Redemptive History or the Event of Redemption," 79–89.

45. Maritain, *On the Philosophy of History*, 28. Lee presupposed that the kingdom of God and the history of salvation is, as Jacques Maritain says, the major task of the theology of history; but the philosophy of history is concerned with world history, or the history of human civilization. Cf. Lee, "Redemptive History or the Event of Redemption," 79.

46. Rad, "Historical Question," 21. Rad proclaimed that how God acts in history, and how His acts affect Israel's life and confession, are the new concern of OT theology at that time.

47. Wright, *God Who Acts*, preface.

48. Stauffer, *Theologie des Neuen Testaments*, 155, quoted in Lee, "Redemptive History or the Event of Redemption," 80. Stauffer stated that Jesus Christ, the ultimate content of time and history, is the center of the design of God's time.

49. Piper, *God in History*, 53–71. Cf. Piper, *Biblical Theology of the New Testament*. Otto Piper, a professor at Princeton Theological Seminary, also discussed the characteristics of "holy history," which might be distinct from secular history, and he emphasized God's sovereignty and providential works in both areas of history.

concepts of salvation history, suggesting Cullmann was considered the most preeminent amongst those scholars.[50]

Lee highlighted Cullmann's criticism that Bultmann had eliminated the redemptive-historical perception of time in the Bible, because he did not understand, according to Cullmann's judgment, the essential Christology, which must be examined within the circle of redemptive history, and the characteristic indivisibility of "Existence and *Heilsgeschichte*."[51] Bultmann, in responding to Cullmann, claimed that the Christ event (*Heilsgeschehen*) is not the kind of concept which can be expressed by salvation history (*Heilsgeschichte*). The crucial differences between them concern their views of the unity of the Bible, Christology, and eschatology,[52] especially whether Christ is the center of redemptive history. Bultmann held that Christ is the eschatological present event "approaching now to you and me," not the fact which was established and discussed as the past event. Therefore, Christ is always the end of time and history to believers.[53]

According to Lee, Bultmann criticized Cullmann's idea in three main areas. Firstly, whenever Bultmann considers history, he bears in mind not *Historie* but *Geschichte*, especially *Geschichtlichkeit*, the historicity of human existence. For Bultmann, the human being is the prior historical reality and anything else is secondary. The event of Christ's redemption for "me" can be experienced not from historical study, but only from "my" personal decision of faith and actual participation in the event.[54] The most essential and centering matter should be "the event of Jesus' salvation," not salvation history. Secondly, Bultmann thinks salvation history is not much more than myth, which is unacceptable to the modern mind. He gave as an example the apostle Paul, who was not limited by

---

50. Lee considered that Cullmann overcame the theology of the nineteenth century's historicism, which claims that the Bible is nothing else than a human production. Cullmann thought that scholars of historicism consider history in the Bible as a symbol of timeless truth. This is, for Cullmann, their misunderstanding of the linear shape of time. Lee seemed to agree with Cullmann.

51. Cullmann, *Christology in the New Testament*, 326.

52. Cullmann accepts that all events in the OT connect to the Christ event, but Bultmann rejects the OT as God's specific revelation of redemption. Cullmann takes the main source of discussion from the Acts and the Gospel of Luke, but Bultmann uses the Gospel of John and the Pauline epistles. Cullmann considers Christ is the center of time, but Bultmann says Christ is the end of time and history.

53. Bultmann, *History and Eschatology*, 151–53.

54. Ibid., 110–19.

temporal matters and actively demythologized them in order to obtain an existential interpretation (Rom 6:4–11, 14:17; Gal 2:20). Thirdly, Bultmann also criticized Cullmann for not differentiating history from myth or saga, even though they are explicitly distinct.

Responding, Cullmann said that the core of Christian *kerygma*, since the early period of the Christian church, is salvation history (*Heilsgeschichte*) through Christ.[55] If the historical facts in the Bible were, for Cullmann, disregarded or just symbolized to stress the existential decision of Christians, then the historical reality of God's revelation would be despised. Further, Cullmann's eschatology differs from Bultmann's in that "the end" began after Christ's first advent, but its fulfilment will come at His second advent. The essential difference between Cullmann (redemptive-historical eschatology) and Bultmann (existential present eschatology) about the end is between the "already . . . not yet" and the "no longer . . . not yet." Finally, Cullmann responded on the relationship between history and myth by saying that even the events which happened in real history are treated like myths by Bultmann.[56] Both agreed that there are myths or sagas in the Bible, but disagreed on the principles to identify myths and on how to treat them. Bultmann considers that the pre-existence, the virgin birth, the resurrection, the ascension, and the second advent of Christ, as well as the final judgment and the theory of penal substitution, are to be treated as entirely mythical in the Bible. However, Cullmann believes that only the narratives "in the beginning and in the end" are myths or sagas and thus these can be demythologized. But if we separate the mystical from the historical narratives, then the history of the beginning and the end would, for Cullmann, become timeless, and the essential redemptive-historical characteristics are then not necessarily deprived of the original intention of the New Testament authors. Cullman claimed that Paul and John used mystical expressions to deliver only "the events of redemptive history," in spite of discerning the beginning and the end matters as not being historical. Both Cullmann and Bultmann admit that there are some mystical factors in the Bible, but Cullmann prefers to amalgamate the mystical into the historical while Bultmann wants to distinguish them from his own hermeneutical goal.

Lee accepted both ideas of redemptive history from Cullmann and Bultmann and tried to fuse them, producing a new resolution: "All events

55. Culllmann, *Christ and Time*, 29–32.
56. Ibid., 95.

on the RH line affect on the whole human being and have meaning, but only if they were accepted as repeated events to individual believers are they considered to be salvation events."[57] Thus, for Lee, theologians and historians should ask the basic question as to whether salvation history (*Heilsgeschichte*) or the event of redemption (*Heilsgeschehen*), is the right hermeneutical perspective of the New Testament, and the answer should not be one or the other, but both of them. Lee suggested a "redemptive-historical and existential soteriology," as provided by Emil Brunner, as an answer.[58] Lee's answer is not logically appropriate, because he does not issue any reason for integrating the ideas of Cullmann and Bultmann into one. Lee expressed his wish for a deeper and more serious discussion on this subject at the fourth World Council of Churches (WCC)[59] General Assembly, which was held from 4–20 July 1968 in Uppsala, Sweden, and later in Korea. However, his wish was not realized due to some reasons which we will discuss later in this chapter.

Wie Chai, Professor of New Testament in the Korean Methodist Theological Seminary, examined the redemptive-historical perspective of Luke and his understanding of the Holy Spirit in 1968.[60] Chai presupposed "the historical and analytical methodology" of interpretation as being necessary for the right understanding of the biblical text; we should see the "Spirit" through the historical context of Luke and then He must be understood as "the power of history," creating a new era and simultaneously accomplishing the end of history, which is the judgment. Thus, the "Spirit" is to be considered as the *alpha* and *omega* of history.

According to Chai, Luke understood the *pneuma* (the Spirit) as "the driving motive and power" of the phenomena of the kingdom of God, defining the center of redemptive history as the transcendental dimension of that divine nation.[61] In other words, the periods of the kingdom of God, which are divided by the *pneuma* into the time of "Israel," "Jesus," and the "Spirit," should be defined through the functions of the Holy Spirit. Eventually, Chai claims, there is no perception of the personality of the Holy Spirit in Luke's understanding of the *pneuma*.

57. Lee, "Redemptive History or the Event of Redemption," 89.
58. Brunner, *Christian Doctrine of the Church*, 367–74.
59. The WCC is the broadest and most inclusive among the many organized expressions of the modern ecumenical movement—a movement whose goal is Christian unity. See World Council of Churches, "What is the World Council of Churches?"
60. Chai, "The Understanding of Holy Spirit," 119–27.
61. Ibid., 123.

Chai also explained that Luke, as a Hellenist, depicted the advent of the Holy Spirit (power) in a very dramatic and poetic way, and thus it was not necessarily a real supernatural phenomenon or miracle.[62] He added that without this contextual understanding of the miracle, people might descend into religious fanaticism, believing irrationally in miracles. Luke originally intended to emphasize the fact that "the power of the Spirit" focused on global mission. Afterwards, Luke's understanding of the Spirit is as the dynamic agent of applying God's redemptive history and the generating force in the realization of the kingdom of God in this world. According to this redemptive-historical perspective, we are living in the time of the Holy Spirit. I submit that Chai's article cannot be accurately designated as the redemptive-historical approach of interpreting the Bible, although he employs the term in his exegesis. Chai misunderstands the term *redemptive history* as the methodology of historical criticism, but it should not be applied to the school of *Heilsgeschichte*.

Rak-Jae Choi (1937–2010), Professor of New Testament in Chong-Shin Theological Seminary (1973–1980), discussed redemptive history as a possible methodology for New Testament hermeneutics.[63] He began his article by meditating on two biblical statements in Isa 64:1–2 and 1 John 1:1–3, saying that they ably show the foundation of Christianity in the supernatural and historical incarnation of Jesus Christ and His saving ministry. He added that the formation of the Bible was a part of the divine works in God's redemption. Thus, Choi thought that the highest intention of a Christian's theological study should be the proper interpretation of this work of God's redemption, namely, the history of redemption throughout Scripture.

According to Choi, this redemptive-historical reality, which is the very core, and a unique feature, of Christianity, was already plainly manifested in its founder Jesus Christ and His instructions, then further preserved and transferred to the Christian church through the traditions of the apostles, and finally through God's deliberate formation of the New Testament.[64] The text thus has this redemptive-historical background and must be read through a lens which reflects the progress of that redemptive history. This is regarded as the right principle for the New Testament hermeneutic, and Choi consequently rejects three of its rivals: the alle-

---

62. Ibid., 125.

63. Choi, "New Testament Hermeneutics and the History of Redemption," 51, 59–66.

64. Ibid., 64.

gorical method, proof-text methodology, and the fragmentary approach. Choi's perspective of redemptive-historical hermeneutics is based on the theories of Reformed theologians like Machen,[65] Vos,[66] and especially Gaffin.[67] Choi's article was the first introduction of a Reformed view of redemptive history to Korean Presbyterian churches in the early 1970s. However, its weakness is that this view only gives us a unilateral understanding of the subject.

This period, from the 1960s to the early 1980s in Korea, produced several theological articles about redemptive history in an attempt to introduce the ideas of Western theologians. For example, Gwang-Shik Kim, a retired professor of Yon-Sei University, introduced Oscar Cullmann as a redemptive-historical theologian, briefly examining Cullman's biography and his literature.[68] Young-Bae Cha, Professor of Systematic Theology in Chong-Shin Theological Seminary, wanted to outline the *Heilshistorische Theologie* by introducing several redemptive-historical theologians like Cullmann, von Rad, Wolfhart Pannenberg, and Schilder.[69] Cha contended that Schilder renders mostly a correct theology of redemptive history. Hyung-Yong Park, Professor of New Testament in Hap-Dong Theological Seminary, showed that the redemptive-historical perspective appeared in the Pauline epistles, such as Romans, Ephesians, and Colossians,[70] and also that redemptive history is a consistent keynote in Paul's letters, suggesting it is essential for interpreting Pauline theology.

Those studies of redemptive history by, for example, Dong-Shik Chi and Chang-Kyu Lee, were comparatively more developed than those in the previous period, but they were still only introductory material or translations of Western theological books. There was no thorough attempt to understand the subject of redemptive history comprehensively and remove the serious misunderstandings which existed in Korea. However, in this period Korean Presbyterian churches gradually became familiar with the term.

---

65. Machen, *Christianity and Liberalism*, 70.

66. Vos, "Christian Faith and the Truthfulness of Bible History," 299; Vos, *Inaugral Address*, 14.

67. Gaffin, *Resurrection and Redemption*, 15.

68. Kim, "Oscar Cullmann," 75–82.

69. Cha, "'Theology of Salvation History," 20–29.

70. Park, "Study on the Redemptive-Historical Perspective," 102–13.

1980s to 2010: Introspection and Diversification of Theology

The Korean Protestant church began to be more introspective after its centennial year in 1985, largely because of the negative aspects of sudden church growth in the previous period. Bong-Ho Son, a professor at Seoul National University, had already pointed out problems resulting from the rapid growth of Korean churches, such as the shortage of qualified leaders, the image of Christianity as being immature, and the problem of uncommitted or selfish Christians.[71] The by-products of rapid church growth were the charismatic movement, the low moral standing of Korean churches, compromise within evangelicalism,[72] confusion with regard to Min-Jung theology,[73] and indigenous theology,[74] which spread in influence more widely than before.[75] Under the influence of worldwide postmodernism, renouncing any traditional authority and accepting diversity of thought was considered an unavoidable fashion in Korean churches. These factors have significantly contributed to the slowdown of Korean Protestant church growth during the last twenty years.

However, despite all these challenges, the redemptive-historical perspective within the Korean church progressed more in terms of its understanding and application during this period. Jong-Chil Park, Professor of Old Testament in Ko-Shin University, published his *The Redemptive-Historical Interpretation of the Scriptures* in 1986.[76] This was the first

71. Son, "Some Dangers of Rapid Growth," 333–47. Son alerted readers to the dangers of an overemphasis upon quantitative church growth. The shamanistic background of the Korean church contributes to the growth but endangers the church due to characteristics such as "the extreme eagerness for secular blessing but the negligence of social responsibility."

72. Kim, *Problems of the Modern Protestant Churches*, 5.

73. Lee, "Korean Christian Thought," 312. Min-Jung theology is universally recognized as a genuine Korean theology, but is not entirely supported by all Korean churches because it was developed by liberal theologians like Byung-Moo Ahn, Nam-Dong Suh, Yong-Hak Hyun, and Hee-Suk Moon. Min-Jung means "the people or the masses," who are politically oppressed, economically exploited, socially alienated, and uneducated, and thus Min-Jung theology seeks the liberation of the people from their depression. This theology has been criticized by Reformed theologians because of its radical deviation from the traditional way of interpreting Scripture.

74. Kim, "Is Christianity a Korean Religion?" 162–68. This theology was developed by Korean Methodist theologians like Sun-Hwan Byun and Sung-Bum Yoon in the 1960s. They claimed to understand the gospel by means only of the Korean situation, rather than Western traditions. The theology has only recently gained popularity.

75. Ahn, "Recent Theological Trends in Korean Churches," 119–26.

76. This book is composed of four parts: Scriptures and Hermeneutics;

Korean-authored book dealing with the subject of redemptive history, and it opened a new horizon for the understanding of the hermeneutical approach of redemptive history in Reformed Korean churches. However, this book was seriously deficient, as it provided only a collection of short essays and articles which Park had written previously on various topics, such as "The Relationship between the Two Testaments," "How to Read Scripture," "Document Theory or the Word of God?" "The Truth of *Tolledoth*[77] in Genesis," and "Liberation Theology and Scriptural Text." In his later treatise in 1987,[78] Park insightfully described the philosophical perspectives of redemptive history by focusing on the Dutch homiletical controversy.

According to Park, Barthian scholars, like Wilhelm Vischer,[79] and Hans Hellbardt,[80] acknowledged the continuity between the two testaments, but disregarded the progress of history in the Old Testament for learning about the coming incarnate Christ from historical texts, while Bultmann identified OT history as "a heap of contradictions," which was inappropriate for examining the meaning of history, except for seeing the failures of sacred covenants.[81] Park suggests that Friedrich Baumgärtel is hermeneutically close to Bultmann, because he mainly understands the Old Testament as the failure of various covenants and judgments on God's people.[82] On the other hand, Von Rad is closer to Barth because of his typological interpretation, which mostly finds types of Christ in the OT,[83]

Redemptive-Historical Interpretation of Scriptures; Examples of Redemptive-Historical Preaching; several essays about reality, peace, and the Christian life.

77. A Hebrew word meaning history, or genealogy, or generation (Gen 2:4, 5:1, 6:9, 10:32).

78. Park, "Study on the Controversies of the Redemptive-Historical Interpretation and Application (Preaching) of the Scriptures," 31–121. This treatise consists of six chapters: Definitions of Redemptive history and Problems; History of Philosophical Redemptive-Historical Hermeneutics; Biblical Structure of Redemptive History; Controversies over Reformed Perspective of Redemptive History and its Application; Evaluation of the Concepts of Reformed Theologians; Conclusion and Hope. The treatise overlapped with the previous book to some extent, especially in its description of an historical survey of redemptive history.

79. Vischer, *Witness of the Old Testament to Christ*.

80. Hellbardt, *Das Alte Testament und das Evangelium*.

81. Park, "Redemptive-Historical Interpretation of the Scriptures," 13–24.

82. Westermann, *Essays on Old Testament Hermeneutics*. This work has also been translated into Korean.

83. Rad, *Theologie des Alten Testaments*, vol. 2.

provides a relationship with the NT, but sacrifices the specific meaning of God's saving history, thus undermining the unity of Scripture.[84] For example, the story of Joseph's life in Genesis is illuminated by typology, illustrating Christ's forsakenness and suffering for God's salvation, but the specific characteristics of Joseph and his life in salvation history can be disregarded. Park evaluates these methodologies as being improper, and suggests instead the redemptive-historical methodology of Holwerda, a representative debater in the Dutch controversy. Park examined the structure of redemptive history in Scripture, intending to discover an authoritative significance for redemptive history but, disappointingly, he only discusses concepts handled by the Reformed theologians of Holland.[85] His conclusion was the same as that of Trimp, who evaluated the debate in Holland.[86] But Park's research did show some progress with regard to the concept of redemptive history in the Korean Presbyterian church in that it was a first step in studying redemptive-historical hermeneutics more comprehensively.[87]

Sung-Jong Shin, Professor of New Testament in Chong-Shin Theological Seminary, pointed out areas of concern about preaching in the Korean church in the 1980s, and suggested redemptive-historical methodology as a solution.[88] He first identified the problems of using historical texts of Scripture as models for human instruction or illustration. According to Shin, the timeless modelling of biblical events or figures is misleading for it can reduce salvation history to secular history, disregarding its historical uniqueness and the reality of the events. He called this method of interpretation "fragmentary" and "atomic," as Schilder had originally done.[89] For example, one may preach exactly the

84. Park, *Redemptive-Historical Interpretation of the Scriptures*, 22.

85. Park, "Study on the Controversies of the Redemptive-Historical Interpretation," 63–79, 105–19.

86. Trimp, *Heilsgeschiedenis en prediking*, 72–106.

87. Park continued to publish his studies until the early 1990s. These are: *Redemptive-Historical Interpretation of the Old Testament*; *Redemptive-Historical Understanding of the Psalms*.

88. Shin, "Problems of the Korean Pulpit Based on the Hermeneutical Position," 54–63.

89. Greidanus, *Sola Scriptura*, 62–63. Schilder called the illustrative interpretation of historical texts "the fragmentary interpretation" because it shatters redemptive history into many fragments and isolates the text (event, person) from the totality of Scripture (redemptive history). "Atomic" refers to the isolation within the text from the "inner coherence" and the "central thrust" of the text.

same message in this method from different texts, such as Matt 11:1–6 and John 20:24–29, Gen 22 and Matt 15:21, but in doing so the historical characteristics and differences are disregarded. Shin also pointed out that biographical preaching can be humanistic as well as arbitrary, and thus unbiblical.

Shin suggested redemptive-historical methodology as an alternative appropriate biblical interpretation, enumerating three advantages. Firstly, it excludes the illustrative function for dealing with historical texts as preaching-texts. Secondly, it includes competent exegesis which interprets the biblical text itself, employing two principles, namely, the organic interpretation (seeing the text through the whole scheme of redemptive history) and the integral interpretation (seeing events from the unique text itself).[90] Finally, Shin concluded that preaching would be powerful, not because of a preacher's ability, but due to the power of the Holy Spirit working through the Word itself. This article challenged many preachers in Korean churches and thus the original book, *Sola Scriptura*, which this article mainly quoted, was soon translated into Korean in 1989.

N. H. Gootjes, a Dutch Professor of Systematic Theology in Ko-Shin Graduate School, also published a book in order to introduce redemptive-historical preaching and its application.[91] Gootjes included twenty-four sermons in that book,[92] showing how redemptive-historical preaching is composed, and how to use redemptive history from the biblical text. He explained the principles of the method in three ways—as "God prior to anything else," "the progress of history," and "salvation." According to Gootjes, preachers should not take man as the starting point of interpretation, because Scripture describes primarily what God does and how He does it, and then only secondarily describes the human response to God's ministry. The gospels' authors explicitly expressed the object of their writings as preaching Christ as the Son of God, and preachers of the gospel should not miss this essential point as otherwise the preaching would

---

90. Shin, "Problems of the Korean Pulpit Based on the Hermeneutical Position," 62.

91. Gootjes, *Between Exegesis and Sermon*.

92. The sermon titles include: "The Lies of Abraham" (Gen 12:10–20); "The Death of Nadab and Abihu" (Lev. 10:1–3); "Salvation and Law" (Deut 6:6–7); "Bearing the Cross" (Matt 10:38); "The Mission of the Church" (Acts 13:1–5), etc. These sermons cannot be said to be appropriate for providing models for redemptive-historical preaching because they are mostly brief and move into the text hastily without examining the historical and literary background.

not be redemptive-historical. These principles provided clear criteria for judging what redemptive-historical preaching is.

Sung-Kuh Chung, Principal of Dae-Shin University, studied the redemptive-historical concept in depth and published a book presenting its principles and methodology in 1988.[93] This treatise consisted of eight chapters: the Prolegomena; Recent Interest in Redemptive-Historical Preaching (RHP); the Beginning of RHP; Reconsideration of Exemplary Preaching and its Problems; the Principles of RHP; the Method of RHP and a Comparison with Other Types of Preaching; Evaluation; then, finally, his Conclusion. In his Prolegomena, Chung mainly emphasized redemptive-historical methodology as the consistent thrust of Scripture, while taking the method of expository preaching as its base.

Chung explained the recent increase of interest in redemptive-historical methodology at a ThM program in Chong-Shin Graduate School, which studied redemptive-historical preaching using the Korean translations of Greidanus's *Sola Scriptura* and Clowney's *Preaching and Biblical Theology*. Chung found the origin of redemptive-historical preaching in the works of Dutch Calvinists in the 1930s, when the dialectical theology of Karl Barth permeated Reformed churches in Holland and when, at the same time, a group of theologians rose against the traditional subjectivism and spiritualism of the period. The Dutch redemptive-historical preaching movement started from this background. Chung also defined the principles of redemptive-historical preaching as being the same as Gootjes's.

Chung provided a more concrete method to develop redemptive-historical preaching, which consisted of six steps: recognition of the historical text; selection of the proper text; historical interpretation; organic interpretation; textual-thematic preaching; relevant preaching.[94] Chung's book was used as a redemptive-historical preaching text when the Korean homiletical debate occurred in 1998 and its use continued until recently. Although the redemptive-historical proponents in the debate are Chung's pupils, they misunderstood Chung's redemptive-historical preaching principles and I will discuss this in more detail in chapter 6.

Won-Tae Suk, Principal of Go-Ryo Theological Seminary, published a textbook on redemptive-historical preaching, *Redemptive-Historical Principles of Homiletical Theology*, which demonstrates a distinctive

---

93. Chung, *Principles and Methods of Redemptive-Historical Preaching*.
94. Ibid., 36–44.

understanding of redemptive history. He finds the ground of redemptive history in historic Calvinism, which he understands as a comprehensive biblical thought and life system, with a systematic interpretation of the Scriptures and with the idea of God-centeredness, which especially emphasizes God's sovereignty and proclaims God's authority over the origin, course, and end of all things. Suk defines history as an outcome of God's sovereign ruling over the world. Redemptive history is explained as:

> . . . the on-going historical process, on which God set the great plan, according to His delight and sovereign will, that is, saving His elect people under sin from eternal punishment through the redemption of Jesus Christ His Son, which had been previously revealed in Scriptures, and is fulfilled in the church, the body of Christ in the world.[95]

This definition of redemptive history distinctly emphasizes the sovereignty of God and includes the function of the church.

For Suk, world history is the stage for God's unfolding redemptive history. All things, including world history, are God's means for accomplishing His overarching purpose, the redemption of His people. Hence, history will never be purposelessly or meaninglessly repeated. If the objective of redemptive history were accomplished, then world history would come to an end. Suk opens his book with the proclamation: "Redemptive history centers on world history; Jesus Christ is the center of redemptive history; the redemptive history of Jesus Christ unfolds through the movements of His body, the church; the movements of Jesus Christ's church is activated by way of *kerygma*, namely, preaching."[96] Thus Suk's concept of redemptive history makes a monistic, teleological, and ecclesiological theory of history, emphasizing the *kerygma* of Christ's church as the kernel of human history. We will discuss this in more detail in chapter 7.

Jong-Kil Byun, Professor of New Testament in Ko-Shin Theological Seminary, published his doctoral dissertation in 1997, in which he dealt with the relationship between the progress of redemptive history and the ministry of the Holy Spirit in the text of John 7:39.[97] Byun tried to examine the progress of the Holy Spirit's ministry, especially in the

---

95. Suk, *Redemptive Historical Principles of Homiletical Theology*, 68–69.

96. Suk, Ibid., "Introduction."

97. Byun, "The Holy Spirit Was Not Yet." This thesis has been published in Korean with the title, *The Holy Spirit and Redemptive History*.

period before and after Christ's glorification, through the redemptive-historical perspective. He defined the term *redemptive history* like Trimp, saying "the whole of the divine acts which happened, happen and shall happen in history according to the eternal counsel of God, in so far as this is concerned with bringing salvation, redemption and restoration to mankind."[98] He seemed to understand redemptive history as a series of historical events in the Bible, such as creation, the fall of humanity, Abraham's calling, the Exodus, the incarnation of Christ, the cross and resurrection, ascension, Pentecost, and the second advent of Christ.[99]

Byun discussed the progress of the concept of redemptive history in the Church Fathers, such as Irenaeus, Tertullian, Origen, Chrysostom, and Augustine, then in the thought of Reformed theologians like Calvin, Kuyper, Herman Bavinck, and Ridderbos, exegeting the text of John 7:37–39 carefully. He concluded that the differences in the ministry of the Holy Spirit after Christ's glorification are "abundant grace," "indwelling in the church," and "the Spirit of the glorified Jesus," stressing that this new era of the Holy Spirit as the Paraclete should be explained in terms of the "progress of RH."[100] This study is significant, as Byun is the first Korean to examine the controversial aspect of pneumatology, especially John 7:37–39, from a Reformed biblical theology and redemptive-historical perspective.

Deuk-Il Shin, Professor of Old Testament in Ko-Shin University, wrote about redemptive history as a hermeneutical perspective in 2002.[101] He discussed redemptive history as a comprehensive concept relating to a variety of other themes, such as covenant, kingdom of God, promise, and fulfilment. He contends that the idea of redemptive history is a theological presupposition that is set up and anticipated by the Bible itself. For Shin, it is therefore inappropriate to interpret Old Testament texts without the correct application of redemptive-historical methodology.

---

98. Trimp, *Heilsgeschiedenis en prediking*, 37, quoted in Byun, *Holy Spirit and Redemptive History*, 22–23. Byun also indicated that Hofmann used the term *redemptive history* in Christian theology in the nineteenth century and that it was introduced into Reformed theology by Ridderbos by way of Oscar Cullmann.

99. Byun, *Holy Spirit and Redemptive History*, 23–24. Byun intended to point out a major stream or change of divine acts in the Scriptures. He appeared to consider the main text to be John 7:39.

100. Ibid., 215–225.

101. Shin, "Centre of the Old Testament in Debate and Redemptive History," 39–64.

More recently, Sung-Joo Kim has published a creative work in which he attempts to arrange all the covenants of Scripture along the lines of redemptive history.[102] He finds a close relationship between redemptive history and covenantal history in Scripture and suggests the concept of "covenantal redemptive history" for a more satisfying interpretation of the Bible. The kingdom of God is, for Kim, a comprehensive, consistent theme throughout the Bible, and the key to the theme is redemptive history, which is processed by the way of divine covenant.[103] This idea is mainly based on the work of William J. Dumbrell, Graeme Goldsworthy, Ridderbos, and Vos, but shows development in that all the covenants of Scripture are rearranged under the redemptive-historical perspective.[104]

This period, therefore, can be identified as the time when the concept of redemptive history flourished in the Korean Presbyterian Church.[105] There has been significant progress, as well as development, in accepting and applying redemptive-historical principles in hermeneutics and homiletics since the late 1980s. Several books relating to redemptive-historical preaching have been published, emphasizing the importance of a redemptive-historical framework for correct interpretation and preaching of the Scriptures. The term *redemptive history* has come to be held as a banner of orthodox doctrine and interpretation, the attachment of these words being recognized as a very Reformed theological position.

This flood of literature dealing with redemptive history is not, however, necessarily beneficial to a proper understanding and right application of redemptive history. There are also significant misconceptions, as well as confusion, over redemptive history in those writings, and subsequently conflict over the pros and cons of redemptive-historical preaching emerged in this period. We will briefly discuss this conflict later in this chapter, but in more detail in chapter 6. We now need to survey the cause and nature of this confusion.

---

102. Kim, *Redemptive History and God's Covenant for the Kingdom*.

103. Ibid., 167–71.

104. Dumbrell, *Covenant and Creation*; Goldsworthy, *Gospel and Kingdom*; Ridderbos, *Coming of the Kingdom*; Vos, *Biblical Theology*.

105. Kim, "Is it Right to Keep Redemptive-Historical Preaching in This Way?"

Redemptive History: Confusion

The understanding of redemptive history by the Korean Presbyterian Church is varied and confused, with many misunderstandings, and is in need of clarification. I begin this section by describing the confusion which exists over redemptive history in Korean churches.

Firstly, there are differing opinions about the origin of redemptive history in Korea. Dong-Shik Chi suggested its origins lay with theologians of German Pietism in the eighteenth century, especially J. A. Bengel.[106] Young-Bae Cha described Irenaeus of Lyons as the first scholar to promote the idea of redemptive history who was influenced not by Greek philosophy or myth, but rather by the Pauline epistles and the canonical book of Revelation.[107] Sung-Kuh Chung claims redemptive-historical preaching emerged with the Dutch Calvinists in the late 1930s.[108] Gootjes pointed out simplistically that redemptive history originated with the Bible itself.[109] Chang-Gyun Chung also finds the origin of redemptive-historical preaching in Scripture and biblical theology.[110] These explanations are not completely wrong, because the differences arise from different views of redemptive history. For example, D. S. Chi views redemptive history as a hermeneutical methodology, while Sung-Kuh Chung regards it as an homiletical approach, and Y. B. Cha considers it as one of the theological trends. Gootjes and Chang-Gyun Chung view it differently, as an implicit structure within Scripture. If redemptive history is intrinsic within Scripture, rather than superimposed from without, then the origin of redemptive history must be found in Scripture itself rather than in any specific theological school.[111] There still remains, however, the challenge of selecting the more appropriate way of viewing redemptive history from among these different perspectives.

Secondly, there are also basically different approaches to redemptive history, which might be perceived either as relating to hermeneutics or

---

106. Chi, "Modern Theology and the Concept of Redemptive History," 199.

107. Cha, "Theology of Salvation History," 20; cf. Lawson, *Biblical Theology of Saint Irenaeus*.

108. Chung, "Principles and Methods of Redemptive-Historical Preaching," 18–19.

109. Gootjes, *Between Exegesis and Sermon*, 195–97; cf. "How to Do Redemptive-Historical Preaching,"

110. Chung, *Preaching Beyond the Stereotyped Ideas*, 40–41.

111. This view is common among Reformed biblical theologians such as Vos, Ridderbos, and T. R. Schreiner. Cf. Ladd, *Theology of the New Testament*, 32.

homiletics. Those who initially introduced redemptive history to Korea, like Dong-Shik Chi, Chang-Kyu Lee, Wie Chai, and Gwang-Shik Kim, mainly discussed the hermeneutical or philosophical aspects of redemptive history, rather than the homiletical..[112] On the other hand, later proponents of redemptive history, like Sung-Jong Shin and Gootjes, focused mainly on the homiletical implications of redemptive history, while still others, like Young-Bae Cha, Sung-Kuh Chung, and Jong-Chil Park, dealt with its theological aspects. For example, Gootjes is concerned only with competent biblical preaching in the handling of redemptive history,[113] while Cha recognizes redemptive history as a comprehensive theology, rather than partly a methodology including hermeneutics or homiletics.[114] Park and Chung, however, incorporate the redemptive-historical hermeneutical method into Reformed preaching.[115]

This difference of focus concerning redemptive history is due not only to individual preferences but also to changing trends and theological developments in Korean church history itself. One example is that redemptive history was first introduced as a Western concept in the 1960s, but was highlighted in terms of hermeneutics in the 1970s. From the late 1980s the stress was more on homiletics, but from the early 1990s Korean churches have sought to attain a balance between hermeneutics and homiletics. Thus the difference in the weighting of redemptive history on the side of either hermeneutics or homiletics should be understood as illustrating changes in theological trends in Korean churches.

Thirdly, many Presbyterians, such as Jei-Ho Han[116] and Soon-Kil Huh,[117] assume that redemptive history represents the essence of the hermeneutics of Reformed theology. Sung-Kuh Chung, a representative theologian of Reformed homiletics in Korea, expressed redemptive-historical preaching as being the most desirable methodology among all

112. See the section "1960s to 1980s: Church Explosion" in this chapter. Cf. Cullmann, "Christ and Time"; Ott, *Geschichte und Heilsgeschichte in der Theologie Rudolf Bultmanns*; Braaten, *History and Hermeneutics*.

113. Chung, "Principles and Methods of Redemptive-Historical Preaching," 14–15.

114. Cha, "Theology of Salvation History," 20–29.

115. Park, "Study on the Controversies of the Redemptive-Historical Interpretation," 116–19; cf. Chung, *Reformed Homiletics*, 53: Chung thinks the problems and struggles of the contemporary Korean Church arose out of the separation between theology and preaching; thus he contends both elements need to be integrated into one dimension.

116. Han, *Biblical Interpretation and Preaching*.

117. Huh, *Reformed Preaching*.

the available approaches, in his magnum opus *Reformed Homiletics* in the early 1990s. This raised unnecessary misunderstanding and confusion in identifying redemptive-historical preaching with Reformed hermeneutics and homiletics. Many preachers[118] in Korean Reformed Presbyterian churches have been advocating redemptive history, considering it equivalent to orthodox Presbyterian theology. However, as Jong-Chil Park pointed out, the theology written under the banner of redemptive history has never been represented as being identical with Reformed theology, but instead has been fused with different theologies which include historical criticism and existentialism.[119]

Fourthly, the question as to whether redemptive history should be viewed as history, or as part of the revelation of Scripture, is also discussed in the literature relating to redemptive history in Korea. This is not due merely to confusion within Korean churches, for it is more intricate and even Western theologians struggle with this question. As we have explored in chapter 2,[120] there have been various views on redemptive history, which are based on how Scripture is to be viewed. For example, Cullmann identifies redemptive history with history, to which Scripture itself significantly attests, centering on the event of Jesus Christ,[121] while Bultmann considers redemptive history as the event or events of man's encountering God or His revelation.[122] On the other hand, Vos defines redemptive history as the history of God's special revelation, with which Scripture should be identified.[123] As we need to clarify these definitions of redemptive history before proceeding to discuss and evaluate the Korean debate, I will discuss this matter later in this chapter.

Fifthly, there are misconceptions over the relevance of redemptive history for contemporary churches. Theologians like Jee-Chan Kim regard redemptive-historical preaching as an old fashioned method that

---

118. For example, cf. Jang, "Study on the Homiletics of C. E. Macartney;" Sho, "Study on Hebrews Chapter Eleven."

119. Park, "Study on the Controversies of the Redemptive-Historical Interpretation," 36.

120. See section "Existentialism, " subsection "Relations to Redemptive History" and section "Reformed Biblical Theology," subsection "Characteristics and Influence" in chapter 2.

121. Cullmann, *Salvation History*, 45.

122. Bultmann, "History of Salvation and History," 274–80.

123. Vos, "Idea of Biblical Theology," 15–16; cf. *Biblical Theology*, 14.

should be abolished or renewed.[124] However, Kim does not identify those aspects of redemptive-historical preaching which he considers are outdated, or discuss how to make redemptive-historical preaching more relevant. This matter of relevancy has been considered differently according to the respective views of redemptive-historical proponents. For example, if it is regarded as originating with German Pietism, or even with the Dutch Calvinists of the 1930s, can redemptive history then be recognized legitimately as being irrelevant to the contemporary situation? However, most proponents of redemptive history, like Jong-Chil Park and Chang-Gyun Chung, think differently, claiming that the redemptive-historical perspective is deeply rooted in Scripture itself and is useful at any time for application to hermeneutics and homiletics.[125] There are differences, therefore, among Korean proponents of redemptive history concerning their respective understandings of it. But how did these differences arise?

Different Theological Windows

We should remind ourselves that there are different theological windows from which Korean theology might be examined in the context of Korean Presbyterian churches. Jong-Sung Lee suggested the two dimensions of "conservatism and liberalism," while Dong-Shik Ryu refers to three dimensions of "conservatism, progressivism, and liberalism," and Geun-Hwan Kang claims there are four dimensions of "conservatism, evangelicalism, progressivism, and liberalism."[126] These distinctive theological trends explain how conceptions of redemptive history have developed differently among Korean proponents.

Theological conservatism in Korea clings to those theological traditions which missionaries established in the early days of Protestantism,

---

124. Kim, "Is it Right to Keep Redemptive-Historical Preaching in This Way?" Kim believed that redemptive-historical preaching arose from the hermeneutic and homiletic debate in the Netherlands in the 1930s and 1940s, but that it had disappeared after 1944. Although Trimp tried to reignite the controversy, he was not successful. Kim then felt that it was unnatural for the old fashioned approach to flourish in Korea as it had by then run its course.

125. Chung, "Ground of Redemptive-Historical Preaching," 7. Chung says that redemptive-historical preaching is the necessary corollary of Reformed biblical theology and should be recognized not as one of several preaching methodologies but as the grounding principle in which biblical preaching must be rooted.

126. Kang, "Theological Trends Developed through Historical Streams of the Protestant Church of Korea," 143–71.

and does not welcome modern theological thought like that of *Heilsgeschichte*, which theologians like Bultmann and Barth used extensively. For example, Yune-Sun Park first warned about Barth's theology,[127] insisting that his view of Scripture is crucially different from the Reformed position. This warning stirred members of Korean Presbyterian churches in the 1950s, and contributed to their rejection of Barthian theology at a time when it began to influence Korean churches in general. For this reason, some scholars like Harold Hong criticize the theological conservatism that held the Korean peninsula firmly in its grasp and blocked other types of theological thought.[128]

On the other hand, theological liberalism in Korea received various theological influences from the Western world in the same period, advocating "the idea of freedom" which was oriented towards progressive, open scholarship.[129] This theological trend in Korea began in the middle of the 1930s and was established by the 1960s. According to Dong-Shik Ryu,[130] a professor at Yon-Sei University, theological liberalism relating to redemptive history was planted in Korea in the 1960s.[131] For example, Nam-Dong Seo introduced Bultmann's concept of *Heilsgeschichte*, and Chang-Kyu Lee responded quickly to it, comparing Bultmann with Cullmann in 1966.[132] Ik-Hwan Moon (1918–1994), Professor of Old Testament in Han-Shin Theological Seminary, unhesitatingly accepted higher criticism in the late 1950s and began to introduce a critical view of history through his articles.[133] While these liberal theologians discussed

---

127. Park, "Criticism on Barth's View of Revelation," 32–35, 77. Park criticized Barth's dualistic view of revelation, which divides revelation into "supra-temporal" (*Urgeschichte*) and "temporal" areas, originating from Platonism that separates spirit from body, because the latter was considered as evil but the former as good. Scripture consistently stresses, however, a revelation representing not only the spiritual world but also the temporal world.

128. Hong, "Past, Present, and Future of the Korean Church," 22.

129. This phrase is a banner of Han-Shin Theological Seminary, which is the denominational seminary of Ki-Jang (The Presbyterian Church in the Republic of Korea).

130. Kim, "Trends of Korean Theology," 128–36. Ryu divides the periods of the Korean Protestant church according to the perspective of the theological liberalism of Korea, such as the periods of "forthcoming" (1885–1930), "establishment" (1930–1960), and "development" (1960–2000).

131. Ryu, "Review," 93–95, 102.

132. See the section "Theological Turbulence and Schism" in this chapter.

133. Moon, "Redemptive History and Creation History," 45–70.

redemptive history, the conservative group hardly mentioned the term or the concept in their literature in the 1960s.

Evangelicalism in Korea, which is not necessarily Reformed or conservative,[134] began to appear from the 1960s after schism in the largest Presbyterian denomination. The two largest Presbyterian groups, Hap-Dong and Tong-Hap, separated from each other in 1959 because the latter joined the WCC. The Hap-Dong group was critical of the WCC for embracing a more liberal theology, but the Tong-Hap group supported the organization.[135] Thus the Presbyterian Church in Korea was divided almost equally, with nearly seven thousand local churches and more than two million members in each. The Tong-Hap group, more open to accepting theological inclusiveness, has been recognized as the "new evangelicalism" or "moderated conservatism," regarding the original theological conservatism as an "erroneous and irrelevant type of thought" for modern minds.[136]

This trend, thus, embraces various kinds of theology, especially neo-orthodox Barthian theology, criticizing the limits and narrowness of the alleged fundamentalism, which was the traditional theology in Korean Presbyterian churches. Myung-Yong Kim, Professor of Systematic Theology in Jang-Shin College,[137] criticized the theology of Korean Reformed churches for rejecting the theology of Barth, Brunner, Niebuhr, and Moltmann, who were each globally recognized as great Reformed theologians, and following instead the narrower theology of Machen and Van Til.[138]

These distinctive theological trends in Korean churches inevitably contributed to different understandings of redemptive history in Korean literature, so that the reception and modification of the redemptive-historical concept in Korean churches has been mostly processed along these

---

134. Kim, "Trends of Korean Theology," 130–31. In Europe, Evangelicalism means the thought and theology, of the Reformers, as opposed to Roman Catholicism or theological liberalism. In Korea it is recognized as theological neutralism, a position between extreme conservatism and the liberalism, or New Evangelicalism in the United States, which emphasizes evangelism of the gospel without questioning or debating controversial doctrines like the Virgin Birth of Christ.

135. Song, "Historical and Theological Analysis of Schism," 24.

136. Kim, "Criticism on New Evangelicalism," 37–50. Cf. Ashbrook, "New Evangelicalism."

137. Jan-Shin College is based in the Tong-Hap denomination. Its official English name is Presbyterian College and Theological Seminary, but it is usually called Jang-Shin College in Korean churches.

138. Kim, *Open Theology and Right Ecclesiology*, 200–209.

lines. For example, Rak-Jae Choi described redemptive history through Reformed or theological conservatism, but Gwang-Shik Kim did so through a theologically liberal framework in the same period. That is one reason why those who are theologically conservative are uninterested in the early introduction of hermeneutical aspects of redemptive history, while liberals are not so interested in the later debate of redemptive-historical preaching. We need to look in more detail later in this chapter at the relationship of the Korean understanding of redemptive history and Western authors responsible for redemptive-historical literature.

Denominational Backgrounds and Restriction

Different theologies also closely relate to the backgrounds of church denominations in Korea. Joshua Song described the history of schism in the PCK from 1969 to 2005. His analysis was that the causes for these divisions were historical, political, sociological, and theological factors. According to Song, the theological factors are especially complex and deeply related to international theological movements.[139] Once the churches divided into different denominations, they either did not cooperate with each other or they compromised, particularly on theological issues. It would therefore have been extremely difficult, if not impossible, to have exchanged open discussion on any theological issue across denominational barriers.

Western thought and theologies in relation to redemptive history have also left their mark on the theological attitudes and assumptions of Korean theologians and ministers. Jong-Hyun Sung, a New Testament professor in Jang-Shin Theological Seminary, who mapped out the various influences on denominational seminaries in the 1980s, claimed that Jang-Shin Seminary had been influenced by traditional redemptive-historical school scholars like Cullmann, C. H. Dodd, Leonhard Goppelt, and A. M. Hunter. Nevertheless, it is surprising that no Jang-Shin professor shows interest in the redemptive-historical homiletical debate in Korea and no explanation of this fact is provided.[140]

---

139. Song, "Historical and Theological Analysis of Schism," 305–6.
140. Sung, *Introduction to the New Testament*, 90.

Links to Western Theologians

Nearly all Korean theologians who favor, and write on, redemptive history have an affinity with Western theologians of redemptive history. For example, Gwang-Shik Kim introduced Cullmann as a representative theologian of redemptive history,[141] and also translated Heinrich Ott's book on redemptive history[142] in the mid-1970s. Kim himself was directly affected theologically by Cullmann and Ott, in the relationship of teacher and pupil, during his theological studies in Basel University in the 1960s. Kim recollected that he often had the opportunity to meet Cullmann in a school dormitory, Theologisches Alumneum, and listen to him on "*schon aber noch nicht*" ("already but not yet") which is the essential content of his theology of redemptive history.[143] This meeting with Cullmann served as a stimulus for developing a closer relationship with Ott and translating his books.[144]

Nam-Dong Seo, who first introduced the term *redemptive history* in Korean literature in the late 1950s, acknowledged that his own theological concept of redemptive history, as well as other subjects like the kingdom of God, was influenced by several Western theologians, especially Bultmann, Niebuhr, and Tillich.[145] Bultmann's writings, such as *Primitive Christianity* and *History and Eschatology*, and Tillich's *Protestant Era* and *Interpretation of History*, had admittedly a crucial impact on Seo's thought and methodology.[146] Niebuhr's consciousness of history also helped Seo equip himself with a mature understanding of the Christian interpretation of history and further his interest in the hermeneutics of history.

Wie Chai, who mentioned the perspective of Luke's redemptive history in the 1960s, also owed the theological development of his concept of the kingdom of God mainly to theologians like Cullmann and Carl Braaten.[147] Most Korean scholars, such as Nam-Dong Seo, Gwang-Shik

---

141. Kim, "Oscar Cullmann," 75–82.

142. Ott, *Geschichte und Heilsgeschichte in der Theologie Rudolf Bultmanns*.

143. Kim, "Oscar Cullmann," 75.

144. Ibid., 76. When Kim once asked Cullmann about the paradoxical relationship between philosophical existentialism and Cullmann's concept of redemptive history, Cullmann replied that Kim would do better to seek the answer from Ott, because Cullmann himself was not a philosopher but a scholar of the Bible.

145. Seo, "Theologians and their Writings by Which I Have Been Affected," 69–71.

146. Seo also translated Bultmann's *History and Eschatology* into Korean.

147. Cullmann, "Christ and Time"; Braaten, *History and Hermeneutics*.

Kim, Ik-Whan Moon, and Wie Chai, who discussed the hermeneutical subject of redemptive history in the earlier period from the 1950s to the 1960s, are classified as being theologically liberal or progressive in Korea and had close connections with German theologians like Bultmann and Cullmann.

The later proponents of redemptive history and more conservative theologians are, in contrast, closer to the two specific theological trends belonging to the Netherlands and the United States. On the one hand, Rak-Jae Choi, who introduced a Reformed view, especially the concept of redemptive history of Vos and Ridderbos,[148] formed his hermeneutical perspective of redemptive history in his studies at WTS, Philadelphia. This school highlighted the biblical theology of Vos and also the redemptive-historical approach of Ridderbos and Gaffin. Choi's theological position relates directly to the Reformed tradition of Vos, Ridderbos, and Gaffin. The frequent and crucial quotations from those theologians in Choi's writings attest to his academic affinity with them.[149] Hyung-Yong Park, who discussed the redemptive-historical perspective in 1977,[150] had also previously studied at WTS and quotes often from Ridderbos and Vos, clearly depending on them.

On the other hand, Sung-Kuh Chung, who first introduced redemptive-historical preaching to the Korean Presbyterian Church, graduated from the Free (Vrije) University in Holland where he received his Doctor of Theology in Homiletics. Chung focused on the principles and methods of redemptive-historical preaching, which Dutch theologians like Schilder and Holwerda had controversially discussed earlier and Greidanus and Trimp reviewed later. Chung's introduction of redemptive-historical preaching expressed mainly the transposition of the Dutch discussion of the subject, and included not only the explanation of its principles but also some unnecessary details of the debate.

Jong-Chil Park, who extensively discussed redemptive history as a hermeneutic and homiletical methodology, mostly refers to the ideas of Dutch theologians, especially Holwerda. Although Park had not studied in Dutch theological institutions, he indirectly encountered Dutch

---

148. Choi, "New Testament Hermeneutics and the History of Redemption," 59–66, 51. This article was originally Choi's thesis for his MTh from Westminster Theological Seminary.

149. Choi, "Revelation and the Bible," 64–70; "Paul's Eschatology," 67–76; *Kingdom of God*; *Seeing Christ in Scripture*.

150. Park, "Study on the Redemptive-Historical Perspective," 102–13.

advocates of redemptive history, like Gootjes, in Korea and was affected by their writings. These references to Western theologians, and the transposition of the Western theological debate directly or indirectly into Korean churches, reflect the dependence of Korean redemptive-historical scholars on Western theologians.

Those dependent on Western theologians can be classified into three groups with regard to redemptive history. The first group includes Korean liberal theologians, like Gwang-Shik Kim and Nam-Dong Seo, who discussed mainly its hermeneutical aspects and are directly related to German theologians like Cullmann, Barth, and Bultmann. In the second group are the more conservative theologians, who introduced the Reformed view of redemptive history and directly relate to American theologians like Vos, Ridderbos, and Gaffin. The third group comprises other conservative scholars, like Sung-Kuh Chung and Jong-Chil Park, who mostly discussed redemptive-historical preaching directly or indirectly and were connected with Dutch theologians specializing in its methodology and its debate.

The basic teachings and definitions of redemptive history by Western theologians, from whom Korean proponents of redemptive history have learned and quoted, need to be reviewed briefly at this point.

Definitions of Redemptive History

We have examined the roots of various understandings of redemptive history, with analysis of related scholars, in chapter 2. However, there may still be some remaining confusion over the definition of redemptive history. We need to review briefly those various definitions comparatively in order to identify the concepts of redemptive history and the resultant perspectives regarding redemptive-historical preaching.

Oscar Cullmann

Cullmann has been most frequently mentioned with regard to the subject of *Heilsgeschichte* as one major exponent of the *heilsgeschichtlich* (salvation-historical) approach in Korean literature.[151] This identified

---

151. Cf. Chang, "Redemptive-Historical Preaching and Biblical Theology," 12–24; this article was an interview with a redemptive-historical preacher, Jei-Ho Han, who identified Cullmann as the initiator in the 1930s of the use of the expression "salvation

Heilsgeschichte with the "economy of salvation," which actually means "the divine sequence of events." But the German word *Heilsgeschichte* has, for Cullmann, several controversial elements. On the one hand, theologians in the German-speaking world almost automatically link the expression *salvation history* to a specific theological group—the *Heilsgeschichtler* (belonging to the salvation history school) in the nineteenth century—because adherents of that school wrote the expression on their banners.[152] Misunderstandings arose that anyone using the term was influenced by those earlier ideas.

On the other hand, the term *salvation history* is not found in Scripture itself. However, Cullmann claims that the expression is closely related to the NT Greek word *oikonomia,* meaning plan or economy, and renders the "plan of salvation."[153] Therefore, Cullmann defines salvation history as "a connected series of events, within God's plan (or economy) of salvation, which belongs to history, and of which the centre and norm is Christ's death on the cross."[154] In this basic concept of salvation history, the tension between the "already fulfilled" and the "not yet completed" of God's plan is considered by him to be the key to the whole theology of the NT.[155] Cullmann thought that Scripture itself attests to the idea of salvation history as the central theme of theology, and thus it should be read with that clear perspective in mind.

---

history" as synonymous with *Heilsgeschichte.* Han was, however, not correct because the German word was already used by Bengel in the eighteenth century, and also by Hofmann and "the school of Heilsgeschichte" in the nineteenth century. See the section "Historical Background" in chapter 1.

152. Cullmann, *Salvation in History,* 75. Cullmann thought that the school of salvation history was greatly dependent upon the Hegelian philosophy of the time. Cf. Cullmann, *Heil als Geschichte.*

153. See the "Definition" section in chapter 1. Cullmann argued that the biblical Greek word *oikonomia* renders the "plan of salvation" (Rom 11:25; 1 Cor 4:2, 15:51) or "economy of the mystery of God" (Eph 3:9). He taught that the idea that "God carries out his plan in connection with specific, temporal events," included in the NT meaning of *oikonomia,* is intended in the whole New Testament.

154. Cullmann, *Salvation in History,* 78.

155. Ibid., 166–85.

Rudolf Bultmann

Bultmann, introduced to Korean churches as a distinguished opponent of Cullmann's *heilsgeschichtlich* approach,[156] admittedly struggled with the concept of salvation history.[157] For Bultmann, the meaning of history in the phrase *history of salvation* is unclear and refers to nothing other than the succession of events in time and space. The idea of the history of salvation, in which history and myth are connected, in Bultmann's judgment originally appeared in Jewish apocalyptic speculation and was modified by Cullmann, with the mid-points having been pushed back on the Christ's time-line.[158]

Bultmann thought there can be no real "salvation occurrence" in that kind of mystical history. He explained that the appearance of Christ signifies the eschatological event that puts an end to the old aeon, or time, and thus there can be no more history and also no more history of salvation.[159] Consequently Bultmann said, "For as much as I would agree with the statement that the occurrence of salvation is Christian theology's real theme, as little could I see this salvation-occurrence in what Cullmann speaks of as the history of salvation."[160] For Bultmann, salvation occurrence (*Heilsgeschehen*) is more important than salvation history (*Heilsgeschichte*) in the New Testament, and the latter is to be abandoned due to its irrelevance.

According to Bultmann, Christian existence as a "new creation" must be understood as an eschatological mode of existence, which means to exist in constantly new decisions of faith.[161] Briefly, the history of salvation, recognized as the apocalyptic and narrative sequence of events in Israel, was terminated with Christ's appearance and then Christians began to exist in the following eschatological era while constantly making decisions with regard to Christ's ethical imperatives. This view, I suggest, approximates to the philosophy of history advocated by Heidegger.

---

156. Lee, "Redemptive History or the Event of Redemption," 79–89. Cf. Chi, "Modern Theology and the Concept of Redemptive History," 197–210.

157. Bultmann, "History of Salvation and History," 268–84. Cf. "Heilsgeschichte und Geschichte," 659–66. In its original form this article is subtitled "A Review of Oscar Cullmann, *Christ and Time*."

158. Cullmann, *Christ and Time*, 94–95.

159. Bultmann, "History of Salvation and History," 281.

160. Ibid., 274.

161. Ibid., 283–84.

There is, therefore, a deep division between Cullmann and Bultmann over the concept of redemptive history, and thus confusion can arise in reading both authors side by side. Bultmann seeks the positive meaning of history in the phrase of salvation history, while Cullmann revives the concept of primitive Christianity; the former was affected by philosophical positivism, and the latter by early theologians like Irenaeus.

Karl Barth

Barth initially would have nothing to do with the concept of *Heilsgeschichte*, because he thought revelation, which belongs to the eternal world of God, cannot be found in history, which is the transitory or rebellious world of humans.[162] He utilized instead the term *Urgeschichte* (primal history) in his early period of writing in *Church Dogmatics I*. He writes: "Even human nature and human history in general have no independent signification. They point to the primal history (*Urgeschichte*) played out within them between God and the one man, and all other men as His people."[163] History then belongs to the temporal world that is considered by Barth to be the object of God's judgment: "The whole history of the Church and of all religion takes place in this world. What is called the 'history of our salvation' is not an event in the midst of other events, but is nothing less than the Crisis of all history."[164] The latter term here means the encountering of the two different worlds, for example, the righteous God with rebellious man, and brings in the judgment of God. Revelation thus occurs not in the human historical realm but at the intersection where God's world of salvation and the world of human history meet, and it is the "end of history."[165]

Barth might, in his early period, have more preferably used the expression *Urgeschichte* rather than *Heilsgeschichte*, but he changed his view,[166] later accepting the perspective of salvation history when he wrote

---

162. Barth, *Epistle to the Romans*, 77. Barth said, "History is the display of the supposed advantages of power and intelligence which some men possess over others, of the struggle for existence hypocritically described by ideologists as a struggle for justice and freedom, of the ebb and flow of old and new forms of human righteousness, each vying with the rest in solemnity and triviality."

163. Barth, *Church Dogmatics* II/2, 8–9.

164. Barth, *Epistle to the Romans*, 57.

165. Rottenberg, *Redemption and Historical Reality*, 149–50.

166. Barth, *How I Changed My Mind*, 61–72. Barth divided his theological journey

his *Church Dogmatics* III.[167] He began to claim that all other history must be read in the light of *Heilsgeschichte*:

> The history of salvation is the history, the true history which encloses all other history and to which in some way all other history belongs to the extent that it reflects and illustrates the history of salvation; to the extent that it accomplishes it with signs and intimations and examples and object lessons.[168]

This concept of salvation history is not different from what the school of *Heilsgeschichte* in the nineteenth century taught. However Barth redefined the history of salvation:

> What is meant is the history of the covenant of grace instituted by God between Himself and man; the sequence of the events in which God concludes and executes this covenant with man, carrying it to its goal, and thus validating in the sphere of the creature that which from all eternity He has determined in Himself . . . This history is from the theological standpoint *the* history.[169]

Salvation history for Barth, then, is nothing less than the history of the covenant of grace, and all other history belongs to it.

However, Barth's concept of *Heilsgeschichte* clearly differs from both that of Cullmann and Bultmann. Barth criticized Cullmann's perspective on the basis that the crucial thing in the New Testament is the vertical saving act of God in Christ.[170] On the other hand, Barth rejected Bultmann's teaching in that the demythologizing or discarding of the elements of salvation history could be an inappropriate approach to Scripture. Barth said:

> It resulted in an attempt to penetrate to a 'historical' kernel which is supposed to give us the true, i.e., 'historical' Word of

---

into five periods: before 1928, 1928–38, 1938–48, 1948–58, and after 1958. He changed his mind about salvation history, especially in the period from 1938–48 when he completed four volumes of *Church Dogmatics*, from vol. II, part one, to vol. III, part two, lecturing at the University of Basel.

167. Rottenberg, *Redemption and Historical Reality*, 151.

168. Barth, *Church Dogmatics* III/1, 60. Barth also says, "To distinguish it from world history . . . the conservative theology of the 19th century called it the history of salvation. The expression is materially correct and important."

169. Ibid., 59.

170. Cullmann, *Salvation in History*, 16.

> God—the only trouble being that in the process it was unfortunately found that with the discarding of saga we do not lose only a subsidiary theme but the main point at issue, i.e., the biblical witness.[171]

Differing from Bultmann, Barth accepts in salvation history not only the historical factors, which can be verified through scientific analysis, but also the non-historical or pre-historical events, namely, saga, which are not traceable by an historicist's research.

These differences highlight for us again the complexity of the term *Heilsgeschichte* and we also find Barth's inconsistent understanding of the term is problematic. I regard the underlying problem here to be rooted in the prevailing idea of philosophical positivism which refuses to recognize the historical process of God's saving action as real history. Barth pointed this out, but simultaneously proclaimed that the biblical history is to be reckoned with as being both history and saga.[172]

Geerhardus Vos

Vos, the father of Reformed biblical theology, sought for the meaning and definition of biblical theology and its directly related term redemptive history not from contemporary philosophy, but from Scripture itself. Biblical theology is, for Vos, the history of special revelation.[173] Vos mainly discussed the relationship between the historical processes of redemption and revelation in his magnum opus *Biblical Theology*. To Vos, revelation is a function, namely, an interpretation, of redemption, and thus the history of revelation is an essential strand within the history of redemption as a whole. For him, the redemption of God does not abruptly cut into history only at a single point, in contrast to the thought of existentialist theologians like Bultmann, but it consists in the long history of God's covenantal activity up to its final fulfilment in Christ.[174]

---

171. Barth, *Church Dogmatics* III/1, 82. For Barth, the biblical history of creation is pure saga, which is defined as an intuitive and poetic picture of a pre-historical reality of history which is enacted once and for all within the confines of time and space (p. 81). In this understanding, Christ's crucifixion and resurrection events in the gospels become the narratives of the once-for-all event in the form of saga.

172. Ibid., 81–82.

173. Vos, *Biblical Theology*, 23.

174. Gaffin, "Introduction," xvi.

According to Vos, biblical theology, which is the history of special revelation, is nothing less than the interpretation of the history of redemption. Both the history of revelation and the history of redemption comprise essentially the same content, that is, God's redemptive acts in history. Therefore biblical theology, for Vos, has an inseparable connection with the history of redemption. Gaffin asserts, "It is difficult to resist the conclusion that the biblical-theological method or, better, the redemptive-historical orientation exemplified by Vos is, to date, the most fruitful and pointedly biblical realization of the Reformation insistence that Scripture interprets Scripture."[175]

In Vos's concept of the history of redemption there are no theological or philosophical pitfalls, which lead the reader into a maze. While Bultmann and Barth are struggling with the definition of *Geschichte*, to vindicate it from the nineteenth century philosophical approach, Vos affirms the integral tie between truth and history from a biblical perspective. The history of redemption, for Vos, is not some special kind of history, which was prevalent in the contemporary existential theology as the notion of a detemporalized *Geschichte*, but a square and obviously acceptable history, which is the history of revelation depicted by Scripture itself. Vos confirms this:

> Revelation is not an isolated act of God, existing without connection with all the other divine acts of supernatural character. It constitutes a part of that great process of the new creation . . . The revelation of God being not subjective and individual in its nature, but objective and addressed to the human race as a whole, it is but natural that this revelation should be embedded in the channel of the great objective history of redemption and extend no further than this.[176]

Here we find that Vos's delineation of redemptive history is different from that of Cullmann, Bultmann, and Barth, for he is expressing and demanding the close relationship between revelation and redemptive history. Vos sought for the biblical understanding of redemptive history, and this is rather more creative and orthodox than that given by the theologians of *Heilsgeschichte*. This is the first case, in the Reformed world, that the term and its related concept are defined in terms of revelation. Gaffin highlights this point: "In the case of Scripture, the redemptive-historical

---

175. Ibid., xviii.
176. Vos, *Redemptive History and Biblical Interpretation*, 8.

structure or framework established by Scripture itself is the contextual factor having the broadest bearing on a given text."[177]

Herman Ridderbos

Ridderbos also emphasized the relationship between redemptive history and Scripture: "Scripture has a history. It is a product of God's revelatory activity in the history of redemption. Therefore the revelatory character of the Bible should not be separated in a mechanical fashion from RH."[178] He also affirmed that redemptive history crucially affected the process of the canonization of the New Testament. For Ridderbos, the significance of the Bible and the nature of its authority can properly be understood only by closely relating Scripture to redemptive history.[179] This affirmation implies a circular corollary that redemptive history constitutes Scripture and thus it can only be understood by Scripture itself. We cannot find an explicit definition of redemptive history in Ridderbos's literature, only the recognition of it as the foundation for interpreting the New Testament.

Klaas Schilder

Schilder views history as the fulfilment of God's counsel; everything in the world follows the plan of God's plan—a plan which does not allow two kinds of history. Although Barth and the theologians of *Heilsgeschichte* differentiated between sacred and secular history, Schilder dislikes that distinction and emphasizes the unity of history: "Both the so called 'sacred' history and the profane history occur in the same realm, on earth, in our world, in time, among men of flesh and blood."[180] He added:

> Reformed people . . . believe that the Counsel of God has planned all things according to his will, that God fulfils that Counsel, that he reveals himself in Christ to save the world; that it follows from this that history is a unity, and that this unity,

---

177. Gaffin, "Introduction," xxii.
178. Ridderbos, *Redemptive History*, ix.
179. Ibid.
180. Schilder, *Heidelbergsche Catechismus*, vol. 1, 178, quoted in Greidanus, *Sola Scriptura*, 122.

which includes the unity of 'redemptive history,' is apparent (to faith) in Holy Scripture which relates of this history . . .[181]

Schilder's description is in line with Calvin and Luther, as well as with Vos's dependence on the Bible.[182] He went further to define redemptive history in 1946 as "the successive realization in time of God's thoughts of peace for us according to his fixed plan, and the fulfilment in time of this work-program which Father, Son, and Spirit decided upon before time."[183] Here we find more focus on God's work-plan in time. Schilder later added the function of revelation in redemptive history, saying, "Revelation exists in God's counsel and, according to his plan, is imparted in time, progressing from strength to strength, from nucleus to periphery, from twilight to noontide."[184] This definition is more doctrinal than Vos's and yet follows Scripture closely and practically.

Sidney Greidanus

Greidanus tried to find a clear definition of the history of redemption and finally claimed to have found a reason why no precise definition of redemptive history had been given in church history—that it is intimately related to God's revelation and, in fact, redemptive history is itself revelation.[185] While Greidanus viewed redemptive history as being identical with God's revelation, Vos distinguishes between them.[186] Thus Greidanus suggested the preferable expression *redemptive revelational*

---

181. Schilder, "Concerning the Unity of 'Redemptive History' in Connection with Preaching," 365, quoted in Greidanus, *Sola Scriptura*, 123.

182. Schilder's description of history is in accord with Calvin's notion of God's decree, creation, providence, and fulfilment in history.

183. Schilder, *Ref*, XXI (1946), 225. Cf. *Heidelbergsche Catechismus*, vol. 2, 263, quoted in Greidanus, *Sola Scriptura*, 123.

184. Greidanus, *Sola Scriptura*, 124.

185. Ibid., 121.

186. Ibid. Cf. Vos, *Biblical Theology*, 6. Greidanus says that redemptive history is intimately related with God's revelation; in fact, redemptive history is itself revelation. Vos says that the two processes (redemption and revelation) are not entirely co-extensive, for revelation comes to a close at a point where redemption still continues. For Vos, redemptive history extends further than revelation, as redemptive history is engaged in the subjective-individual acts of God's redemption, like regeneration, justification, conversion, sanctification, and glorification, whereas revelation accompanies only the process of objective-central redemption.

history rather than that of redemptive-history.[187] He contends that there are essentially three postulates in the redemptive-historical approach: real history, a unity, and progress, so God realizes His plan of redemption on the horizontal plane of history, which in turn constitutes the essential characteristics of Scripture, that is, its unity and progress. We can then see from Scripture that this one progressing history is centered in Christ and anchored in the eternal decree of God.[188] Scripture therefore shows us the embedded unity and progress of this Christ-centeredness. As a corollary of his approach, Greidanus suggests that the terms *redemptive history* and *revelational history* should be used interchangeably, the features of the one applying equally to the other. This concept agrees closely with that of Schilder.

As we have seen above, the original Western concepts of redemptive history are complex and somewhat confusing, resulting in inevitable confusion concerning redemptive history in Korean churches, particularly over the terms *history* and the *redemption of God*, which both converge into the question of how to read and interpret the Bible. To put the point differently, each concept of history and revelation, and their relation to each other is an essential issue in Western and in Korean Protestant theology. These points relate directly to the question of how to read and interpret the Bible, consequently resulting in a different understanding of redemptive-historical hermeneutics.

We have already examined these points in chapter 2, concentrating on three methods which are prevalent in biblical hermeneutics: historical criticism (or historicism), existentialism, and Reformed biblical theology. We now proceed in the next chapter to explore the present status of redemptive history in Korean Protestant theology and homiletics.

187. Ibid.
188. Ibid., 124.

6

The Debate in Korea
Homiletics and Redemptive History

WE HAVE ALREADY EXPLORED three hermeneutical roots of redemptive-historical perspectives[1] and also the homiletical redemptive-historical debates within Reformed circles in the Netherlands and America.[2] The historical background to the different, sometimes confused, understandings of redemptive history by Korean theologians and preachers in Korea was also examined in the previous chapter.

In this chapter we describe and assess how the Korean debate emerged and developed.

The Redemptive-Historical Debate in Korea: Its Homiletical Context.

The numerical growth in Korean Protestant churches in the 1970s and 1980s had a profound, often negative, influence on qualitative church growth.[3] One negative influence was in relation to preaching, which became a matter of deep concern for many Reformed scholars and church leaders. For example, Sung-Kuh Chung suggested that "the sermon is the mirror of the Korean church. I would like to mention again that the Korean church has grown through the intensive Bible study and the

---

1. Refer to chapter 2.
2. Refer to chapters 3 and 4.
3. Refer to the section "1960s to 1980s: Church Explosion" in chapter 5.

preaching of the early Korean preachers," who had ministered from the 1950s to the 1970s.[4] However, he acknowledged that by 1986 Protestant preaching was generally characterized by a more superficial approach which sought to entertain and make people happy, with an emphasis on testimonies, and with sermon content geared to numerical growth as well as local church success.[5] This is sometimes referred to as "the crisis of preaching," and is now examined in more detail.

Crisis of Preaching

The crisis regarding preaching is related to the rapidly decreasing number of members and adherents in Protestant churches in Korea during the last twenty years, which contrasts sharply with a numerical increase in the same period for Roman Catholicism and also Buddhism. A media research in 2006 reported that 58 percent of the Korean people do not respect or trust Protestant churches.[6] Jae-Chul Lee, pastor of The 100th Anniversary Memorial Church, regrets that the Korean church has lost the ability to contribute beneficially to society, but instead has become the target of scathing criticism from unbelievers.[7] This criticism is due in part to the increasing number of nominal Christians in churches who fail to practice their Christian principles in the community or in their own homes. Their poor life styles are rarely challenged by vital biblical preaching, and even preachers themselves are not beyond reproach for their inconsistent behavior. The current Protestant church "crisis of preaching" is intimately linked to this poor standard of preaching, with its negative impact on church life.

This crisis has at least two integral aspects which are relevant to this research. One is that of understanding the biblical text and the other is that of applying the biblical text responsibly to the congregation. Here is the challenge of moving between "the two horizons" of the biblical and contemporary worlds. The preaching often fails to handle the text competently and adequately, frequently deviating from the authorial intent of the original writer. Within the Reformed confessional context such preaching would be regarded as defective and no longer

---

4. Chung, *Korean Church and Reformed Faith*, 20.
5. Chung, *History of Preaching in the Korean Church*, 395.
6. "The Greatest Cause."
7. Lee. "At the Centre of the Crisis in Preaching Are the Mega-Churches."

recognized as God's Word. Rather it would be viewed as an expression of mere human opinions.

The unexpected church expansion in Korea in the 1970s and 1980s required the immediate introduction of more Christian workers, but this resulted in the hasty provision of additional ministers and evangelists, many of whom were ill-equipped and inexperienced due to inadequate theological training in some non-accredited seminaries.[8] In this situation complaints were made by church officers and members concerning "the absence of true preaching," and some referred to what they called "the crisis of preaching."[9] Complaints about preaching continued to be made even when ministers had been well trained; the complaints concerned the irrelevance of such preaching for the daily lives and problems of the hearers. Chang-Bok Chung, a professor of homiletics in Jang-Shin Theological Seminary, describes today's preaching in Korea as unclear in interpreting the biblical text, laden with meaningless words, and with excessive time given to stories about the preacher himself.[10] People therefore become bored and dissatisfied with such preaching and tend to lose confidence in preaching. Sometimes attempts are even made to introduce other methods and programs as substitutes for preaching.[11]

Response

Recognizing the serious nature of the problem, PCK leaders adopted various strategies to overcome this crisis. One significant response was to reflect on the history of preaching and compare it critically with contemporary preaching. According to Sung-Kuh Chung, the PCK had majored on one style of preaching, that of topical preaching, and had done so for about one hundred years.[12] The reason for this was that early Western missionaries had preached in that way and so it was firmly established as a tradition for preaching. Focusing mainly on examples from the lives of people, allegories, and experiences in order to interest and communicate with the congregation, topical preaching had helped the early Christians for several decades. However, in the second part of the twentieth cen-

---

8. Song, "Historical and Theological Analysis of Schism," 310–11.
9. Park, *Homiletics Today*, 15–19.
10. Chung, *Introduction to the Homiletics of the Korean Church*, 284.
11. Kim, *Expository Preaching as Architectures*, 19.
12. Chung, *History of Preaching in the Korean Church*, 18.

tury, and especially from around the 1980s, dissatisfaction was expressed regarding this type of preaching as people became better educated and their social, family, and personal needs changed. New preaching styles were consequently introduced into some theological seminaries like Chong-Shin, so that expository preaching was highlighted as a more suitable way of satisfying people's contemporary needs.[13]

This concern for better and "true preaching" increased and led to the introduction to Korean churches of many homiletical textbooks, with Korean scholars translating some Western homiletical textbooks into Korean. Among these were: Barth's *Homiletik: Wesen und Vorbereitung der Predigt*, translated by Keun-Won Park (1981); J. Daniel Baumann's *Introduction to Contemporary Preaching*, translated by Chang-Bok Chung (1983); Andrew Blackwood's *The Fine Art of Preaching*, translated by Chang-Bok Chung (1983); Jay Adams's *Pulpit Speech*, translated by Dong-Sik Chon (1984); Trimp's *De Preek*, translated by Seo-Hee Ko, Deuk-Il Shin, and Man-Soo Han (1986); Timothy Keller's *Reformed Homiletics*, translated by Eun-Jae Lee (1993);[14] and James W. Cox's *Preaching* (1999). In addition, Korean authored books, such as Chang-Bok Chung's *An Introduction to Homiletics* (1992) and Joo-Young Lee's *Modern Homiletics* (1985), were also published in the Korean language. More than thirty additional homiletical textbooks were published in this period, mostly emphasizing the expository method and redemptive-historical hermeneutics as the appropriate approach to preaching, and affirming that Scripture should constitute the main content of sermons.[15]

Introduction of Redemptive-Historical Preaching

In the early 1980s, redemptive-historical preaching as a contemporary approach, when introduced to the PCK, created considerable interest on the part of scholars and preachers alike. When Greidanus's *Sola Scriptura* was published in Canada in 1970, it was not long before many Korean scholars, like Sung-Kuh Chung, Sung-Jong Shin, and Soo-Kyung Kwon, utilized and taught its contents. Chung adopted it as a homiletics textbook for the ThM course from 1980 in Chong-Shin Seminary. Previously

13. Chung, *Reformed Homiletics*, 346.

14. This book is translated from Keller's lecture notes on homiletics at WTS Philadelphia, with his permission.

15. Lee, *Introduction of Homiletics*, 71.

there had been no book dealing with redemptive-historical preaching in Korea.[16] Shin summarised the message of Greidanus's work in a theological journal in 1985, challenging preachers to reconsider their old-fashioned approaches of exemplary and topical preaching.[17]

Gootjes introduced redemptive-historical preaching through comparing conventional and redemptive-historical preaching. He described redemptive-historical preaching as recognizing redemptive history in Scripture, with the need to acknowledge the purpose of the given text (John 5:39, 20:31) in interpreting it, and to emphasize this in preaching. Gootjes also characterized redemptive history as stressing the progress of revelation history, which is most highlighted in the salvation found in Christ.[18] Although these principles were well-known in biblical hermeneutics, redemptive-historical preaching was officially launched in Holland. Gootjes also discussed redemptive-historical issues in relation to Greidanus's *Sola Scriptura* in 1987, and in "The Function of Examples in Historical Texts of Scripture,"[19] and "Redemptive Historical Interpretation Regarding Historical Texts of Scripture,"[20] in 1988. Soo-Kyung Kwon translated *Sola Scriptura* into Korean, with Greidanus's permission, and published it with the Korean title *Principles of Redemptive Historical Preaching* in 1989.

In this same period, Clowney's *Preaching and Biblical Theology* was also translated into Korean in 1982, and gave effective support to disseminating the principles of redemptive-historical preaching in Korea. This book was expected to revitalize Korean preaching, as it relevantly emphasized that a mature, biblical understanding of the authority and characteristics of preaching demanded a new perspective on biblical theology.[21] This translation of Clowney's book was then studied as a homiletical textbook in seminaries in relation to Greidanus's *Sola Scriptura*, and as a result there was increased interest in, and desire for, redemptive-historical preaching by the mid-1980s. One Masters program student in

---

16. Chung, "Principles and Methods of Redemptive Historical Preaching," 16.

17. Shin, "Problems of the Korean Pulpit Based on the Hermeneutical Position" 54–63.

18. Gootjes, "How to do Redemptive-Historical Preaching?"

19. Gootjes, "Function of Examples in Historical Texts of Scripture," 115–31.

20. Gootjes, "Redemptive Historical Interpretation Regarding Historical Texts of Scripture," 19–36.

21. Clowney, *Preaching and Biblical Theology*, 5 (Korean translation, translator's preface.)

Chong-Shin subsequently wrote a thesis in 1985 on the principles of both Greidanus and Clowney regarding redemptive-historical preaching.[22]

In addition, Korean homiletical textbooks on redemptive-historical preaching began to be published in this period; these include Gootjes's *Between Exegesis and Sermon: The Practice of Redemptive Historical Preaching* (1987); Sung-Kuh Chung's *Reformed Homiletics: Redemptive Historical and Expository Preaching* (1991); and Won-Tae Suk's *Redemptive Historical Principles of Homiletical Theology* (1991). These additional textbooks gave further impetus to the teaching of the redemptive-historical approach in seminaries so that it was soon widely believed that this was the most biblical way for preachers to proclaim God's Word in Korean churches. However, despite this growing acceptance and popularity of redemptive-historical preaching in Korea, opposing views emerged at the same time, provoking animated debates and arguments. A debate regarding redemptive-historical preaching eventually occurred in the late 1990s and we now turn to discuss this homiletical debate in more detail.

Homiletical Redemptive-Historical debate

What are the origins of the Korean redemptive-historical debate? Or, to put the question differently, why did this debate occur in Korea? What were the main arguments and issues? These questions are now addressed in this section.

Origin

Since redemptive-historical preaching was mainly introduced by and through Greidanus's *Sola Scriptura* and Clowney's *Biblical Theology and Preaching*, the development of redemptive-historical preaching, and also the redemptive-historical debate, was largely dependent on these two authors. For example, Sung-Kuh Chung maintains that, "Our preaching should be 'RH expository preaching' which means that it is based on grammatical, historical, and theological interpretation of the texts,"[23] in this way integrating redemptive-historical preaching with the currently accepted expository method of preaching. However, I submit that this

---

22. Kim, "Study on Principles of Redemptive History."
23. Chung, *Reformed Homiletics*, 345.

insistence was not original to Chung, for he himself depended on, and mainly recycled, Greidanus's principles concerning preaching.[24]

The teaching of Greidanus and Clowney was not the only influence on Korean scholars in their accepting and developing the principles of redemptive-historical preaching and debating these homiletical issues. For example, Jong-Chil Park suggested that although the earlier Dutch debate might be disregarded as having nothing to do directly with Korean churches, yet the arguments raised in that Dutch debate did relate to Korean Presbyterian churches. This is because the issues which inevitably arise in preaching God's message to a sinful world are similar in nature and remedy irrespective of location or culture, as the message is timeless, transcultural and international.[25]

On this account, Korean scholars like Jong-Chil Park and Sung-Jong Shin wanted to apply the principles of redemptive-historical preaching and lessons directly from the Dutch debate to Korean churches in order to foster an improved biblical content and structure for sermons. Similar views or perspectives found in the Dutch redemptive-historical debate were naturally shared with church leaders in other countries, such as Korea.

Ignition of the Controversy

The Korean debate broke out in July 1998 in a monthly Christian journal, *Geu-Mal-Seum*, in which redemptive-historical preaching was specifically dealt with for the purpose of improving the theological content of preaching in Korean churches. *Geu-Mal-Seum* is the annexed journal to *Mok-Hoi-Wa-Shin-Hak*, (meaning "Pastoral Ministry and Theology") which was launched in July 1989 in order to provide a competent companion and guide especially for Korean church ministers and Christian workers. The journal claimed that: "Through *Pastoral Ministry and Theology*, we have strived to propagate the criteria for biblically healthy church ministry and also for evangelical theology since its foundation."[26] Since its foundation *Geu-Mal-Seum* had mainly dealt with the sermons

---

24. Greidanus, *Sola Scriptura*, 213–33.
25. Park, "Redemptive-Historical Interpretation and Preaching," 40.
26. This journal belongs to the On-Nu-Ri Church, which is oriented to a broader evangelicalism than Reformed theology; it cannot therefore be said to provide precisely sound criteria for Reformed churches.

of evangelical theologians and ministers in and outside Korea, involving popular as well as deeper and broader studies of biblical texts. A series of articles in November 1998, which were specially edited and aimed at assisting redemptive-historical preaching in Korea, had the title "To Discuss Redemptive Historical Preaching," and these articles initiated a controversy.

In the first article, entitled "The Ground of Redemptive-Historical Preaching and its Derived Problems," Chang-Gyun Chung demonstrated that Reformed biblical theology is the foundational presupposition of redemptive-historical preaching.[27] Chung first of all affirmed that interpretation and communication are the two foundational stones for preaching, because the former guarantees "the validity" and the latter preserves "the vitality" of preaching. He then defined "redemptive-historical" in the term "redemptive-historical preaching" as reflecting the perspective of a biblical, theological interpretation of texts, and "preaching" as reflecting the necessary communication of that biblical interpretation to the congregation here and now.[28] For Chung, any preaching which lacks a thorough biblical theological interpretation of the text is invalid, as also is preaching which does not adequately deliver that interpretation to the congregation. Reformed biblical theology, especially that of Vos, which recognizes Scripture as being the revelation of God's redemptive acts in history, can, for Chung, be a suitable ground and framework for redemptive-historical preaching.[29]

Nevertheless, Chung identified a tendency in some preaching in which "biblical theological interpretation" was considered an obstacle to relevant preaching, and this on the part of those who tended to emphasize "application here and now," especially in exemplary or ethical preaching. Chung also recognized, but was unhappy with, another tendency, that a "biblical theological interpretation" expressed in preaching is assumed to be good preaching, even without application and sensitivity to the situations and needs of the hearers. Chung thought that the issues between these two tendencies were also essential arguing points between the redemptive-historical and exemplary groups, as we examined in chapter 3.

To assess these problems relating to redemptive-historical preaching, Chung raised several questions: Does the text in redemptive-historical

27. Chung, "Ground of Redemptive-Historical Preaching."
28. Ibid., 6.
29. Bornemann, "Toward a Biblical Theology," 117.

preaching function only as the "window" through which we see past history? Can redemptive-historical preaching be only a fossilized instruction? Is it necessary always to mention Christ in the preaching and opening of a biblical text? Is it inevitable that a congregation will find it too difficult to understand redemptive-historical preaching?[30]

Chung provided his own answers to these questions. He thought that historical biblical texts not only reveal objective historical facts but also link those facts to our circumstances today.[31] Redemptive-history did not end with the Bible, he insisted, but continues God's work of saving His people. Redemptive-historical preaching should, therefore, not be fossilized instruction, but rather lively and influential participation in God's redemptive work.[32] Chung also affirmed that "Christ-centeredness" is not an obsessive imposition of Christ on each and every biblical text, but rather identifying and highlighting Christ's redemption throughout the organic structure of redemptive history in the entire Scripture. In this way it is the principles which are being emphasized in the context of redemptive history, and whether the text provides an example and is therefore man-centered or otherwise.[33] Chung claimed that redemptive-historical preaching itself is not necessarily difficult to exercise, but it is more likely the inability or lack of effort on the part of a preacher in seeking to illuminate the dynamic link between the "then and now" which consequently makes it difficult for the congregation to follow the preaching.[34]

Some of the problems raised in relation to redemptive-historical preaching thus do not relate exclusively to redemptive-historical preaching itself, for there are other deficiencies like the preacher's poor ability or lack of preparation or flair in communicating the message. According to Chung, as the biblical theological perspective recognizes the organic unity and diversity of God's revelation of redemptive history throughout the whole of Scripture, it then highlights the text's central message, namely, Christ's salvation of His people, which facilitates relevant, meaningful application.[35] Therefore, redemptive-historical preaching should

---

30. Chung, "Ground of Redemptive-Historical Preaching," 10–13.
31. Ibid., 11.
32. Ibid., 12.
33. Ibid., 12–13.
34. Ibid., 13.
35. Ibid., 10.

necessarily be understood not as a preaching model but as a principle in which preaching should be rooted.[36] This solution by Chung is not very different from what Clowney himself taught,[37] and we will discuss this in more detail later.

Jong-Kil Byun, in the second article entitled "The Meaning and Limits of Redemptive-Historical Preaching," again described the introduction of the Dutch debate into Korean churches. According to Byun, Trimp's *Preaching and the History of Salvation* practically retrieved the redemptive-historical controversy from its long dormant state and revitalized it.[38] Nevertheless, Byun followed Trimp in his error that the Dutch debate was not swayed by the wrong definition of the term *example* but rather by the different perspectives on the historical text.[39] In addition, Byun claimed that several texts in the NT like Rom 15:4; 1 Cor 10; Jas 5; and Heb 11 support and validate the use of historical figures and events in the OT as examples or instruction for believers today.[40]

Byun then distinguished carefully between the terms *example* and *imitation*, suggesting that although we cannot imitate Elijah when he prayed effectively for rain to be withheld for three and a half years, yet we are authorized in taking his prayerful example and being challenged by his sincere faith in almighty God.[41] Similarly, we do not, and cannot, imitate Christ's crucifixion, but we can follow His example in principle and be prepared to make sacrifices in order to do God's will. According to Byun, liberal theologians tend to imitate Christ's self-denial or ethical life alone, while sometimes disregarding, or even denying, the uniqueness of His redemptive works.[42] Partly because of this tendency, Reformed theologians strongly oppose the exemplary interpretation of Christ's life, but Byun affirmed the importance of taking biblical persons as examples, as that is what Paul and Peter commanded (1 Cor 4:16, 11:1; Phil 3:17; 1 Thess 1:6; 1 Pet 2:21). For Byun, the very fact that Jesus Christ lived with

---

36. Ibid., 7.

37. Clowney, *Preaching and Biblical Theology*, 5–6. See the section "Background: Westminster Theological Seminary and Edmund Clowney" in chapter 4.

38. Byun, "Meaning and Limit of Redemptive-Historical Preaching," 14.

39. Ibid., 17.

40. Ibid., 18–20.

41. Ibid., 20.

42. Ibid., 21.

His people for thirty-three years had the purpose of providing not only words, but also an example of behaving and living.[43]

Byun has described fairly the strengths and weaknesses of redemptive-historical preaching. Such preaching can make a useful contribution in highlighting the whole contour of Scripture with its center in Christ; it also calls attention to the position and meaning of the text within the redemptive-historical scheme, thus cautioning against an irresponsible use of biblical characters or historical events as contemporary ethical models. On the negative side, redemptive-historical preaching can often overlook the continuity of believers in the OT and NT. This is a weakness, for in the OT the believers were God's people like ourselves, with highs and lows of faith and unbelief, transgressions and failures, answers to prayer, and spiritual delight, which all provide instruction and challenge for us today. In addition, redemptive-historical preaching overlooks the works of Christ and the Holy Spirit in the OT, because it sees in it only the future coming of Christ.[44] Redemptive-historical preaching, therefore, can tend to neglect the varied profitable instruction that is embedded in historical biblical texts, which, in turn, points to deficiencies in redemptive-historical preaching.

Nevertheless, Byun suggests a solution for the Dutch debate; instead of the usual practice of opposing redemptive-historical preaching and exemplary preaching, one should rather think more in terms of "right preaching" versus "wrong preaching," because the opposition between redemptive-historical and exemplary preaching creates theological confusion.[45]

Byun's evaluation of the Dutch debate is similar to, and dependent on, that of Trimp's; for Byun, the deficiencies of redemptive-historical preaching can be overcome by reading historical biblical texts not just as history but as the words of God, which are the unique and ultimate standards for our faith and life. The words of God are given to us through history, and so we must read them historically as well as theologically. This way of reading is consistent with Reformed principles of biblical hermeneutics, which we have broadly examined in chapter 2.[46]

---

43. Ibid., 21.
44. Ibid., 22.
45. Ibid., 23.
46. See the section "Reformed Biblical Theology" in chapter 2.

Besides the above two articles, there are four others in that same series: Gyu-Hyun Chae's "How to Preach Old Testament in the RH way" (24–29); Jung-Woo Kim's "Christological Preaching of the Psalms" (30–49); Jei-Ho Han's "Theory of RH Preaching and its Application"(50–57); and Seo-Taek Kim's "Practice of RH Preaching" (58–67). Each of these articles appears to treat redemptive-historical preaching distinctively, but in fact they are theoretically and practically similar to those we have examined above.

Criticism of Redemptive-Historical Preaching in Korea

The above discussion in *Geu-Mal-Seum* stimulated more criticism of redemptive-historical preaching. A Christian weekly newspaper, *Ki-Dok-Shin-Moon*, which belongs to PCK (Hap-Dong), published a new section in its pages in the latter part of 1998 under the title "Meeting with Reformed Theology," in order to identify, discuss, and give direction on important theological themes. Redemptive-historical preaching was selected for the first issue as the subject which needed urgent attention. To open this series, Jee-Chan Kim was invited to give a scholarly view on the question, "Is RH preaching the right kind of preaching?"

Kim began with his own personal experience of redemptive-historical preaching. When he was a seminarian in the late 1970s and early 1980s, Chong-Shin Seminary taught him redemptive-historical preaching in his first year and he was attracted to its Christ-centered interpretation, as well as its broad perspective of redemptive history and vigorous biblical-theological approach. He was tired of the conventional exemplary and illustration-centered preaching to which he had been accustomed. However, he soon felt the inadequacy of redemptive-historical preaching as it seemed to him boring and narrow in its use of the redemptive-historical method by preachers. Eventually, dissatisfied over his own preaching, he abandoned the method but heard that his peers were reproached by their senior pastors for not participating in redemptive-historical preaching in their churches.

After completing his doctoral studies in Holland, Kim returned to Korea in the late 1980s, but was dismayed by the continuing popularity of redemptive-historical preaching in Korea despite its deficiencies and limitations.[47] It was startling for Kim to see the special edition of *Geu-*

---

47. Kim, "Is it Right to Keep Redemptive-Historical Preaching in This Way?"

Mal-Seum in November 1998 given over to a discussion of redemptive historical preaching. The articles in this issue mostly assumed that redemptive-historical preaching should be retained in its original form, but modified for further development as it had already become outdated in Holland.[48] Kim's studies in Holland led him to recognize that the inherent problems of redemptive-historical preaching in both Holland and Korea could not be addressed by slight modifications, such as refusing exemplary elements and excessively inserting Christ into the text. For Kim, the crucial problem with the redemptive-historical scheme was to read Christ into the text too early, bypassing the first steps of Reformed hermeneutics such as an essential grammatical-literal analysis of the text, rather than proceeding directly to a canonical-theological interpretation.[49] Kim maintained that, in practice, Korean redemptive-historical preaching normally neglected this first step of exegesis.[50]

Kim illustrated this defective approach of redemptive-historical preaching with a practical example from Gootjes's sermon on Gen 12:10–20. From the text, Gootjes maintained that the essence of redemptive-historical preaching in this context should be what God had done, rather than Abraham's lie.[51] Kim identified three themes which Gootjes had preached from the text. Firstly, the fact that God is almighty; secondly, Abraham's lie placed God's promise of Abraham's offspring in danger; thirdly, God saved Sarah from danger so that the Messiah should eventually be born through her line. Gootjes concluded that God had already foreseen and planned our salvation three thousand years before it was actually accomplished, and thus that is a major factor why God saved Sarah from harm in Pharaoh's palace. Kim questioned whether this was the right message from the text and the one that the author originally intended. Kim claimed that the text should rather be read in the closer context of God's promises in Gen 12:1–3, and then understood as a fulfiment of the promise that God would bless those who blessed Abraham and would curse those who cursed him.[52]

Kim clearly criticizes redemptive-historical preaching as being deficient in neglecting what should be the earlier preparatory work

---

48. Ibid.
49. Ibid.
50. Ibid.
51. Gootjes, *Between Exegesis and Sermon*, 16–22.
52. Kim, "Is it Right to Keep Redemptive-Historical Preaching in This Way?"

of grappling with the text. He suggested that a return to text-centered preaching, which is even more thoroughly biblical no matter what style of preaching is adopted, could overcome the problem.[53] Kim maintained that Scripture is not to be interpreted by redemptive-historical principles with the object of its becoming lively and dynamic. Scripture was formed in and through God's redemptive history; thus as the living words of God it still underlies God's redemptive work today.[54] Kim insisted that if we focus attention on the actual text itself we may then hear the word of God's redemptive history, and so he redefined redemptive-historical preaching as hearing and proclaiming the voice of the text itself.[55]

I submit that Kim's criticism reflects his own experience and also the current status of homiletics in Korea. His concluding remarks are, in my judgment, very similar to Greidanus's assessment of the Dutch debate, and we will return to that point later in the chapter.[56]

Refuting the Criticism

Hae-Moo Yoo responded strongly to Kim's criticism, although agreeing with his thesis concerning the defects in the Korean style of redemptive-historical preaching. However, he disagreed significantly with Kim's approach.[57] He queried Kim as to when redemptive-historical preaching in Korea had been established in a Korean style, as Kim, in his previous essay, did not show how redemptive-historical preaching had been introduced to Korea or to his seminary in Chong-Shin. Consequently Yoo suspected that Kim was saying that the Dutch debate and its annexed redemptive-historical preaching were introduced in the late 1970s and early 1980s. However, as we examined earlier,[58] the Dutch debate was introduced to Korea at the latest in the late 1970s and early 1980s through Greidanus's book.

Yoo then rejected Kim's claim that redemptive-historical preaching had enjoyed a lengthy popularity in Korea, even after Kim himself had

53. Ibid. Cf. Greidanus, *Sola Scriptura*, 214.
54. Ibid.
55. Ibid.
56. See the section "Assessment and Suggestions" in chapter 3.
57. Yoo, "Refute against."
58. See the section "Introduction of Redemptive-Historical Preaching" in this chapter.

returned from abroad. For Yoo, Kim had too readily generalized from his own experience of redemptive-historical preaching and so tended to distort the facts[59] and forget that ethical instruction and man-centered preaching had dominated Korean preaching for a considerable period. However, Yoo was pleased that redemptive-historical preaching had become a key issue for debate.[60]

Yoo also disagreed with Kim's judgment on Gootjes's preaching for disregarding the immediate context and grammatical-historical exegesis.[61] He noted that Gootjes had referred to God's covenant in Gen 12: 2–3 as part of the immediate context, and had actually applied the grammatical-historical interpretation first, before the canonical-theological interpretation.[62] However, Yoo here misses the point in that Kim actually referred, for the close context, to God's saving Sarah from Pharaoh's mischief. For Kim, referring to our salvation through Christ from the text is not a sufficient consideration of the immediate context. I submit that to view the text primarily as the accomplishment of God's promise to Abraham (Gen 12:1–3) is correct in terms of the closer context, so Kim's judgment of Gootjes's preaching is partly correct.

Yoo then rejected Kim's assumed opposition between the grammatical-historical and the canonical-theological approaches and instead regarded them as being interrelated and interdependent in hermeneutics. In practice, redemptive-historical preaching is likely to read quickly into the text, linking it with Christ, but without necessarily disregarding grammatical-historical principles. Yoo also suggests that Kim's scheme was premature in criticizing redemptive-historical preaching.[63]

Kim's response was that Yoo had misunderstood his intention concerning redemptive-historical preaching, for he had only wanted to improve, commend, and build up a proper redemptive-historical approach, but through the right process of the grammatical-literary approach.[64] Kim's defense was that of viewing redemptive-historical preaching from a more objective perspective, rather than the customary and previously one-sided understanding so typical in Korean churches.

---

59. Yoo, "Refute against."
60. Ibid.
61. Kim, "Is it Right to Keep Redemptive-Historical Preaching in This Way?"
62. Yoo, "Refute against."
63. Ibid.
64. Kim, "To Answer Hae-Moo Yoo's Refutation."

For example, whereas Greidanus's *Sola Scriptura* objectively described the Dutch debate and provided the third way of text-centered preaching, which was a step beyond that of both redemptive-historical and exemplary preaching, its Korean version was arbitrarily titled as *Principles of Redemptive-Historical Preaching*, and so appeared to be supporting the redemptive-historical approach. In addition, Greidanus's methodology was criticized rather scathingly by Gootjes in the introduction to the book. In Kim's view, the translated book had hindered readers from viewing the redemptive-historical debate more objectively and helpfully.

Kim also pointed out Yoo's misunderstanding about the longevity of redemptive-historical preaching in Korea. He believed that redemptive-historical preaching in Korea had progressed over a long period without any criticisms from outside, or even serious challenges from within.[65] Kim added that he had himself raised the problems concerning redemptive-historical preaching, and his proposed third way for resolving the problems had been previously indicated in Greidanus's *Sola Scriptura*,[66] and so his criticisms and suggestions were not intended to undermine or distort redemptive-historical preaching; rather, he was only applying Greidanus's criticisms of redemptive-historical preaching to Korean theologians and preachers for their further reflection.

There are, however, several significant differences between Kim and Yoo in recognizing redemptive-historical preaching and its problems. Firstly, Kim conceived of redemptive-historical preaching as having an inherent problem, that of largely neglecting the grammatical-historical interpretation and reading redemptive history too quickly into the biblical text, while Yoo assumed that the redemptive-historical approach involved undertaking an initial grammatical-historical exegesis before reading redemptive history into the text. Secondly, Kim claimed that the dilemma between redemptive-historical and exemplary preaching should be resolved through text-centered preaching, whereas Yoo suggested the solution should be Christ-centered redemptive-historical preaching rather than exemplary preaching, because the former was more successful in removing what he called the "ethical" or "man-centered" preaching which had dominated in Korean Protestant churches. Thirdly, while Kim was more aware of the serious problems associated with Korean redemptive-historical preaching, Yoo considered exemplary

65. Ibid.
66. Ibid.

and human-centered preaching in Korea to be more of a problem. These discrepancies between the two scholars in viewing redemptive-historical preaching will be examined more carefully later in this chapter.

There were other participants in this debate, and Jae-Yul Sho, a pastor in PCK (Hap-Dong), gathered all these debates together in a book.[67] We need to examine each debate briefly in order to be comprehensive in our coverage, in an attempt to understand more clearly all the issues and distinctions relating to this complex redemptive-historical homiletical debate in Korea.

Sho described Kim's criticism of redemptive-historical preaching as a mistaken generalization, as Kim's objection had been expressed in the late 1970s and early 1980s when there was no active discussion of redemptive history in Korea. For this reason Sho rightly pointed out that Kim was not contributing, nor responding, to the redemptive-historical debate at all; rather Kim's objection was rooted in his own experience of redemptive-historical preaching in that early period—preaching which could hardly at that time be described as redemptive-historical preaching for it was more christological in its manner, which was then the popular method.[68] It was not until Greidanus's *Sola Scriptura* and Clowney's *Biblical Theology and Preaching* were introduced to Korea in the mid-1980s that redemptive-historical principles were clearly and practically applied to preaching, and discussed in Korean churches.[69]

Sho also rejected Kim's claim that text-centered preaching should be restored and that it is consistent with Reformation teaching and the practice of *sola scriptura*. For Sho, to remain in the grammatical-historical interpretation of the text is nothing more than following a mere Jewish approach, while Reformed hermeneutics goes one step further to find the relation of the text to Christ in light of its canonical interpretation.[70] Another valuable point made by Sho was that, even if the grammatical-historical interpretation were applied, the preacher and congregation might still not discover Christ from OT texts without using and applying the redemptive-historical perspective. Sho therefore insists that preachers

---

67. Sho, *Debate of Redemptive-Historical Preaching*, 4. According to Sho, he and Geun-Ho Lee wrote essays quickly refuting Kim's criticism of redemptive-historical preaching after Kim's first essay was reported, and sent them to the *Christian Journal*, but they did not appear in the journal, with no reason given.

68. Sho, "Review," 31–35.

69. Kim, "Study on Principles of Redemptive History," 4.

70. Sho, "Review," 41.

should presuppose God's redemption through Christ before and during the interpreting of the text.

Se-Yoon Kim, a renowned NT professor, supports Sho at this point: "The OT by itself has no meaning to us Christians. Only when seen under the light of the perfect, full revelation in Christ, can its meaning arise."[71] I agree with Se-Yoon Kim here, but Sho's judgment of Jee-Chan Kim was too harsh because the latter did emphasize the final step for the preacher in carefully examining the relation of the specific text to the NT, especially in terms of Christ's accomplishment of salvation.[72]

Sho also supported Gootjes's approach in his sermon on Abraham's lie (Gen 12:10–20) and felt that points made by Gootjes concerning God's divine omnipotence and faithfulness in honouring His promises were faithful to the text. He insisted that Gootjes's conclusion, that "God saved Sarah from Pharaoh's palace, foreseeing already Jesus Christ for our redemption three thousand years beforehand," linked superbly with the NT, especially Gal 3:16 which refers to God's covenant with Abraham and his seed, that is, Jesus Christ. Sho argued that Gootjes was more canonical and systematic in understanding the text with its redemptive-historical perspective.

Finally, Sho's own perspective on the Dutch redemptive-historical debate was that it involved the issue of epistemology. For example, does one know truths about God inductively by collating observable information, like people's experiences of God, then analyzing it carefully and rationally to reach general truths about God, or does one use a deductive approach to draw out specific religious knowledge from the objective content of Scripture as God's Word which reveals His redemptive, historical acts? Sho claimed the latter, maintaining that preaching should thus rely on a deductive approach.[73]

Geun-Ho Lee, a PCK (Hap-Dong) pastor, also opposed Kim's position, affirming that, "True respect for Scripture ought to draw out its rules for interpretation from itself other than outwardly added rules. The apostles' rules of interpreting Scripture disallowed such rules as grammatical-literary presupposition. Thus, literary interpretation conflicts with an RH interpretation."[74] According to Lee, apostolic interpretation

---

71. Kim, *What is Salvation?* 100–101.
72. Kim, "Is it Right to Keep Redemptive-Historical Preaching in This Way?"
73. Ibid., 45–49.
74. Lee, "Refutation on Jee-Chan Kim's Criticism," 18.

by the apostles, such as Peter and Paul, was dominated by the inspiration of the Holy Spirit, focusing on the cross event, and they re-interpret the whole of history in that light. Such hermeneutical rules, Lee felt, cannot be obtained merely by analyzing the literary structure of the OT text, and so he concluded there is no necessary connection between the literary interpretation and an appropriate redemptive-historical interpretation.[75] I disagree with Lee here, if only for the reason that his view disregards the very Reformed hermeneutical principles he espouses and which are clearly elucidated by Reformed scholars like Berkhof,[76] Thiselton,[77] Goldingday,[78] and even Vos.[79]

Another journal, *The Pastoral Monthly*, published a special edition in 2001 on redemptive-historical preaching, with the title "A New Paradigm of Preaching: Redemptive-Historical Preaching".[80] This title implies that redemptive-historical preaching provides a new solution for problems inherent in conventional preaching in Korean churches. There were five articles on redemptive-historical preaching, which we need to examine briefly in order to appreciate fully the progress of redemptive-historical homiletics after the debate in 1998 and 1999.

Sung-Jong Shin pointed out the limits of typological interpretation and proposed redemptive-historical preaching in its place.[81] For Shin, typology means interpreting the OT, based on Col 2:17, as the shadow, or type, of the antitypes in the NT, but he insists that there are essential weaknesses in this approach in that not everything in the OT can be interpreted typologically in terms of NT accomplishments; consequently, there is a danger of falling into allegory, which, in turn, disregards the text's historicity.

For Shin, the redemptive-historical approach has the potential to fall into dispensationalism, with its division between Israel and the church, arbitrary division of biblical history into seven dispensations, and misinterpretation of biblical prophecies to suit the pre-established schemes

---

75. Ibid.
76. Berkhof, *Principles of Biblical Interpretation*, 67–74, 113–15.
77. Thiselton, *Two Horizons*, 10–17.
78. Goldingay, *Models for Interpretation of Scripture*, 8–9, 167–71.
79. Vos, *Redemptive History and Biblical Interpretation*, 19–20.
80. "New Paradigm of Preaching," 48–77. The articles of five proponents of redemptive-historical preaching were included in this edition: Sung-Jong Shin, Sung-Choon Oh, Geum-Nam Choi, Ki-Hong Kim, and N. H. Gootjes.
81. Shin, "Bible is the Drama of God," 48–52.

of dispensations.⁸² In contrast to this, Shin claimed that the redemptive-historical perspective enabled him to view the Bible as divine drama, with Gen 1–12 as the prelude, the first act from Gen 12 to Malachi, the interlude occurring during the inter-testamental history between the OT and NT, the second act from Matthew to Jude, and Revelation as the final scene.⁸³ However, the tendency to divide biblical history into several dispensations was also found in earlier redemptive-historical proponents like Augustine of Hippo and Joachim of Fiore.⁸⁴

Shin summarised the strengths of redemptive-historical preaching in six ways: (1) it clearly recognizes the contour and structure of Scripture; (2) it helpfully interprets the meaning of world history by viewing Christ as the center of history; (3) it highlights the progression of God's revelation by closely relating the two testaments; (4) in addition to being instructive it is also historical and evangelical; (5) it facilitates expository preaching; (6) it gives greater clarity and liveliness to preaching.⁸⁵

On the negative side, Shin refers to five weaknesses in redemptive-historical preaching: (1) it is difficult to preach without knowing the whole contour of redemptive history; (2) it is rather difficult to interpret many parts of Scripture as having a direct relation to redemptive history; (3) redemptive-historical preaching is in danger of becoming monotonous; (4) such preaching cannot avoid the criticism that ordinary people in the congregation have difficulties in understanding redemptive-historical preaching; (5) it is hard to obtain resources to create special sermons for weddings, funerals, and specific anniversary occasions.

Sung-Choon Oh, a professor in Jang-Shin Theological Seminary, emphasized the necessity for preaching to be full of the stories related by Christ, rather than the Korean church practice of filling sermons with human stories of epic events or remarkable feats of sacrifice and service.⁸⁶ He challenged, "Have we invited Christ and let Him do His work in us

---

82. Grudem, *Systematic Theology*, 1240.

83. Shin, "Bible is the Drama of God," 51–52.

84. See the section "Background: Redemptive History in New Testament Theology" in chapter 1. Cf. Rottenberg, *Redemption and Historical Reality*, 27. Augustine divided the world into two: the city of God (*de civitate Dei*) and the other realm, that is, the secular world. Joachim taught that the Father, the Son, and the Holy Spirit are manifested in different dispensations that follow one another in successive historical eras.

85. Shin, "Bible is the Drama of God," 52.

86. Oh, "Let's Make Preaching Overflowing with the Stories of Christ!" 53–58.

or conversely have we been speaking only people's stories beside Christ? However, the Holy Spirit does work where God's stories are heard."[87] For Oh, the words from and about God describe how He loved His people, and what He did for them.

This special edition of *The Pastoral Monthly* regarded Oh's approach as constituting practical redemptive-historical preaching, but I disagree and view it more like Barth's christological preaching in emphasizing only God's redemptive event in Christ[88] without highlighting the historical unity and progression of events relating to Christ throughout both testaments. Here is another example where an article such as Oh's reveals confusion in Korea as to what redemptive-historical preaching is.

Geum-Nam Choi, a PCK (Hap-Dong) pastor, also emphasized God-centered rather than human-centered preaching and complained there were currently two main types of popular preaching in Korea: legalistic and exemplary.[89] Their common ground is that they highlight man. This concerned Choi and he suggested the solution was to focus on the preaching of grace, which highlights God's grace, that is, what God has done rather than what people should do to enjoy happiness here and now. According to Choi, legalistic preaching is associated with *Ki-Bok-Shin-Ang* (bliss-pursuit belief) which originates from shamanism, focusing only on secular blessing and prosperity while disregarding Christian duties and ethics; this teaching had been widely acknowledged as a formidable challenge for Christians to overcome in Korean churches.[90] In that redemptive-historical preaching essentially highlights how God reveals Himself in historical facts in relation to our salvation, Choi thought that the redemptive-historical approach should be applied in order to transform legalistic preaching into grace-centered preaching.

While Choi described redemptive-historical preaching as consistently illuminating God's sovereignty over history and thus focusing the preacher's attention fully on God Himself,[91] I submit that his description of redemptive-historical preaching is only partial rather than comprehensive. However, to emphasize only the principles of God-centeredness

---

87. Ibid., 53.
88. Barth, *Homiletik*, 54.
89. Choi, "Not to Lose God," 59–65.
90. Ibid., 61–62.
91. Ibid., 63.

is not the whole of redemptive-historical preaching and I will elaborate on this later in the chapter.

Ki-Hong Kim, a pastor in PCK (Tong-Hap), provided his own principles in order to construct his version of redemptive-historical preaching. For Kim, redemptive-historical preaching begins with the consciousness of the gravity of human sin and the urgency of salvation, proceeds with the assurance that God is the only way to salvation through His only Son, whom He sent to die in our stead then raised from the dead, and closes with a sensitive awareness of the congregation's spiritual hunger and the current affliction in their lives, and their responsibility to turn their interests from worldly things to the eternal.[92] Kim's own remedy for making redemptive-historical preaching effective is to stress the gospel as the supreme truth from which people can experience God's free forgiveness, eternal life, and power to live holy lives.

Kim observed that theological students in Korea often inadvertently made subjects such as "Build up our righteous country," "Be spiritually stronger in times of hardship," "Help our poor neighbours," "Pray to get power," or "Set the right goals for your life" the central theme of their preaching.[93] These themes do not immediately relate to gospel truths. Other examples of popular sermon themes are: "Enjoy true rest in Christ," "Believe in Jesus the healer and live healthy lives," "Live with the power of the Lord," "God grants us victory." However, these themes are seriously deficient in that any religious figure can be substituted for Christ and so the preaching would not be distinctively Christian.

Kim attempted to modify the foregoing themes in order to place them more firmly within the context of the Christian gospel, so as to be more christocentric which, for Kim, would then represent redemptive-historical preaching. This approach by Kim is similar to an approach in the American redemptive-historical debate, which we examined in chapter 4, namely, that biblical application is "assimilation" of oneself with the text so that the believer may enjoy the "eschatological present" in the text.[94] This approach mainly focuses on the cognitive aspect of belief and disregards the behavioural aspect. Adams criticized this approach

---

92. Kim, "Training of RH Reasoning and Construction of Preaching," 66–68.

93. Ibid., 69.

94. Dennison, "Redemptive-Historical Hermeneutic and Preaching," 27. See sections in chapter 4: "The Extreme Wing of Redemptive-Historical Preaching" and "Dilemma: Explication versus Application."

as being influenced by Barth, who tended to leave application to God's revelatory encounter with the congregation.[95]

One example of this from Kim is his redemptive-historical sermon, with the title "Living Sacrifice," on Gen 22:6–14. The thesis is "Realise yourself as a living sacrifice in the worship service!" Kim makes three major points: one, "a sacrifice is to be killed;" two, "the sheep has died instead;" and three, the challenge: "thus live as a sacrifice." Kim's third point has the message, "Isaac becomes the only one living and coming down from the altar, due to the substitutionary death of the sheep. So do I. Thus, I become a living sacrifice for my entire life. Do you know that you are a living sacrifice before God?"[96] I submit that this sermon, though cleverly reasoned, lacks application as to how to live as a living sacrifice in this world. While Kim suggests his sermon is an example of responsible redemptive-historical preaching, I view it as being problematic in that it is somewhat irrelevant to today's congregation.

Gootjes also offered examples of redemptive-historical preaching in Korean churches, but for him the term *redemptive* involves the focus of the whole Scripture, while the term *historical* signifies the unique facts of redemption. He thus regards redemptive-historical preaching essentially as highlighting the redemption of Christ, which can be traced throughout from Genesis to Revelation.

Gootjes refers to embarrassing sermons he had heard during his long residence in Korea. One example was from the text of 1 Sam 6:12, which records the cows pulling the Ark all the way to Beth Shemesh while lowing all the time. The preacher used this text to illustrate maternal love for children, concluding it was natural for a mother to weep over her children when she sent them for study abroad or into marriage, acts similar in principle to the cows lowing as they headed for Beth Shemesh. Gootjes rightly criticized this sermon as distorting the text by ignoring God's action in the event, and thus disregarding God's special providence that revealed to the Philistine leaders the undeniable fact that the God of Israel was in control of the wondrous incident.[97] From this text we

---

95. See section "The Opponents of Exclusive Redemptive-Historical Preaching" in chapter 4. Cf. Barth, *Homiletik*, 94, 104. For Barth, preaching means to explain the biblical text to the contemporary congregation so that they may have the foundation and hope of their life only in Christ. In this concept, there is no concrete application, which homiletic scholars like J. Adams propounded.

96. Kim, "Training of RH Reasoning and Construction of Preaching," 71.

97. Ibid., 75–76.

should have learned the truth that there is no other god than the God of Israel, Jehovah, to whom we should give appropriate worship. I agree here with Gootjes's criticism, for this principle should have been primarily elucidated from the text.

Another example from Gootjes's experiences of misinterpreted sermons is that of a pastor who when preaching on Luke 7:37–38 concentrated exclusively on the woman herself and the fact that she sacrificed to the Lord. But, from the context in verses 36–50, Luke clearly focuses on Jesus Christ, not the woman. Gootjes reconstructed the sermon, with the first point being that, although a transgressor, the woman came to Jesus. Secondly, she is changed, for her weeping expresses repentance, while her anointing of Jesus signifies her deep gratitude and love for Jesus as her Savior, which is in contrast to Simon the Pharisee. In this way, Jesus demonstrates what saving belief is and proclaims that which is His prerogative to do. Again I concur with Gootjes.

Besides these articles, other scholars and preachers have participated in the redemptive-historical debate in Korea. For example, Do-Soon Yoo, a pastor of PCK (Hap-Dong), supported the necessity of redemptive-historical preaching, as the entire Bible consists of redemptive-history, so that to preach on a biblical text is to preach redemptive-history.[98] Others, like Seo-Taek Kim, Jung-Woo Kim, and Jei-Ho Han, have also expressed their views on this debate, mostly supporting redemptive-historical preaching in principle. However, as we have examined in the above essays, most scholars and preachers have misunderstood redemptive-historical preaching and confuse it with christological preaching or grace preaching.

Present Status

In 2002, Jee-Chan Kim suggested text-centered christological preaching as the substitute for the conventional redemptive-historical preaching. Kim highlighted the necessity and legitimacy of christological preaching, asserting that the OT ought to be primarily interpreted christologically, otherwise the OT would be irrelevant for God's people today. OT and NT believers are directly related through Jesus Christ, so it is necessary and legitimate for the OT texts to be understood as messages for the covenant people in the NT period as well as for the Israelites in the OT.

98. Yoo, "Why should we do RH preaching?" 73–129.

As a corollary, the biblical stories should be recognized as one unified story woven throughout both the OT and NT, and so a christological approach to Scripture needs to be combined with redemptive-historical preaching.[99]

However, Kim disagreed with the conventional Korean practice of hastily reading a redemptive-historical framework into the text, because the redemptive-historical approach was originally a comprehensive perspective to view the whole contour of God's redemptive works in Scripture. It had been erroneously practiced in Korea, as Gootjes skipped the first step of interpreting the text and found the redemptive-historical meaning by arbitrarily relating the text to NT events. Kim thought this fault was becoming inherent in conventional redemptive-historical preaching. He therefore opted for the *sola scriptura* principle which meant, for him, interpreting the text within its immediate context, then exploring canonically—a method of preaching which could only be appropriately described as christological preaching.[100] Kim is not actually criticizing redemptive-historical preaching itself, but rather its flawed practice in Korean churches.

Kim provided an example of such preaching from Josh 5:1–9. He identified the text as consisting of three paragraphs: Joshua's immediate obedience to God's command for the Israelites to be circumcised (5:1–3), the reason for the national ritual (5:4–7), and God's announcement of the termination of the Israelites' disgrace (5:8–9). Analyzing its structure and context, Kim expounds the text as highlighting the comparison between the old and new generations: the latter obeyed God's order (v. 3) whereas the former disobeyed (v. 6), so that the national circumcision signifies how the new generations owe faithful obedience to God.

However, Kim attests that a Korean pastor preached differently on this text, believing that it describes the "self-consciousness of the Israelites as God's covenant people," and also "their consciousness of dependence on God alone."[101] Kim sees this way of preaching as disregarding the text's immediate and close context, because the text immediately tells us that the Israelites' enthusiastic obedience to God was more important than physical circumcision. The text also relates to Jeremiah's proclamation that the Israelites were uncircumcised in their hearts (Jer 9:25–26), which

---

99. Kim, "Historical Books and Christological Preaching," 50–52.
100. Ibid., 53–54.
101. Ibid., 55.

points directly to Rom 2:25, where to keep the law validates circumcision but breaking the law renders it void.

Circumcision, therefore, was originally the mark of God's covenant people, but now the sign shifts to faith acting with Christ's love (Gal 5:6, 6:15). The real circumcision is not physical, but is rather a supernatural operation which cuts off the disobedient tendency towards God through the absolute but painful crucifixion of the self at the cross with Christ (Rom 6:6; Gal 2:20, 6:14). Therefore, for Kim, the text of Josh 5:1–9 teaches that the baptism of the heart, that is, thorough obedience to God, is required to enter God's kingdom. Kim urged people to be circumcised in heart, like the new generation which needed to be circumcised before entering the Promised Land.[102]

Finally, Kim suggested practical principles in constructing christological sermons on historical texts. According to Kim, OT historical texts depict the history of the Israelites as a nation from their time in Egypt to the destruction of the temple by Babylon in 586 BC, but this history was evidently oriented so that Jesus Christ should be the climax and purpose of this grand narrative of God's covenant people. When preaching OT historical texts, therefore, preachers should elucidate how they are connected to Christ. If this is done well, christological preaching is undertaken and Christ is being proclaimed as the ultimate and unique accomplishment of OT history.[103]

Nevertheless, I suggest Kim's sermon on Josh 5:1–9 also has a crucial defect as it disregards the immediate context, and also fails to give adequate emphasis to God's act in the deliverance of the Israelites, which is recorded in the text. One commentator states that God silenced all the enemies of the Israelites (v. 1) and let the new generation have the seal of belonging to God's covenant people (vv. 2–7), which eventually rolled away the "reproach of Egypt" (vv. 8–9).[104] God ultimately glorified Himself in this event, by saving His people through the miracle of the drying up of the river Jordan and renewing His covenant with the Israelites.[105] The text intends to highlight the saving act of God, rather than circumcision itself or the comparison between the obedience, or otherwise, of the

102. Ibid., 58–59.
103. Ibid., 59.
104. Henry, "Commentary on Joshua 5:1–9."
105. Wiersbe, *Wiersbe's Expository Outlines on the Old Testament*, 214. By this circumcision the Israelites might escape from the reproach that their God was not strong enough to take them into Canaan.

two generations to God. I submit that Kim's sermon cannot be categorized as an adequate example of text-centered preaching.

Kim also appears to misunderstand the nature of christological preaching, which requires the avoidance of specific pitfalls such as obsessively mentioning Christ. According to Chang-Gyun Chung, there is no need to insert Christ or the cross event unnaturally into the historical text to obtain christological preaching.[106] Greidanus also adds that christocentric preaching does not hinge on the discovery of the types of Christ, because to hear the acts of God in historical texts is to hear the act of Christ.[107] Bryan Chapell also maintains that a sermon becomes Christ-centered not because it finds a reference to Christ in the message but because it recognizes that the text legitimately serves in the great drama of God's redemption of His people.[108] To be brief, God-centered preaching is Christ-centered preaching, because to proclaim God as He has revealed himself is to make known the nature and character that are eternally manifested in Christ (Heb 13:8).[109] Kim arbitrarily connects the text to Christ through circumcision, although it is only the secondary message in the context, and so his view of christological preaching is somewhat forced and defective.

Chang-Hoon Kim, a professor in Chong-Shin Theological Seminary, briefly evaluated redemptive-historical preaching in a theological journal in 2007. He acknowledges that the redemptive-historical approach contributes to the right perspective on the unity and progression of Scripture, and highlights the essential theme of Scripture as being God's redemption through Christ, which we should proclaim emphatically while avoiding pitfalls in biblical interpretation such as anthropocentricism, allegory, spiritualizing, and moralizing.[110] But Kim also refers to several problems which have arisen in the redemptive-historical approach, especially amongst the exclusive, unilateral, and extreme proponents of redemptive-historical preaching, like the Dutch scholars in the 1930s, and those today, such as Goldsworthy and Chapell. Kim identifies the latter two scholars with the Dutch redemptive-historical proponents, but I submit that this is misplaced for Goldsworthy and Chapell are out

---

106. Chung, "Christological Preaching's Traps and Faults."
107. Greidanus, *Sola Scriptura*, 224–25.
108. Chapell, *Christ-Centered Preaching*, 301.
109. Ibid., 304.
110. Kim, "Evaluation of Redemptive-Historical Preaching," 137.

of step with redemptive-historical exclusivists because they endeavor to avoid Christmonism.

The first problem, for Kim, of redemptive-historical preaching is the exclusion of exemplary preaching, although such preaching is legitimate in texts like 1 Cor 10, Heb 11, and Jas 5. As Elizabeth Achtemeier maintains, the history of the church, the new Israel in Christ, recapitulates the history of the old Israel; the faith and acts of the Israelites become ours also in Christ.[111] Thus their examples in OT history should not be excluded in biblical or redemptive-historical preaching.

The second problem is the propensity of the redemptive-historical approach to distort biblical interpretation in initially reading Christ into the text, disregarding basic principles like exploring the text, proceeding to the close context, and finally interpreting the text in the light of the entire contour of Scripture. For example, although Isa 7 should be interpreted in the immediate context, showing God's sovereign control of history as well as His saving of the Israelites despite their disloyalty, it is often used as a prophecy of Christ.[112] However, as noted previously, this neglect of the initial steps in biblical interpretation is the result of faulty redemptive-historical preaching, not of redemptive-historical preaching per se.

The third problem relating to redemptive-historical preaching, for Kim, is its disdain for the varied aspects of preaching. For example, Chapell claims that if the instruction does not embrace the proper understanding of Christ's redemptive work as the motivation and power for vitalizing that instruction, the preacher subsequently utters mere Pharisees' instruction.[113] This is correct in the sense that Christ provides the foundation and support for the new lives of all Christians and empowers them to live according to God's will. However, Kim interprets Chapell's position as in effect disregarding a person's free will, whereas we must emphasize human responsibility to promote spiritual maturity and holiness.[114] He adds that although preaching has many aspects such as *kerygma*, *didache*, and *paraklesis*, redemptive-historical preaching claims only one goal and so lacks respect for the diverse aspects of preaching.[115]

---

111. Achtemeier, *Preaching from the Old Testament*, 25–26.
112. Kim, "Evaluation of Redemptive-Historical Preaching," 142–45.
113. Chapell, *Christ-Centered Preaching*, 19.
114. Kim, "Evaluation of Redemptive-Historical Preaching," 145.
115. Ibid., 146.

However, I regard this criticism as being directed only at a faulty expression of redemptive-historical preaching.

Kim himself proposes what he calls the "(Trinity) God-centered RH approach," because such preaching seeks to apply God's revealed will in today's world and thus can overcome the pitfalls in much of redemptive-historical preaching.[116] I think this evaluation is helpful, but Kim confuses the current proponents of biblical or Christ-centered preaching with the Old Dutch scholars in their view and practice of redemptive-historical preaching. As a result confusion remains in Korea over redemptive-historical preaching and the different positions of redemptive history proponents.

Recently, the *Pastoral Monthly* has again drawn attention to Christ-centered preaching and redemptive-historical preaching respectively in its special editions. In the edition titled "The Sermon: Why It Should Be Christ-centred," Yoon-Jae Lee, a pastor in PCK (Ki-Jang), points out that preaching without Christ is produced through uncertainty of the power of the biblical *kerygma* and is oriented only for church growth, according too much attention to congregational feedback rather than to God's words, and with an exclusively entertaining psychological appeal to people.[117] For Lee, a preacher needs to experience Christ in the text while reading and meditating on the Bible with Christ's perspective, and thus seeing Christ in all the Scriptures. Geum-Nam Choi refers to the deteriorating situation regarding preaching in Korean churches due to the unbalanced focus on the external, numerical growth of the church rather than on the proclamation of biblical truth. Choi claims to be able to recover biblical preaching through Christ-centered redemptive-historical preaching.[118]

In the edition entitled "Talks On Redemptive-Historical Preaching," Chul-Won Seo, a scholar in PCK (Hap-Dong), maintains that God's economy of creation includes the fulfilment of creation's goal, namely, the completion of salvation, for which God alone has been working though human history; these redemptive and divine works of redemption are

---

116. Ibid., 147–48. Kim defines "God-centered RH preaching" as an approach to finding God, who creates the world, controls its history and is true to His covenant, and to proclaiming the truth of salvation through Christ. In addition, this approach also highlights the Holy Spirit who illuminates and applies the truth to us.

117. Lee, "Preaching with Christ Being Evaporated," 60–67.

118. Choi, "Let's Go Back to the Christ-Centered Redemptive-Historical Preaching," 52–59.

recorded in Scripture. Christian preaching, therefore, should center on God alone as creator and redeemer.[119] Seo identifies God-centered preaching with redemptive-historical preaching itself. Soon-Jin Choi, Professor of Old Testament in Torch Trinity Graduate University, also assumes that redemptive-historical preaching presupposes historical continuity between the OT and NT in Christ; the OT should therefore be interpreted with a christocentric perspective,[120] which Choi believes is the essence of redemptive-historical preaching. Choi acknowledges that his position is that of Clowney's in *Preaching Christ in All of Scripture*.[121] However, I question whether even finding Christ in the OT text can be identified with redemptive-historical preaching, despite support being given to that view by many scholars like Soon-Jin Choi and Jae-Yoon Lee. I will discuss this matter in more detail later in the chapter.

Despite the various positions taken by Korean scholars on redemptive-historical preaching in Korea, and reported on in papers and theological journals in the country, there remain serious misunderstandings over the nature and practice of redemptive-historical preaching today. How do these misconceptions relate to the Western controversies regarding redemptive history? We need to examine the influences of the Dutch and American debates on the Korean debate in its understanding and misunderstanding of redemptive-historical preaching.

The Influence of Western Redemptive-Historical Debates

As we have examined above, the Korean redemptive-historical debate has been essentially and profoundly influenced by the preceding Western debates. First of all, the Korean redemptive-historical debate was genetically a reproduction of its Western precedents: the Dutch and American redemptive-historical debates. Most participants in the debate adopted the arguments of Western scholars such as Greidanus, Trimp, and. Clowney. For example, Chang-Gyun Chung argues in a manner based on Clowney's reasoning, Jong-Kil Byun judges redemptive-historical preaching as Trimp did, while Jee-Chan Kim criticizes such preaching on the basis of Greidanus's theory.

---

119. Seo, "Focus of Preaching," 44–53.
120. Choi, "Can Christ be found in the OT?" 60–70.
121. Ibid., 61.

When we compare the three debates, it is clear that both the American and Korean debates depended on the previous Dutch debate regarding the principles and nature of redemptive-historical preaching. The Dutch debate established redemptive-historical principles for interpreting historical text. The American debate developed these principles into the eschatological perspective of Vos's biblical theology, whereas the Korean debate rearranged them as practical issues for a Korean style of redemptive-historical preaching. The first Dutch debate was initially introduced into the American situation by Clowney in the 1960s, and later into the Korean by Sung-Jong Shin in the 1980s. The first debate became the theoretical basis, or reference point, for the two later debates. The Korean debate owed much of its development to both of the previous two debates.

The first debate originated from the New Direction movement in Holland. The second, the American debate, found its origin in Clowney's redemptive-historical preaching formulation, based on Vos's biblical theology. The third, the Korean debate, began with the introduction of Greidanus's *Sola Scriptura*, which describes how the first debate in Holland occurred, progressed, and ended, and then also with Clowney's *Biblical Theology and Preaching* being introduced into Korean churches. The last debate depended, in its start, process, and entire argument in terms of its content, on the first and second debates.

The first debate focused on how to interpret historical text correctly, whereas the second focused on the application issue. The third debate concentrated on the faults of redemptive-historical preaching in Korea, especially the issue of neglecting, or even ignoring, the grammatical-historical interpretation; this was an essential point of Greidanus's evaluation of the first debate in his book. In addition, the third debate also took the application issue as one of the major problems in redemptive-historical preaching. The previous two debates were thus revived, but in a more specified and focused manner, in the third debate.

The major conflict in the first debate was whether a preacher should exclude or include the exemplary or illustrative function of historical text in preaching, that is, the conflict was between exclusivism and inclusivism. The second debate struggled with how God's Word could be appropriately applied to the congregation and, more specifically, how Vos's biblical theology legitimately established the relation of the indicative to the imperative in his Pauline ethics. The Korean debate dealt mainly with whether or not the redemptive-historical approach has inherently major deficiencies for interpreting Scripture. Critics of redemptive-historical preaching, like Jee-Chan Kim, criticized the redemptive-historical approach as having an inherent problem, that of too quickly reading the redemptive history frame into the text, while the proponents of redemptive-historical preaching claimed the problem was due rather to the flawed practice of redemptive-historical principles, which originally engage a valid interpretation of the text.

The first debate was fundamentally rooted in theological differences between Neo-Calvinists and the Old Calvinists, which had been latent in the GKN denomination since its foundation. The debate exposed the theological dissidence in the church and resulted in ecclesiastical schism.[122] The second debate set its theological basis on Vos's biblical theology, but the essential issue regarding Vos's approach to application in the Pauline texts was left untouched. The third debate focused on how to understand redemptive-historical preaching, which was introduced into Korean churches through the books of Greidanus and Clowney. The third debate was eventually entirely affected by the previous two debates through those books, because they became the immediate context for the debate's ignition, process, and result. Subsequently the third redemptive-historical debate was embedded with theological features, through the strengths and weaknesses, and understandings and misunderstandings, of the Dutch and American debates.

For redemptive-historical preaching to develop in Korea, it is necessary to highlight its strengths, but also to face the challenge of its weaknesses. On this account, the third redemptive-historical debate needs to be evaluated and I now intend to evaluate this debate in Korea more critically.

Evaluation of the Korean Redemptive-Historical Debate

What are the significant, constructive points, or otherwise, in the Korean redemptive-historical debate? Is there a possibility of resolving some of these issues or gaining from the debate? These questions will now be explored.

---

122. See section "Background" in chapter 3.

Strengths

The Korean debate reveals several distinctive strengths. Firstly, the debate offered an opportunity to reflect on contemporary preaching, especially on how to interpret the sermon text, and this could only be a useful and fruitful exercise. As we examined earlier in this chapter, redemptive-historical preaching was only introduced into Korean churches in the 1980s as an attempt to meet the crisis in preaching which Korean churches had experienced since the 1970s. Eventually the controversy over redemptive-historical preaching naturally led to discussion regarding conventional preaching, which mainly concentrated on the congregation's own sense of material needs and success rather than on the message of the biblical text itself.[123] For example, Geum-Nam Choi referred to legalistic or exemplary preaching as enervating the Christian gospel, preventing us from viewing the big picture of God's kingdom,[124] while Chang-Hoon Kim pointed out the ill-effects of anthropocentric, allegorical, or moralistic preaching in Korean churches.[125] As a result, the debate enabled Korean preachers to view in retrospect these unbiblical, harmful aspects of popular preaching.

Secondly, it also challenged Reformed preachers to view critically the redemptive-historical preaching which had been practiced in Korean pulpits since the early 1980s. An example is Jee-Chan Kim's criticism of Korean style redemptive-historical preaching, like Gootjes's, as reading the redemptive history framework too quickly into the text. Jong-Kil Byun criticized redemptive-historical sermons for disregarding both the work of the Holy Spirit in the OT and the relationship between the Israelites and NT believers,[126] and Eung-Yul Ryu pointed out the dangers of redemptive-historical preaching.[127] Regardless of the validity of this form

---

123. Lee, "Preaching with Christ Being Evaporated," 61–63. Cf. Chung, *History of Preaching in the Korean Church*, 394–97.

124. Choi, "Not to Lose God," 65. According to Choi, this preaching led people to struggle between self-achievement and a sense of guilt and resulted in a concern for worldly matters rather than heavenly ones. One's perspective or sense of values is greatly affected by how one understands God's redemptive history.

125. Kim, "Evaluation of Redemptive-Historical Preaching," 132; "Let Us Overcome the Pulpit Crisis with 'God-Centered' preaching."

126. Byun, "Meaning and Limit of Redemptive-Historical Preaching," 22.

127. Ryu, "Redemptive-Historical Preaching," 78–88. According to Ryu, the reasons for redemptive-historical preaching being criticized in Korea are: disregarding the immediate meaning of the text in search of Christ, unconditionally rejecting

of preaching, such criticisms opened the minds of people to the pitfalls of faulty redemptive-historical preaching. In brief, the debate provided the opportunity to identify what became known as faulty redemptive-historical preaching.

Thirdly, the debate firmly positioned redemptive-historical preaching in the history of preaching in Korea. Beyond the confusion, the debate ultimately helped to clarify the beginnings of redemptive-historical preaching in Korea as occurring in the late 1970s and early 1980s. Although Jee-Chan Kim misguidedly said that redemptive-historical preaching had already been popular in the late 1970s, he admitted he had overstated his case.[128] Ko-Shin University professor Sang-Kyu Lee also confirmed this point that a new movement of preaching began to appear from the early 1980s in the history of preaching in Korea.[129] That new movement was, according to Lee, redemptive-historical preaching.

Fourthly, the debate provided Korean preachers with various resources relating to the redemptive-historical approach, enabling them to benefit from these in their preaching. For example, Chang-Gyun Chung introduced hermeneutical presuppositions of redemptive-historical preaching and various critics of it, such as Greidanus and Krabbendam; Jong-Chil Park offered essential quotations from Schilder, Trimp, and Gootjes; while Jae-Yul Sho compiled the fundamental arguments of Korean scholars relating to redemptive-historical preaching. If it had not been for the redemptive-historical debate, such valuable materials would not have been made available. To put it differently, a preacher was more able to view objectively the redemptive-historical approach due to the resources obtained throughout the debate.

On the whole, the Korean debate contributes to the development of redemptive-historical preaching in Korea. It had been unilaterally introduced and so it was understood that redemptive-historical preaching was the most appropriate way to expel the problems of conventional preaching in Korean churches.[130] However, the debate became so epochal that the status of redemptive-historical preaching in Korea was drastically changed from its unilateral and exclusive position to one that is more

---

exemplary preaching, and wrongly treating application in preaching.

128. Kim, "To Answer Hae-Moo Yoo's Refutation."

129. Lee, "Talk over the Korean Pulpit," 13.

130. Kim, "To Answer Hae-Moo Yoo's Refutation." Kim declared that the translation in 1989 of Greidanus's *Sola Scriptura* into Korean as *Principles of Redemptive Historical Preaching* implied the propagating of redemptive-historical preaching.

discreet, especially in the way of applying it. Thus, the debate has actually enabled the further development of redemptive-historical preaching in Korea.

Weaknesses

The distinctive weaknesses of the Korean redemptive-historical debate also need to be identified. Firstly, the arguments in the debate remained at the primary level of hermeneutics. Redemptive-historical preaching fundamentally relates to hermeneutical principles; thus a discussion on it, if it is to be fruitfully performed, requires proper examination of its hermeneutical roots, as we have previously examined.[131] However, the debate exhibits only statements concerning the phenomenal aspects of the redemptive-historical approach, for example, the strengths and weaknesses of redemptive-historical preaching, but nothing concerning its hermeneutical or philosophical roots. For example, Chang-Gyun Chung discussed briefly the position and the problems of an erroneous type of redemptive-historical preaching,[132] while J. K. Byun merely introduced the Dutch debate, with his own suggestions for resolving the issues;[133] and S. J. Shin added the features of redemptive-historical preaching by comparison with typological preaching.[134] These scholars barely mentioned the crucial hermeneutical roots of redemptive-historical preaching. I submit that greater depth and understanding of the background is required in relation to redemptive-historical hermeneutics.

Secondly, the debate was only partial, rather than comprehensive, compared with the Dutch debate, pursuing only a small number of issues regarding redemptive-historical preaching, namely, that of too quickly reading a redemptive-historical frame into the text and that of being too human-centered in preaching, whereas the Dutch debate dealt with the whole range of redemptive history, that is, with all the problems relating to exemplary and redemptive-historical preaching. For example, Jee-Chan Kim only pointed out the crucial problem of redemptive-historical preaching as neglecting the first step of exegesis in the historical text,[135]

---

131. See chapter 2.
132. Chung, "Ground of Redemptive-Historical Preaching."
133. Byun, "Meaning and Limit of RH Preaching," 14–23.
134. Shin, "Bible is the Drama of God," 48–52.
135. Kim, "Is it Right to Keep Redemptive-Historical Preaching in This Way?"

and Chang-Hoon Kim described major problems with regard to such preaching, but there was no comprehensive theological and homiletical discussion of it.[136]

In addition, the debate mainly focused on redemptive-historical preaching, not on exemplary preaching. Thus, Hae-Moo Yoo claimed that it was not the time to relinquish but to further develop redemptive-historical preaching, because there were many more problems in moral and human-centered preaching in Korea than in redemptive-historical preaching.[137] I submit that for a more satisfying and balanced discussion of redemptive-historical preaching, a more wide-ranging discussion is required, which includes exemplary preaching. In Korea, as we have seen, that has been widely recognized as being closely connected to *Ki-Bok-Shin-Ang*, which has had an unhelpful impact on Korean churches.

Thirdly, the debate was too much dominated by a few books which introduced the Western debates, especially those of Greidanus, Trimp, and Clowney. For example, Jee-Chan Kim, a major critic of redemptive-historical preaching, essentially borrowed his view of redemptive-historical preaching from Greidanus, while Hae-Moo Yoo criticized his approach. Kim also defended himself by depending on Greidanus, and thus the debate between the two scholars could not develop further.

Fourthly, the debate inadvertently confused christological preaching with redemptive-historical preaching. For example, Hae-Moo Yoo interchanged redemptive-historical preaching with Christ-centered preaching in his argument,[138] and similarly Jee-Chan Kim substituted christological preaching for redemptive-historical preaching.[139] In addition, Geum-Nam Choi proclaimed that Christ-centered preaching and redemptive-historical preaching are actually the same, in that if a preacher practices Christ-centered preaching his sermon is already placed in the context of redemptive history.[140] However, the two approaches are very different. In the Dutch debate, the exemplary preachers also sought to encourage christocentric preaching, by drawing a line directly from the text to Christ. This approach has its dangers, being under Barthian influence, even advocating a dehistoricized redemptive-historical preaching,

---

136. Kim, "Evaluation of Redemptive-Historical Preaching," 132.

137. Yoo, "Refute against."

138. Ibid.

139. Kim, "Historical Books and Christological Preaching," 50–51.

140. Choi, "Let's Go Back to the Christ-Centered Redemptive-Historical Preaching," 59.

in so as far as it disregards questions of historicity, progression, and unity of a text within the entire context of redemptive history.

We now need to underline disagreements in the Korean redemptive-historical debate. The Korean debate, as we have noticed, consisted of several disagreements, specifically on the following issues of the redemptive-historical approach:

1. A too rapid insertion of a redemptive-historical framework into the biblical text and omitting a grammatical-historical interpretation.

2. The exclusion of exemplary or illustrative use of historical texts in preaching.

3. An obsession with Christ-centeredness, so as to always mention Christ regardless of the context.

4. The difficulty for the preacher in composing the message and also for the ordinary congregation to then understand what is preached.

5. The ignoring, or at least neglect, of ethical application and the underlining of human responsibility.

6. The resulting reaction of the congregation to the irrelevance of the preaching to their lives.

However, as we found in chapters 3 and 4, these issues were mostly dealt with in the Dutch and American debates. For example, the first issue actually relates to the "schematism, speculation, and objectivism" with which Greidanus characterized the exclusive redemptive-historical approach.[141] The others also directly or indirectly connect with the conflicting issues in the Dutch and American debates and I will offer a possible solution of these issues in the following section.

Most of the proponents of redemptive-historical preaching in Korea, unlike those redemptive-historical exclusivists or extremists in the Western debates, only partly embrace the exemplary or illustrative use of historical text. For instance, although Sung-Kuh Chung points out that monolithic example-centered preaching has the associated problems of psychologizing, spiritualizing, and moralizing the historical text, thus disregarding the unique history of God's salvation and ultimately making it utterly human-centered, he nevertheless submits that if redemptive-historical principles are primarily kept, then the exemplary use of the

---

141. Greidanus, *Sola Scriptura*, 174. See the section "Assessment and Suggestions" in chapter 3.

historical text is possible, as when Nehemiah used King Solomon as an example of warning against gentile marriage.[142] In addition, Gootjes explains that human faith and acts in historical texts can be examples for us when they relate to God's redemptive acts.[143]

These redemptive-historical advocates do not seem to exclude the exemplary function of the text, but rather limit it by redemptive-historical rules of interpretation, especially the authorial intent of the text. Then, as for this moderate redemptive-historical group, conventional exemplary preaching should be modified by the redemptive-historical way of exemplary preaching. Eventually there should have been discordance between monolithic exemplary and moderate redemptive-historical preaching. However, the former group barely responds, while most redemptive-historical advocates agree on the necessity of an exemplary function accompanying redemptive-historical preaching. Ultimately, the Korean debate could not develop to the extent that it would influence Reformed preachers enough to change their practical sermon-making in terms of redemptive-historical principles.

Despite claims to the contrary, redemptive-historical preaching in Korean churches has not been well understood or properly utilized in them. Holding the contrary view, Young-Min Go, a professor in PCK (Hap-Dong), relates that there have been various types of preaching, such as textual, situational, exemplary, inductive, and prophetic, proposed and practiced in Korean churches since the 1970s, and he asserts that among them expository preaching and redemptive-historical preaching have most broadly appealed to Korean preachers. However, while the former has undergone considerable discussion and has eventually been agreeably accepted, the latter, in terms of practice, remains still a challenge, or even strange, to Korean preachers.[144] I therefore submit that redemptive-historical preaching needs more appropriate in depth discussion before it can be fully accepted and practiced in Korean Reformed pulpits.

There have been some misunderstandings over redemptive-historical preaching, especially currently among redemptive-historical advocates in Korea, and I now turn finally in this chapter to discuss several restrictions to further development of this debate in Korea.

---

142. Chung, "Principles and Methods of Redemptive Historical Preaching," 22–28, 58–59.

143. Gootjes, "Function of Examples in Historical Texts of Scripture," 115–31.

144. Go, "Redemptive-Historical Preaching."

Further Development

I suggest that the redemptive-historical preaching debate in Korea is not developing positively for several reasons. Firstly, Korean culture, unlike in the West, is deeply rooted in Confucianism and this is part of the difficulty in fostering a more extensive and helpful debate. For example, as we saw earlier in this chapter, Jee-Chan Kim and Hae-Moo Yoo launched an open debate, but it quickly ended without agreement. The Confucian culture, which considers open criticism of another's view as a personal attack, or an expression of contempt,[145] helps to block further discussion between scholars. In Korean society, even those who have studied abroad are reluctant to criticize publically the opinions of other scholars.

In addition, the debate is further stifled because many Korean scholars are unfamiliar with, or inept in, academic debate, which requires refined and critical examination of specific issues, as well as an engagement in more detached logical and non-emotional discussion. For example, Jee-Chan Kim's argument about redemptive-historical preaching became somewhat subjective rather than objective,[146] and eventually Hae-Moo Yoo pointed out that Kim's method of discussion was not appropriate for a scholar.[147] Yoo also felt that Kim had revealed malevolent intentions regarding the validity of Gootjes's redemptive-historical preaching.[148] Yoo's criticism of Kim seemed rather scathing, and even personal, although Yoo himself had suggested more constructive criticism was necessary for fruitful discussion. The debate between Kim and Yoo eventually became so affected by personal slander that it was unable to go further. I submit that for further development of the debate, more skilful and objective academic discussion is required.

Finally, the limited number of participants in the debate, and their lack of academic proficiency, has hindered the debate from developing to the extent that a fruitful result is possible. Yoo attests that there are not many Korean preachers who are well educated in grammatical-historical interpretation.[149] Likewise, not many Korean scholars have sufficient experience in redemptive-historical principles. Some scholars, like Jong-Chil Park, appear to be familiar with redemptive history but

---

145. Keum, *Confucianism and Korean Thoughts*, 23.
146. Kim, "Is it Right to Keep Redemptive-Historical Preaching in This Way?"
147. Yoo, "Refute against."
148. Ibid.
149. Ibid.

do not actively engage in the debate.¹⁵⁰ These deficiencies have served to hinder progress in the redemptive-historical controversy and the debate has stalled without any of the issues being resolved.

I now suggest solutions to this impasse in the debate.

Suggestions

I submit that some answers in the Korean redemptive-historical debate can possibly be acquired from the previous Dutch and American debates. Most participants in the Korean debate were in fact searching for a solution from the two previous Western debates. Jee-Chan Kim suggested text-centered preaching, instead of the redemptive-historical approach, to address the problem of schematically reading the redemptive-historical frame into the text, but this idea was originally propounded by Greidanus.¹⁵¹ Chang-Hoon Kim also proposed Greidanus's historical and organic interpretation,¹⁵² which secures the meaning of the text in its own historical context and then highlights the literary connection of the text with its progression and fulfilment in the context of the whole of Scripture.¹⁵³

On the other hand, Sung-Kuh Chung thought that a proper redemptive-historical approach would never disregard the basic rules of biblical interpretation, namely, the grammatical-historical interpretation.¹⁵⁴ If a preacher were to apply the hermeneutical principles of the redemptive-historical approach correctly, his preaching would start with the original meaning of the text. I concur with Chung's position on this point.

On the matter of excluding the exemplary use of historical texts, Jong-Kil Byun attempts to find the solution in Trimp's definition of the

---

150. Park, "Redemptive-Historical Interpretation and Preaching," 40–53.

151. Kim, "Is it Right to Keep Redemptive-Historical Preaching in This Way?"

152. Greidanus, *Sola Scriptura*, 218–24. Greidanus contends that organic interpretation goes along with the redemptive history side's christocentric interpretation, but the danger of arbitrariness, in which one reads Christ into the text, can be precluded by taking seriously the historical interpretation.

153. Kim, "Evaluation of Redemptive-Historical Preaching," 144–45.

154. Chung, "Preaching and Redemptive-Historical Interpretation," 227. For Chung, the more important thing is to realize the meaning and contour of God's redemptive history which the author of the text intended to reveal, rather than to explore the literary context, the relationship between before and after the text, or the contemporary historical situation.

term *example* in the NT. Trimp defines this as meaning a characteristic part of the whole history of redemption, so that it can be a warning or instruction for today's Christian.[155] Chang-Hoon Kim also supports Byun in that various scriptural texts like 1 Cor 10, Heb 11, and Jas 5 justify the exemplary use of historical text.[156] Although the followers of the Dutch redemptive-historical group, like Do-Soon Yoo and Jae-Yul Sho, retain the position of excluding the exemplary use of historical texts,[157] most moderate redemptive-historical advocates like Eung-Yul Ryu acknowledge the legitimacy of exemplary preaching which fundamentally recognizes the essential message of the text in its redemptive-historical canonical context.[158] While there may not be as much disagreement over exemplary preaching in Korea as in the Dutch debate, the avoidance of exemplary preaching in pursuing redemptive-historical preaching should be placed in the context of efforts to overcome the undermining influence of *Ki-Bok-Shin-Ang*.

The problem of obsessively mentioning Christ regardless of context may be resolved by Chang-Gyun Chung's proposition that Christ-centeredness is defined by Christ taking the center place in the organic whole of the Scriptures, rendering it unnecessary always to mention Christ in the text.[159] Chapell supports this, if the preaching is faithful to the christocentric nature of all Scripture and to God's redemptive purpose.[160] Even the two opposing parties in the Dutch debate concurred that christocentric preaching does not simply draw a direct line from every text to Christ, but rather that it signifies the fullness of God's revelation in Christ from a specific point of redemptive history.[161] Thus, proper redemptive-historical preaching is not determined by how many times one mentions Christ, or how well the text connects to Christ, but by how rightly the text is interpreted in the light of redemptive-historical hermeneutical principles, that is, the historicity, progression, and unity of redemptive history.

In relation to the perception that redemptive-historical preaching is too difficult to understand, C. G. Chung maintains that the difficulty

155. Byun, "Meaning and Limit of Redemptive-Historical Preaching," 16–17. Cf. Trimp, *Preaching and the History of Salvation*, 96–101.

156. Kim, "Evaluation of Redemptive-Historical Preaching," 138–142.

157. Yoo, "Why Should We Do RH Preaching?" 82–84.

158. Ryu, "Redemptive-Historical Preaching," 82–83.

159. Chung, "Ground of Redemptive-Historical Preaching," 12.

160. Chapell, *Christ-Centered Preaching*, 301–5.

161. See the section "The Features of Redemptive Historical Preaching" in chapter 3.

is not redemptive-historical preaching itself, but rather the preacher's inability to employ it correctly and to be responsible for, and responsive to, the needs of the congregation.[162] According to Clowney, genuine redemptive-historical preaching is difficult to use and apply: "Christological preaching calls for careful comparing of Scripture with Scripture, extensive use of concordances, and a lifetime commitment to Bible study, meditation, and prayer."[163] John Frame also attests that redemptive-historical preaching is not easy for a beginner,[164] requiring long and patient effort to prepare appropriately for. it. However, I submit that redemptive-historical preaching, if competently and prayerfully prepared, is suitable for preachers and congregations alike.

Disregarding ethical application and human responsibility are complicated issues in the American debate, as we saw in chapter 4. However, Eung-Yul Ryu states that the most serious fallacy of redemptive-historical advocates, also held by Gootjes and Sung-Kuh Chung, is the view that application is unnecessary for relevant preaching. Their view is mistaken, because Scripture was originally oriented for the salvation, and also the sanctification, of believers.[165] Ryu's contention is consistent with the views of Clowney and Goldsworthy. Clowney affirmed that the redemptive-historical approach necessarily yields ethical application, because we are faced with ethical commands whenever we meet God's redemptive work culminating in Christ.[166] Goldsworthy also emphasizes that the essence of preaching is to make the congregation pledge to follow God's Word and so apply the Word to their hearts and wills.[167] Chappell strengthens this point by saying that application is the personal consequence of scriptural truth so that application actually fulfils the redemptive purpose.[168] The best biblical preaching, for these Reformed scholars, is the one that is most faithful to the objectives of Scripture, and thus redemptive-historical preaching should be oriented for radical change, namely, the salvation and sanctification of the congregation.

162. Chung, "Ground of Redemptive-Historical Preaching," 13.
163. Clowney, "Preaching Christ From All the Scriptures," 190.
164. Frame, "Ethics, Preaching, and Biblical Theology." See the section "Opponents of Exclusive Redemptive-Historical Preaching" in chapter 4.
165. Ryu, "Redemptive-Historical Preaching," 83–88.
166. Clowney, *Preaching and Biblical Theology*, 80.
167. Goldsworthy, *Preaching the Whole Bible as Christian Scripture*, 121.
168. Chappell, *Christ-Centered Preaching*, 210.

Nonetheless, the application issue is also complicated in the Korean debate. For example, proponents of redemptive-historical preaching, such as Do-Soon Yoo, adopt the position of the extreme redemptive-historical wing in the American debate,[169] which insists that application should be the ministry not merely of humans but of the Holy Spirit. For this reason, a preacher needs to exercise caution and not try to apply the text arbitrarily to the congregation, but rather take them to the text.[170] Sung-Kuh Chung also takes a similar position to that of Greidanus, who affirms that the Word itself has already contained application in its theocentric explication.[171] This issue connects directly to the controversy over the "explication versus application" issue in the Dutch and American debates.

I now raise a significant dilemma in these redemptive-historical debates. The overarching dilemma in the Korean redemptive-historical debate, as also in the Dutch and American debates, is principally the conflicting tension between God-centeredness and man-centeredness, in which the contemporary struggle in Reformed preaching emerges. A preacher who focuses on the congregation is likely to highlight in the text man's will and efforts rather than God's sovereign acts of delivering His people. This is easily illustrated in exemplary or human-centered preaching. On the other hand, a preacher who stresses God-centeredness in the text tends to disregard man's responsibility.

Western pulpits have also faced this tension. William Willimon points out that contemporary preachers, whether conservative or liberal, refer to overtly man-centered preaching in the pulpit.[172] However, Lindblad insists that Christ's appointed preachers with a Reformed faith will seek to emulate the apostle Paul in preaching nothing but Christ and Him crucified, rather than promoting people (1 Cor 2:2).[173] The Western redemptive-historical debates, especially the debates concerning "redemptive-historical versus exemplary" and "biblical theological versus traditional," reflect the struggle and anxiety for responsible and improved preaching in Reformed circles.

169. Yoo, "Why should we do RH preaching?" 105–29.

170. Dennison, "Biblical Theology and the Issue of Application," 149.

171. Greidanus, *Sola Scriptura*, 160.

172. Willimon, *Peculiar Speech*, 9, quoted in Lindblad, "Redemptive History and the Preached Word," part 1, Introduction, May 2005, 25.

173. Lindblad, "Redemptive History and the Preached Word," part 1, Introduction, May 2005, 25.

The essence of this disagreement is that between "autonomy" and "heteronomy," which can be expressed as human-centeredness versus God-centeredness. Put differently, when redemptive-historical preaching deals with life after salvation, that is, the order of salvation, and the roles that both God and man have, then the issue of God's sovereignty and, on the other hand, the responsibility of humans, becomes a key issue in the debate.

This fundamental dilemma underlies other differences in the redemptive-historical debates, and so a common criterion needs to be identified for evaluating redemptive-historical sermons. Vos's biblical theology can be an appropriate criterion, because participants in the American and Korean debates generally accept and respect Vos as having a more acceptable hermeneutical basis for redemptive-historical preaching.

Conclusion

In this chapter I have delineated the homiletical debate in Korean Reformed churches and shown that these churches have been confused by the links with the Western debates. I suggest the need of reevaluation and reconstruction of redemptive-historical theology in the Korean church along the line of Reformed principles.

In the next chapter I will offer my conclusion, with a brief introduction to Won-Tae Suk, who has been faithful in the pursuit of a Korean expression of redemptive-historical preaching which is consistent with the principles and tradition of Reformed theology.

7

Conclusion

With Samples of Korean Redemptive-Historical Preaching

I DESCRIBED THE BACKGROUND to, and development of, the debates concerning redemptive-historical hermeneutics and homiletics in Reformed circles, especially in Holland, America and Korea, in chapter 1. I then explored in chapter 2 the history of hermeneutical theories relating to redemptive history within NT theology and identified three roots of the redemptive-historical perspective. In chapter 3 the Dutch debate was outlined and examined critically, especially its relation to the historical and ecclesiastical background. I also explored, in chapter 4, the origin, progress, and influence of the American redemptive-historical debate, while comparing it with the Dutch debate. In chapter 5 I traced the understanding of redemptive history during the history of the Korean Protestant church, before discussing in detail, in chapter 6, the redemptive-historical homiletical debate in Korea, in the context of the earlier Western debates.

Findings

Having critically examined the redemptive-historical homiletical debates which occurred in Holland, America, and Korea, I have reached, and already indicated earlier, several significant conclusions about redemptive-historical hermeneutics and homiletics.

Firstly, there has been serious confusion and misunderstanding in claiming that redemptive-historical preaching originated in the Dutch theological context, especially from Schilder during the redemptive-historical debate in the 1930s. American redemptive-historical preaching, formulated by Clowney, was actually based on Vos's biblical theology. In Korea, Won-Tae Suk's redemptive-historical preaching was independently developed by himself from his own study of Scripture with mediation and prayer, although I qualify this by acknowledging other theological influences upon him.

Secondly, any attempt to bracket these redemptive-historical debates as one continuous debate would be a major mistake. The context is crucial for understanding each debate, as each context differs from the others. Disregarding this important fact subsequently leads to a misunderstanding of the debate. The context of the Dutch debate was the struggle between Kuyper's Neo-Calvinism and Dutch Pietism in the GKN. The American debate resulted from excessive support for Vos's biblical theology, which inevitably led to a confrontation with experiential Calvinism. The Korean debate occurred due to the confusion over redemptive-historical preaching in relation to the Dutch debate.

Thirdly, it is extremely helpful if the hermeneutical roots of redemptive-historical preaching are examined beforehand in order to achieve a responsible understanding of the redemptive-historical approach to Scripture. Any redemptive-historical approach should be carefully examined and assessed along the above hermeneutical lines before adapting it as an approach to Scripture.

Fourthly, there are misconceptions in Korean Reformed churches in assuming that christological, or Christ-centered, preaching is the same as redemptive-historical preaching. Redemptive-historical preaching is both God-centered and Christ-centered, whereas Christ-centered preaching is not necessarily redemptive-historical preaching. According to Vos, redemptive-historical preaching should recognize four features of revelation: "historical progressiveness," "its actual embodiment in history," "the organic nature of the historical process observable in revelation," and "practical adaptability."[1]

In the context of reaching these conclusions after considerable research and reflection, there are six ways in which this study offers an

---

1. Vos, *Biblical Theology*, 5–7.

original and important contribution to learning. These were mentioned early in chapter 1, but I underline them again at this point.

One contribution is that I am the only scholar who has adopted a non-polemical approach to the Dutch debate. A second contribution is that, unlike others, I have identified cultural and theological issues as major factors in the Dutch debate. A third area is that I challenge the common assumption of scholars that the Dutch debate was merely continued in America. My research demonstrates that this assumption is unfounded. A fourth contribution is that no one else has compared the Dutch and American redemptive-historical preaching debates and in an objective manner. The fifth contribution is that in comparing the Dutch and American debates I have related them in detail to developments in the Korean redemptive-historical preaching debate. This has not previously been done.

There is a sixth area where I make a contribution to learning, as I am the first researcher to provide a significant introduction to Won-Tae Suk, a major Korean redemptive-historical preaching minister, preacher, and academic who also authored an important homiletical textbook in Korean on redemptive-historical preaching. Many of his sermons have been published, but I intend to introduce him in this concluding chapter as one main example in Korean Reformed churches of redemptive-historical preaching. I would like to include other examples of Korean preaching for comparison and critical evaluation. The consideration of other Korean preachers will demand extensive research.

Why introduce only one representative Korean redemptive-historical preacher at this late stage? Won-Tae Suk, already referred to in chapter 5,[2] is my chosen sample for several reasons.

Firstly, there are several preachers who have been regarded as leading redemptive-historical preaching proponents in Korea, but I suggest that only three have preached within a consistent redemptive-historical perspective and also authored textbooks on the subject. These are Gootjes,[3] Sung-Kuh Chung,[4] and Won-Tae Suk.[5] Gootjes's book introduced redemptive history into the Ko-Shin denomination, but he left Korea before it was critically examined in the Korean debate. Chung's book

---

2. See the section "1980 s to 2010: Introspection and Diversification of Theology" in chapter 5.
3. Gootjes, *Between Exegesis and Sermon*.
4. Chung, *Principles and Methods of Redemptive-Historical Preaching*.
5. Suk, *Redemptive Historical Principles of Homiletical Theology*.

has been the most frequently quoted in the theses of seminarians and has been given considerable status by students and some academics. However, his book recycles the arguments of Western redemptive-historical proponents and, what is more disappointing, he fails to express his own view or provide critical evaluation of Western writers. In contrast, Suk's book presents his own thoughts about redemptive-historical preaching; he later became aware of Western scholarship on the subject yet approached redemptive-historical preaching within a creative Korean context. Consequently, I regard Suk as an interesting example of Korean redemptive-historical preaching.

A second reason for choosing Suk is that he has achieved a helpful balance between the theory and practice of redemptive-historical preaching, whereas some proponents, such as Jong-Chil Park, overemphasized theoretical aspects, especially the hermeneutical history of redemptive-historical preaching.[6] In contrast, most redemptive-historical preaching proponents, like Geum-Nam Choi[7] and Yoon-Jae Lee,[8] as we saw in chapter 6, focus on the practical aspect, but are also guilty of confusing redemptive-historical preaching with Christ-centered preaching. A very small number of scholars, however, including Sung-Kuh Chung and Won-Tae Suk, are balanced in discussing both redemptive-historical preaching theory and practice.

Thirdly, Suk has been more consistent than other Korean advocates in applying redemptive-historical principles in church ministries. Suk ministered as a PCK pastor for over fifty years and published over eighty books containing his collected sermons and lectures. All these sermons express Suk's redemptive-historical perspective. Sung-Kuh Chung, a respected redemptive-historical preaching leader, acknowledges Suk's prominence and consistency in such preaching, with a unique perspective.[9]

---

6. Park, *Redemptive-Historical Interpretation of the Scripture*.

7. Choi, "Let's Go Back to the Christ-Centered Redemptive-Historical Preaching," 52–59. Choi contended that Korean churches should recover biblical preaching through Christ-centered RH preaching, but he confused redemptive-historical preaching with Christ-centered preaching.

8. Lee, "Preaching with Christ Being Evaporated," 60–67. Lee claimed that a Korean preacher needs to experience Christ in the text while meditating on Scripture, but for him that experience is only to be existential rather than historical.

9. Chung, "Study on Won-Tae Suk's Preaching."

A fourth reason for introducing Suk is that I have access to his primary sources. I have heard him preach often, but I am also aware how other preachers and academics in Korea respect him as a preacher and theologian who wrestled with redemptive-historical preaching.

Methodology

My chosen method in considering Suk's published sermons is that of using only a limited sample. There are 1,543 published sermons of Suk in thirty-four volumes. I have consulted most of these volumes, but have majored on identifying references in these sermons to redemptive history and to evaluating the ways in which Suk presents this. I have not examined each of the 1,543 sermons in detail for several reasons.

Firstly, because the existing confusion and misunderstanding in Korea over the history and nature of the redemptive-historical preaching debate is considerable, the extensive background was essential in order to be able to identify and assess redemptive-historical preaching responsibly before considering in any detail the sermons of Korean preachers.

Secondly, I am not using Suk's sermons as a case-study; rather I am sampling and introducing him, though not in a random manner. I have read through many of the sermons and also scanned many of them electronically for references to, and examples of, redemptive-historical preaching. My more modest aim and focus is to introduce one example of Korean Reformed preaching.

I regard Suk as a suitable choice as a practical example and theorist of Korean redemptive-historical preaching. In outlining the three stages of Suk's development of redemptive-historical preaching and the types of preaching he recognizes, I will refer briefly to a significant number of his sermons.

Won-Tae Suk

Won-Tae Suk is Emeritus Pastor of Gyeong-Hyang Presbyterian Church, a leading Reformed church for over three decades in Korea. He planted the church in 1973, serving as its senior pastor for thirty-one years until retirement in September 2004 at the age of seventy. He also founded Goryo Theological Seminary in 1976. In addition, Suk founded a new denomination, Reformed Goryo Presbyterian Church, and developed it as a significant denomination among the nearly two hundred Protestant denominations in Korea.[10] As a famous pastor, respected educator, and prominent preacher and leader, Suk has influenced many Christian ministers, even beyond his denomination.

What are the influences on Suk's thought and theology which contributed to his understanding of redemptive-historical preaching? Suk's conversion occurred at the age of eighteen in September 1934 in Changwon,[11] when he became convinced of the major importance of the Scriptures for believers and for evangelizing, and that the Holy Spirit works through Scripture and its proclamation.[12] Another crucial influence on Suk was his sense of divine call around 1953 to be a preacher. He later advanced to Koshin College in Pusan for theological education.[13] Koshin was established in 1946 by its founders, Nam-Sun Joo (1888–1950) and Sang-Dong Han (1901–76),[14] who had refused to worship in the Shinto religion and experienced severe persecution under the Japanese colonial government.[15] One object of the college was to maintain the values of the Korean martyrs and orthodox theology. Suk was profoundly influenced in the formation of his faith and theology at the college.

10. Han-Mee-Joon and Gallup Korea, *Research Report–The Religious Concepts and Activities of Korean Protestants*, 303–306. According to this report, Reformed Goryo Presbyterian Church (or PCK Goryo) is one of the leading ten Presbyterian denominations in Korea.

11. Changwon was a small rural village in the southern part of the Korean Peninsula which has now become a large city, with a population of about 500,000 in 2007.

12. Suk, "The Lord Opened My Spiritual Eyes!" When Suk listened to the preaching on Isaiah 53 that night he realized that Christ was silent before Pilate and others at his trial, and was lashed and speared, before finally being killed on the cross, all because he was offering himself as a sacrifice for our sins. Suk bowed and wept all night until the dawn prayer bell rang. From then on he understood the Christian message and everything in the world seemed totally new to him.

13. It was formerly called Korea (or Goryo) Theological Seminary but changed to this name in 1970 when registering as a college with the Educational Ministry Department of Korea, since there was already an educational institution with the same name.

14. Oh, "History of Koshin College," 107.

15. Kim, *Korean Church History*, 210. Shinto is the doctrine that the Japanese people are directly descended from the Sun goddess and thus they are believed to become gods when they die for the nation. Korean churches had suffered from a severe ordeal due to Japan's enforcement of Shinto worship from the middle of the 1930s to Independence Day, 15 August 1945. The colonial government built Shinto shrines all over the country, thinking that to have Korean people worship Japanese gods who died in battles for Japan was very important for japanizing Koreans. Cf. Clark, *History of the Church in Korea*, 221–22.

Sang-Dong Han's influence[16] on Suk was particularly significant, especially through his preaching which was permeated with "the thought of God" and His glory and sovereignty as expressed through Scripture, as well as with his own solitude and suffering for Christ. These characteristics are also found in Suk's preaching. Suk was influenced also in terms of preaching while he was a church apprentice under Han.

Yune-Sun Park, former president of Koshin College, also deeply influenced Suk's approach to Scripture. Park, a graduate of WTS, Philadelphia in 1936, returned to Korea[17] and began to lead Korean churches into a clearer understanding of Calvinist theology. The focus of Park's theological education was Calvinist Reformed principles, such as God centeredness, *sola scriptura*, *sola gratia*, and *sola fide*.[18] Suk was attracted to these principles through Park's sermons and through reading his voluminous books, even though he could enjoy Park's teaching in class. Suk recently acknowledged that he came to appreciate biblical theology when his previous avid reading of Scripture was given more enlightenment through Park's sermons and books based on Reformed biblical theology. Park provided Suk with considerable insight into Reformed biblical theology, and from this base Suk began his journey in redemptive-historical theology.[19] Chi-Mo Hong affirmed that Park always emphasized that "thought relied on revelation," and this was embodied in Suk's writings. Thus, "it is no exaggeration to say that Won-Tae Suk is a person who has faithfully and exhaustively followed Park's Reformed thoughts."[20]

---

16. Han was regarded as a "living martyr" and characterized as "all the way walking with the Lord" in any circumstance, even to death. Cf. Kim, "Sang-Dong Han, a Master Who Lives the Life of All the Way Walking With the Lord," 15–16.

17. Park graduated from Soong-Sil College in 1931 (English Literature major), and from Pyeong-Yang Theological Seminary in 1934. He then entered Westminster Theological Seminary where he was under the influence of J. Gresham Machen and studied the apologetics of Cornelius Van Til. Park came to a certainty that the Scriptures have the supreme authority which comes from God's words. Later he confessed that the education in WTS helped him to recognize the faith of Calvinism (or the Reformed faith) and hold it firmly from then on. Cf. Park, *Obsessed with His Word*, 69–75.

18. Chung, *Korean Church and Reformed Faith*, 210.

19. Suk, "Gyeong-Hyang Presbyterian Church and Goryo Theological Seminary."

20. Hong, "Book Review," 278.

Three Stages of Suk's Redemptive-Historical Preaching

Suk's redemptive-historical preaching can be divided into three stages during his ministry: its inception (1966–1972), development (1973–1991), and proliferation (1992 to the present). This division reflects significant changes in Suk's ministry and preaching. For example, Suk finished his Pusan ministry in 1972, moving to Seoul to plant Gyeong-Hyang Presbyterian Church in 1973. He published his definitive redemptive-historical preaching textbook in 1991.

The inception period (1966–1972) shows that Suk's preaching was firmly rooted in Calvinist theology, with its God-centeredness. For example, the sermon titled "O Sun! Stand Still!" (Josh 10:12–13) represented Suk's firm belief in Scripture. For Suk, darkness was prevented by Joshua's prayer and God's command, although such a happening may not occur again for it was a unique occasion in Scripture.[21] Suk has a complete, often literal, acceptance of what is written in the Bible. In the sermon "The Barley Bread Movement" (Judg 7:1–23) Suk claims that Gideon's camp was like a small loaf of bread which could raise a great deliverance movement when God held it in His hand; likewise modern church movements are like a small loaf, but under God they can achieve an enormous amount.[22] This comparison seems allegorical and subjective, but it observes the symbolism in Suk's redemptive-historical preaching principles that we discuss below.

The sermon series "The Culture of the Lost Son and Christianity" (Luke 15:11–32) affirmed that the lost son most valued himself (autonomy) and so left his father and lost the blessedness to be enjoyed in his father's house. For Suk, the culture of lost sons is illustrated in biblical history in events such as Cain's homicide, the fall of God's sons in Noah's time, the construction of the Tower of Babel, Esau's selling of his birthright, Jeroboam's self-willed worship of idols (1 Kgs 12:28–33), and Judas Iscariot's betrayal to satisfy his greed. This culture originates in those who refuse to love and honour God first in their lives; however, Christianity is the movement of returning people to God the Father, through Jesus Christ.[23] This is not redemptive-historical preaching, although Suk uses historical incidents as illustrations. However it is characterized by focusing especially on God and His relationship with men as His beloved but lost children.

21. Suk, *O Sun! Stand Still!* 39–52.
22. Suk, *Barley Bread Movement*, 275–81.
23. Suk, *Culture of the Lost Son and Christianity*, 19–89.

Suk also affirmed in "The Image of the True Church" (1 Pet 2:1–5) that God called and nurtured the elect through the church for the accomplishing of His economy of redemption. The church movement existed from the primeval struggle between the seed of the woman and the serpent, continuing differently for the godly Noah and his household. Abraham's family line was then distinguished from that of other people, becoming a collective worship movement in a centralised holy place (the tabernacle and then the temple) from Moses's era to the period of the Israelite kings, finally becoming the universal church movement in the NT era. God's redemptive history has unfolded through the church movement.[24] In this practical way, Suk's redemptive-historical perspective was clearly represented in his early preaching.

The second period (1973–1991) exhibited the development of Suk's redemptive-historical perspective and subsequently the formation of his redemptive-historical preaching theological principles, highlighting God's sovereignty. The sermon "The Genuine Meaning of History" portrayed various perspectives of history, such as cycle, struggle, repetition, biography, and progress; however, the more correct perspective is that of the living God as the host of history, God's redemption as its goal, and Christ as the center. Thus all history proceeds towards this goal and centers on redemptive history.[25]

The sermon series "The Sovereignty of God" (1 Chr 29:11–13) emphasized that God sovereignly saves some people, not all, from danger and death. God sovereignly created everything in the universe, controlling the inanimate and biological worlds, the righteous and unrighteous, and people therefore ought to be responsible in honoring God.[26] In addition, the sermon "The Eyes Viewing on History" (Dan 8:1–3) highlighted the grace and insight of Christians in being able to acknowledge God's sovereignty. Subsequently, redemptive history is the core of history, providing purpose and significance, and is the means of accomplishing God's redemption.[27]

The sermon "Redemptive History and the Church Movement" (Matt 16:13–20) established the essential four features of redemptive history, namely,

---

24. Suk, *O Sun! Stand Still!* 62–71.
25. Suk, *Citizen of the World*, 207–213.
26. Suk, *People Who Had Won*, 349–355.
27. Suk, *Eyes Viewing on History*, 175–181.

1. The centrality of redemptive history in history.
2. Christ as the center of redemptive history.
3. The church as the specific organization for the movement of redemptive history.
4. The preaching of the church as the means of accomplishing redemptive-history.

The sermon defined redemptive history as the fact of God's redemptive plan being achieved progressively in history, concluding that God's redemption movement is being unfolded to the world through the church as Christ's body, which He purchased. World history will end when redemptive history is fulfilled.[28]

The third period (1992 to the present) shows the extension of Suk's redemptive-historical perspective into areas such as preaching and ministry. I have established that the term *redemptive history* appeared in more than 150 sermons from 1992 to 2002, whereas only fifty-three sermons adopted the terms and concept in the development period (1973–1991) when the stress was more on God's sovereignty, the Reformed faith, ecclesiology, and eschatology, rather than on redemptive history itself. In this third period, Suk's redemptive-historical hermeneutical principles, which we discuss later, have been more prominent and applied to all aspects of church ministries through sermons like "The Year of 98 in the Hands of God,"[29] "The Way of History,"[30] "Recollecting the History,"[31] "God shall be God Himself!"[32] "The Way of the Israelites,"[33] "The Church in History,"[34] "This World and the World to Come,"[35] and "By Scripture Alone."[36]

I now explore Suk's redemptive-historical and homiletical principles.

---

28. Ibid., 183–189.
29. Suk, *Way of History*, 8–15.
30. Ibid., 287–295.
31. Suk, *Glory of Christ*, 387–393.
32. Suk, *Star Wars*, 317–325.
33. Suk, *May the Lord Increase Us a Thousand Times More Than the Present!* 391–398.
34. Suk, *Revival of the Church*, 309–315.
35. Suk, *This World and the World to Come*, 383–431.
36. Suk, *By Scripture Alone*, 289–296.

Hermeneutical and Homiletical Principles

Suk's concept of redemptive history contains seven basic elements: God the creator, His sovereign will in redemption, people to be redeemed, Jesus Christ the redeemer, the divine revelation of this redemption, the church as the institution of this glorious redemption movement, and the historicity of that redemption.[37] Suk defines redemptive history as having these basic elements:

> RH is an historical process whereby God, according to His delightful will and plan, first reveals in the Scriptures the work of salvation through the redemption of Jesus Christ for His people who were corrupted by sin, and then accomplishes the divine plan by way of the movement of the Church in the ground of real history.[38]

Suk assumes several theological principles in, and from, the above definition. Initially he recognizes redemptive history as the integration of history with salvation, and insists that the author and subject of redemptive history is God alone.[39] His definition also implies that the object of redemptive history is God's people, who were spoilt by sin. It also infers that redemptive history has been consistently revealed in Scripture, which is the exclusive text for redemptive history. This redemptive history drama renders Jesus Christ and His church as its main characters, while its stage is the world and its history.[40]

This concept of redemptive history highlights history as revelatory and monistic, redemptive-historical events like the fall, then the crucifixion of Christ, confirming that God's will of saving His people was achieved through history, which has a revelatory function.[41] Secular and redemptive history should not be separated in God's redemptive will.[42] This understanding of redemptive history is not new, as in the eighteenth century Jonathan Edwards (1703–1758) taught that everything in human

---

37. Ibid., 66–68.
38. Suk, *Redemptive Historical Principles of Homiletical Theology*, 68–69.
39. Ibid., 69.
40. Ibid.
41. Ibid., 61.
42. Ibid., 62.

history is subservient to Christ's redemptive history.[43] For Edwards, nothing can frustrate this work as all that happens in history serves to fulfil it.

While, for Suk, redemptive history has an inseparable relation with world history, Jesus Christ, the church, and preaching, how does redemptive history relate to them? Firstly, as we have seen, redemptive history functions in the center of world history, while Suk insists that Scripture reveals the essential nature and purpose of mankind (Dan 7–8 and Rev 17:9–10).[44] From this apocalyptic literature, Suk underlines the scriptural principle that the dominant seven empires in world history are the plaza for the history of God's redemptive purpose.[45]

Secondly, redemptive history specifically represents Christ as its center. Christ's coming was anticipated and revealed in Scripture, for example, through various figures and types (Gen 3:15, 4:25—5:32, 6:1, 9:1 and Luke 3:36–38. Exod 3:1–5 and Acts 7:30–38. Exod 13:20–22, 14:1–31, 15:22–27, 16:1–36, 17:1–7; Num 9:16–23; Deut 8:15 and 1 Cor 10:1–11. Num 17:1–11, 21:4–9, 35:6–33; Deut 34:9; Judg 2:16; 1 Sam 7:12; Jer 23:5 and Acts 2:30. Dan 8:9–27, 11:29–30 and Rev 16:13–14. Esth 9:23–28 and John 16:33).[46]

Thirdly, Christ's redemptive-historical movement unfolds through the history of the church He established. The church is necessary, comprising God's people who endeavor to accomplish God's will (Isa 43:1–7, 21; 1 Cor 1:2; Eph 1:4–14). Suk asserts that the church began not from Pentecost, but from the beginning of the economy of God's redemption.[47] However, he provides more detail, with scriptural justification, indicating that the church's history progressively revealed various redemptive-historical patterns, like the altar in the patriarchal period, the tabernacle from Moses to Samuel, the temple in the period of the kings, the synagogues in the post-exilic period, the universal catholic church in the New Testament period, and, finally, the heavenly church in the final consummation of redemptive history, and then for ever.[48]

Fourthly, Suk maintains that the redemptive-historical movement highlights preaching as the vital means of achieving the goal of redemptive

---

43. Edwards, *History of the Work of Redemption*, 19, 197, 255. Cf. Machen, *New Testament*, 31–32.

44. Suk, *Redemptive Historical Principles of Homiletical Theology*, 74.

45. Ibid., 185.

46. Ibid., 103–22.

47. Ibid., 123.

48. Ibid., 123–33.

history. Suk recognizes various types of preaching movements in history: from the fall to the patriarchal period; the priestly proclamation in the wilderness church period; the prophetic preaching before the kings of Israel and Judah; the interpretative preaching in the post-exilic period; John the Baptist's preaching as the forerunner of Christ; then, climatically, Christ heralding the *kerygma*. Since then it has been harvest time for the church and the world, until Christ's second coming.[49] The distinctiveness of Suk's redemptive-historical view is that while other redemptive-historical scholars have a high view of preaching in the redemptive purpose, they do not express it as strongly as Suk, who regards preaching as the essential means for consummating the redemptive-historical goal. The church and its preaching within redemptive history are indispensably related, with Christ at the center of redemptive history.

Suk's redemptive-historical perspective can be characterized in several ways. Firstly, it is the fruit of his intense study of Scripture, in fact of his "long-time study and meditation on the Scriptures."[50] He claims he "solely relied upon the Scriptures." I add that he did so, but only in that he received and reflected upon a biblical theology through Yune-Sun Park's teaching, then modified it somewhat. Suk did not study redemptive history under Western Reformed scholars, like Schilder, Vos, and Clowney, but those scholars would have been in substantial agreement with him. Nevertheless, for Suk, Scripture is the eye with which to view the history of redemption.[51]

Secondly, Suk underlines God's sovereignty in creation, providence, and salvation (Gen 1:1; John 3:16; Rom 3:28, 5:6–9; Eph 2:8; 1 John 4:9–10). God's rule is almighty, omniscient, benevolent, purposeful (Ps 107:8; Rom 8:28), and moving toward its ultimate goal (Rom 11:36).[52] Suk refuses to discuss redemptive history except within the context of divine sovereignty, Scripture, Jesus Christ, the church, and preaching.[53]

Thirdly, as we noticed, his teaching features a monistic and teleological concept of history. This concept is Augustinian, for Augustine also described history as marching from a specific point to an absolute goal.[54]

---

49. Ibid., 134–46.

50. Shin, "Reverend Won-Tae Suk's View on History and Redemptive History," 370.

51. Suk, *Eyes Viewing on History*, 181.

52. Suk, *Let's Live With Gospel!* 292–297.

53. Suk, *Redemptive Historical Principles of Homiletical Theology*, 13–33.

54. Augustine, *City of God*, XXI:17, 788.

This goal is, for Suk, the fulfilment of God's salvation of His people and its subsequent glorification of God.[55]

Fourthly, Suk concentrates all the church's efforts especially on the *kerygma* (preaching). His redemptive-historical perspective encourages people to devote themselves to the church, with mottos like "With Christ (or His church) our goal, our life the means." The value and object of a Christian's life should be in his or her participation in the church movement.[56]

Suk's redemptive-historical preaching is grounded in the following three principles: God's absolute sovereignty, the progression of history, and Christ-centeredness.[57] Firstly, God's sovereignty is an all-encompassing principle for Suk's preaching, as it is the fundamental principle of Calvinist theology.[58] Suk's homiletical textbook begins with the description of God's sovereignty.[59]

Secondly, the progression of history is also a corollary of the first principle, for God's redemptive history is a progressive, continuous process in history, which God controls.[60] Suk claims that the researching of biblical history, culture, tradition, language, and figures is necessary for grasping specific redemptive-historical events in Scripture because they become more meaningful for contemporary people.[61]

Thirdly, Christ-centeredness is the most common principle for Dutch and American redemptive-historical preaching, as we saw in chapters 3 and 4.[62] However, there is often a misunderstanding in Korea that drawing a line from historical texts to Christ and the cross is the major feature of Christ-centeredness which, it is assumed, must then constitute redemptive-historical preaching. The focus, however, should not be on mentioning Christ repeatedly, but on the adequate recognition of God's progressive redemptive action in the text's historical context.[63] In fact, the proclamation from all of Scripture of the sovereign God and

---

55. Suk, *Way of History*, 291–92.
56. Suk, *Eyes Viewing on History*, 189.
57. Suk, *Redemptive Historical Principles of Homiletical Theology*, 150–51.
58. Suk, "Future of Calvinist Theology," 48.
59. Suk, *Redemptive Historical Principles of Homiletical Theology*, 13–33.
60. Ibid., 150–151.
61. Ibid., 151.
62. Refer to the section "Evaluation of the Korean Redemptive History Debate" in chapter 6.
63. Chapell, *Christ-Centered Preaching*, 302–3.

His redemption is necessarily both God-centered and Christ-centered. To avoid viewing history dualistically, and engaging in obsessively christocentric preaching, as Barth does,[64] Suk suggests that redemptive-historical preaching requires unqualified faith in Scripture as God's supreme revelation, with divine sovereignty uppermost.

These principles concur with Sung-Kuh Chung's three redemptive-historical preaching principles: God-centeredness, historical progression, and God's redemptive movement as the center of history.[65] According to Chung, redemptive-historical preaching always approaches an historical text from God's viewpoint rather than from a human one. There are two poles in redemptive history: God and man.[66] A preacher should speak of both when preaching historical texts, but must speak first of God and what He intended to reveal through that text, and this, for Chung, is the essence of redemptive-historical preaching.[67] Suk's first and second principles are the same as Chung's, while his third principle, with its Christ-centeredness, which means for Suk the centrality of redemptive history in world history, corresponds with Chung's third.

Types of Suk's Redemptive-Historical Preaching

Suk's sermon collection demonstrates that his redemptive-historical preaching is not limited to a specific type of preaching, such as expository preaching, which Sung-Kuh Chung is more likely to confine to redemptive-historical preaching.[68] Suk considers that redemptive-historical preaching may adopt various methods, such as textual, expository, and thematic preaching. Textual preaching, for Suk, describes preaching with the title and themes taken from the biblical text, but which is not expository.[69] His sermons represent his preaching as being mostly textual, as in "New Wine in New Skins" (Matt 9:14–17),[70] "Whose Sins Brought

---

64. Greidanus, *Sola Scriptura*, 141–46.
65. Chung, *Reformed Homiletics*, 361–69.
66. Gootjes, *Between Exegesis and Sermon*, 195.
67. Chung, *Reformed Homiletics*, 364.
68. Ibid.
69. Suk, *Redemptive Historical Principles of Homiletical Theology*, 281–82.
70. Suk, *Let's Go to Move the Mountain!* 17–28.

This?"(John 9:1–7),[71] "The Church Purchased by His Blood" (Acts 20:17–37),[72] etc.

Suk's textual preaching contains and conveys redemptive-historical preaching features. For example, the sermon "The Gospel of Resurrection" (1 Cor 15:1–58) has five themes from the text: the gospel as being historical (1–11); the resurrection as the basis for our faith and essential for the church's existence and life (12–19); Christ's resurrection declared as the first fruit of the resurrection of all believers (20–28); faith in the resurrection as the only power to overcome the present world (29–34); our resurrected body will be a glorified body, with eternal life (35–58).[73] We see here redemptive-historical textual preaching which is faithful to the redemptive-historical preaching principles we identified earlier.

Suk holds that the prototype of preaching is the exegesis of Scripture,[74] and in this concurs with Chung.[75] However, Suk describes expository (or exegetical) preaching as modified textual preaching, which interprets a part of Scripture whether words, a passage, a paragraph, or an entire chapter. In contrast, Chung adopts H. W. Robinson's definition, which we examined in chapter 3.[76] For Suk, preaching based on a text is transmitted through an historical, grammatical, and literary study of a passage in its context, which the Holy Spirit applies to the preacher.[77] For example, in the the sermon "The Redemptive Historical Implication of Recapturing Zion" (2 Sam 5:6–10), Suk described first the historical and literary context of David's recapturing of Zion through examining scriptural texts before and after the event (Gen 14:18; Josh 10:1, 3, 15:8, 18:28; Judg 1:21, 19:10–11; Ps 76:2) and then explained that Zion symbolized the OT church and the NT also adopted this name (Ps 74:2, 87:5, 102:13, 128:5, 132:13–17, 133:3; Isa 51:16; Rom 11:26; Gal 4:26; Heb 12:22; 1 Pet 2:6; Rev 14:1). Finally, just as David recaptured Zion, the fortress,

---

71. Suk, *Let's Spirit Up!* 113–20.

72. Suk, *What is this?* 105–14.

73. Suk, *Life Like Eagle*, 109–15.

74. Suk, *Redemptive Historical Principles of Homiletical Theology*, 286.

75. Chung, *Reformed Homiletics*, 280.

76. Ibid., 279. Cf. Robinson, *Expository Preaching*, 20; Robinson, *Biblical Preaching*, 30: "Expository preaching is the communication of a biblical concept, derived from and transmitted through a historical, grammatical, and literary study of a passage in its context, which the Holy Spirit first applies to the personality and experience of the preacher, then through the preacher, applies to the hearers."

77. Suk, *Redemptive Historical Principles of Homiletical Theology*, 285–86.

and made it God's dwelling place, Christ also recaptured His people from the enemy to form His church.[78] Here we find the redemptive-historical expository preaching of which Chung speaks. It is debatable, however, whether this is textual or expository preaching, as considerable symbolism is adopted.

In addition, Suk is likely to adopt a thematic style for redemptive-historical preaching. Thematic preaching gives more weight to the selected title than to the text; everything in the sermon relates to the title. For example, a Korean pastor's thematic sermon titled "The Living Water of the Desert" (Isa 35:1–7) has the following themes: there is no living water in the desert, no flowers or plants, no way in to lodge or exit. Chung considers this preaching at variance with redemptive-historical preaching, for it disregards the text's authorial intent, namely, God's redemptive revelation that He would save the Israelites (Isa 35:4).[79] I agree with Chung.

However, Suk skilfully adapts a thematic style to redemptive-historical preaching. For example, the thematic sermon "The Line of Reformed Faith" (1 Kgs 18:30–46) portrayed the theme, with five serial sermons, as: the line of biblicist faith, the line of covenantal faith, repenting faith, obtaining faith, and living faith.[80] In these sermons, Suk claimed that the reformation wrought through Elijah relied on God's words alone (18:32, 36) and followed the orthodox covenant of his forefathers (18:30–31). Elijah called for the Israelites to repent of their doublemindedness between God and Baal on the basis of God's gracious works (18:32–35) and turned their hearts to the true God, who listened to his servant's prayer and answered through a miraculous sign (18:21–24, 39). Elijah embodied the life of faith, radically purging out sin and evil doings, anticipating the fulfilment of God's promise, and eventually seeing the blessed result of that promise, which was the rain of grace (18:40–46). Then Suk, in a considerable leap, declared that this line of Elijah's faith continued through the Reformed line of faith, relying on *sola scriptura* and then on living dynamically in the church movement to win God's people through faith in Jesus Christ.[81]

---

78. Suk, *Attraction of Christians*, 31–38.
79. Chung, *Reformed Homiletics*, 382–84.
80. Suk, *Line of Reformed Faith*, 229–69.
81. Ibid., 268–69.

Although thematic, these sermons should be classified as redemptive-historical preaching, for they highlight God, the revelation of God's covenant, the need of sinners to be saved, and God's salvation. Suk attempts to show that various types of preaching can belong to redemptive-historical preaching if they follow the principles identified earlier. Exemplary preaching, regarded as inconsistent with redemptive-historical preaching in the Dutch debate, can be adapted to that preaching using Suk's approach. Suk occasionally utilized the so called exemplary preaching, which was alleged by the redemptive-historical group in the Dutch debate to disparage and disregard the redemptive-historical characteristics of historical texts,[82] to deliver crucial Christian instruction. However, his exemplary sermons, like "The Faith of the Daughter" (Mark 5:25–34),[83] "Abigail's Blessing" (1 Sam 25:32–35),[84] "Daniel Highly Esteemed by God" (Dan 10:10–12),[85] "Do You See This woman?" (Luke 7:36–50),[86] and "Mary Magdalene" (John:20:11–18),[87] initially recognize Scripture as God's special revelation of divine redemption, then take historical events or figures as illustrations or models to be followed by Christians who live in that same redemptive-historical context.

For example, the sermon "Mary Magdalene" carefully examined other related texts first before affirming that Mary had been a "night person" captured by Satan (Luke 8:2). However, on meeting Jesus she changed to a "person of new morning" (Luke 8:2–3a), so people could see Mary with a new beginning (Luke 8:3b). Mary was led to the scene of the cross and the resurrection, becoming the first resurrection witness (John 20:11–18). Suk highlights the grace bestowed on Mary to become such a witness. According to Schilder, this historical text should emphasize no one except Jesus Christ. However, as we discussed in chapter 3, Reformed redemptive-historical preaching like Clowney's may take human examples like Mary Magdalene to enforce the text's message, which is applied relevantly to the hearer. Likewise, Suk's exemplary preaching is firmly based on redemptive-historical principles, as it takes historical events or figures in texts as examples to enforce the truth of God's sovereign action

---

82. Refer to the section "Criticisms of the Exemplary Approach" in chapter 3.
83. Suk, *Armageddon War and World Mission*, 221–28.
84. Suk, *Let's Live with Gospel!* 317–24.
85. Suk, *God Said*, 131–37.
86. Suk, *Human Revolution*, 257–64.
87. Suk, *Human Clone*, 353–60.

in redemptive history. I submit that in this sense Suk's exemplary preaching can be regarded as redemptive-historical exemplary preaching, and different to that which the Dutch redemptive-historical group and the extreme wing of redemptive-historical preaching in America opposed.

A Korean proponent of the Dutch style redemptive-historical approach criticized one example of Suk's exemplary preaching, "Joseph the Devoted Son" (Gen 46:28–30), claiming that it was an ill-conceived sermon, as a preacher who wanted an ethical application should avoid historical texts. He therefore concluded that Suk was mistaken in using that text to instruct on filial piety.[88] However, I disagree. Suk's sermon was topical, not textual, and so was comparatively free of the text while recognizing the redemptive-historical context and God's covenant. Suk affirmed: "Joseph was being obedient to his father in his juvenile period (Gen 37:1–13); then gave proper respect and support to his father in his adolescent period (Gen 37:18–38, 39:1–12); he did his filial duty to the end as succeeding his father's testament (Gen 47:27–31, 50:1–12, 22–28)."[89] I submit that Suk highlights man's duty in the context of redemptive history, that is, God's covenant, and thus the emphasis of his sermon is more on persuasion than on human-centered ethical instruction. To limit didactic texts like the Ten Commandments for use in Christian ethics is, in fact, to fall into the trap of the dilemma in the Dutch redemptive-historical debate.

Redemptive-Historical Preaching: Practical Methodology

Suk suggests the following as aids in the practical preparation of redemptive-historical preaching:

1. Reading Scripture as God's Word which reveals His redemptive will for mankind.

2. Research and study of the text's historical background, including contemporary historical figures, politics, economy, culture, education, philosophy, language, and tradition.

3. Exegesis of the text according to the basic biblical principle, in which Scripture interprets Scripture in the original language.

---

88. Yoo, "Why Should We Do RH Preaching?"
89. Suk, *Promises of Blessings*, 175–81.

4. Correct understanding of various symbols in Scripture.[90]

According to Suk, biblical symbols have various groups of types. For example, the burning bush and Bethel's ladder are symbols of God's presence, while the OT ritual system, the Passover, and the priesthood symbolize a system of God's salvation. In the NT, various events, metaphors, and actions of Christ symbolize His messiahship and His kingdom which will soon be consummated.[91] These symbols are to be appropriately interpreted for redemptive-historical preaching, avoiding an allegorical interpretation.

Suk offers a guideline for the legitimate use of symbols, such as a reciprocal relationship between symbols, unity (coherency), and entailing a certain object, that is, the final revelation of Jesus Christ the Son of God (Heb 1:1–3).[92] Suk's guideline concerning biblical symbols corresponds with Clowney's diagram for typology in redemptive history. For the latter, a historical event symbolizes a truth of God's revelation at the first level, which progresses through redemptive history, and finally arrives at its fulfilment in Christ.[93] Clowney's diagram also requires the progressive relation between symbols along redemptive history (unity), and finally their fulfilment in Christ as the goal. Suk's guideline for biblical symbolism harmonizes with Clowney's suggestion for legitimate typology in redemptive-historical preaching. It is not easy to tell symbols from allegory, but Suk's guideline helps to avoid the pitfall of allegory, which disregards the historicity of the texts.

In addition, Suk has five features to identify the central contents of redemptive-historical preaching:[94] God's sovereign self-revelation of salvation; the salvation through Christ the Mediator; the salvation conferred to the covenant people; the newness and relevancy of the salvation; and the finality and lastingness of the salvation. For Suk, redemptive-historical preaching should contain these five elements. Preaching without recognition of Scripture as God's sovereign self-revelation of salvation can never be a proper redemptive-historical preaching. For the One who speaks in many times and in various types is the very God, the Sovereign One (Heb 1:1–3), by whom redemptive history was originated, from

90. Suk, *Redemptive Historical Principles of Homiletical Theology*, 152–54.
91. Ibid., 153.
92. Ibid., 154.
93. Clowney, *Preaching Christ in All of Scripture*, 32.
94. Suk, *Redemptive Historical Principles of Homiletical Theology*, 154–56.

whom it proceeded, and who will fulfil it.[95] Also, preaching disregarding that Jesus Christ is the only mediator of God's salvation is essentially illegitimate for redemptive-historical preaching, for there is one mediator between God and men, the man Christ Jesus, who gave Himself as a ransom for all men (1 Tim 2:5), and there is no other name under heaven by which salvation may be given (Acts 4:12).

Suk adds that redemptive-historical preaching, as a homiletical methodology, adopts four fundamental elements of preaching: *kerygma* (proclamation of the gospel itself), *didache* (interpretation of the gospel for teaching), *paraklesis* (exhortation to believe the gospel), and *homilia* (application of the results of the gospel).[96] For Suk, *kerygma* means Jesus Christ Himself, conceived by the Holy Spirit, who proclaimed the kingdom of God with miraculous signs, suffered and died for our sins, was resurrected for our righteousness, ascended to heaven, lives forever on the throne to execute an everlasting priesthood, saves His people through the church movement by the Holy Spirit, and will finally judge and reward. This is the gospel of salvation and eternal life. *Didache* means to teach why Christ became incarnate, died, was raised, and will return. *Paraklesis* means exhortations such as "Jesus died on the cross because He loves you. Thus, you must believe in Jesus!" *Homilia* means the application of the result of the belief: "Then, you and your household will be saved!" "Thence, you will live forever!" "You will be blessed!" In this sense, Suk affirms that true preaching goes back to Scripture itself and is achieved when these four elements are used in balance.[97]

Redemptive-Historical Preaching: Biblical Examples

Suk finds three reliable examples of redemptive-historical preaching in Scripture: Peter's preaching at Pentecost, Stephen's preaching at his martyrdom, and Paul's preaching at the Areopagus. The rationale for this choice can be briefly described. Firstly, Suk highlights Peter's preaching at Pentecost as the prototype of Christian preaching. It was the first preaching of the apostles after Christ's resurrection and the actual vehicle for the birth of the Christian church, opening a new era of church history. Peter's preaching became the archetype of all ecclesiastical historical

---

95. Ibid., 154.
96. Ibid., 157–58.
97. Chun, "*Won-Tae Suk's Perspective on Preaching,*" 405.

preaching.⁹⁸ In addition, Peter's preaching (Acts 2:14–47) is a biblical redemptive-historical preaching model, proclaiming God who sovereignly performed wonders and fulfilled His revelation given to Joel (11, 14–21). It testified of Jesus Christ, incarnated, crucified according to God's will, resurrected, ascended, sender of the Holy Spirit, and sitting on the throne of God (22–35). It was preached mainly to the covenant people (39) and seeks their salvation (40–41). For Suk, Peter's sermon was based on God's absolute sovereignty, a redemptive-historical perspective, the Holy Spirit, biblicism, and covenantal theology. Furthermore, it was certainly soteriological, ecclesiastical, and homiletical preaching, for it comprised the necessary homiletical elements of *kerygma, didache, paraklesis,* and *homilia*.⁹⁹

Secondly, for Suk, Stephen's preaching (Acts 7:1–53) was thoroughly rooted in the redemptive history of the OT. It proclaimed the God of the Israelites as the true God who accomplished the covenant of redemption through Abraham's altar (1–8), Joseph's deliverance (9–16), Moses's exodus movement (17–35) and the wilderness church (38–43), and through theocracy and the holy temple in Canaan (44–50), but finally through Jesus Christ (51–53). Suk contends that Stephen's preaching met all his requirements for redemptive-historical preaching.¹⁰⁰

Thirdly, Paul's preaching to the Greek Gentiles at Areopagus (Acts 17:22–34) is another biblical model of evangelizing redemptive-historical preaching. Paul began by referring to the Gentiles' religious practice, then introduced God as the creator and ruler of the universe. He informed the Gentiles that man's very existence and activities are dependent on God (24) and His rule and purpose is that they seek and know Him (27). Finally, Paul urged the people to repent of idol worship and believe that God will judge the world with justice by Jesus Christ, the proof of which is Christ's resurrection (29). Some were cynical, while a few believed (32–34). Suk insists that Paul's preaching was redemptive-historical preaching.¹⁰¹

Each sermon has a different preacher, context, congregation, and result. Peter's sermon was delivered to the God-fearing Jews in Jerusalem from various parts of the Roman Empire, while Stephen's was to

---

98. Suk, *Redemptive Historical Principles of Homiletical Theology*, 160.
99. Ibid., 165–67.
100. Ibid., 168–74.
101. Ibid., 74–180.

opponents of the gospel (7:52–53) and Paul's to the Greeks in Athens (17:22). Peter's preaching was fruitful, but Stephen's preaching raised extreme opposition and resulted in martyrdom for the preacher (7:54–60). Paul's preaching also divided the people (17:32–34). In these biblical examples there is no stereotyped redemptive-historical preaching, but different patterns and results, yet, for Suk, the indispensable principles of redemptive-historical preaching were honored.

Evaluation

Firstly, was Suk's redemptive-historical preaching theory original? Sung-Kuh Chung acknowledged that there were unique aspects to Suk's redemptive-historical approach. However, he questioned whether Suk's redemptive-historical preaching was more specifically related to Western scholars like Schilder, Clowney, and Greidanus. His question is relevant, for it was not until the literature of the above theologians had been introduced that Suk began to discuss the term *redemptive history*. According to Chung, Korean pastors began to open their eyes to the idea of redemptive-historical preaching from the 1980s, only after Clowney's *Preaching and Biblical Theology* and Greidanus's *Sola Scriptura* were translated into Korean in 1972 and 1989 respectively.[102] Significantly, Suk began to promote his redemptive-historical preaching theory from the early 1990s,[103] leading Chung understandably to assume that Suk's redemptive-historical preaching was related to these redemptive-historical scholars, especially the Dutch redemptive-historical tradition in the 1930s.

However, I am unhappy with Chung's assumption. For one thing he does not provide any firm connection between Suk's theory and that of the Dutch debate. That is a serious weakness. Furthermore, Suk's redemptive-historical conception and use of the term *redemptive history* appeared even earlier than Chung suggests. Chung wrongly claims that Suk did not know about the redemptive-historical approach in the 1970s because there were no redemptive-historical sermons by Suk in the 1970s and 1980s.[104] Suk's redemptive-historical concept and its term appeared early in the 1970s in his sermons. For example, Suk mentioned redemptive history at the establishment of Gyeong-Hyang Church in 1973: "I

---

102. Chung, "Study on Won-Tae Suk's Preaching," 81–82.
103. Ibid., 78.
104. Ibid.

have really appreciated God's great providence along the economy of God's redemptive history, in which God now gives birth to Gyeong-Hyang Church . . . Thanks! Thanks! Give thanks to God!"[105]

Suk had used the term even earlier, in 1971: "When a supernatural thing happens in history, history should not refuse it; for we call it Christ's redemptive history."[106] Furthermore, he mentioned specific terms like "God's economy of redemption" and "God's redemptive history" in sermons like "The Image of the True Church" delivered in the 1960s.[107]

In addition, Suk's redemptive-historical concept is evident in the early 1970s: "The world is in God's hand so it can't be accidental. History is also in God's hand so it can never be fortuitous. You, and I, and all of us are in God, so fatalism is not true for us";[108] "The world history of the year 1972 can't be accidental. It moved in and according to God's hand. The history of our church in 1972 is not the outcome of fortuity but of God's direct control";[109] "The Church can be likened to the greatest central motor in the factory of history of the earth. And the core energy to operate that motor is Jesus Christ . . . Thus the Church is the very producer of the greatest and most valuable thing, that is, Christ's redemption."[110] For these reasons, we can affirm that Suk's distinctive redemptive-historical perspective was expressed before any Western redemptive-historical preaching material was introduced into Korea.

Secondly, Suk's redemptive-historical preaching has shown consistency from the 1960s to the present. Sung-Kuh Chung also admits this : "I wonder how he grasped such RHP, and how he has consistently preached with touching the grand contour of RH throughout his entire life . . ."[111] This shows that Suk's redemptive-historical preaching has developed consistently through his preaching during his fifty years of ministerial life. Chung also assesses Suk's redemptive-historical perspective as being unique in its emphasis on the Reformed view of Scripture and on relating this to God's sovereignty.[112]

105. Compilation Committee of Gyeong-Hyang 30 Years History, *Thirty Years History of Gyeong-Hyang Church*, 107.
106. Suk, *20 Years' History of Students For Christ*, 6.
107. Suk, *O Sun! Stand Still!* 63.
108. Suk, *Is it by God or by Accident?* 24.
109. Ibid., 34.
110. Suk, *O Sun! Stand Still!* 82–83.
111. Chung, "Manifestation of Calvinistic Preaching, Won-Tae Suk," 59–60.
112. Chung, "Study on Won-Tae Suk's Preaching," 82.

Thirdly, Suk's redemptive-historical perspective has the merit of faithfully reflecting the traditional Reformed view of Scripture as it is described in the historic Westminster Confession of Faith. Suk's theory begins with uncompromising faith in Scripture as God's Word, whereas Greidanus considers it, especially historical texts, as "word-paintings" which are a remake of God's acts in history, not history itself.[113] Accordingly, Suk's approach to Scripture is acceptable to both the redemptive-historical and exemplary approaches in the Dutch debates and also in the American debate.

Suk's redemptive-historical approach primarily accords with Vos's biblical theology, which we examined in chapter 2, in that both are based on Reformed theological principles that begin from the thought of the sovereign God and from Scripture as His infallible, supernatural revelation.[114] From one perspective, Suk's approach can be considered an effective antidote to negative, critical approaches to the Bible or to heretical movements in Korea; Vos described Reformed biblical theology as a most effective means of defense against critical approaches.[115] Moreover, Suk's redemptive-historical perspective is at variance with the redemptive-historical views of Barth, Bultmann, and Cullmann. For Suk, Scripture does not separate *Geschichte* (subjective history) from *Historie* (objective history); the *kerygma* of Christ and His disciples testifies to its historical reliability, while God's revelation is not distinguished from Scripture itself.[116]

Fourthly, Suk's redemptive-historical preaching can be considered as more relevant when compared with other redemptive-historical approaches in the Dutch and American debates. The Dutch style redemptive-historical preaching was used to interpret unilaterally the redemptive-historical significance of the text, so did not escape the criticism that it failed to affect people in the pew.[117] The extreme wing of redemptive-historical preaching in the American debate also principally excluded application of the text and faced similar criticism. To make

---

113. Greidanus, *Sola Scriptura*, 214.

114. Vos, "Idea of Biblical Theology," 5. "God in so far as He has revealed Himself, is the object of Theology . . . To let the image of God's self-revelation in the Scriptures mirror itself as fully and clearly as possible in his mind, is the first and most important duty of every theologian."

115. Ibid., 22.

116. Suk, *Redemptive Historical Principles of Homiletical Theology*, 69–72.

117. Krabbendam, "Hermeneutics and Preaching," 235–36.

it worse, the refusal of the use of application can lead one into Barth's assimilation of preaching, with just the explication of the text without any application.[118] However, as we saw earlier, Suk's approach embraces the exemplary function and employs application without violating redemptive-historical principles.

Fifthly, there are weaknesses in Suk's redemptive-historical preaching, for it draws a line directly from historical texts to Jesus Christ, or from an OT event to an NT event without any clear rationale. For example, Suk proclaimed in "The Occupation Zone" (2 Kgs 25:1–12) that people have been captured by fear and death because of sin (Rom 7:14), just as Jerusalem was occupied by Babylon and the Jews there were brutally killed.[119] Suk drew a line between the Babylonian Captivity and Paul's description of the deplorable human condition under the captivity of sin and death. This approach, the so called "historical equation mark," was criticized in the Dutch debate as disregarding historical texts through psychologizing and spiritualizing.[120] However, this type of sermon only appeared in the early period when Suk's redemptive-historical approach was undeveloped.

Again, Suk's equation of OT symbols with Christ in the NT seems somewhat intuitive and unclear to a congregation. We understand that the Passover symbol points to God's salvation, but that the collapse of the walls of Jericho should be a symbol of Christ is unacceptable. Even though Suk provides a guideline for the legitimacy of symbols, he has no justification for using Jericho in this way.[121] Korean proponents of redemptive-historical preaching often confuse allegory and symbolism, with Suk sometimes employing allegorical symbolism. One example is Suk's description of Rahab's red string as signifying the confession of faith and the assurance of salvation in the OT, while now meaning that Christ's cross is our token of salvation.[122] In fact, to consider the red string as representing, or pointing, to the cross of Christ is an ancient allegorical

---

118. Barth, *Homiletics*, 118–19. Barth likened preaching to the lip movements of someone reading Scripture with care; preaching was recital, the recital without addition or interpretation of the biblical message alone. He did not trust "application." He says, "Pastors must aim their guns beyond the hills of relevance."

119. Suk, *O Sun! Stand Still!* 378–85.

120. Refer to the section "Criticisms of the Exemplary Approach" in chapter 3.

121. Suk, *Redemptive Historical Principles of Homiletical Theology*, 153–54.

122. Suk, *Promises of Blessings*, 275–82.

approach, and is severely criticized by proponents of Reformed biblical theology like Seung-Kuh Lee.[123]

Furthermore, Suk's approach has been deficient in terms of theological interaction with other Korean and Western redemptive-historical theologians. His theology is somewhat independent of the Dutch and American debates with the result that he has been unable to benefit from them. Consequently the main weakness in Suk's redemptive-historical preaching is that it has not benefited from constructive or negative criticism from academics.

Korean Style Redemptive-Historical Preaching

The major concern in introducing Suk in this chapter has been to sample Korean redemptive-historical preaching, particularly the practical aspect of Suk's preaching. Suk has been acclaimed as "a maestro of Reformed preaching" among contemporary preachers in Korea. Sung-Kuh Chung studied Suk's preaching and evaluated him as a prominent Reformed preacher.[124] According to John Stott, five theological convictions should undergird preaching: convictions about God, Scripture, the church, the pastorate, and preaching.[125] Chung affirmed that if we searched for one example that exactly fits the above convictions in Korea, it would be Won-Tae Suk.

Suk has firm convictions about the church and preaching. While most Reformed ministers in Korea have an unwavering conviction about God and Scripture, few have as strong a conviction concerning the church and preaching. Suk insisted that "Human history without the Church would be unthinkable. The Church movement is metaphysically the essence, content, and meaning of history. For the Church heralds and reveals the age to come in this age and becomes the sign of history."[126] This high view of history assumes God's sovereignty in all human affairs, and history as the unfolding of the divine purposes with the central feature of building, expanding, and ultimately completing the church at the *parousia* of Jesus Christ, which signals the *telos* and consummation of history in Christ. In addition, Suk affirmed that the preaching undertaken by the

---

123. Lee, "Reformed Biblical Theology and Preaching," 371.
124. Chung, "Study on Won-Tae Suk's Preaching,'" 57.
125. Stott, *Between Two Worlds*, 92–115.
126. Suk, *Revival of the Church*, 315.

church is God's predetermined will and method to call His people into His kingdom, the church.[127] For Suk, the only time when there will be no more preaching will be when the number of people to be saved is fulfilled at the end. Hence, preaching is integral to history. Suk himself always feels excited and humbled by being appointed to this precious work.[128] This sense of the divine importance of preaching is rooted in his perspective of redemptive history.

Suk's preaching can also be considered as being representative of redemptive-historical preaching in Korea. Sung-Kuh Chung described Suk's preaching as redemptive-historical preaching rather than traditional topical preaching.[129] As we examined earlier, redemptive-historical preaching had only been adequately dealt with in Chung's *Reformed Homiletics* and Suk's *Redemptive Historical Principles of Homiletical Theology*, despite the fact that there are many other Korean homiletical books.[130] Chung had briefly introduced the principles of redemptive-historical preaching, especially those relating to the Dutch debate. However, Suk's own understanding of that preaching is more comprehensive and based on the Reformed biblical theology he had received from Yune-Sun Park. Chung acknowledged that Suk's approach and principles are more original even than those of earlier redemptive-historical scholars in Holland.[131] I suggest that Suk developed his own understanding of such preaching within the Reformed tradition and am therefore justified in referring to his teaching and practice as Korean style redemptive-historical preaching. Suk clearly rooted redemptive-historical preaching within a firm Korean cultural context, yet in close harmony with Western Reformed theology.

---

127. Suk, *This World and the World to Come*, 2.
128. Suk, *O Sun! Stand Still!* 2.
129. Chung, "Study on Won-Tae Suk's Preaching," 78.
130. Refer to the section "Introduction of Redemptive-Historical Preaching" in the first part of chapter 6.
131. Chung, "Study on Won-Tae Suk's Preaching," 82, 85.

Bibliography

Note on Korean Language Titles

Books and articles which have been translated into Korean from English, or occasionally from another European language, are entered under that language, followed by the Korean language title in brackets. They are indicated as translations by the phrase "Translated into Korean." Original Korean language items are entered under an English title translated from the Korean by the author, followed by the Korean title in brackets. Korean language periodical titles within a bibliograpical entry are given in translated English form, followed by the Korean title.

Aageson, James W. *Written Also for Our Sake: Paul and the Art of Biblical Interpretation.* Louisville: John Knox, 1993.
———. "Written Also for Our Sake: Paul's Use of Scripture in the Four Major Epistles, with a Study of 1 Corinthians 10." In *Hearing the Old Testament in the New Testament*, edited by Stanley E. Porter, 152–81. Grand Rapids: Eerdmans, 2006.
Achtemeier, Elizabeth. *Preaching from the Old Testament.* Louisville: Westminster John Knox, 1989.
Adams, Jay. E. *Preaching with Purpose.* Grand Rapids: Zondervan, 1982.
———. *Pulpit Speech [설교학].* Translated into Korean by Dong-Sik Chon. Seoul: Ji-Hwei, 1984.
———. *Truth Applied: Application in Preaching.* London: Wakeman Trust, 1990.
Ahn, Myung-Jun. "Recent Theological Trends in the Korean Churches." *Gospel and Theology [복음과신학]* 3 (2000) 119–26.
Alexander, Joseph. A. "The Plan and Purpose of the Patriarchal History." *BRPR* 27 (1855) 24–39.
Allen, Edgar Leonard. *Existentialism from Within.* London: Routledge & Kegan Paul, 1953.
Anderson, Robert. *The Bible and Modern Criticism.* London: Hodder & Stoughton, 1905.

Ashbrook, William A. "The New Evangelicalism —The New Neutralism." *Central C. B. Quarterly* 2.2 (1959).

Asselt, Willem J. van. *The Federal Theology of Johannes Cocceius (1603–1669)*. Translated by Raymond J. Blacketer. Studies in the History of Christian Thought 100. Leiden: Brill, 2001.

Augustine. *Basic Writings of Saint Augustine*. Vol. 1. Edited by Whitney J. Oates. New York: Random House, 1948.

———. *The City of God*. New York: Modern Library, 1993.

Aune, David. "Allegory." In *The Westminster Dictionary of New Testament and Early Christian Literature and Rhetoric*, 30–33. Louisville: Westminster John Knox, 2003.

———. "Typology." In *The Westminster Dictionary of New Testament and Early Christian Literature and Rhetoric*, 479. Louisville: Westminster John Knox, 2003.

Bahnsen, Greg L. *Van Til's Apologetic: Readings and Analysis*. Phillipsburg, NJ: P & R, 1998.

Baker, David L. "Biblical Theology." In *NDT*, edited by Sinclair B. Ferguson and David F. Wright, 96–99. Leicester: Inter-Varsity, 1988.

———. *Two Testaments, One Bible: The Theological Relationship Between the Old and New Testaments*. 3rd ed. Nottingham: IVP Academic, 2010.

Barr, James. *Old and New in Interpretation: A Study of the Two Testaments*. London: SCM, 1966.

Barth, Karl. *Church Dogmatics*. 2/2: *The Doctrine of God*, edited by G. W. Bromiley and T. F. Torrance. Translated by G. W. Bromiley et al. Edinburgh: T. & T. Clark, 1983.

———. *Church Dogmatics*. 3/1: *The Doctrine of Creation*. Translated by J. W. Edwards et al. Edinburgh: T & T Clark, 1982.

———. *The Epistle to the Romans*. Translated by Edwyn C. Hoskyns. London: Oxford University Press, 1933.

———. *Homiletics*. Translated by G. W. Bromiley and D. E. Daniels. Louisville: Westminster John Knox, 1991.

———. *Homiletik: Wesen und Vorbereitung der Predigt [설교학 원강]*. Translated into Korean by Keun-Won Park. Seoul: Jeon-Mang Sa, 1981.

———. *How I Changed My Mind*. Edinburgh: Saint Andrew, 1969.

———. "Preface to the Second Edition." In *The Epistle to the Romans*. Translated by Edwyn C. Hoskyns. London: Oxford University Press, 1933.

Barton, John. *Biblical Interpretation*. Oxford: Oxford University Press, 1988.

———. "Historical-Critical Approaches." In *The Cambridge Companion to Biblical Interpretation*, edited by John Barton, 9–19. Cambridge: Cambridge University Press, 1998.

Baumann, J. Daniel. *An Introduction to Contemporary Preaching [현대 설교학 입문]*. Translated into Korean by Chang-Bok Chung. Seoul: Emmaus, 1991.

Bavinck, Johan Herman. *De toekomst van onze kerken*. Bruinisse, Netherlands: Van der Wal, 1943.

Bebbington, David. *Evangelicalism in Modern Britain: A History from the 1730s to the 1980s*. London: Unwin Hyman, 1989.

———. *Patterns in History: A Christian Perspective on Historical Thought*. Grand Rapids: Baker Book House, 1990.

Beeke, Joel R. *The Quest for Full Assurance*. Edinburgh: Banner of Truth, 1999.

Berkhof, Louis. *Principles of Biblical Interpretation*. Grand Rapids: Baker, 1950.

Betz, Hans Dieter. "Gerhard Ebeling (1912–2001) in Memoriam." *Journal of Religion* 82 (2002) 347–48.
Blackwood, Andrew. *The Fine Art of Preaching [설교학: 설교는 예술이다]*. Translated into Korean by Gwang-Chul Park. Seoul: Word of Life, 1983.
Blair, H. E. "The Time and the Event" ["시간과 사건"]. *TTR [신학지남]* 108 (1939) 36–44.
Bornemann, Robert. "Toward a Biblical Theology." In *The Promise and Practice of Biblical Theology*, edited by John H. Reumann. Minneapolis: Fortress, 1991.
Braaten, Carl. E. *History and Hermeneutics*. New Directions in Theology Today 2. Philadelphia: Westminster, 1966.
Bratt, James D. *Dutch Calvinism in Modern America: A History of a Conservative Subculture*. Grand Rapids: Eerdmans, 1984.
———. *History and Hermeneutics [역사와 해석학]*. Translated into Korean by Wee Chai. Seoul: Christian Literature Society of Korea, 1969.
Bray, Gerald. *Biblical Interpretation: Past and Present*. Leicester: IVP, 1996.
Brown, Colin, ed. *New International Dictionary of New Testament Theology*, vol. 3. Grand Rapids: Zondervan, 1986.
Bruce, F. F. "Biblical Criticism." In *NDT*, edited by Sinclair B. Ferguson and David F. Wright, 93–96. Leicester: Inter-Varsity, 1988.
———. "History and the New Testament." In *History, Criticism and Faith*, edited by Colin Brown. Leicester: Inter-Varsity, 1976.
Brunner, Emil. *The Christian Doctrine of the Church, Faith, and the Consummation*. Dogmatics 3. Philadelphia: Westminster, 1962.
Bultmann, Rudolf. *Existence and Faith: Shorter Writings of Rudolf Bultmann*. London: Collins, 1964.
———. "Heilsgeschichte und Geschichte." *Theologische Literaturzeitung* 73 (1948) 659–66.
———. "Hermeneutics and Theology." In *The Hermeneutics Reader*, edited by Kurt Mueller-Vollmer, 241–55. New York: Continuum, 2000.
———. *History and Eschatology: the Presence of Eternity*. New York: Harper & Row, 1957.
———. *History and Eschatology [역사와 종말론]*. Translated into Korean by Nam-Dong Seo. Seoul: Christian Literature Society of Korea, 1968.
———. "History of Salvation and History." In *Existence and Faith: Shorter Writings of Rudolf Bultmann*, 268–84. Translated by Schubert M. Ogden. London: Collins, 1964.
———. *The History of the Synoptic Tradition*. Oxford: Basil Blackwell, 1963.
———. *Jesus and the Word*. New York: Charles Scribner's Sons, 1958.
———. *Jesus Christ and Mythology*. New York: Charles Scribner's Sons, 1958.
———. *The Presence of Eternity*. New York: Harper & Brothers, 1957.
———. "The Problem of Ethics in Paul." In *Understanding Paul's Ethics: Twentieth Century Approaches*, edited by Brian S. Rosner, 195–216. Translated by Christoph W. Stenschke. Grand Rapids: Eerdmans, 1995.
———. *Theology of the New Testament*, vol. 1. Translated by Kendrick Grobel. London: SCM, 1952.
———. *Theology of the New Testament*, vol. 2. Translated by Kendrick Grobel. London: SCM, 1955.

Burrell, David James. *The Sermon: Its Construction and Delivery.* New York: Fleming H. Revell, 1913.

Butterfield, Herbert. *Christianity and History.* London: Bell, 1949.

———. *History and Human Relations.* London: Collins, 1951.

Byun, Jong-Kil. *The Holy Spirit and Redemptive History [성령과 구속사].* Seoul: Association of Reformed Faith and Acts, 1997.

———. "The Meaning and Limit of Redemptive-Historical Preaching" ["구속사적 설교의 의미와 한계"]. *Geu-Mal-Seum [그 말씀]* (November 1998) 14–23.

Calhoun, David B. *Princeton Seminary: The Majestic Testimony.* Edinburgh: Banner of Truth, 1996.

Calvin, John. *Commentaries on the Epistles of Paul the Apostle to the Romans.* Calvins Commentaries 19. Translated by John Owen. Grand Rapids: Baker Book House, n.d.

———. *The Institutes of the Christian Religion*, edited by John T. McNeill. Louisville: Westminster John Knox, 1960.

Cara, Robert J. "Redemptive-Historical Themes in the Westminster Larger Catechism." In *The Westminster Confession into the 21st Century: Essays in Remembrance of the 350th Anniversary of the Westminster Assembly*, vol. 3, edited by J. Ligon Duncan, 55–76. Fearn, Scotland: Mentor, 2004.

Carrick, John. *The Imperative of Preaching: A Theology of Sacred Rhetoric.* Edinburgh: Banner of Truth, 2002.

———. "Redemptive-Historical Preaching: A Critique." In *Reformed Spirituality: Communing With Our Glorious God*, edited by Joseph A. Pipa and J. Andrew Wortman. Taylors, SC: Southern Presbyterian, 2003.

Cha, Young-Bae. "A Theology of Salvation History" ["구원사 신학"]. *TTR [신학지남]* 173 (1977).

Chai, Wie. "The Understanding of Holy Spirit as Viewed from Luke's Redemptive Historical Perspective" ["누가의 구속사관에서 본 성령이해"]. *Christian Thoughts [기독교사상]* 12 (1968) 119–27.

Chang, Byung-Doo. "Redemptive-Historical Preaching and Biblical Theology" [" 구속사적 설교와 성경신학"]. *Geu-Mal-Seum [그 말씀] (February 1997) 12–24.

Chapell, Bryan. *Christ-Centered Preaching.* Grand Rapids: Baker Academic, 2005.

Che-Il Young-Do Church History Compilation Committee. *The 100 Years' History of Che-Il Young-Do Church (1896–1996) [제일영도교회 100년사(1896–1996)].* Pusan, Korea: Che-Il Young-Do Church History Compilation Committee, 1997.

Chi, Dong-Shik. "Modern Theology and the Concept of Redemptive History" [" 현대신학과 구속사 개념"]. In *Theological Forum [신학논단] 18*, 197–210. Seoul: Theological College of Yon-Sei University, 1962.

Childs, Brevard S. *Biblical Theology in Crisis.* Philadelphia: Westminster, 1970.

———. *Biblical Theology of the Old and New Testaments.* Minneapolis: Fortress, 1993.

———. "Interpretation in Faith: The Theological Responsibility of an Old Testament Commentary." *Interpretation* 18 (1964) 432–49.

Choi, Geum-Nam. "Let's Go Back to the Christ-Centered Redemptive-Historical Preaching" ["그리스도 중심의 구속사적 설교로 돌아가자"]. *The Pastoral Monthly [월간목회]* (March 2010) 52–59.

———. "Not to Lose God" ["하나님을 놓치지 않는다"]. *The Pastoral Monthly [월간목회]* (April 2001) 59–66.

Choi, Rak-Jae. *The Kingdom of God. [하나님의 나라].* Seoul: Bible Union, 1986.

———. "The New Testament Hermeneutics and the History of Redemption" ["신약해석학과 구속사"]. *TTR* [신학지남] 165 (1973) 59–66.

———. "Paul's Eschatology" ["바울의 종말론"]. *TTR* [신학지남] 184 (1979) 67–76.

———. "The Revelation and the Bible" ["계시와 성경"]. *TTR* [신학지남] 175 (1976) 64–70.

———. *Seeing Christ in Scripture* [성경에서 그리스도를 보라]. Seoul: Sung-Yak, 2007.

Choi, Soon-Jin "Can Christ Be Found in the OT?" ["구약에서 그리스도를 발견할 수 있는가?"]. *The Pastoral Monthly* [월간목회] (January 2001) 60–70.

Chun, Jae-Ki. "Won-Tae-Suk's Perspective on Preaching" ["석원태 목사의 설교관"]. In *Festschrift of Reverend Won-Tae Suk's Fifty Years of Sacred Ministry* [우성 석원태 목사 성역 50년 기념문집], 399–408. Seoul: Gyeong-Hyang, 2004.

Chung, Chang-Bok. *An Introduction to Homiletics: A Basic Principle and Practice for the Korean Pulpit* [설교학 서설]. Seoul: Emmaus, 1992.

———. *Introduction to the Homiletics of the Korean Church*. [한국교회의 설교학 개론]. Seoul: Worship and Preaching Academy, 2001.

Chung, Chang-Gyun. "Christological Preaching's Traps and Faults, and Resolution" ["기독론적 설교의 함정과 오류, 그리고 극복"]. *Geu-Mal-Seum* [그 말씀] (December 2002) 18–29.

———. "The Ground of Redemptive-Historical Preaching and its Derived Problems" ["구속사적 설교론의 근거와 제기되는 문제들"]. *Geu-Mal-Seum* [그 말씀] (November 1998) 6–13.

———. *Preaching beyond the Stereotyped Ideas* [고정관념을 넘어서는 설교]. Suwon, Korea: Hap-Dong Graduate School of Theology Press, 2002.

Chung, Sung-Kuh. *A History of Preaching in the Korean Church* [한국교회 설교사]. Seoul: Chong-Shin University, 1986.

———. *Korean Church and Reformed Faith: Focusing on the Historical Study of Preaching in the Korean Church*. Seattle: Time, 1996.

———. "A Manifestation of Calvinistic Preaching, Won-Tae Suk" ["칼빈주의 설교의 화신 석원태 목사"]. In *Festschrift of Reverend Won-Tae Suk's Fifty Years of Sacred Ministry* [우성 석원태 목사 성역 50년 기념문집], 58–60. Seoul: Gyeong-Hyang, 2004.

———. "Preaching and Redemptive-Historical Interpretation" ["설교와 구속사적 해석"]. *The Pastoral Monthly* [월간목회] (July 2005) 226–29.

———. "The Principles and Methods of Redemptive-Historical Preaching" ["구속사적 설교의 원리와 방법"]. *TTR* [신학지남] 214 (1987) 14–60.

———. *The Principles and Methods of Redemptive-Historical Preaching* [구속사적 설교의 원리와 방법]. Seoul: Korea Calvinism Institute, 1988.

———. *Reformed Homiletics: Redemptive-Historical and Expository Preaching* [개혁주의 설교학]. Seoul: Chong-Shin University Press, 1991.

———. "A Study on Won Tae Suk's Preaching" ["석원태 목사의 설교를 논함"]. In *Soli Deo Gloria* [하나님께 영광을], 57–86. Seoul: Gyeong-Hyang, 1994.

Clark, Allen D. *A History of the Church in Korea*. Seoul: Christian Literature Society of Korea, 1971.

Clark, R. Scott. *Recovering the Reformed Confession*. Phillipsburg, NJ: P & R, 2008.

Clement of Rome, *1 Clement*. http://www.ccel.org/ccel/schaff/anf01.toc.html.

Clements, Keith W. *Friedrich Schleiermacher: Pioneer of Modern Theology*. London: Collins, 1987.

Clowney, Edmund P. *Preaching and Biblical Theology*. Phillipsburg, NJ: Presbyterian & Reformed, 1961.

———. *Preaching and Biblical Theology. [설교와 성경신학]*. Translated into Korean by Jung-Hoon Kim. Seoul: Christian Education Institute, 1982.

———. "Preaching Christ From All the Scriptures." In *The Preacher and Preaching: Reviving the Art in the Twentieth Century*, edited by Samuel T. Logan. Phillipsburg, NJ: Presbyterian & Reformed, 1986.

———. *Preaching Christ in All of Scripture*. Wheaton, IL: Crossway, 2003.

———. "Presbyterianism." In *NDT*, edited by Sinclair B. Ferguson and David F. Wright, 530–31. Leicester: Inter-Varsity, 1988.

Cobb, John B. *Living Options in Protestant Theology: A Survey of Method*. Philadelphia: Westminster, 1962.

Cochrane, Arthur C. *The Existentialists and God: Being and the Being of God in the Thought of Søren Kierkegaard, Karl Jaspers, Martin Heidegger, Jean-Paul Sartre, Paul Tillich, Etienne Gilson, Karl Barth*. Dubuque, Iowa: University of Dubuque Press, 1956.

Collins, G. N. M. "Federal Theology." In *EDT*, edited by Walter A. Elwell, 444. 2nd ed. Grand Rapids: Baker Book House, 2001.

Collins, John. "Is a Critical Biblical Theology Possible?" In *The Hebrew Bible and Its Interpreters*, edited by William Henry Propp et al., 1–17. Winona Lake, IN: Eisenbrauns, 1990.

Committee for Compiling Goryo History. *25 Years' History of Goryo Presbyterian Church [고려 (반고소) 25년사]*. Seoul: Gyeong-Hyang, 2002.

Compilation Committee of Gyeong-Hyang 30 Years History. *Thirty Years History of Gyeong-Hyang Church: 1973–2003 [경향교회 30년사: 1973–2003]*. Seoul: Gyeong Hyang, 2003.

Conkin, Paul K. and Roland N. Stromberg. *The Heritage and Challenge of History: The History and Theory of History*. New York: Dodd, Mead, 1969.

Conn, Harvie M. "Studies in the Theology of the Korean Presbyterian Church: An Historical Outline," part 1. *WTJ* 29 (1966) 24–58.

———. *Studies in the Theology of the Korean Presbyterian Church [한국 장로교 신학사상]*. Translated into Korean from four serial essays published in *WTJ*. Seoul: Korea Society for Reformed Faith and Action, 1988.

Cook, E. D. "Existentialism." In *NDT*, edited by Sinclair B. Ferguson and David F. Wright, 243–44. Leicester: Inter-Varsity, 2005.

Copleston, Frederick. *Contemporary Philosophy: Studies of Logical Positivism and Existentialism*. London: Burns & Oates, 1963.

Cornick, David. *Letting God Be God: The Reformed Tradition*. London: Darton, Longman & Todd, 2008.

Cotterell, Peter and Max Turner. *Linguistics & Biblical Interpretation*. Downers Groves, IL: IVP, 1989.

Cox, James W. *Preaching. [설교학]*. Translated into Korean. Seoul: Christian Digest, 1999.

Crowell, Steven, "Existentialism." In *The Stanford Encyclopedia of Philosophy*, edited by Edward M. Zolta. http://plato.stanford.edu/archives/win2010/entries/existentialism.

Cullmann, Oscar. *Christ and Time: The Primitive Christian Conception of Time and History*. Translated by Floyd V. Filson. London: SCM, 1957.

———. "Christ and Time" ["그리스도와 시간"]. Translated into Korean by Wie Chai. In *The Collection of Christian Thoughts of the World* [세계기독교사상전집] vol. 11. Seoul: Shin-Tae-Yang-Sha, 1975.

———. *Christology in the New Testament*. London: SCM, 1959.

———. *Heil als Geschichte: Heilsgeschichtliche Existenz im Neuen Testament*. Tübingen, Germany: J. C. B. Mohr, 1965.

———. *Salvation in History*. New York: Harper & Row, 1967.

Dabney, Robert L. *Sacred Rhetoric*. Edinburgh: Banner of Truth, 1979.

Davies, Eryl. "Korea's Debt to a Welshman: Robert Thomas." *Heath Evangelical Church Magazine* (May/June 1993).

———. "The New Hermeneutic," part 1. *Foundations* 9 (1982) 47–55.

———. "The New Hermeneutic," part 2. *Foundations* 12 (1984) 29–36.

Davis, John Jefferson. *Foundations of Evangelical Theology*. Grand Rapids: Baker Book House, 1984.

De Jong, Peter Y., "Introduction to . . . M. B. Van't Veer, 'Christological Preaching on Historical Materials of the Old Testament.'" 1983. http://www.spindleworks.com/library/veer/intro.htm.

De Vries, John Hendrik, "Biographical Note." In *To Be Near Unto God*, by Abraham Kuyper, 5–14. Translated by John Hendrik de Vries. Grand Rapids: Baker Book House,1970.

De Vries, P. "Hegel, Georg Wilhelm Friedrich." In *EDT*, 2nd ed., edited by Walter A. Elwell. Grand Rapids: Baker Book House, 2001.

De Witt, John R. "Contemporary Failure in the Pulpit." *TBT*. 210 (1981) 19–24.

———. *What is the Reformed Faith?* Edinburgh: Banner of Truth, 1981.

Dennison, Charles G. "Preaching and Application: A Review." *Kerux* 4.3 (1989) 44–52. http://www.kerux.com/doc/0403R1.asp.

———. "Some Thoughts on Preaching." *Kerux* 11.3 (1996) 3–9. http://www.kerux.com/doc/1103A1.asp.

Dennison, James T. "Born of the Virgin Mary: Matthew 1:1–25." *Kerux* 18.3 (2003). http://www.kerux.com/doc/1803A3.asp.

———. "Building the Biblical Theological Sermon," part 1: Perspective. *Kerux* 4.3 (1989) 30–43. http://www.kerux.com/doc/0403A3.asp.

———. "Geerhadus Vos." In *Bible Interpreters of the 20th Century: a Selection of Evangelical Voices*, edited by Walter A. Elwell and J. D. Weaver, 82–92. Grand Rapids: Baker, 1999.

———. "Introduction." *Kerux* 1.1 (1986) 2–3. http://www.kerux.com/doc/0101.asp.

———. "John 2: Structure and Biblical Theology." *Kerux* 11.1 (1996) 3–13. http://www.kerux.com/doc/1101A1.asp.

———. "Life, Light, Lamb and the Logos: John 1:1–18." *Kerux* 1.1 (1986) 30–36. http://www.kerux.com/doc/0101A4.asp.

———. "Paul on the Damascus Road: Acts 9:1–19." *Kerux* 2.2 (1987) 21–28. http://www.kerux.com/doc/0202A3.asp.

———. "The Shepherd-Lord: Psalm 23." *Kerux* 15.1 (2000) 50–55. http://www.kerux.com/doc/1501.asp.

———. "What is Biblical Theology?: Reflections on the Inaugural Address of Gerhardus Vos." *Kerux* 2.1 (1987) 33–41. http://www.kerux.com/doc/0201A4.asp.

Dennison, William D. "Biblical Theology and the Issue of Application in Preaching." In *Reformed Spirituality*, edited by Joseph A. Pipa and J. Andrew Wortman. Taylors, SC: Southern Presbyterian, 2003.

———. "Indicative and Imperative: The Basic Structure of Pauline Ethics." *CTJ* 14 (1979) 55–78.

———. "The Redemptive-Historical Hermeneutic and Preaching." *Kerux* 21.1 (2006) 11–39. http://www.kerux.com/doc/2101A2.asp.

Dijk. D. van. "Tot onze leering." *Pro-Ecclesia* (1940/41).

———. *Pro-Ecclesia* 6 (1941).

Dijk, Klaas. *De dienst der prediking*. Kampen: Koj, 1955.

Dooyeweerd, Herman. *In the Twilight of Western Thought*. Nutley, NJ: Craig, 1960.

———. *A New Critique of Theoretical Thought*, vol. 1: *The Necessary Presuppositions of Philosophy*. Translated by David H. Freeman and William S. Young. Philadelphia: Presbyterian and Reformed, 1953.

———. *Roots of Western Culture*. Toronto: Wedge, 1979.

Douma, J. "Calvijn over historische stoffen." *De Heraut* 3292, 3300 (1941).

———. "Exemplarische prediking." *De Heraut* 3336 (1942).

Driver, S. R. *The Book of Genesis*. London: Methuen, 1905.

Dumbrell, W. J. *Covenant and Creation [언약과 창조]*. Translated into Korean by Woo-Sung Choi. Seoul: Christian, 1999.

Ebeling, G. *Word and Faith*. London: SCM, 1963.

Edwards, Jonathan. *A History of the Work of Redemption*. Edinburgh: Banner of Truth, 2003.

Eerdman, W. C. "God's Great Economy" ["하나님의 크신 경륜"]. *TTR [신학지남]* 37 (1928) 5–12.

Erickson, Millard. *The New Evangelical Theology*. London: Marshall, Morgan & Scott, 1968.

Farrar, F. W. *History of Interpretation*. Grand Rapids: Baker, 1961.

Ferguson, Sinclair B. "Exegesis." In *The Preacher and Preaching: Reviving the Art in the Twentieth Century*, edited by Samuel T. Logan. Phillipsburg, NJ: Presbyterian and Reformed, 1986.

———. "Introduction." In *Grace and Glory: Sermons Preached in the Chapel of Princeton Theological Seminary*, by Geerhardus Vos. Edinburgh: Banner of Truth, 1994.

Findley, Gary. Review of *Christ-Centered Preaching: Reedeming the Expository Sermon*, by Bryan Chapell. *Kerux* 11.1 (1996) 37–41. http://www.kerux.com/kerux/doc/1101R1.asp.

Flender, Helmut. *St. Luke: Theologian of Redemptive History*. Translated by Reginald Fuller and Ilse Fuller. London: SPCK, 1967.

Flückiger, F. "Heilsgeschichte und Weltgeschichte." *EvT* 18 (1958).

Frame, John M. *The Doctrine of God*. Phillipsburg: P & R, 2002.

———. *The Doctrine of the Kingdom of God*. Phillipsburg: P & R, 1987.

———. "Ethics, Preaching, and Biblical Theology." *IIIM Magazine Online* 1.11, (1999). http://reformedperspectives.org/article.asp/link/http:%5E%5Ereformedperspectives.org%5Earticles%5Ejoh_frame%5EPT.Frame.Ethics_Preaching_BT.html/at/Ethics,%20Preaching,%20and%20Biblical%20Theology.

Frame, John M. and Leonard J. Coppes. *The Amsterdam Philosophy: A Preliminary Critique*. Phillipsburg: Harmony, 1972.

Free Reformed Churches of North America, "Our History." http://frcna.org/about-us/our-history.
Furnish, Victor Paul. *The Love Command in the New Testament*. Nashville: Abingdon, 1972.
———. *Theology and Ethics in Paul*. Louisville: Westminster John Knox, 2009.
Gaffin, Richard B. "Biblical Theology and the Westminster Standards." *WTJ* 65 (2003) 165–79. http://beginningwithmoses.org/bt-articles/188/biblical-theology-and-the-westminster-standards.
———. "Introduction." In *Redemptive History and Biblical Interpretation: The Shorter Writings of Geerhardus Vos*. Phillipsburg, NJ: Presbyterian and Reformed, 1980.
———. "Redemption and Resurrection: An Exercise in Biblical-Systematic Theology." In *A Confessing Theology for Postmodern Times*, edited by Michael S. Horton. Wheaton, IL: Crossway, 2000.
———. "Reformed Hermeneutics," part 1. 1998. Audio. http://www.sermonaudio.com/sermoninfo.asp?SID=72210833151.
———. "Reformed Hermeneutics," part 2. 1998. Audio. http://www.sermonaudio.com/sermoninfo.asp?SID=72210847321.
———. "Reformed Hermeneutics," part 3. 1998. Audio. http://www.sermonaudio.com/sermoninfo.asp?SID=72210858432.
———. *Resurrection and Redemption: A Study in Paul's Soteriology*. 2nd ed. Phillipsburg: P & R, 1987.
———. "Systematic Theology and Biblical Theology." *WTJ* 38 1976) 281–99.
Go, Young-Min. "Redemptive-Historical Preaching, Is it the Best Methodology for Preaching?" ["구속사적 설교, 최선의 설교방법론인가?"]. *The Pastoral Monthly [월간목회]* (January 2011) 54–59.
Goldingay, J. *Models for Interpretation of Scripture*. Grand Rapids: Eerdmans, 1995.
Goldsworthy, G. *Gospel and Kingdom [복음과 하나님의 나라]*. Translated into Korean by Young-Chul Kim. Seoul: Bible Union, 1991.
———. *Preaching the Whole Bible as Christian Scripture*. Leicester: Inter-Varsity, 2000.
Gootjes, N. H. *Between Exegesis and Sermon: The Practice of Redemptive Historical Preaching [구속사적 설교의 실제]*. Seoul: Christian Literature Crusade, 1987.
———. "Book Introduction" ["책을 소개하며"]. In Greidanus, *Sola Scriptura [구속사적 설교원리]*, 11–25. Translated into Korean by Soo-Kyung Kwon. Seoul: S.F.C., 1989.
———. "The Function of Examples in Historical Texts of Scripture" ["성경의 역사적 본문에 있어서 모범의 기능"]. *Korea Theological Journal [고려신학보]* 14 (1987) 115–31.
———. "How to do Redemptive-Historical Preaching?" ["구속사적 설교 어떻게 할 것인가?"]. *The Pastoral Monthly [월간목회]* 83 (1988) 78–83.
———. "Luke 4:16 — Redemptive-Historical or Exemplary?" *Kerux* 3.2 (1988) 20–24. http://www.kerux.com/doc/0302A2.asp.
———. "Redemptive Historical Interpretation Regarding Historical Texts of Scripture" ["성경의 역사적 본문에 대한 구속사적 해석"]. *Korea Theological Journal [고려신학보]* 16 (1988) 19–36.
Goppelt, Leonhard. *Theology of the New Testament*, vol. 1. Translated by John E. Alsup. Grand Rapids: Eerdmans, 1981.
———. *Typos: The Typological Interpretation of the Old Testament in the New Testament*. Translated by Donald H. Madvig. Grand Rapids: Eerdmans, 1982.

Goryo Theological Seminary. *Soli Deo Gloria [하나님께 영광을]*. Seoul: Gyeong-Hyang, 1994.

Gowan, Donald E. *Reclaiming the Old Testament for the Christian Pulpit*. Edinburgh: T & T Clark, 1981.

Graaf, S. G. de. *From Creation to the Conquest of Canaan*. Promise and Deliverance 1. St. Catharines, Ontario: Paideia, 1977.

Grace Orthodox Presbyterian Church. "Our History: Grace Orthodox Presbyterian Church 1967-2007." http://graceopcpgh.org/OurHistory.htm.

Grant, Robert M. *A Short History of the Interpretation of the Bible*. Philadelphia: Fortress, 1984.

"The Greatest Cause: 58% of Church Membership Decrease is 'Loss of Image'" [" 교인감소 최대 원인 58% '이미지 실추'"]. *Christian Today* (27 July 2006). http://www.christiantoday.us/sub_read.html?uid=8430&section=section8.

Green, William Henry. "The Structure of the Old Testament." *BRPR* 37 (1865) 161-87.

———. "Theology of the Old Testament." *BRPR* 25 (1853) 102-20.

Greenville Presbyterian Theological Seminary. *2010-2013 Academic Catalog*.

Greenville Presbyterian Theological Seminary. "Faculty." http://www.gpts.edu/faculty.

Greidanus, Sidney. *The Modern Preacher and the Ancient Text: Interpreting and Preaching Biblical Literature*. Grand Rapids: Eerdmans, 1988.

———. *Preaching Christ from the Old Testament*. Grand Rapids: Eerdmans, 1999.

———. *Principles of Redemptive Historical Preaching. [구속사적 설교의 원리]*. Translated into Korean from *Sola Scriptura* by Soo-Kyung Kwon. Seoul: SFC, 3rd ed. 1997.

———. *Sola Scriptura*. Eugene, OR: Wipf and Stock, 2001.

Grosheide. F. W. *Hermeneutiek: ten dienste van de bestudeering van het Nieuwe Testament*. Amsterdam: Van Bottenburg, 1929.

Grudem, Wayne. *Systematic Theology: An Introduction to Biblical Doctrine*. Nottingham: Inter-Varsity, 2010.

Guthrie, Donald. "The Historical and Literary Criticism of the New Testament." In *Biblical Criticism: Historical, Literary and Textual*, by R. K. Harrison et al. Grand Rapids: Zondervan, 1978.

———. *New Testament Theology*. Downers Grove, IL: IVP Academic, 1981.

Habermas, G. R. "Rationalism." In *EDT*, edited by Walter A. Ewell, 985-87. New ed. London: Paternoster, 1995.

Hamilton, Ian. "Wherein Consists Reformed Spirituality?: Greenville Seminary Theology Conference Focuses on 'Communing with Our Glorious God.'" *Presbyterian and Reformed News* 8.1 (2002) 10-13. http://banneroftruth.org/uk/resources/articles/2002/wherein-consists-reformed-spirituality/.

Han, Jei-Ho. *Biblical Interpretation and Preaching [성경해석과 설교]*. Seoul: Literature Publishing Banner of Truth, 1995.

Han-Mee-Joon and Gallup Korea, eds. *Research Report-The Religious Concepts and Activities of Korean Protestants [한국 교회 미래 리포트]*. Seoul: Tyrannus, 2005.

Hanson, R. P. C. *Allegory & Event: A Study of the Sources and Significance of Origen's Interpretation of Scripture*. London: SCM, 1959.

Harnack, Adolf von. *What is Christianity?* New York: Putnam's, 1901.

Harris, Horton. *The Tübingen School: A Historical and Theological Investigation of the School of F. C. Baur*. Grand Rapids: Baker Book House, 1990.

Harrisville, R. A. "Von Hofmann, Johann Christian Konrad (1810–1877)." In *Historical Handbook of Major Biblical Interpreters*, edited by Donald K. McKim. Leicester: Inter Varsity, 1998.

Hart, D. G. and John R Muether. "Why Machen Hired Van Til." *Ordained Servant* 6 (1997) 65–68. http://www.opc.org/OS/MachenVanTil.html.

Hasel, Gerhard. *New Testament Theology: Basic Issues in the Current Debate*. Grand Rapids: Eerdmans, 1972.

———. *Old Testament Theology: Basic Issues in the Current Debate*. Grand Rapids: Eerdmans, 1972.

Hays, Richard B. *The Moral Vision of the New Testament*. Edinburgh: T & T Clark, 1996.

Heidegger, Martin. *Being and Time*. Oxford: Blackwell, 1962.

———. *On the Way to Language*. New York: Harper & Row, 1971.

Hellbardt, Hans. *Das Alte Testament und das Evangelium*. München: Kaiser, 1938.

Helm, Paul. *Faith and Understanding*. Edinburgh: Edinburgh University Press, 1997.

Henry, Matthew. "Commentary on Joshua 5:1–9." In *Concise Commentary on the Whole Bible* by Matthew Henry. http://www.christnotes.org/commentary.php?com=mhc&b=6&c=5.

Hill, David. *Greek Words and Hebrew Meanings: Studies in the Semantics of Soteriological Terms*. London: Cambridge University Press,1967.

Hill, Michael. "Theology and Ethics in the Letter to the Romans." In *The Gospel to the Nations: Perspectives on Paul's Mission*, edited by Peter Bolt and Mark Thompson, 249–62. Leicester: Apollos, 2000.

Hodge, A. A. *The Life of Charles Hodge*. New York: Charles Scribner's Sons, 1880.

Hoekstra, T. *Gerefomeerde homiletiek*. Wageningen: Zomer & Keuning, 1926.

Hofmann, J. C. K. von. *Interpreting the Bible*. Translated by Christian Preus. Minneapolis, MN: Augsburg, 1972.

Holland, Tom. *Contours of Pauline Theology*. Fearn, Scotland: Mentor, 2004.

Holwerda, B. *Begonnen hebbende van Mozes*. Netherlands: Copiëerinrichting van den Berg, 1974.

———. *De betekenis van verbond en kerk voor huwelijk, gezin en jeugd*. Goes, Netherlands: Oosterban & Le Cointre, 1958.

———. *Dictaten: historia revelationis Veteris Testamenti*. Kampen, Netherlands: Committee for the Publication of the Lecture Notes of the late Prof. B. Holwerda, 1954.

———. "De heilshistorie in de prediking." *Gereformeerd Theologisch Tijdschrift* 43, (1942).

———. *Populair-wetenschappelijke bijdragen*. Goes, Netherlands: Oosterbaan & Le Cointre, 1962.

Hong, Chi-Mo. "Book Review: Theological Books and Textbooks for Laity" ["서평: 신학 서적 및 평신도 교제"]. *GTJ [고려신학]* 7. (2002) 277–84.

Hong, Harold S. "Past, Present, and Future of the Korean Church: General Picture of the Korean Church; Yesterday and Today." In *Korea Struggles for Christ: Memorial Symposium for the Eightieth Anniversary of Protestantism in Korea*, edited by Harold S. Hong et al. Seoul: Christian Literature Society of Korea, 1966.

Horton, Michael S. "What Are We Looking For in the Bible?" *Modern Reformation* 5.3 (1996) 4–8. http://www.modernreformation.org/default.php?page=articledisplay&var1=ArtRead&var2=64&var3=issuedisplay&var4=IssRead&var5=6.

Hughes, Philip. E. "The Truth of Scripture and the Problem of Historical Relativity." In *Scripture and Truth*, edited by D. A. Carson and John D. Woodbridge, 173–94. Grand Rapids: Zondervan, 1983.

Huh, Soon-Gil. *Fifty Years History of Korea Theological Seminary [고려신학대학원 50년사]*. Seoul: Young Mun, 1996.

———. *History of the Korean Presbyterian Church in Korea [장로교회사: 장로교회 (고신) 50주년 희년 기념]*. Pusan, Korea: Committee of Church History of the Presbyterian Church in Korea (Koshin), 2002.

———. *Reformed Preaching [개혁주의 설교]*. Seoul: Christian Literature Crusade, 1996.

Hunter, A. M. *The Message of the New Testament*. Philadelphia: Westminster, 1954.

Huyser, J. "Exemplarische prediking." *GTT* 50 (1950).

Hyun, Yung Hoon. "A Study on Reverend Won-Tae Suk's Leadership Compared with Biblical Leadership." ThM diss., Torch Trinity Graduate School of Theology, Seoul, 2004.

"The Index of *Shin-Hak-Jee-Nam* from 1918 to 1971" ["신학지남 색인목록"]. *TTR [신학지남]* 254 (1998) 311–73.

Jang, Chang-Soo. "A Study on the Homiletics of C. E. Macartney" ["C. E. Macartney 의 개혁주의 설교신학 연구"]. ThM diss., Chong-Shin University, 2004.

Johnson, Thomas K. *Dutch Reformed Philosophy in North America: Three Varieties in the Late Twentieth Century*. MBS Texte 81. Berlin: Martin Bucer Seminar, 2007. http://www.bucer.org/uploads/tx_org/mbstexte081.pdf.

Ka, Jin-Soo. *Master Church 100 [마스터 교회 100]*. Seoul: Kook-Min Daily News, 2000.

Kaiser, Walter C. *Toward an Old Testament Theology*. Grand Rapids: Zondervan, 1978.

Kaiser, Walter C. and Moises Silva. *An Introduction to Biblical Hermeneutics: The Search for Meaning*. Grand Rapids: Zondervan, 1994.

Kalsbeek, L. *Contours of a Christian Philosophy: An Introduction to Herman Dooyeweerd's Thought*. Toronto: Wedge, 1975.

Kang, Geun-Hwan. "Theological Trends Developed through Historical Streams of the Protestant Church of Korea" ["한국교회 신학의 흐름과 전망"]. *Korean Theological Journal [한국신학논총]* 22 (2001) 143–72.

Kannengiesser, C. "Biblical Interpretation in the Early Church." In *Historical Handbook of Major Biblical Interpreters*, edited by Donald K. McKim. Leicester: Inter Varsity, 1998.

Keller, Timothy. *Reformed Homiletics. [개혁주의 설교학]*. Translated into Korean by Eun-Jae Lee. Seoul: Compass House, 1993.

Kent, John. "History." In *NDCT*, edited by Alan Richardson and John Bowden. London: SCM, 2002.

Kerux. "Biblical Theology Primer." http://www.kerux.com/primer.asp.

Keum, Jang-Tae. *Confucianism and Korean Thoughts*. Seoul: Jimoondang, 2000.

Kierkegaard, Søren. *Kierkegaard's Concluding Unscientific Postscript*. Translated by D. F. Swenson and W. Lowrie. Princeton, NJ: Princeton University Press, 1941.

Kim, Chang-Hoon. "The Evaluation of Redemptive-Historical Preaching" ["구속사적 설교의 평가"]. *Gospel and Practical Theology [복음과 실천신학]* (Winter 2007) 132–52.

———. "Let Us Overcome the Pulpit Crisis with 'God-Centered' Preaching" ["위기의 강단 '하나님 중심 설교'로 회복하자!"]. *Christian Newspaper* [기독신문] (18 April 2011). http://www.kidok.com/news/articleView.html?idxno=69727.

Kim, Eui-Hwan. "A Criticism on New Evangelicalism" ["신복음주의 비판"]. *TTR* [신학지남] 166, (1974) 37–50.

Kim, Gwang-Shik. "Oscar Cullmann, a Theologian of Redemptive History" ["구속사 신학자 오스카 쿨만"]. *Christian Thoughts* [기독교사상] 211 (1976) 75–82.

Kim, Heung-Soo. "Is Christianity a Korean Religion?: One Hundred Years of Protestant Churches in Korea" ["기독교는 한국의 종교인가?: 한국 개신교의 100년"]. *Evangelical Review of Theology* 30 (2006) 162–68.

Kim, Hyo-Sung. *The Problems of the Modern Protestant Churches: Apostasy, Compromises, Confusions* [현대교회의 문제: 배교, 타협, 혼란]. Seoul: Yet-Shin-Yang, 2001.

Kim, Hyung-Kyu. "Sang-Dong Han, a Master Who Lives the Life of All the Way Walking With the Lord" ["한상동, 여주 동행의 삶을 산 지도자"]. In *Preaching of Korean Church leaders: Han Sang Dong*, edited by Korea Institute for Advanced Theological Studies, 8–25. Seoul: Hong-Sung-Sa, 2009.

Kim, Jee-Chan. "Historical Books and Christological Preaching" ["역사서와 기독론적 설교"]. *Geu-Mal-Seum* [그 말씀] (December 2002) 50–59.

———. "Is it Right to Keep Redemptive-Historical Preaching in This Way?" ["구속사적 설교 이대로가 좋은가?"]. *Christian Newspaper* [기독신문] (4 November 1998) 17.

———. "To Answer Hae-Moo Yoo's Refutation" ["유해무 교수의 반론을 답하여"]. *Christian Newspaper* [기독신문] (13 January 1999) 17. http://www.kidok.com/news/quickViewArticleView.html?idxno=29717.

Kim, Ki-Hong. "Training of RH Reasoning and Construction of Preaching" ["구속사적 논지 훈련과 설교의 작성"]. *The Pastoral Monthly* [월간목회] (April 2000) 66–71.

Kim, Kyung-Jae. "The Trends of Korean Theology" ["한국신학의 태동과 흐름"]. *Christian Thoughts* [기독교사상] 518 (2002) 128–36.

Kim, Myung-Yong. *Open Theology and Right Ecclesiology*. Seoul: Jang-Shin University Press, 1997.

Kim, Se-Yoon. *What is Salvation?* [구원이란 무엇인가?]. Seoul: True Words, 1993.

Kim, Seo-Taek. *Expository Preaching as Architectures* [건축술로서의 강해설교]. Seoul: Hong Sung Sa, 1998.

Kim, Sung-Joo. *Redemptive History and God's Covenant for the Kingdom* [구속사와 하나님의 나라]. Seoul: The Remnants [남은자], 2007.

Kim, Yang-Sun. *History of the Korean Church in the Ten Years Since Liberation* [한국기독교해방 10년사]. Seoul: Religious Education Committee of the Korean Presbyterian Church, 1956.

Kim, Young-Jae. *Korean Church History* [한국 교회사]. Seoul: Ire Seo Won, 2004.

Kim, Young-Kuh. "A Study on Principles of Redemptive History: Centering on S. Greidanus and E. P. Clowney" ["구속사적 설교론: 그레이다누스와 클라우니를 중심으로"]. ThM diss., Chong-Shin Theological Seminary, 1985.

Klapwijk, Jacob. "The Struggle for a Christian Philosophy: Another Look at Dooyeweerd." *Reformed Journal* 30 (1980) 12–15.

Koole, J. L. "Het soortelijk gewicht van de historische stoffen van het Oude Testament." *GTT* 65 (1965) 81–104.

Krabbendam, Hendrick. "Hermeneutics and Preaching." In *The Preacher and Preaching: Reviving the Art in the Twentieth Century*, edited by Samuel T. Logan. Phillipsburg, NJ: Presbyterian and Reformed, 1986.

Kroner. "History and Historicism." *JBR* 14 (1946) 131–34.

Kummel. W. G. *The New Testament: The History of the Investigation of its Problems*. London: SCM, 1970.

Kuyper, Abraham. *Lectures on Calvinism*. Grand Rapids: Eerdmans, 1931.

———. "A Pamphlet on the Reformation of the Church." Translated by Herman Hanko. *The Standard Bearer* vols. 54–63 (1977–86). Search box: http://standardbearer.rfpa.org.

———. *Principles of Sacred Theology*. Translated by John Hendrik De Vries. Grand Rapids: Eerdmans, 1965.

———. *To Be Near Unto God*. Translated by John Hendrik de Vries. Grand Rapids: Baker Book House, 1979.

Ladd, G. E. *The New Testament and Criticism*. Grand Rapids: Eerdmans, 1989.

———. "The Search for Perspective." *Interpretation* 25 (1971) 41–62.

———. *A Theology of the New Testament*. Grand Rapids: Eerdmans, 1982.

Lawson, John. *The Biblical Theology of Saint Irenaeus*. London: Epworth, 1948.

Lawson, Steven J. *The Expository Genius of John Calvin*. Orlando: Reformation Trust, 2007.

Lee, Chang-Kyu. "Redemptive History or the Event of Redemption" ["구속사냐 구속사건이냐"]. In *Christian Thoughts [기독교사상]* vol. 10, 79–89. Seoul: The Christian Literature Society of Korea. [대한기독교서회], 1966.

Lee, Geun-Ho. "A Refutation on Jee-Chan Kim's Criticism" ["김지찬 교수에 대한 논박"]. In *The Debate of Redemptive-Historical Preaching [구속사 설교 논쟁]*, edited by Jae-Yul Sho, 17–28. Seoul: Mal-Seum Sha-Yeak, 1999.

Lee, Hoon-Koo. *An Introduction of Homiletics [설교학 총론]*. Seoul: Untied Mission Association, 1991.

Lee, Jae-Chul. "At the Centre of the Crisis of Preaching Are the Mega-Churches" ["설교의 위기의 중심에 대형교회가 있다"]. http://www.newspower.co.kr/sub_read.html?uid=12465&section=section4.

Lee, Joo-Young. *Modern Homiletics [현대 설교학]*. Seoul: Sung-Kwang, 1983.

Lee, Jung-Young. "Korean Christian Thought." In *The Blackwell Encyclopaedia of Modern Christian Thought*, edited by Alister E. McGrath, 309–13. Oxford: Blackwell, 1996.

Lee, Sang-Kyu. "Talk over the Korean Pulpit: Preaching in Korean Churches and its History and Evaluation" ["한국교회 강단을 말한다: 한국교회의 설교, 그 역사와 평가"]. Unpublished lecture notes of the 26th Ministers' Theological Seminar "Preaching and Preachers," Seoul Presbyterian Church, 8 November 2004.

Lee, Seung-Kuh. "Reformed Biblical Theology and Preaching" ["개혁주의 성경신학과 설교"]. *Korea Reformed Theology Journal [한국개혁신학 논문집]* 4.1 (1998) 346–74.

Lee, Yoon-Jae. "Preaching with Christ Being Evaporated, and its Problems" ["그리스도가 증발된 설교, 그 문제점"]. *The Pastoral Monthly [월간목회]* (March 2010) 60–67.

Letham, R. W. A. "Reformed Theology." In *NDT*, edited by Sinclair B. Ferguson and David F. Wright. Leicester: Inter-Varsity, 1988.

Lindbeck, George. "Scripture, Consensus, and Community." *This World* 23.4 (1988) 5–24.

Lindblad, Stefan T. "Redemptive History and the Preached Word." *TBT* 500, 502, 505 (2005).
Lloyd-Jones, D. Martyn. *Preaching and Preachers*. Grand Rapids: Zondervan, 1972.
———. *What is an Evangelical?* Edinburgh: Banner of Truth, 1992.
Loetscher, Lefferts. *The Broadening Church: A Study of Theological Issues in the Presbyterian Church Since 1869*. Philadelphia: University of Pennsylvania Press, 1954.
Longenecker, Richard. *Biblical Exegesis in the Apostolic Period*. Grand Rapids: Eerdmans, 1975.
Longfield, Bradley J. *The Presbyterian Controversy: Fundamentalists, Modernists, and Moderates*. Oxford: Oxford University Press, 1993.
Longman, Tremper. *Literary Approaches to Biblical Interpretation*. Foundations of Contemporary Interpretation 3. Grand Rapids: Zondervan, 1987.
Luther, Martin. *Lectures on Genesis*. Luther's Works 1–3, edited by Jaroslav Pelikan. St. Louis, MO: Concordia, 1961.
MacArthur, John F. "The Sufficiency of the Written Word." In *Sola Scriptura!: The Protestant Position on the Bible*, edited by Don Kistler, 151–83. Morgan, PA: Soli Deo Gloria, 1995.
Machen, J. Gresham. *Christianity and Liberalism*. Grand Rapids: Eerdmans, 1977.
———. *The New Testament: An Introduction to its Literature and History*. Edinburgh: Banner of Truth, 1972.
Mackintosh, R. "Introduction to Albrecht Ritschl." In *The Christian Doctrine of Justification and Reconciliation*, by Albrecht Ritschl. Translated by H. R. Mackintosh. Edinburgh: Clark, 1900.
Macquarrie, John. "Demythologizing." In *NDCT*, edited by Alan Richardson and John Bowden. London: SCM, 2002.
———. *An Existentialist Theology: A Comparison of Heidegger and Bultmann*. New York: Harper & Row, 1955.
Maier, Gerhard. *Biblical Hermeneutics*. Translated by Robert W. Yarbrough. Wheaton, IL: Crossway, 1994.
Malpas, Jeff, "Hans-Georg Gadamer." In *The Stanford Encyclopedia of Philosophy*, edited by Edward N. Zolta. http://plato.stanford.edu/archives/win2013/entries/gadamer.
Maritain, Jacques. *On the Philosophy of History*. London: Charles Scribner & Sons, 1957.
Marshall, I. Howard. *New Testament Interpretation: Essays on Principles and Methods*. Grand Rapids: Eerdmans, 1977.
———. *New Testament Theology*. Nottingham: Apollos, 2004.
———. "Redemption." In *NDT*, edited by Sinclair B. Ferguson and David F. Wright, 560. Leicester: Inter-Varsity, 1988.
———. "Salvation." In *NDT*, edited by Sinclair B. Ferguson and David F. Wright, 610–11. Leicester: Inter-Varsity, 1988.
Matera, Frank. J. *New Testament Theology: Exploring Diversity and Unity*. Philadelphia: Westminster John Knox, 2007.
Mayer, Herbert T. "Clement of Rome and His Use of Scripture." *CTM* 42 (1971) 536–40.
McGoldrick, James E. "Every Inch for Christ: Abraham Kuyper on the Reform of the Church." *Reformation & Revival Journal* 3 (1994) 91–99.
———. *God's Renaissance Man: The Life and Work of Abraham Kuyper*. Darlington: Evangelical Press, 2000.
McGrath, Alister E. *Christian Theology*. Oxford: Blackwell, 1994.

———. *Evangelicalism and the Future of Christianity*. London: Hodder & Stoughton, 1993.
McIntire, C. T. "Herman Dooyeweerd in North America." In *Dutch Reformed Theology*, edited by David F. Wells. Grand Rapids: Baker Book House, 1989.
———. *The Legacy of Herman Dooyeweerd: Reflections on Critical Philosophy in the Christian Tradition*. Lanham, MD: University Press of America, 1995.
Mead, James K. *Biblical Theology: Issues, Methods, and Themes*. London: Westminster John Knox, 2007.
Meeter, H. Henry. *The Basic Ideas of Calvinism*. Grand Rapids: Baker Book House, 1990.
Merriam-Webster. "Criticism: Definition and More from the Free Merriam-Webster Dictionary." http://www.merriam-webster.com/dictionary/criticism.
Merrick, Jeffrey. "Roland Stromberg (1916–2004)." *Perspectives on History* 43.3 (2005). http://www.historians.org/perspectives/issues/2005/0503/0503mem2.cfm.
Moffett, Samuel Hugh. *The Christians of Korea*. New York: Friendship, 1962.
Möller, Karl. "Renewing Historical-Criticism." In *Renewing Biblical Interpretation*, vol. 1, edited by Craig Bartholomew et al. Grand Rapids: Zondervan, 2000.
Moon, Ik-Hwan. "Redemptive History and Creation History" ["구속사와 창조사"]. *Theological Study [신학연구]* 10 (1967) 45–70.
Morgan, D. Densil. *The SPCK Introduction to Karl Barth*. London: SPCK, 2010.
Morgan, Robert. "The Bible and Christian Theology." In *Biblical Interpretation*, edited by John Barton. Cambridge: Cambridge University Press, 1998.
———. "Introduction." In *Theology of the New Testament*, by Rudolf Bultmann. Translated by Kendrick Grobel. New York: Scribner, 1970.
Mounier, Emmanuel. *Existentialist Philosophies: An Introduction*. London: Rockliff, 1951.
Murray, David P. "The Dangers of Redemptive-Historical Preaching." http://headhearthand.posterous.com/the-dangers-of-redemptive-historical-preaching.
Murray, John. *Collected Writings*, vol. 2. Edinburgh: Banner of Truth, 1977.
Nam, Young-Whan. *History of Korean Denominations [한국기독교 교단사]*. Seoul: Yung-Moon, 1995.
Nash, Ronald H. *The Meaning of History*. Nashville, TN: Broadman & Holman, 1998.
Needham, N. R. *The Age of the Early Church Fathers*. 2000 Years of Christ's Power 1. London: Grace Publication Trust, 1998.
"A New Paradigm of Preaching: Redemptive-Historical Preaching" ["설교의 새 패러다임: 구속사적 설교"]. *The Pastoral Monthly [월간목회]* (April 2001) 48–77.
Noll, Mark A. "Pietism." In *EDT*, edited by Walter A. Elwell, 924–26. 2nd ed. Grand Rapids: Baker Book House, 2001.
Norris, R. A. "Irenaeus." In *Historical Handbook of Major Biblical Interpreters*, edited by Donald K. McKim. Leicester: Inter Varsity, 1998.
Northwest Theological Seminary. "Faculty, Staff and Board of Directors – James T. Dennison. " http://www.nwts.edu/faculty.htm.
———. "Mission Statement." http://www.nwts.edu/statement.htm.
O'Donovan, Oliver. *Resurrection and Moral Order: An Outline for Evangelical Ethics*. 2nd ed. Leicester: Apollos, 1994.
Ogden, Schubert M. *Christ Without Myth*. New York: Harper & Row, 1961.

Oh, Byeong-Se. "The History of Koshin College" ["고신대학의 역사"]. In *The Characteristics and Highlights of Calvinism [*칼빈주의의 특성과 강조점*]*, edited by Geun-Sam Lee, 101–23. Seoul: Emmaus, 1986.

Oh, Sung-Choon. "Let's Make Preaching Overflowing with the Stories of Christ!" ["예수님의 이야기로 가득하게 하자"]. *The Pastoral Monthly [*월간목회*]* (April 2001) 53–58.

Olson, Roger E. *The Story of Christian Theology*. Leicester: Apollos, 1999.

"The Opposing Statement against Holding the 10th General Assembly of WCC in Pusan, Korea" ["WCC 제10회 부산 총회 개최에 대한 반대 성명서"]. *Chosun Daily News [*조선일보*]* (29 September 2009).

Otto, Heinrich. *Geschichte und Heilsgeschichte in der Theologie Rudolf Bultmanns*. Beiträge zur Historischen Theologie 19. Tübingen, Germany: J.C.B Mohr, 1955.

———. *Geschichte und Heilsgeschichte in der Theologie Rudolf Bultmanns [*역사와 구속사*]*. Translated into Korean by Gwang-Shik Kim. The Collection of Christian Thoughts of the World [세계기독교사상전집] 11. Seoul: Shin-Tae-Yang-Sha, 1975.

Packer, James I. "God." In *NDT*, edited by. Sinclair B. Ferguson and David F. Wright, 274–77. Leicester: Inter-Varsity, 1988.

———. "Infallible Scripture and the Role of Hermeneutics." In *Scripture and Truth*, edited by D. A. Carson and John D. Woodbridge, 321–56. Grand Rapids: Baker Book House, 1992.

———. "Introduction: Why Preach?" In *The Preacher and Preaching: Reviving the Art in the Twentieth Century*, edited by Samuel T. Logan, 1–29. Phillipsburg, NJ: P and R, 1986.

———. "Preaching as Biblical Interpretation." In *Inerrancy and Common Sense*, edited by Roger R. Nicole and J. Ramsey Michaels, 187–203. Grand Rapids: Baker, 1980.

Pailin, David A. "Enlightenment." In *NDCT*, edited by Alan Richardson and John Bowden. London: SCM, 2002.

Park, Cho-Joon. "The Dynamics of Young Nak Presbyterian Church Growth." In *Korean Church Growth Explosion: Centennial of the Protestant Church (1884–1984)*, edited by Bong-Rin Ro and Marlin L. Nelson, 201–10. Seoul: Word of Life, 1983.

Park, Hyung-Ryong "Providence and History." ["섭리와 역사"]. *TTR* [신학지남] 116.10 (1954) 3–7.

———. "Providence and History." ["섭리와 역사"]. *TTR* [신학지남] 128 (1964) 15–24.

Park, Hyung-Yong. "A Study on the Redemptive-Historical Perspective as It Appears in the Pauline Epistles" ["바울서신에 나타난 구속사관 연구"]. *TTR [*신학지남*]* 178 (1997) 102–13.

Park, Jong-Chil. "Redemptive-Historical Interpretation and Preaching, Its Trends and Prospective" ["구속사적 성경해석과 설교, 그 흐름과 전망"]. *Pastoral Ministry and Theology [*목회와 신학*]* (April 1991) 40–53.

———. *Redemptive-Historical Interpretation of the Old Testament [*구속사적 구약성경 해석*]*. Seoul: Association of Reformed Faith and Acts, 1989.

———. *The Redemptive-Historical Interpretation of the Scriptures [*구속사적 성경해석*]*. Seoul: Christian Literature Crusade, 1986.

———. *The Redemptive-Historical Understanding of the Psalms [*시편의 구속사적 이해*]*. Seoul: Young-Moon, 1991.

———. "The Study on the Controversies of the Redemptive-Historical Interpretation and Application (Preaching) of the Scriptures" ["구속사적 성경해석 및 적용 (설교)에 대한 논쟁 연구"]. *Ko-Shin University Journal [고신대학저널]* 15 (1987) 21–121.

Park, Keun-Won. *Homiletics Today [오늘의 설교론]*. Seoul: Christian Literature Society, 1989.

Park, Yune-Sun. "A Criticism on Barth's View of Revelation" ["바르트의 계시관 비판"]. *The Theological Review [신학지남]* 95 (1937) 32–35.

———. *Obsessed with His Word [성경과 나의 생애]*. Seoul: Yung Eum Sa, 1992.

Parker, T. H. L. *Karl Barth*. Grand Rapids: Eerdmans, 1970.

Perry, Lloyd. M. *A Manual for Biblical Preaching*. Grand Rapids: Baker, 1981.

Piper, Otto. "Biblical Theology and Systematic Theology." *JBR* 25 (1957) 106–11.

———. "Biblical Theology of the New Testament." Unpublished manuscript for exclusive use in Princeton Theological Seminary. 1942–1943.

———. *God in History*. New York: Macmillan, 1939.

Plantinga, Alvin. "Two (or More) Kinds of Scripture Scholarship." In *Behind the Text: History and Biblical Interpretation*, edited by Craig Bartholomew et al., 19–57. Grand Rapids: Zondervan, 2003.

———. "When Faith and Reason Clash: Evolution and the Bible." *Christian Scholar's Review* 21 (1991) 8–33.

Plantinga, Theodore. "Understanding Dooyeweerd Better than He Understood Himself." *Philosophia Reformata* 74 (2009) 105–14. http://www.plantinga.ca/PR_2009-2_Article_2.pdf.

Preus, Christian. "Preface." In *Interpreting the Bible*, by J. C. K. von Hofmann. Minneapolis: Augsburg, 1972.

Pronk, Cornelius. "Neo-Calvinism." *Reformed Theological Journal* 11 (1995) 42–56.

———. "Preaching in the Dutch Calvinist Tradition." *The Messenger* 53.5 & 6 (2006). http://banneroftruth.org/uk/resources/articles/2006/preaching-in-the-dutch-calvinist-tradition-1 and http://banneroftruth.org/uk/resources/articles/2006/preaching-in-the-dutch-calvinist-tradition-2.

Rad, Gerhard von. "The Historical Question." *Christian Century* 10 (1959).

———. *Old Testament Theology*, vol. 2, *The Theology of Israel's Prophetic Traditions*. London: SCM, 1975.

———. *Theologie des Alten Testaments*, vol. 1. München: Kaiser, 1958.

———. *Theologie des Alten Testaments*, vol. 2. München: Kaiser, 1960.

Ramm, Bernard. *Protestant Biblical Interpretation: A Textbook of Hermeneutics*. Grand Rapids: Baker Book House, 1970.

Ramsay, William. *St. Paul the Traveller and the Roman Citizen*. London: Hodder and Stoughton, 1898.

Reid, W. S. "Reformed Tradition." In *EDT*, edited by Walter A. Elwell, 997–99. 2nd ed. Grand Rapids: Baker Book House, 2001.

Renninger. W. R. "The New Testament Use of Old Testament Historical Narrative and the Implications for the Exemplary Interpretation of Old Testament Narrative." PhD. diss., Evangelische Theologische Faculteit te Heverlee (Leuven, Belgium), 2000.

Rhodes, Harry A. *History of the Korea Mission, Presbyterian Church U.S.A., 1884–1934*, vol. 1. Seoul: Chosen Mission of the Presbyterian Church U.S.A., 1934.

Rian, Edwin H. *The Presbyterian Conflict*. Grand Rapids: Eerdmans, 1940.

Richardson, Alan. *History, Sacred and Profane*. London: SCM, 1964.
Ridderbos, Herman N. *The Coming of the Kingdom*. Translated by H. de. Jongste. Philadelphia: P & R, 1962.
———. *The Coming of the Kingdom [하나님 나라의 도래]*. Translated into Korean by Hyung-Joo Kim. Seoul: Words of Life, 1991.
———. *Paul: An Outline of His Theology*. Translated by H. de Jongste. Philadelphia: P & R, 1962.
———. *Redemptive History and the New Testament Scripture*. Phillipsburg, NJ: Presbyterian and Reformed, 1988.
Ro, Bong-Rin. "Non-Spiritual Factors in Church Growth." In *Korean Church Growth Explosion: Centennial of the Protestant Church (1884-1984)*, edited by Bong-Rin Ro and Marlin L. Nelson, 159-70. Seoul: Word of Life, 1983.
———. "South Korea." In *World Churches Handbook*, edited by Peter Brierley. London: Christian Research, 1997.
Roberts, James M. "Historical-Critical Method, Theology, and Contemporary Exegesis." In *Biblical Theology: Problems and Perspectives*, edited by Steven J. Kraftchick et al. Nashville: Abingdon, 1995.
Robinson, Haddon W. *Biblical Preaching*. Grand Rapids: Baker Academic, 2001.
———. *Expository Preaching: Principles & Practice*. Leicester: Inter-Varsity, 1986.
Robinson, James M. *A New Quest of the Historical Jesus*. Naperville, IL: Alec R. Allenson, 1959.
Rogers, Jack B. and Donald K McKim. *The Authority and Interpretation of the Bible: An Historical Approach*. London: Harper & Row, 1979.
Rosner, Brian. "Paul's Ethics." In *Cambridge Companion to St. Paul*, edited by James G. Dunn. Cambridge: Cambridge University Press, 2003.
Rottenberg, Isaac C. *Redemption and Historical Reality*. Philadelphia: Westminster, 1964.
Rushdoony, R. J. "Foreword." In *The Case for Calvinism*, by Cornelius Van Til. Philadelphia: P & R, 1963.
Rust, Eric C. *Salvation History*. Richmond, VA: John Knox, 1962.
———. *Towards a Theological Understanding of History*. New York: Oxford University Press, 1963.
Ryu, Dong-Shik. Review of *History and Eschatology*, by Rudolf Bultmann [역사와 종말론 서평]. *Christian Thoughts [기독교사상]* 15 (1958) 93-96.
Ryu, Eung-Yul. "Redemptive-Historical Preaching" ["구속사적 설교"]. *TTR [신학지남]* 296 (2008) 60-91.
Schelhaas, J. "Christus en de historische stoffen in de prediking." *GTT* 41 (1941) 107-28.
Schilder, Klaas. *Christ Crucified*. Translated by Henry Zylstra. Grand Rapids: Eerdmans, 1938.
———. *Christ in His Suffering*. Translated by Henry Zylstra. Grand Rapids: Eerdmans, 1938.
———. *Christ on Trial*. Translated by Henry Zylstra. Grand Rapids: Eerdmans, 1939.
———. *Christus in zijn lijden: overwegingen van het lijdensevangelie*. Kampen: Kok, 1930.
———. *Heidelbergsche Catechismus*. Goes, Netherlands: Oosterbaan & Le Cointre, 1939-1940.

———. "Iets over de eenheid der 'heilsgeschiedenis' in verband met de prediking." *De Reformatie* 11 (1931).

———. "Kerkelijke leven: puten van overeenkomst," part 1. *De Reformatie* 14 (1933-1934).

———. *Wat is de hemel?* Kampen, Netherlands: Kok, 1935.

———. *Zur Begriffsgeschichte des 'Paradoxon': mit besonderer Berücksichtigung Calvins und des nach-Kierkegaardschen 'Paradoxon.'* Kampen: Kok, 1933.

Scholer, David M. "An Introduction to Philo Judaeus of Alexandria." In *The Works of Philo*. Translated by C. D Yonge. Peabody, MA: Hendrickson, 1993.

Seo, Chul-Won. "The Focus of Preaching: the God-Centered Preaching" ["설교의 초점-하나님 중심의 설교"]. *The Pastoral Monthly [월간목회]* (January 2011) 44–53.

Seo, Nam-Dong. "The End and History" ["종말과 역사"]. *Christian Thoughts [기독교사상]* 17 (1959) 58–68.

———. Review of *History and Eschatology*, by Rudolf Bultmann ["역사와 종말론"]. *Theological Study [신학연구]* 4. (1958) 214–16.

———. "Theologians and Their Writings By Which I Have Been Affected" ["내가 영향을 받은 신학자와 저술들"]. *Christian Thoughts [기독교사상]* 81 (1964) 69–71.

Seo, Young-Il. "To Teach and To Reform: The Life and Times of Dr. Yune-Sun Park." ThD. diss., Westminster Theological Seminary, Philadelphia, 1992.

Shearer, Roy E. *Wildfire: Church Growth in Korea*. Grand Rapids: Eerdmans, 1966.

Shedd, William G. T. *Homiletics and Pastoral Theology*. London: Banner of Truth, 1965.

Shin, Deuk-Il. "The Centre of the Old Testament in Debate and Redemptive History as Perspective of Theological Exegesis" ["구약 중심 주제의 논쟁점과 신학적 주석 관점으로서의 구속사"]. *Ko-Shin Theological Journal [고신신학]* (December 2002) 39–64.

Shin, Ho-Sub. "Reverend Won-Tae Suk's View on History and Redemptive History" ["석원태 목사의 역사관과 구속사관"]. In *Festschrift of Reverend Won-Tae Suk's Fifty Years of Sacred Ministry [우성 석원태 목사 성역 50년 기념문집]*, 366–83. Seoul: Gyeong-Hyang, 2004.

Shin, Sung-Jong. "The Bible is the Drama of God" ["성경은 하나님의 드라마다"]. *The Pastoral Monthly [월간목회]* (April 2001) 48–52.

———. "The Problems of the Korean Pulpit Based on the Hermeneutical Position" ["해석학적 입장에서 본 한국 강단의 문제점"]. *TTR [신학지남]* 204 (1985) 54–63.

Sho, Jae-Yul. "A Review on Jee-Chan Kim's 'Is it Right to Keep RH Preaching in This Way?'" ["김지찬 교수의 구속사적 설교 이대로가 좋은가에 대한 논평"]. In *The Debate of Redemptive-Historical Preaching [구속사 설교 논쟁]*, edited by Jae-Yul Sho, 29–49. Seoul: Mal-Seum Sha-Yeak, 1999.

———. "A Study on Hebrews Chapter 11 from the Redemptive-Historical Perspective" ["구속사의 관점에서 본 히브리서 11장 연구"]. ThM diss., Calvin College, Korea, 2003.

Sho, Jae-Yul, ed. *The Debate of Redemptive-Historical Preaching [구속사 설교 논쟁]*. Seoul: Mal-Seum Sha-Yeak, 1999.

Simonetti, Manlio. *Biblical Interpretation in the Early Church: An Historical Introduction to Patristic Exegesis*. Translated by John A. Hughes. Edinburgh: T & T Clark, 1994.

Sohm, Rudolf. *Outlines of Church History.* Translated by May Sinclair. London: Macmillan, 1926.
Son, Bong-Ho "Some Dangers of Rapid Growth." In *Korean Church Growth Explosion: Centennial of the Protestant Church (1884–1984),* edited by Bong-Rin Ro and Marlin L. Nelson, 256–73. Seoul: Word of Life, 1983.
Song, Joshua Yun-Bum. "An Historical and Theological Analysis of Schism in Presbyterian Churches in Korea, 1969–2005." PhD diss., University of Wales, Lampeter, 2006.
Spear, Wayne R. "Word and Spirit in the Westminster Confession." In *The Westminster Confession into the 21st Century,* vol. 1, edited by Ligon Duncan. Fearn, Scotland: Mentor, 2003.
Spier, H. J. "Wijsbegeerte en prediking." In *Wijsbegeerte en levenspractijk,* edited by H. J. Spier and J. M. Spier. Kampen: Kok, 1948.
Sproul, R. C. *The Heart of Reformed Theology.* London: Hodder & Stoughton, 1997.
Spykman, Gordon J. *Reformational Theology: A New Paradigm of Doing Dogmatics.* Grand Rapids: Eerdmans, 1992.
Stacey, John. "Homiletics, Homily." In *NDCT,* edited by Alan Richardson and John Bowden. London: SCM, 2002.
Stauffer, E. *Die Theologie des Neuen Testaments.* Stuttgart: Kohlhammer, 1941.
Steinmetz, David C. "The Superiority of Pre-Critical Exegesis." *Theology Today* 37.1 (1980) 27–38.
Stonehouse, N. B. *J. Gresham Machen: A Biographical Memoir.* 3rd ed. Edinburgh: Banner of Truth, 1987.
Stott, John R. W. *Between Two Worlds: The Art of Preaching in the Twentieth Century.* Grand Rapids: Eerdmans, 1982.
———. *The Preacher's Portrait.* Grand Rapids: Eerdmans, 1961.
———. *What is an Evangelical?.* London: Church Pastoral Aid Society, 1992.
Suk, Won-Tae. *Armageddon War and World Mission [*아마겟돈 전쟁과 선교*].* Won-Tae Suk's Sermon Collection 18. Seoul: Gyeong-Hyang, 2002.
———. *The Attraction of Christians [*그리스도인의 매력*].* Won-Tae Suk's Sermon Collection 31. Seoul: Gyeong-Hyang, 2003.
———. *The Barley Bread Movement [*보리떡 운동*].* Won-Tae Suk's Sermon Collection 2. Seoul: Gyeong-Hyang, 1971. Reprinted in 2002.
———. *By Scripture Alone [*오직 성경만으로*].* Won-Tae Suk's Sermon Collection 34. Seoul: Gyeong-Hyang, 2009.
———. *The Citizen of the World [*세계시민*].* Won-Tae Suk's Sermon Collection 16. Seoul: Gyeong-Hyang, 1987. Reprinted in 1994.
———. *Culture of the Lost Son and Christianity[*탕자문명과 기독교*].* Won-Tae Suk's Sermon Collection 3. Seoul: Gyeong-Hyang, 1972. Reprinted in 2002.
———. "Due Pay for Living in Peace Time" ["평화시대를 사는 값(1)"]. 8 June 2008. http://ghpc.or.kr/board/sermon/list.asp?search=&find=&page=12&DB_name=ghpc_brdS24&idx=2608.
———. *The Eyes Viewing on History [*역사를 보는 눈*].* Won-Tae Suk's Sermon Collection 17. Seoul: Gyung-Hyang, 1992.
———. "The Future of Calvinist Theology" ["개혁주의 신학의 미래"]. In *Festschrift in Commemoration of 20 years of the Reinstatement of Goryo Theological Seminary [*고려신학교복교 20주년기념 논문집*],* 47–68. Seoul: Gyeong-Hyang, 1996.

———. *The Glory of Christ* [그리스도의 영광]. Won-Tae Suk's Sermon Collection 29. Seoul: Gyeong-Hyang, 2001.

———. *God Said* [하나님이 가라사대]. Won-Tae Suk's Sermon Collection 20. Seoul: Gyeong-Hyang, 1993. Reprinted in 2002.

———. "Gyeong-Hyang Presbyterian Church and Goryo Theological Seminary" ["경향과 고려신학교"]. In the tape "The Memorial Sermons on the 26th Anniversary of Gyeong-Hyang Presbyterian Church Foundation" ["교회설립 26주년 감사부흥회 간증설교 테이프"]. 19 April 1999.

———. *Homiletical Principles: Redemptive Historical Theology and Homiletics* [설교학원론]. Seoul: Gyeong-Hyang, 1992.

———. *A Human Clone* [복제 인간]. Won-Tae Suk's Sermon Collection 25. Seoul: Gyeong-Hyang, 1998.

———. *Human Revolution* [인간 혁명]. Won-Tae Suk's Sermon Collection 10. Seoul: Gyeong-Hyang, 1985. Reprinted in 2002.

———. *Is It By God or By Accident?* [하나님이냐 우연이냐]. Won-Tae Suk's Sermon Collection 4. Seoul: Gyeong-Hyang, 1981.

———. *Let's Go to Move the Mountain!* [산을 옮기러 가자!]. Won-Tae Suk's Sermon Collection 5. Seoul: Gyeong-Hyang, 1981. Reprinted in 2002.

———. *Let's Live With Gospel!* [복음과 함께 삽시다!]. Won-Tae Suk's Sermon Collection 21. Seoul: Gyeong-Hyang, 1994. Reprinted in 2002.

———. *Let's Spirit Up!* [힘내기 하자!]. Won-Tae Suk's Sermon Collection 7. Seoul: Gyeong-Hyang, 1981. Reprinted in 2002.

———. *The Life Like Eagle* [독수리 인생]. Won-Tae Suk's Sermon Collection 27. Seoul: Gyeong-Hyang, 1999.

———. *The Line of Reformed Faith* [개혁주의 신앙노선]. Won-Tae Suk's Sermon Collection 9. Seoul: Gyeong-Hyang, 1981.

———. "The Lord Opened My Spiritual Eyes!" ["눈을 여신 주"]. In the tape "The Memorial Sermons on the 26th Anniversary of Gyeong-Hyang Presbyterian Church Foundation" ["경향교회설립 26주년 감사부흥회 간증설교 테이프"]. 7:30 pm, 19 April 1999.

———. *May the Lord Increase Us a Thousand Times More Than the Present!* [현재보다 천 배나 많게 하소서!]. Won-Tae Suk's Sermon Collection 30. Seoul: Gyeong-Hyang, 2002.

———. *O Sun! Stand Still!* [태양아 머무르라]. Won-Tae Suk's Sermon Collection 1. Seoul: Gyeong-Hyang, 1970. Reprinted in 1995.

———. *The People Who Had Won* [이긴 사람들]. Won-Tae Suk's Sermon Collection 6. Seoul: Gyeong-Hyang, 1985.

———. *The Promises of Blessings* [축복의 약속들]. Won-Tae Suk's Sermon Collection 14. Seoul: Gyeong-Hyang, 1985. Reprinted in 2002.

———. *Redemptive-Historical Homiletics* [구속사적 설교신학]. Seoul: Gyeong-Hyang, 2002.

———. *Redemptive Historical Principles of Homiletical Theology* [구속사적 설교신학원론]. 3rd ed. Seoul: Gyeong-Hyang, 2005.

———. *Revival of the Church* [교회의 부흥]. Won-Tae Suk's Sermon Collection 32. Seoul: Gyeong-Hyang, 2004.

———. *The Seven Principles of Christianity* [기독교 7영리]. Seoul: Gyeong-Hyang, 2000.

———. *The Star Wars* [별들의 전쟁]. Won-Tae Suk's Sermon Collection 28. Seoul: Gyeong-Hyang, 2000.

———. *This World and the World to Come [이 세상 오는 세상]*. Won-Tae Suk's Sermon Collection 33. Seoul: Gyeong-Hyang, 2004.
———. *The Way of History [역사의 길]*. Won-Tae Suk's Sermon Collection 26. Seoul: Gyeong-Hyang, 1999.
———. *20 Years' History of Students For Christ [학생신앙운동 20년사]*. Pusan, Korea: National S.F.C., 1971.
———. *What Is This? [이것이 무엇이냐?]*. Won-Tae Suk's Sermon Collection 8. Seoul: Gyeong-Hyang, 1981. Reprinted in 2002.
Sung, Jong-Hyun. *Introduction to the New Testament [신약총론]*. Seoul: Jang-Shin University, 1991.
Swinburne, Richard. *Faith and Reason*. Oxford: Clarendon, 1981.
Taylor, Marion Ann. *The Old Testament in the Old Princeton School (1812–1929)*. San Francisco: Mellen University Research Press, 1992.
Taylor, Roy. "So What?" *Journal of Pastoral Practice* 4.4 (1980).
Thileman. Frank. *Theology of the New Testament*. Grand Rapids: Zondervan, 2005.
Thiselton, Anthony C. *Hermeneutics: An Introduction*. Grand Rapids: Eerdmans, 2009.
———. *The Two Horizons: New Testament Hermenutics and Philosophical Description with Special Reference to Heidegger, Bultmann, Gadamer, and Wittgenstein*. Grand Rapids: Eerdmans, 1980
Tholfsen, Trygve R. *Historical Thinking*. New York: Harper & Row, 1967.
Thomas, Geoff. "Edmund P. Clowney 1917–2005." 2005. http://banneroftruth.org/uk/resources/articles/2005/edmund-p-clowney-1917-2005/.
———. "Learning from the Life of Dr. Klaas Schilder," part 3. 1999. http://banneroftruth.org/uk/resources/articles/1999/learning-from-the-life-of-dr-klaas-schilder-part-iii/.
———. "Powerful Preaching." In *The Preacher and Preaching: Reviving the Art in the Twentieth Century*, edited by Samuel T. Logan. Phillipsburg, NJ: Presbyterian and Reformed, 1986.
Tidball, Derek J. *Who Are the Evangelicals?: Tracing the Roots of Today's Movements*. London: Marshall Pickering, 1994.
Tillich, Paul. *Theology of Culture*. Oxford: Oxford University Press, 1959.
Torrance, Thomas F. *Karl Barth: Biblical and Evangelical Theologian*. Edinburgh: T & T Clark, 1990.
Trimp, C. *Heilsgeschiedenis en prediking*. Kampen, Netherlands: Van den Berg, 1986.
———. *Preaching and the History of Salvation*. Translated by Nelson D. Kloosterman. Scarsdale, NY: Westminster Book Service, 1996.
———. *De preek [설교학 강의]*. Translated into Korean by Seo-Hee Ko et al. Seoul: Christian Literature Crusade, 1986.
Troeltsch, Ernst. *Protestantism and Progress*. London: Putnam's Sons, 1912.
Van Til, Cornelius. *A Christian Theology of Knowledge*. Phillipsburg. NJ: Presbyterian & Reformed, 1969.
———. *The Defense of the Faith*. 3rd ed. Philadelphia: Presbyterian and Reformed, 1967.
———. *The New Hermeneutic*. Presbyterian and Reformed, 1974.
———. *The New Modernism: An Appraisal of the Theology of Barth and Brunner*. Philadelphia: Presbyterian and Reformed, 1973.
Vanderlann, Eldred. *Protestant Modernism in Holland*. London: Oxford University Press, 1924.

VanGemeren, Willem. *The Progress of Redemption: From Creation to the New Jerusalem.* Reading: Paternoster, 1988.

Veer, M. B. van't. "Christological Preaching on Historical Materials of the Old Testament." http://www.spindleworks.com/library/veer/veer.html.

———. "Christologische prediking over de historische stof van het Oude Testament." In *Van den dienst des woords,* edited by R. Schippers, 117–67. Goes, Netherlands: Oosterbaan & Le Cointre, 1944.

———. *GM* 19 (1941).

Virkler, Henry A. *Hermeneutics: Principles and Processes of Biblical Interpretation.* Grand Rapids: Baker Book House, 1981.

Vischer, Wilhelm. *The Witness of the Old Testament to Christ.* Translated by A. B. Crabtree. London: Lutterworth, 1949.

Voight, G. "Joachim of Floris (1135–1202). In *A Religious Encyclopaedia or Dictionary of Biblical, Historical, Doctrinal, and Practical Theology,* vol. 2, edited by Philip Schaff, 1183. 3rd ed. London: Funk & Wagnalls, 1894. http://www.medievalchurch.org.uk/p_joachim.php.

Vos, Geerhardus. *Biblical Theology [성경신학].* Translated into Korean by Seung-Koo Lee.

Seoul: Christian Literature Crusade, 1985.

———. *Biblical Theology: Old and New Testaments.* London: Banner of Truth, 1975.

———. "Christian Faith and the Truthfulness of Bible History." *Princeton Theological Journal* 3 (1906) 289–305.

———. "The Eschatological Aspect of the Pauline Conception of the Spirit." In *Redemptive History and Biblical Interpretation: the Shorter Writings of Geerhardus Vos,* edited by Richard B. Gaffin. Phillipsburg, NJ: Presbyterian and Reformed, 1980.

———. "Eschatology of the New Testament." In *Redemptive History and Biblical Interpretation: the Shorter Writings of Geerhardus Vos,* edited by Richard. B. Gaffin. Phillipsburg, NJ: Presbyterian and Reformed, 1980.

———. "The Idea of Biblical Theology as a Science and as a Theological Discipline." In *Redemptive History and Biblical Interpretation: the Shorter Writings of Geerhardus Vos,* edited by Richard B. Gaffin. Phillipsburg, NJ: Presbyterian and Reformed, 1980.

———. *Inaugural Address.* New York: Anson D. F. and Randolf, 1894.

———. *The Pauline Eschatology.* Phillipsburg, NJ: Presbyterian and Reformed, 1994.

———. "Paul's Eschatological Concept of the Spirit." In *Redemptive History and Biblical Interpretation: the Shorter Writings of Geerhardus Vos,* edited by Richard. B. Gaffin. Phillipsburg, NJ: Presbyterian and Reformed, 1980.

———. *Redemptive History and Biblical Interpretation: the Shorter Writings of Geerhardus Vos,* edited by R. B. Gaffin. Phillipsburg, NJ: Presbyterian and Reformed, 1980.

———. *The Self-Disclosure of Jesus.* New York: George H. Doran, 1926.

———. *The Teaching of Jesus Concerning the Kingdom of God and the Church.* Nutley, NJ: Presbyterian and Reformed, 1972.

Vosteen, J. Peter. "Pastoral Preaching." In *The Preacher and Preaching,* edited by Samuel T. Logan, 397–418. Phillipsburg, NJ: Presbyterian & Reformed, 1986.

———. Review of *Preaching Christ in All of Scripture,* by Edmund P. Clowney. *Kerux* 21.2 (2006) 49–51. http://www.kerux.com/documents/KeruxV21N2R2.htm.

Wallace, Peter J. "The Foundations of Reformed Biblical Theology: The Development of Old Testament Theology at Old Princeton, 1892–1932." *WTJ* 59.1 (1997) 41–69.

Warnock, Mary. *Existentialism*. Oxford: Oxford University Press, 1970.

Weborg, J. "Bengel, J(ohann) A(lbrecht)." In *Historical Handbook of Major Biblical Interpreters*, edited by Donald K. McKim, 289–94. Leicester: Inter Varsity, 1998.

Webster, Ransom Lewis. "Geerhardus Vos (1862–1949): A Biographical Sketch." *WTJ* 40 (Fall 1977 to Spring 1978) 304–17.

Welch, Claude. *Protestant Thought in the Nineteenth Century*, vol. 1, 1799–1870. London: Yale University Press, 1972.

Wells, Paul. "The Historical Critical Method: Can Things Ever Be the Same Again?" *CS* 11.1 (2001).

Wenham, Gordon. "History and the Old Testament." In *History, Criticism and Faith: Four Exploratory Studies*, edited by Colin Brown. Leicester: Inter-Varsity, 1976.

Westermann, Claus. *Essays on Old Testament Hermeneutics*. Richmond, VA: John Knox, 1969.

———. *Essays on Old Testament Hermeneutics [구약해석학]*. Translated into Korean by Moon-Jae Park. Seoul: Christian Digest, 1999.

Westminster Assembly. *The Westminster Confession of Faith: The Larger and Shorter Catechisms of the Westminster Assembly with Scripture References*. Glasgow: Free Presbyterian, 2001.

Wiersbe, Warren W. *Wiersbe's Expository Outlines on the Old Testament*. Wheaton, IL: Victor, 1993.

Willimon, William H. *Peculiar Speech: Preaching to the Baptized*. Grand Rapids: Eerdmans, 1992.

Windsor, Lionel. "Indicative and Imperative in the Letters of Paul." 2004. http://www.lionelwindsor.net/bibleresources/bible/new/Paul_indicative_imperative.htm.

Wink, Walter. *Transformation: Toward a New Paradigm for Biblical Study*. Philadelphia: Fortress, 1973.

Wolfe, Samuel T. *A Key to Dooyeweerd*. Nutley, NJ: Presbyterian & Reformed, 1978.

World Council of Churches. "What is the World Council of Churches?" http://www.oikoumene.org/en/about-us.

Wrede, William. *The Messianic Secret*. Translated by J. C. G. Craig. London: James Clarke, 1971.

Wright, G. E. *God Who Acts*. London: SCM, 1954.

Yarbrough, Robert W. *The Salvation Historical Fallacy?: Reassessing the History of New Testament Theology*. Leiden, Netherlands: Deo, 2004.

Yoo, Do-Soon. "Why should We Do RH preaching?" ["왜 구속사적 설교를 해야만 하는가?"]. In *The Debate of Redemptive-Historical Preaching [구속사 설교 논쟁]*, edited by Jae-Yul Sho, 73–129. Seoul: Mal-Seum Sha-Yeak, 1999.

Yoo, Hae-Moo. "Refute against 'Is it Right to Keep Redemptive-Historical Preaching in This way?'" ["'구속사적 설교 이대로가 좋은가?'에 반론한다"]. *Christian Newspaper [기독신문]* (6th January 1999) 17.

Yoon, Seung-Eun. "Christ's Redemptive-Historical Once-For-Allness" ["그리스도의 구속사적 일회성"], part 1. *Christian Thoughts [기독교사상]* 35 (1960) 108–15.

———. "Christ's Redemptive-Historical Once-For-Allness ["그리스도의 구속사적 일회성"], part 2. *Christian Thoughts [기독교사상]* 36 (1960) 70–74.

Young, William. "Historic Calvinism and Neo-Calvinism." *WTJ* 36.1 (1973).

Name Index

Aageson, James, 124
Achtemeier, Elizabeth, 243
Adams, Jay E., 137, 140, 149–51, 154n94, 155, 157, 163, 219, 237–38
Alexander, Joseph A., 68–69, 72
Anderson, Robert, 47n76
Appenzeller, Henry G., 175
Aquinas, Thomas *See* Thomas, Aquinas, Saint
Aristotle, 83
Arminius, Jacob, 10
Athanasius, Saint, Patriarch of Alexandria, 37
Auberlen, Karl August, 6n21, 19–20
Augustine, Saint, Bishop of Hippo, 17, 36, 81, 195, 235, 272

Baker, David L., 4, 33–34
Baltus, Pietje, 89
Bang, Kee-Chang, 176n14
Barr, James, 38, 43, 49
Barth, Karl, 11–12, 20–21, 38, 40–41, 56–57, 59–60, 65, 70, 78, 97n92, 98, 111, 126, 129, 150–51, 173–74, 183, 190, 193, 201–2, 206, 209–13, 219, 236, 238, 274, 284–85
Barton, John, 44–46, 49, 61
Bauer, Georg Lorenz, 19, 33, 39, 47
Baumann, J. Daniel, 219
Baumgärtel, Friedrich, 190
Baur, Ferdinand Christian, 19, 39, 47, 48n80, 50–51, 136

Bavinck, Johan H., 24, 99, 107, 118, 195
Bebbington, David, 12–13, 32
Beck, Johann Tobias, 6n21, 19–20, 51, 182
Beeke, Joel, 133n237, 154n91
Bengel, Johann Albrecht, 6n21, 18, 181–82, 197
Berdyaev, Nicholas, 55
Berkhof, Louis, 234
Blackwood, Andrew, 219
Blair, H. E., 177
Bousset, Wilhelm, 48
Braaten, Carl, 204
Bray, Gerald, 37n29, 42, 49, 62, 66
Briggs, Charles A., 69–70
Brown, Arthur. Judson, 176n12
Bruce, F. F., 45
Brunner, Emil, 186, 202
Buber, Martin, 55
Bultmann, Rudolf, 6, 21–22, 38, 40–41, 54, 56–58, 60–65, 70–71, 73, 95, 114, 130, 168–69, 173, 182–86, 190, 199, 201, 204–6, 208–12, 284
Bunyan, John, 96
Burrell, David J., 104
Butterfield, Herbert, 32
Byun, Jong-Kil, 28, 38, 194–95, 225–26, 245, 248, 250, 255–56
Byun, Sun-Hwan, 189n74

Calvin, John, 9, 17, 25, 37, 40, 84, 95, 97, 107–8, 158, 162, 195, 214
Cara, Robert J., 138–39

315

NAME INDEX

Carrick, John, 2, 27–28, 137, 140, 149, 155, 159–69, 171
Cha, Young-Bae, 188, 197–98
Chae, Gyu-Hyun, 227
Chae, Pil-Geun, 177
Chai, Wie, 186–87, 198, 204–5
Chapell, Bryan, 116–17, 125, 149, 157, 242–43, 256–57
Chi, Dong-Shik, 181–83, 188, 197–98
Childs, Brevard S., 20, 33, 41, 43, 136
Choi, Geum-Nam, 234n80, 236, 244, 248, 251, 263
Choi, Rak-Jae, 174, 187–88, 203, 205
Choi, Soon-Jin, 245
Chon, Dong-Sik, 219
Chrysostom, John, 35, 195
Chung, Chang-Bok, 218–19
Chung, Chang-Gyung, 28, 197, 200, 223–25, 242, 245, 249–50, 256–57
Chung, Sung-Kuh, 3, 77–78, 173, 193, 197–99, 205–6, 216–19, 221–22, 252, 255, 257–58, 262–63, 274–76, 282–83, 286–87
Clement of Alexandria, 34–35
Clement of Rome, 95
Clowney, Edmund P., 1–2, 26–27, 75, 77, 137, 139–145, 153, 170–72, 220–22, 225, 232, 245–47, 257, 272, 277, 279, 282
Cocceius, Johannes, 18, 72
Cock, Hendrik de, 88
Collingwood, R. G., 22
Conn, Harvie M., 176n12
Cornick, David, 11
Cox, James W., 219
Cullmann, Oscar, 3, 38, 62–63, 73, 173–74, 182, 184–86, 188, 195n98, 199, 201, 203–10, 212, 284

Dabney, Robert L., 157, 160
De Graaf, S. G. See Graaf, S. G. de
De Jong, Peter Y., 126–27
De Wette, Wilhelm, 47, 50
De Witt, John R., 10–11, 149, 152, 155
Dennison, Charles G., 27, 73, 143–44, 147–49, 162
Dennison, James T., 27, 67, 73, 135, 137, 139, 143–46, 153
Dennison, William D., 27, 73, 134–35, 137, 139, 143–44, 156–60, 163–70
Descartes, Rene, 19, 50, 83
Dijk, Douwe van, 100, 103, 106, 110, 121–22
Dijk, Klaas, 24, 25n117, 112n162, 113, 116
Dillmann, A., 67
Dilthey, Wilhelm, 22
Diodorus, 35n19
Dodd, C. H., 203
Dooyeweerd, Herman, 24, 79–85, 126n214
Douma, J., 24–25, 107–9, 118
Driver, S. R., 102
Dumbrell, William J., 196

Ebeling, Gerhard, 22, 63
Edwards, Jonathan, 11, 154, 270–71
Eerdman, W. C., 177

Ferguson, Sinclair B., 160
Frame, John M., 27, 79, 137–139, 142, 149, 152–55, 157, 159, 164–65, 257
Fuchs, Ernst, 22–24, 63
Furnish, V. P., 168–69

Gabler, Johann Philipp, 19, 39, 47, 70–71
Gadamer, Hans Georg, 22
Gaffin, Richard B., 66–69, 73, 135, 137–140, 142, 160–61, 163, 205–6, 212–13
Go, Young-Min, 253
Goldingay, John, 234
Goldsworthy, Graeme, 196, 242–43, 257
Gootjes, Nicolaas Hendrik, 75, 76–77, 119n189, 192, 197–98, 206, 220–21, 227, 230–31, 233, 234n80, 238–40, 252, 254, 257, 262
Goppelt, Leonhard, 4, 46n73, 49, 203
Gowan, Donald E., 114
Graaf, S. G. de, 80
Graf, K. H., 67n178

NAME INDEX

Grant, Robert M., 36n27
Green, William Henry, 68–69, 72
Greidanus, Sidney, 2, 15, 26, 75–79, 91–92, 94, 96, 98–101, 104, 106, 110–14, 116, 119n189, 120–21, 125, 127–30, 173, 205, 214–15, 219–22, 229, 231–32, 242, 245–47, 249, 252, 255, 258, 282, 284
Groen van Prinsterer, G., 88n53
Grosheide, F. W., 41, 109
Gunkel, Herman, 48
Guthrie, Donald, 47, 65
Gutzlaff, Carl, 174

Han, Jei-Ho, 198, 206n151, 227, 239
Han, Man-Soo, 219
Han, Sang-Dong, 265–66
Han, Suk-Jin, 176n14
Hanson, R. P. C., 97
Harnack, Adolf von, 48, 95
Hasel. Gerhard, 4, 33, 41, 42, 46n73, 50, 73, 136, 138n24
Hays, Richard B., 169
Hegel, Georg Wilhelm Friedrich, 19, 31n1, 47, 50, 51n97
Heidegger, Martin, 22, 23, 55, 56, 57–58, 60, 62, 208
Hellbardt, Hans, 190
Hengstenberg, E. W., 68
Herodotus, 156
Herrmann, Wilhelm, 67
Hill, Michael, 169
Hodge, Charles, 68
Hoekstra, Tjeerd, 104, 109, 112n162
Hofmann, J. Chr. K. von, 6n21, 19–20, 37, 51–54, 70, 73, 182, 195n98
Holland, Tom, 5
Holtzmann, H. J., 67
Holwerda, B., 24, 38, 75, 77, 80, 92–93, 96, 100, 102–7, 110, 114–16, 119–22, 125, 128, 131, 191, 205
Hong, Chi-Mo, 266
Hong, Harold, 201
Horton, Michael S., 105n131
Huh, Soon-Kil, 198
Hunter, A. M., 182, 203
Huyser, Philip Jacob, 24, 95, 108–9, 120–22, 127

Ignatius, 17
Iranaeus, 17, 35, 195, 197

Jaspers, Karl, 55
Jerome, 35–36
Joachim, of Fiore, 17, 235
Johnston, Robert, 12
Jonker, W. D., 26
Joo, Nam-Sun. 265
Justin Martyr, 95

Kaiser, Walter C., 16
Kang, Geung-Hwan, 200
Kant, Immanuel, 11n47, 50, 81, 83
Keller, Timothy, 219
Kierkegaard, Søren, 55, 57, 81, 83, 98
Kil, Sun-Joo, 176n14
Kim, Chang-Hoon, 242, 248, 251, 255–56
Kim, Gwang-Shik, 173, 188, 198, 203–6
Kim, Jae-Joon, 177
Kim, Jee-Chan, 28–29, 173, 199–200, 227–33, 239–44, 245, 247–51, 254–55
Kim, Jung-Woo, 227, 239
Kim, Ki-Hong, 234n80, 237–38
Kim, Myung-Yong, 202
Kim, Seo-Taek, 227, 239
Kim, Se-Yoon, 233
Kim, Sung-Joo, 196
Kittel, Gerhard, 179
Kline, Meredith, 73, 138n24, 140
Ko, Seo-Hee, 219
Koole, J. L., 109
Krabbendam, Hendrik, 77, 118, 140, 149–50, 154n93, 155, 157, 171, 249
Kuyper, Abraham, 78, 84–87, 89–91, 99, 108, 195
Kwon, Soo-Kyung, 219–20

Ladd, George Eldon, 4, 38, 41, 44–46, 50, 73, 138n23
Lee, Chang-Kyu, 183–86, 188, 198, 201
Lee, Eun-Jae, 219

NAME INDEX

Lee, Geun-Ho, 232n67, 233–34
Lee, Jae-Chul, 217
Lee, Jae-Yoon, 245
Lee, Jong-Sung, 200
Lee, Joo-Young, 219
Lee, Kee-Poong, 176n14
Lee, Sang-Kyu, 249
Lee, Seung-Kuh, 286
Lee, Yoon-Jae, 244, 263
Lessing, Gotthold Ephraim, 19
Lindbeck, George, 43
Lindblad, Stefan T., 2, 76–77, 137, 140, 258
Lloyd-Jones, D. Martyn, 13, 157, 162n135
Logan, Samuel T., 152n81
Longman, T., 138n23
Luther, Martin, 9, 12, 37, 40, 58, 95, 108, 158, 214

Machen, J. Gresham, 67, 160, 163, 202
Macquarrie, John, 61
Marcel, Gabriel, 55
Marcion, of Sinope, 83n37
Marshall, I. Howard, 65
Marx, Karl, 31n1
Mayer, Herbert T., 95n82
McGrath, Alister, 47, 55
McIntire, John, 174
Mead, H., 136
Meeter, Henry, 11
Menken, Gottfried, 51
Moltmann, Jürgen, 202
Moon, Ik-Hwan, 201, 205
Mounier, Emmanuel, 55
Murray, David, 149, 155
Murray, John, 72, 137, 140, 154, 160

Niebuhr, Reinhold, 56–57, 202, 204
Nietzsche, Friedrich, 55
Nöldecke, Theodor, 67

O'Donovan, O., 169
Oh, Sung-Choon, 234n80, 235–36
Origen, 34, 95, 195
Ott, Heinrich, 204

Park, Cho-Joon, 181

Park, Hyung-Ryong, 176, 179
Park, Hyung-Yong , 188, 205
Park, Jong-Chil, 189–91, 198–200, 205–6, 222, 249, 254–55, 263
Park, Keun-Won, 219
Park, Yune-Sun, 201, 266, 272, 287
Perkins, William, 153
Pfleiderer, Otto, 48
Philo, 34
Pipa, Joseph A., 140
Piper, Otto, 53–54, 70, 73, 183–84
Plantinga, Alvin, 54
Plato, 83
Prinsterer, G, Groen van See Groen van Prinsterer, G.
Pronk, Cornelius, 77, 85, 85n43, 89n54, 91, 126

Rad, Gerhard von, 16, 183, 190
Räisänen, Heikki, 70, 136
Ramm, Bernard, 34, 36n26, 44
Ramsay, W., 112
Ranke, Leopold, 51n97
Renninger, William, 75–77, 100–1, 120–21, 125
Ridderbos, Herman N., 4, 8n30, 62, 72–73, 136, 138n23, 152, 173, 195–196, 197n111, 205–6, 213
Ritschl, Albert, 50, 95
Roberts, John M., 43
Robinson, H. W., 119, 275
Rosner, B., 169
Ross, John, 174
Rottenberg, Isaac C., 3–4
Runia, Klaas, 100n100
Rust, Eric C., 3–4, 64n165, 73
Ryu, Dong-Shik, 200–1
Ryu, Eung-Yul, 248, 256–57

Sartre, Jean-Paul, 55
Schelhaas, J., 101, 104, 113
Schilder, Klaas, 24–25, 38, 75, 78, 80, 92, 97, 100–2, 104–5, 107, 109, 111–14, 117–18, 126–30, 131n229, 171–73, 188, 191, 205, 213–14, 261, 272, 277, 282
Schreiner, T. R., 197n111
Schweitzer, Albert, 50

NAME INDEX

Scleiermacher, Friedrich, 7, 11, 51n97, 52, 94
Semler, Johann Salomo, 19, 39
Seo, Chul-Won, 244–45
Seo, Nam-Dong, 179–80, 201, 204, 206
Shedd, William, 157
Shin, Deuk-Il, 195, 219
Shin, Sung-Jong, 3, 29, 77, 191–92, 198, 219–20, 222, 234–35, 246, 250
Sho, Jae-Yul, 232–33, 249, 256
Son, Bong-Ho, 189
Song, Chang-Geun, 177
Song, Joshua Yung-Bum, 179n23, 203
Song, Nin-Soo, 176n14
Spengler, Oswald, 82
Spier, H. J., 24, 80, 119
Spinoza, Benedictus de, 18n75, 50
Sproul, R. C., 10
Spykman, Gordon J., 138n21
Stauffer, Ethelbert, 182–84
Steinmetz, David, 54
Stoker, H. G., 80
Stonehouse, Ned, 72
Stott, John, 12, 286
Strauss, D. F., 47, 49–50
Stromberg, Roland N., 156
Suh, Kyung-Jo, 176n14
Suk, Won-Tae, 3, 193–94, 221, 259, 261–87
Sung, Jong-Hyun, 203

Tacitus, Cornelius, 156
Taylor, Roy, 149, 153–55
Tertullian, 195
Theodore, Bishop of Mopsuestia, 35, 35n19
Theodoret, Bishop of Cyrrhus, 35n19
Thiselton, Anthony C., 6–7, 23–24, 234
Tholfsen, Trygve R., 33
Thomas, Aquinas, Saint, 36–37, 81
Thomas, Geoff, 126, 140, 142, 157
Thomas, Robert, 174
Thomasius, Gottfried, 51
Tillich, Paul, 56–57, 204
Torrance, Torrance F., 97n92

Toynbee, Arnold, 31n1
Trimp, Cornelius, 2, 26, 75–76, 91, 93, 96, 99–100, 102, 107, 110, 120–21, 130–33, 173, 191, 195, 200n124, 205, 219, 225–26, 245, 255–56
Troeltsch, Ernst, 39, 48–49, 50

Underwood, Horace, 174–75

Van Dijk, Douwe *See* Dijk, Douwe van
Van Prinsterer, G. Groen *See* Groen van Prinsterer, G.
Van Til, Cornelius, 72, 80, 98n95, 144, 164n149, 202
Van't Veer, M. B. *See* Veer, M, B, van't
VanGemeren, Willem, 16, 72, 138n21
Veenhof, C., 24, 80, 100n100, 114, 119
Veer, M. B. van't, 76–77, 97, 100, 102–3, 105, 109–10, 121–26
Vico, Giambattista, 31n1
Virkler, Henry A., 7n26, 19n78, 34n10, 35n20, 36n25
Vischer, Wilhelm, 190
Vollenhoven, D. H. Th, 24, 79
Von Hofmann, J. Chr. K. *See* Hofmann, J. Chr. K. von
Von Rad, Gerhard *See* Rad, Gerhard von
Vos, Gerhard, 5, 28, 33, 37, 38n34, 41, 65–73, 111, 135–36, 140–47, 149, 151n78, 158–59, 162–63, 166–68, 170–74, 196, 197n111, 199, 205–6, 211–12, 214, 223, 234, 246–47, 259, 261, 272, 284
Vosteen, J. Peter, 140, 144

Wallace, Peter J., 68, 69
Warfield, B. B., 68
Warnock, Mary, 55, 56
Webster, R. L., 66–67
Weinel, H., 48n81
Wenham, Gordon, 44
Wernle, Paul, 168n161
Wette, Wilhelm de *See* De Wette, Wilhelm
William I, King of the Netherlands, 88n53

Willimon, William, 258
Wink, Walter, 43
Wolfe, Samuel T., 83n35
Wrede, William, 19, 48, 67, 70, 136
Wright, G. Ernest, 183

Yang, Chun-Paik, 176n14
Yarbrough, Robert W., 4

Yoo, Do-Soon, 239, 256, 258, 278n88
Yoo, Hae-Moo, 29, 229–32, 251, 254
Yoon, Seung-Eun, 180
Yoon, Sung-Bum, 189n74
Young, William, 91–92

Zwingli, Ulrich, 9

Scripture Index

Genesis

1	52–53
1:1	272
1:28	85n43
3:15	16, 103, 271
4.15—5:32	271
6:1	271
9:1	271
9:25–27	16
12	106
12:1–3	16, 228, 230
12:2–3	230
12:10–12	28
12:10–20	228, 233
14:18	275
20	106
22	103, 192
22:6–14	238
45:7	16n57
46:28–30	278

Exodus

3:1–5	271
13:20–22	271
14:1–31	271
15:22–27	271
16:1–36	271
17:1–7	271
20:3	159

Numbers

9:16–23	271
17:1–11	271
21:4–9	271
35:6–33	271

Deuteronomy

8:15	271
26:5–9	16
34:9	271

Joshua

3	275
5:1–9	240–42
10:1	275
10:12–13	267
15:8	275
18:28	275
24:17–18	16

Judges

1:21	275
2:16	271
7:1–23	267
19:10–11	275

1 Samuel

6:12	238–39
7:12	271

2 Samuel

5:6–10	275–76
7	16

SCRIPTURE INDEX

1 Kings

18	121–22, 161n125
18:30–46	276

2 Kings

25:1–12	285

1 Chronicles

29:11–13	268

Esther

9:23–28	271

Psalms

23:1	145
34:15	35n18
74:2	275
76:2	275
78	110, 120
87:5	275
102:13	275
107:8	272
128:5	275
132:13–17	275
133:3	275

Isaiah

7	243
35:1–7	276
35:4	276
43:1–7	271
43:1–21	16n57
43:21	271
51:16	275
64:1–2	187

Jeremiah

9:25–26	240–41
23:5	271
31	16

Daniel

2:44–45	16n57
7–8	271
8:1–3	268
8:9–27	271
11:29–30	271

Hosea

12:4–7	110

Matthew

1:21	5n11
7:18–20	169
9	105n130
11:1–6	103, 192
15:21	103, 192
16:13–20	268–69
28:18–20	85n43

Mark

10:45	5n11

Luke

1:1–4	16n59
3:36–38	271
7:36–50	239
8:2–3	277
15:11–32	267
17	165
24:27	7

John

1:38	7
1:42	7
3:16	272
5:39	220
7:37–39	195
7:39	195n99
8:37–40	110
9:7	7
13:15	161
12:24	102
16:33	271
20:11–18	277
20:24	103
20:24–29	192
20:31	220

Acts

2	8
2:14–47	281
2:30	271
4:12	280
7:1–53	281
7:30–38	271
14:12	7
17:22–34	281–82

Romans

2:25	241
3:28	272
4:23	108
4:23–24	109–10, 120–21
5:6–9	272
5:14	123n204
6:4–11	185
6:6	241
6:17	123n204
7:14	285
8:28	272
11:25	207n153
11:26	275
11:36	272
14:17	185
15:4	225

1 Corinthians

1:2	271
1:18	119
2:1–4	158
2:2	258
4:2	207n153
4:16	225
5:7	169
10	100n103, 109–10, 121, 165, 225, 243, 256
10:1–11	123–25, 271
10:1–13	109
10:4	124
10:5–11	161
10:6	110, 123
10:11	123
11:1	225
12:10	7
14:26–28	7
15	275
15:1–11	62
15:14	129

2 Corinthians

3:6	36

Galatians

2:20	185, 241
2:20–21	159
3:16	233
4:26	275
5:1	169
5:6	241
5:35	169
6:14	241
6:15	241

Ephesians

1:4–14	16n58, 271
1:7–10	5n15
1:7–12	5n16
1:10	17
2:8	272
3:9	207n153

Philippians

2:5	120
2:8	115
3:17	123n204, 225

Colossians

2:17	234

1 Thessalonians

1:16	225
3:7	123n204

2 Thessalonians

3:9	123n204

1 Timothy

2:15	280

2 Timothy

1:13	123n204

Hebrews

1:1–3	279
7:2	7
11	100n103, 109–10, 121–23, 161, 165, 225, 243, 256
11:3–31	122
12:22	275
13:8	242

James

5	110, 121, 165, 225, 243, 256
5:10	109
5:13–18	109, 121–22
5:16–18	100n103

1 Peter

2:1–5	268
2:6	275
2:21	225
5:3	123n204

1 John

1:1–3	187
4:9–10	272

Revelation

14:1	275
16:13–14	271
17:9–10	271

www.ingramcontent.com/pod-product-compliance
Lightning Source LLC
Chambersburg PA
CBHW050615300426
44112CB00012B/1519